Twentieth Century Angli

The Great Theologians

A comprehensive series devoted to highlighting the major theologians of different periods. Each theologian is presented by a world-renowned scholar.

Published

Twentieth Century Anglican Theologians

From Evelyn Underhill to Esther Mombo

Edited by

Stephen Burns, Bryan Cones, and
James Tengatenga

WILEY Blackwell

The right of Stephen Burns, Bryan Cones, and James Tengatenga to be identified as the authors of the editorial material in this work has been asserted in accordance with law.

Registered Offices
John Wiley & Sons, Inc., 111 River Street, Hoboken, NJ 07030, USA
John Wiley & Sons Ltd, The Atrium, Southern Gate, Chichester, West Sussex, PO19 8SQ, UK

Editorial Office
The Atrium, Southern Gate, Chichester, West Sussex, PO19 8SQ, UK

For details of our global editorial offices, customer services, and more information about Wiley products visit us at www.wiley.com.

Wiley also publishes its books in a variety of electronic formats and by print-on-demand. Some content that appears in standard print versions of this book may not be available in other formats.

Library of Congress Cataloging-in-Publication Data

Names: Burns, Stephen, 1970– editor. | Cones, Bryan, editor. | Tengatenga, James, editor.
Title: Twentieth century Anglican theologians : from Evelyn Underhill to Esther Mombo / edited by Stephen Burns, Bryan Cones, and James Tengatenga.
Description: Hoboken, NJ : Wiley-Blackwell, 2021. | Series: The great theologians | Includes bibliographical references and index.
Identifiers: LCCN 2020035241 (print) | LCCN 2020035242 (ebook) | ISBN 9781119611189 (paperback) | ISBN 9781119611318 (adobe pdf) | ISBN 9781119611356 (epub)
Subjects: LCSH: Theologians. | Anglicans.
Classification: LCC BT28 .T845 2021 (print) | LCC BT28 (ebook) | DDC 230/.30922–dc23
LC record available at https://lccn.loc.gov/2020035241
LC ebook record available at https://lccn.loc.gov/2020035242

Cover Design: Wiley
Cover Image: "My Risen Body" by Wes Campbell. The picture adorns the chapel of Pilgrim Theological College, Melbourne. Used by kind permission of Wes Campbell and Pilgrim Theological College. https://wesartblog.wordpress.com/

Set in 10/12pt Galliard by SPi Global, Pondicherry, India

10 9 8 7 6 5 4 3 2 1

Contents

List of Contributors

Neil Bach Anglican Evangelical Fellowship, Melbourne, Australia

Michael Battle General Theological Seminary, New York, USA

Stephen Burns Pilgrim Theological College, University of Divinity, Melbourne, Australia

Christopher R. Brewer Templeton Religion Trust, Nassau, The Bahamas

Ian C. Browne Diocese of Peterborough, UK

Michael Peter Cadwell Diocese of Massachusetts, USA

Chen Yongtao Nanjing Union Theological Seminary, China

Ashley Cocksworth Roehampton University, London, UK

Emmy Corey Emory University, Atlanta, USA

Bryan Cones Diocese of Chicago, USA

Titre Ande Georges Diocese of Aru, Democratic Republic of Congo

Julie Gittoes Diocese of London, UK

C.I. David Joy Kerala United Theological College, Thiruvananthapuram, India

Ryan Kuratko Diocese of New York, USA

John C. McDowell St Athanasius College, University of Divinity, Melbourne, Australia

Mark Meynell Langham Trust, London, UK

Lizette Larson Miller Huron University College, London, Canada

Natalie K. Watson Sacristy Press, Durham, UK

Robert MacSwain School of Theology, University of the South, Sewanee, USA

James Tengatenga School of Theology, University of the South, Sewanee, USA

James Walters London School of Economics, London, UK

Philip Wickeri Hong Kong Shen Sung Hui, Hong Kong

Sean Winter Pilgrim Theological College, University of Divinity, Melbourne, Australia

Preface

This idea for this book emerged when Stephen Burns co-taught a class on Twentieth Century Anglican Theologians with Kwok Pui-lan at Episcopal Divinity School (EDS) in Cambridge, Massachusetts, where both he and Pui-lan were on faculty. Pui-lan and Stephen were agreed that no existing book could serve as a core text for the class, given the Anglo-centric or North Atlantic bias of so much of the literature that exists. Stephen thanks Pui-lan for seeking alternatives to the usual suspects in that class, as in so much of her work.

James Tengatenga sojourned at EDS as a visiting scholar, while he was still chair of the worldwide Anglican Consultative Council, and between his roles as Bishop of Southern Malawi and (currently) Distinguished Professor of Anglican Studies at University of the South in Tennessee. Bryan Cones was also at EDS for an "Anglican Year" to complement his long formation in the Roman Catholic tradition before being ordained as a deacon, then presbyter, in the Episcopal Diocese of Chicago.

Bryan later spent a spell in Melbourne, to study for a doctorate, with Stephen as supervisor (with the thesis later published as *This Assembly of Believers* by SCM Press, 2020), and where he (Bryan) also served as pastor in an Anglican-Uniting ecumenical congregation. Stephen is professor at Pilgrim Theological College, a college of the Uniting Church in Australia in the ecumenical University of Divinity. It was then that the book started to take form.

In a longer view, the origins of this book are likely to somehow be in Stephen's conversations with Ann Loades, beginning in her classes at Durham University and continuing after that, through her supervision of his doctorate and since that time. For many, Ann has been a guide to the Anglican tradition, is a principal authority on a number of those who feature in the book (Underhill, Sayers, and Farrer especially), and is rightly the subject of a chapter by Stephen. The book owes much to Ann's commitment to listening to "voices from the past" (see e.g., Loades 2000) as well as to her determination to notice and draw attention to who has been excluded by the usual suspects.

Stephen and Bryan started work on the book and asked James to join them, and the three drew in the team of writers to whom we are so grateful, as those at Wiley-Blackwell who have worked with us throughout the project. We also want to thank Paul Barker, a bishop in Melbourne, for helping us find writers on Morris and Stott.

Across the book as a whole, the writers are Anglicans and from other Christian traditions, and from numerous countries around the world, variously writing about others from their own most familiar cultures, and across them. For all that a book like this still needs more voices – and not least, despite our efforts, more voices of women and those from beyond the West – we have tried to push the circle wider, as it were, so responding to the lack of a suitable textbook for Pui-lan and Stephen's class. We hope that this book encourages others to keep pushing for wider inclusions, as best they can. We encourage others to prepare a further volume.

During Bryan's stay in Melbourne, as well as on many other occasions around the household table Stephen shares with his spouse Judith Atkinson, Judith, an Anglican priest, would often comment that the thing she most appreciates about her tradition is that "no matter how faith changes or grows, [she] can always be at home" in it, as there is in practice almost no view Anglicanism does not encompass, whatever the "official" position when such a position is possible to ascertain. This can of course be confronting to any quest for conformity, should that be sought; yet it can also be comforting, not least when whatever the local Anglican scene is, is grim. While the Anglican churches are currently marked by friction and deeply scarred by discord – with Melbourne, for example, just one microcosm of the larger divisions – in its own small way this book points to massive and challenging diversity all at once, cheek-by-jowl, unmerged. Readers may well find perspectives they think odd, as well as, hopefully, some in which they take delight. So be it. Anglican forebears in – and contemporaries influenced by – the Benedictine tradition might well see this diversity, as we do, as a clue to "never lose hope in God's mercy" (Rule of Benedict 4).

A Note on Referencing

Every effort has been made to establish a consistent pattern of referencing across the book. References are found in parenthesis in the text (e.g., Kwok 1995, p. 1; Kwok and Burns 2016, p. 2) and fuller information can be found by cross-reference to the list of "References" at the end of every chapter. Additional notes, where used, are also found at the end of the chapters. In most cases, this is straightforward and obvious. Matters are complicated, however, in various cases: for example, if books were published in different places at once – generally both sides of the North Atlantic – with differing titles given to the same work; if writers have relied on anthologies and readers of their subject's previously published or unpublished work put together by persons other than the subjects themselves; if later editions of books made emendations to earlier versions; and when over time multiple editions have been produced by a variety of publishers. Notwithstanding all these factors, the main intent is to signal what seem to be the most readily available versions of texts at the time of this publication.

References

Kwok, P.-l. (1995). *Discovering the Bible in the Non-biblical World*. Maryknoll, NY: Orbis.

Kwok, P.-l. and Burns, S. (eds.) (2016). *Postcolonial Practice of Ministry: Leadership,* *Liturgy, and Interfaith Engagement*. Lanham, MD: Lexington.

Loades, A. (2000). *Feminist Theology: Voices from the Past*. Oxford: Polity.

Un/Usual Suspects

Stephen Burns and Bryan Cones

Incompleteness is a merit of Anglicanism, at least according to some of its most lauded expositors and advocates (Ramsey 1936, p. 220). Incompleteness marks this collection, just as it does other texts about the same tradition, and perhaps needs must. In the first place, it is hard to get a complete view when even determining what might count as "Anglican" is contested, with different views of the sources, edges, and focus of the tradition.[1] At the very least, though, Anglicanism by its name suggests a pertaining to the English, with a locus of its identity in the Angles/Atlantic/British Isles. Evidently, over time, and through both mission and the colonial expansion of empire – and not just one or the other – it has given the germs for related ecclesial forms in a variety of different cultures (see Sachs 1993; Ward 2007; Kaye 2008; Chapman et al. 2015).

The term "Anglican" itself only came into common use in the nineteenth century – with the "Anglican Communion" endorsed by the first Lambeth Conference of 1867, twenty years after talk of a "Communion" emerged (Avis 2018). Identifying which churches belong to the Anglican Communion is presently the most obvious way to determine what is Anglican. Formal lists of course exist, and the website of the Anglican Communion keeps an up-to-date record.[2] Yet aside from such lists, it can be difficult to see what might be Anglican: some Anglican churches are identified by their geography, for example, "The Anglican Church of Australia," "The Anglican Church of Kenya," while other Anglican churches are identified by geography but not by tradition, for example, "The Church of Melanesia," "The Church in the Province of the Indian Ocean." Some Anglican churches use the descriptor "Episcopal": "The Scottish Episcopal Church," while "The Episcopal Church" (TEC) is not just that for the United States but also provinces outside the United States (hence, its name was shortened from its former one, "The Episcopal Church in the USA" [ECUSA]). Brazil has "The Episcopal Anglican Church of Brazil." One Anglican church uses the term "Anglican Communion" in its name, though this is seen to readers of English only in translation: Nippon Sei Ko Kai ("The Anglican Communion in Japan"). The Anglican Church in Hong Kong uses Cantonese in its title, while the church in New Zealand leads with Maori in its full title, "The Anglican Church in Aotearoa, New Zealand and Polynesia." Some churches that are part of the Anglican Communion are united churches, The Church of South India being a case where Anglicans are joined with Methodists and Presbyterians, The Church of North India adding to those traditions Brethren and Pentecostals. In vibrant interfaith environments such as these, Christians have perhaps more readily united. Further complications are now present in that in some parts of the world, the descriptor "Anglican" is claimed by groups that are not part of the Anglican Communion while claiming Anglican heritage, "The Anglican Church in North America" (ACNA) a key case in point, where it is TEC that is part of the Anglican Communion, despite ACNA claiming to be more "authentically" Anglican. That leaders of ACNA have been ordained as bishops by those from "inside" the Communion means that lines are murky – and differences great. Note also divergence even in propositions, that is, whether churches deem themselves to be "of" or "in" a setting: New Zealand has "in," Australia, "of." Australia, mentioned first above, is an example of one of the most divided Anglican settings in the world, despite the singular "church." In fact, "Anglican churches in Australia" might be more apt to the ascendant very conservative evangelicalism akin to ACNA not only in Sydney but increasingly across the country, and brittle anglo-catholic ritualism in sharp decline, cheek by jowl. Australia's "inadequately incorporated pluralism" (Varcoe 1995, p. 192) is perhaps a vivid microcosm of the larger global Anglican picture.

Shared history does not then yield a simple map of the Anglican Communion. But whatever status churches claim within or without the "Anglican Communion," Anglicans have some shared relation to the 1534 Act of Supremacy, which declared Henry VIII – and not the Vicar of Rome – the "supreme head" of the Church of England. Hence, that 1534 Act looms in much Anglican thinking, with an absence of theses or confessions akin to Protestant precedents, placing Anglicanism somewhat outside a trajectory shared by several other churches of the Reformation. While documents do exist in which convictions of the nascent new English church are specified – notably the 39 Articles of Religion – their status in Anglican provinces around the world that inherited them has wavered, and certainly by today is quite diverse. This in part reflects the ongoing dispute about what period or epoch of history is or might be key for Anglicanism, with more or less weight being placed on, for example, the Reformations era, medieval continuities, and "the early church" with its ecumenical councils. It has often been noted that Anglicans have harbored an affection for "patristics," and also that Anglicans have rarely been recognized – or seen themselves – as "systematic" theologians like those spawned in other traditions, both Protestant and Catholic. Sometimes Anglicanism has been seen as involving a "pastoral" way of doing theology (e.g., Wright 1980, p. 3), or even a sophisticated take on "common practice" (Hardy 1989). In whatever mode, "untidiness," "baffling of neatness," and such like (Ramsey 1960, p. 220) often echoes in much theology by Anglicans. According to Robert McAfee Brown (not himself an Anglican), trying to describe Anglicanism in a simple way might lead one to "despair," yet the tradition's resistance to simple definition is at the same time a source of its "greatness" (as cited by Wolf 1979, p. v).

The question of whether or not Anglicanism carries any special doctrines of its own became a quite animated debate in the latter part of the twentieth century (about which discussion has circled around Sykes 1978; for more on the history of the tradition, see Avis 2002, with Avis becoming something of a flag carrier for ongoing attention to this question, e.g., Avis 2018). Whether special doctrines are or are not asserted as part of Anglican identity, "approach" rather than "content" as it were often tends to take precedence in defining the tradition, and in various ways: with Anglicans regarding themselves as those who are or at their best might be "always open" (Giles 1999), "know what they often don't know" (Hanson 1965, p. 132, citing Howard Johnson), value being "gentle" (Hanson 1965, p. 141), and perhaps even represent "the appearance of a type of human being the world doesn't otherwise see" (Hanson 1965, p. 132, again citing Howard Johnson)!

While documents such as the Chicago-Lambeth Quadrilateral suggest that Anglican theology is located in a balance of authorities drawn into theological reflection, how those authorities are to be weighted in the balance is by no means agreed. The Chicago-Lambeth Quadrilateral of 1888 proposes that Old and New Testaments, the Nicene Creed, "gospel sacraments" of baptism and eucharist, and "historic episcopate" – though "locally adapted" – define the Anglican inheritance. Yet it is not just the balance of identified aspects of the quadrilateral that invites questions, for as Hanson notes, "we have Scriptures, Creeds, Sacraments, and Ministry, but no people . . . The people who constitute the Church are ignored" (Hanson 1965, p. 57).

Sometimes, in lieu of confessional documents, "common prayer" has been said to be the locus of Anglican doctrine (see Hefling and Shattuck 2006; Platten and Knight 2011; yet especially Earey 2013 on how wide notions of common prayer may be). However, Books of Common Prayer emerging from different locations are marked by difference as well as similarity, and those to which variants might all trace their genealogy (those of 1549, 1552, 1559; less so maybe 1662, which settled into long practice) were themselves expressions of incremental development in liturgical practice and so invite some measure of conjecture about the reforms they projected. Whatever stands in the more distant past, through the twentieth century liturgical diversity accelerated to a point where current provisions' commonality is now sought less in texts (as more so in the past) but rather in elusive qualities that might suggest some "family resemblance" (see Buchanan 2012).[3]

The Chicago-Lambeth quadrilateral was itself the product of an early Lambeth Conference, with the Lambeth conference of bishops from around the so-called Communion identified as one of four structures in which Anglican connections and "bonds of affection" would later come to be said to rest, the others being the office of the Archbishop of Canterbury, a more select meeting of regional bishops (the "primate" or presiding bishop of each province), and from the late twentieth century (1971 onwards) a more representative group – including laypersons – from diverse locations, the Anglican Consultative Council (ACC). Just one arm of the ACC is the International-Anglican Liturgical Consultation (IALC), a forum for bringing forward good practice that is the fragile latter-day legacy of this "family" of churches with books of common prayer. The ACC meets intermittently, while the steady practice of Lambeth Conferences every decade has recently been troubled for the only time apart from during World War II. The current battle lines are about divergent understandings of homosexuality, about which scripture, creeds, sacraments, and episcopacy may say little, at least in common. The current impasse is a signal instance of how "Anglican theology" can be difficult to expound; a complete picture, were that to be possible, would be quite unlikely to reveal easy ways to agreement.

If the shape and sources of Anglican theology are not straightforward to determine, an alternative approach to taking hold of the tradition might consider what persons within it have had to say. This book takes that angle – but is aware of traps, particularly given that accounts of Anglicanism have often tended to be very Anglo-centric (for criticism of and counterpoints to Anglo-centricism see especially Douglas and Kwok 2000). In these, the wider Communion can be at best marginal,[4] or employ schemas that use "party" categories ("catholic," "evangelical," "liberal," etc.) commonly used in the English church but which are not equivalent across wider cultures.[5] These outlooks obscure contexts that are vital to wider understanding or impose categories that at the very least morph in migration. While studies in "Anglican spirituality" in twentieth century have been abundant (e.g., Mursell 2001; Rowell et al. 2001; Schmidt 2002; Loades 2015), and sometimes conceive the tradition broadly,[6] narratives of Anglican *theology* have sometimes been entirely limited to UK contexts (note the figures discussed in Sedgwick 2005) or otherwise stretched only across the North Atlantic to encircle North America (e.g., Boak Slocum 2015; McMichael 2015). There has also been a tendency to privilege those who do something like systematic theology – somewhat strangely perhaps given at least sometime resistance to the designation – while excluding other modes, including, but by no means limited to, "spirituality."[7] Such studies can look far from complete – "skewed," to echo William Wolf (Wolf 1979, p. viii) – when considered from many parts of the Communion, still too much pertaining to the English, to put it mildly (then note the divide between "global" and "global west" in Morris (2016) and Sachs (2017), albeit sensitively explored in the general introduction to both). What is more, such accounts of Anglican theology may well unwittingly exclude those who – for example, by virtue of their gender – have, until recently at least, been unable to teach theology in academic and/or ecclesial settings in the United Kingdom (see Sayers 1943; Maltby and Shell 2019 for ways in which theology nonetheless emerged), quite apart from those of different genders in many places beyond the United Kingdom (see Kwok et al. 2012).

Aware of incompleteness, and yet also determined to recognize not only "standard divines" (as a chapter title in Sykes et al. 1998, pp. 176–187) but some "unusual suspects," *Twentieth Century Anglican Theologians* considers the work of twenty-three persons. They are both more and less familiar figures in estimates of most esteemed modern Anglican theologians. They come from five continents, include women as well as men, and in some cases those who are associated with other Christian traditions in addition to Anglicanism. Some of them have served as deacons, priests, or (arch)bishops, while others are defiantly lay. Some have worked from academic institutions while others have not. They are variously identified with different theological approaches – "conservative," "progressive," and so on, with all sorts of possibilities of one descriptor being ancillary to another or more – with the descriptors signaling somewhat different things in different contexts, in any case. Some may in some respects be controversial, causing consternation to other Anglicans apart from anyone else. And they wrote or write in either more popular or specialist modes across a range of theological disciplines – spirituality as well as systematics, pastoral as well as historical theology, and sometimes beyond conventional disciplinary boundaries. They were selected in accordance with a number of criteria:

(i) Not only must the theologian have lived half of their life in the twentieth-century (with living subjects around or over retirement age at the time of publication),[8] but

(ii) they must (even if multiply-belonging, that is, also to another tradition) identify with a member church of the Anglican Communion. This, however, includes the united churches in contexts where Anglican churches no longer exist (as in India [Church of South India, 1946–, and Church of North India, 1970–], Pakistan [Church of Pakistan, also 1970–], and in a very different scenario, China), with the situation of the united churches introducing a dynamic that itself impacts questions of Anglican identity.

Then:

(i) The theologian must have had some international influence as well as shaping the thought of the church in their particular context(s); and

(ii) they must have produced significant texts in one genre of theology or another, although attention to their influence through an ecclesial role and ministry is by no means put aside.

These criteria make for both guidance and limits around our selection of subjects, though we recognize in-/exclusions are interesting to debate, and the company we have represented remains partial. The skein of people on which we focus involves, *but expands*, attention to figures from the Church of England, UK and North Atlantic settings – that is, it honors some of those commonly, and rightly, considered of influence but complements and challenges them in a wider circle of peers – as it signals the influence of theologians from around wide stretches of the Communion. Each chapter outlines the theologian's social-political and cultural contexts, sketches a biography with an emphasis on the figure's theological scope, whilst not excluding attention to what they have made known of their personal lives, political commitments, prayer, ministry, and so on. It outlines two or three key themes in the work of the theologian,[9] and *possibly*, one way or another, makes some exploration of how the theologian approaches and articulates the doctrine of divine incarnation in Christ Jesus (in general, see Macquarrie 1990; Macquarrie 1998).[10] So the common-place assumption of an earlier generation of Anglican theology, that it "owes many of its characteristics to the central place held within it by the Incarnation" (Ramsey 1960, p. 27) is tested by shifting optics from the period encircling Frederick Gore on to William Temple in the United Kingdom through to a wider range of persons in a plethora of settings.

While short descriptors do not do justice to the depth and breadth of their work, which the following chapters go on to represent more roundly, to gain an immediate sense of the scope of this book's exploration of twentieth century Anglican theologians the chapters in turn focus on the following:

• Evelyn Underhill (England, 1875–1941), among other "firsts," the first woman to teach theology to Anglican clergy in Britain, and author of highly influential texts *Mysticism* (Underhill 1911) and *Worship* (Underhill 1936) among many other works, but because of the lack of official church role or university base, is often overlooked in purviews of Anglican theologians.

- William Temple (England, 1881–1944), wartime Archbishop of Canterbury, social theologian and ecumenist, often rightly recognized for his subsequent influence on the Anglican tradition – especially its relationships to wider society, for example in *Christianity and Social Order* (Temple 1942).
- T. C. Chao (China, 1888–1979), a pioneering Chinese theologian, and the first to consider the confrontation between Christian doctrine and Chinese traditions, unjustly neglected in other studies of Anglicanism, no doubt at least in part because Anglicanism ceased to exist in China, being submerged into the state church.
- Sadhu Sundar Singh (India, 1889–1929), an underrecognized Indian convert from Sikhism with a remarkable popularity and international reach in a short life; famously situating Christianity with aspects of Indian religious traditions.
- Dorothy L. Sayers (England, 1893–1957), both creative and unconventional, and who gained a massive audience far exceeding her academic and clerical peers through her shaping influence on radio – *The Man Born to be King* (e.g., Sayers 1943) – the performing arts, and literature, but curiously excluded from many lists of Anglican theologians, perhaps because of the genres in which she wrote.
- Austin Farrer (England, 1904–1968), widely acknowledged as the most significant Anglican theologian of the century, working with then-contemporary philosophical trends and through a highly influential ministry of preaching (with many sermons then published) as an Oxford college don.
- Michael Ramsey (England, 1904–1988), an Archbishop of Canterbury widely appreciated for his shaping influence on subsequent Anglican theology and spirituality, distilled in, for example, his classic *The Gospel and the Catholic Church* (Ramsey 1936) and *From Gore to Temple* (Ramsey 1960).
- Donald MacKinnon (Scotland, 1913–1994), a Scottish Episcopalian who was a Cambridge professor with distinctive eclectic, interrogative, and critical tones to his work, and who strongly influenced a generation and more of British theological leadership, including as doctoral supervisor to David Ford and Rowan Williams.
- Leon Morris (Australia, 1914–2006), a biblical scholar who popularized certain interpretations of Jesus' death across much modern Anglicanism and beyond; and while more conservative than most of those more usually considered in purviews of Anglican theology, is representative of some of Anglicanism's contemporary evangelical strongholds.
- K. H. Ting (China, 1915–2014), a bishop with a major influence on the ecumenical movement internationally as well as in the public resurgence of Christianity in China after the Cultural Revolution; missed from many surveys of Anglicanism.
- John A. T. Robinson (England, 1919–1983), a bishop who promoted so-called "secular" theology in the best-selling *Honest to God* (Robinson 1963) produced other influential studies, particularly of the New Testament.
- John Macquarrie (Scotland, 1919–2007), a Scottish theologian who worked in both United Kingdom and United States teaching institutions, wrote the influential

Principles of Christian Theology (Macquarrie 1977), and is widely acknowledged as Anglicanism's foremost "systematic" theologian.

- John Stott (England, 1921–2011), a well-known English preacher who found huge international reach around much of the Anglican Communion, shaping both the doctrine (for example, through *The Cross of Christ* [Stott 1986]) and ethical thought of conservative evangelicalism, of which he became the doyen.
- William Stringfellow (United States, 1928–1985), lay theologian, lawyer, and political activist; close to the Jesuit activist Daniel Berrigan and applauded by the Reformed Karl Barth, he has been widely appreciated.
- Desmond Tutu (South Africa, 1931–), perhaps the best-known Anglican of the century, prized for his advocacy of the marginalized; chair of the renowned Truth and Reconciliation Commission in his "post-apartheid" country.
- John Pobee (Ghana, 1937–2020), an ecumenical theologian whose work pioneered sympathetic assessment of African "traditional religions," and a leading contributor to the study of African religions, surprisingly underacknowledged for the significance of his contributions in a tradition becoming more conscious of its non-Western weight of gravity.
- Ann Loades (England, 1938–), the first woman to be granted a CBE (Companion of the British Empire) medal for services to theology, and the first woman President of the Society for the Study of Theology. Her *Searching for Lost Coins* (Loades 1987) was a powerful early exploration of Christianity and feminism (see also Loades 2000).
- Kenneth Leech (England, 1939–2015), an edgy English practical theologian, firmly located in parish (rather than academic) settings, in books like *True Prayer* (Leech 1979) and *True God* (Leech 1985) unusually combining emphasis on both spirituality and social justice.
- Carter Heyward (United States, 1945–), a lesbian feminist theologian at the vanguard of progressive Anglicanism, and one of the irregularly ordained first wave of women priests known as the "Philadelphia 11."
- David Brown (Scotland, 1948–), a Scottish philosophical theologian whose work includes major reassessment in overlapping space between natural theology, sacramentality, and the dynamics of tradition, as well as work on core doctrines of Trinity (*The Divine Trinity*, [Brown 1985]) and incarnation (*Divine Humanity*, [Brown 2011]).
- David Ford (Ireland, 1948–), a creative Irish theologian criss-crossing theological styles within a distinctive (Pentecostal-influenced) celebratory tone – exemplified in *Jubilate: Theology in Praise* (Hardy and Ford 1984) – as well as shaping distinctive approaches to interreligious dialogue.
- N. T. (Tom) Wright (England, 1948–), whose work spans schemas of early Christianity to popular media, and whose strong biblical focus has both endeared him to and alienated him from evangelical constituents within contemporary Anglicanism.
- Esther Mombo (Kenya, 1957–), the first African Anglican female and feminist theologian to rise to wide international attention, and whose work is engaged with both Anglican and Quaker traditions and issues of gender and sexuality arising in African contexts (e.g., Wafula et al. 2016).

Between the opening subject of this book, Evelyn Underhill – the first woman to teach Anglican clergy in England – and the closing focus on Esther Mombo – the first African Anglican woman to rise to prominence, a half-century after Underhill's death – huge change might be charted. Along the way, quite considerable differences will be seen to exist between the various theologians from the span of time under consideration in this collection, and there is sometimes large space between their convictions. Readers looking for a "core" of Anglican theology expressed across all the thinkers represented here may well be quite frustrated, as aligning and reconciling the biblical "word studies" of Leon Morris – as an example of a writer toward one pole – and the self-identifying "radical" voice of Carter Heyward – in another place – may likely struggle, as startlingly different ideas are at play as to what constitutes "theology." In looking for common themes across numerous authors, it may be noted at least that war and its aftermath (see e.g., Wilkinson 1978) looms large in the thought of at least some of those who lived through the early or middle years of the twentieth century (Dorothy L. Sayers and Donald MacKinnon being just two examples), while gender and sexuality became a key touchstone for many by the turn into the present millennium. In terms of their actions, while some are noted for being personally kind to "down and outs" (e.g., Leon Morris), others have been heavily involved in political life and movement for social change (most notably, Desmond Tutu).

The reader will also be aware that some chapters unfolding here refer more to the "evangelical quadrilateral" than to the Chicago-Lambeth Quadrilateral (e.g., the one on John Stott), and that subjects aligned to particular traditions within the wider diversity of the Church of England are found to be in disagreement with others allied to the same tradition (e.g., Leon Morris' presumed criticism of Tom Wright). Some subjects will be seen to be lifelong Anglicans, while others came to the tradition later, in their cases having first been long identified with other churches, or investing strongly in pan-denominational movements even while committed to Anglicanism (e.g., John Stott). It may be striking to some readers (perhaps depending on the ecumenical openness of their local forms of Anglicanism) that numerous of the subjects here (both long-term and later Anglicans) were in various ways deeply enmeshed in ecumenical work (among others, T. C. Chao and William Temple), while many also evidently prize ideas about Anglicanism's particular sympathy toward and ability for something like "unity by inclusion" (see Stancliffe 1991). Again perhaps depending on readers' local versions of Anglicanism, circling in thinkers from churches that united in the course of the twentieth century (e.g., T. C. Chao and T. H. Ting in China) may not at first seem obvious, yet the emphasis on their contexts may help to invite questions about the (often unacknowledged or uncritically normed) environments from which other writers express their own ideas. Thinking outside the West may come from settings that are either evidently interreligious and in which Christianity is marginal (India) or in which Christianity was at times actively suppressed (China) (for insights into these contexts, see e.g., Wickeri 2000; Wickeri and Wickeri 2007; Lott et al. 2013), and may yield clues to Western readers that press back against a history of ideas being carried, for better and worse, from the West to those in colonies and other elsewheres.

We intend this collection to help recalibrate narrowly focused, exclusive lists of recent Anglican theologians, so fundamentally reorienting its topic toward the contemporary global contexts of Anglicanism, the breath of its uneasy embrace, in all its fragility. While "unity by inclusion" may now be tested to breaking point by current intra-Anglican circumstances, we hope that this book challenges readers to imagine how Anglicanism might yet survive with substantial variance unmerged. The figures represent a range of important and vibrant Anglican voices from Evelyn Underhill to Esther Mombo. That both "bookends" are women itself signals intent with our collection to lift up "unusual suspects" and the subtitle stands in intentional relief against Michael Ramsey's survey from Charles Gore to William Temple (Ramsey 1960), or like-kind (e.g., Page 1967: "from Temple to Robinson," naming and focusing on men in the West).

For very different reasons, many other diverse figures might have been contenders to be subjects in this anthology; for example, A. M. (Donald) Allchin (Wales), Aiyadurai Jesudasen Appasamy (India), Niam Atteak (Palestine), Sarah Coakley (England), Philip Culbertson (the United States), Don Cupitt (England), Gregory Dix (England), Verna Dozier (the United States), Alan Ecclestone (England), Matthew Fox (the United States), Hans Frei (the United States), Monica Furlong (England), Daniel W. Hardy (the United States/England), Michael Harper (England), David Jenkins (England), Broughton Knox (Australia), Kwok Pui-lan (Hong Kong/ the United States), Sally MacFague (the United States), John Mbiti (Kenya), Arvind P. Nirmal (India), James F. Packer (England/Canada), Barney Pityana (South Africa), Oliver Quick (England), Maggie Ross (England/the United States), Vinay Kumar Samuel (India), Lamin Sanneh (the Gambia/ the United States), Harry Sawyerr (Sierra Leone), Israel Selvanayagam (India), John Spong (the United States), Stephen Sykes (England), John V. Taylor (England), Jenny Te Paa (New Zealand), V. H. Vanstone (England), Miroslav Volf (Croatia/the United States), Esther de Waal (England), Benedicta Ward (England), Maurice Wiles (England), Charles Williams (England), and Rowan Williams (Wales).[11] Of course, such further study would reveal both deeper vibrancy and even more tension. May *Twentieth Century Anglican Theologians* encourage discovery and enjoyment of those featured in this book and others in their turn.

Notes

1 Contrast, for example Countryman (1999) and Bartlett (2007) in the same "Traditions of Christian Spirituality" series, with the former focused on poets.

2 https://www.anglicancommunion.org/structures/member-churches.aspx (accessed July 15, 2020).

3 Buchanan (2012) provides a very detailed survey, with his introduction dealing with the work of International Anglican Liturgical Consultation.

4 For example, Chapman (2012) considers the Communion in the final chapter. As does Wells

(2011). Sykes et al. (1998) model problems by drawing almost entirely on North Atlantic perspectives (John Pobee contributes a chapter from elsewhere). Note also that Sykes et al. also includes very little writing by women, with only that of Mary Tanner, Fredrica Harris Thompsett, and Grace Davie (and Davie a co-author of a chapter). The earlier 1988 edition of the same book had Tanner and Thompsett only.

5 Note the organization of Spencer (2012), for example.

6 It is instructive to compare Allchin (1988) and Loades (2015), on the same topic. The

emphases are quite different, with the latter very much broader.

7 For example, Sedgwick (2005) considers six white male university professors in British universities.

8 At the start of the project, we did not know the age of Esther Mombo, being unable to find any publicly available information. However, that aside, there seemed good sense in "book-ending" the project with this woman.

9 A partial model for this is the sections on "achievement" and "agenda," which appear in many chapters of Ford with Muers (2005), while Kennedy (2011) has also shaped our thinking. See also Kerr (2007). As editors, we have not imposed a rigid scheme for content upon authors, so as not to flatten out the richness of difference either from the subjects' experience or from their interpreters in this collection.

10 Kennedy (2011) refracts the work of various theologians through a particular theme, that of justice and peace. In our book on twentieth century Anglicans, incarnation might seem obvious as a connecting theme given the influence and legacy of *Lux Mundi* (see Wainwright 1988) on many subsequent Anglicans, at least many of the usual suspects – though our expansive list of theologians also to some extent challenges this focus.

11 Indeed we had hoped that some of these persons would have been included in this book, but chapters fell through.

References

Allchin, A.M. (1988). Anglican spirituality. In: *The Study of Anglicanism* (eds. S. Sykes, J. Booty and J. Knight), 351–364. London: SPCK.

Avis, P. (ed.) (2002). *Anglicanism and the Christian Church: Theological Resources in Historical Perspective*. London: SPCK.

Avis, Paul. (ed.) (2018). Anglican ecclesiology. In *The Oxford Handbook to Ecclesiology* (ed. Avis, Paul). Oxford: Oxford University Press.

Bartlett, A. (2007). *A Passionate Balance: An Anglican Tradition*. London: DLT.

Boak Slocum, R. (2015). *The Anglican Imagination: Portraits and Sketches of Modern Anglican Theologians*. Farnham: Ashgate.

Brown, D. (1985). *The Divine Trinity*. London: Duckworth.

Brown, D. (2011). *Divine Humanity: Kenosis and the Construction of a Christian Theology*. London: SCM Press.

Buchanan, C. (2012). *Anglican Eucharistic Liturgies, 1985–2010: The Authorized Rites of the Anglican Communion*. Norwich: Canterbury Press.

Chapman, M.D. (2012). *Anglicanism: A Very Short Introduction*. Oxford: Oxford University Press.

Chapman, M.D., Clarke, S., and Percy, M. (eds.) (2015). *The Oxford Handbook of Anglican Studies*. Oxford: Oxford University Press.

Countryman, W.L. (1999). *The Poetic Imagination: An Anglican Tradition*. London: DLT.

Douglas, I.T. and Kwok, P.-l. (eds.) (2000). *Beyond Colonial Anglicanism: The Anglican Communion in the Twenty-First Century*. New York, NY: Church Publishing.

Earey, M. (2013). *Beyond Common Worship: Anglican Identity and Liturgical Diversity*. London: SCM Press.

Ford, D.F. with Muers, R. (eds.) (2005). *The Modern Theologians: An Introduction to Christian Theology Since 1918*. Oxford: Wiley Blackwell.

Giles, R. (1999). *Always Open: Being an Anglican Today*. Cambridge, MA: Cowley.

Hanson, A.T. (1965). *Beyond Anglicanism*. London: DLT.

Hardy, D.W. (1989). Theology through philosophy. In: *The Modern Theologians: An Introduction to Christian Theology in the Twentieth Century* (ed. D.F. Ford), 30–71. Oxford: Blackwell.

Hardy, D.W. and Ford, D.F. (1984). *Jubilate: Theology in Praise*. London: DLT.

Hefling, C. and Shattuck, C. (eds.) (2006). *The Oxford Guide to the Book of Common Prayer: A Worldwide Survey*. New York, NY: Oxford University Press.

Kaye, B. (2008). *An Introduction to World Anglicanism*. Cambridge: Cambridge University Press.

Kennedy, P. (2011). *Twentieth Century Theologians: A New Introduction to Modern Christian Thought*. London: I.B. Taurus.

Kerr, F. (2007). *Twentieth Century Catholic Theologians*. London: Continuum.

Kwok, P.-l., Berling, J.A., and Te Paa, J. (eds.) (2012). *Anglican Women on Church and Mission*. New York: Morehouse.

Leech, K. (1979). *True Prayer: An Invitation to Christian Spirituality*. London: Sheldon.

Leech, K. (1985). *True God: An Exploration of Christian Spirituality*. London: Sheldon.

Loades, A. (1987). *Searching for Lost Coins: Explorations in Christianity and Feminism*. London: SPCK.

Loades, A. (2000). *Feminist Theology: Voices from the Past*. Oxford: Polity.

Loades, A. (2015). Anglican spirituality. In: *The Oxford Handbook of Anglican Studies* (eds. M.D. Chapman, S. Clarke and M. Percy), 149–164. Oxford: Oxford University Press.

Lott, E.J., Thangaraj, M.T., and Wingate, A. (eds.) (2013). *Discipleship and Dialogue: New Frontiers in Interfaith Engagement – Essays in Honour of Dr. Israel Selvanayagam*. Delhi: ISPCK.

Macquarrie, J. (1977). *Principles of Christian Theology*. London: SCM Press.

Macquarrie, J. (1990). *Jesus Christ in Modern Thought*. London: SCM Press.

Macquarrie, J. (1998). *Christology Revisited*. London: SCM Press.

Maltby, J. and Shell, A. (eds.) (2019). *Anglican Women Novelists: From Charlotte Bronte to P.D. James*. London: Bloomsbury.

McMichael, R. (ed.) (2015). *The Vocation of Anglican Theology*. London: SCM Press.

Morris, J. (ed.) (2016). *The Oxford History of Anglicanism, Volume IV: Global Western Anglicanism, 1910-Present*. Oxford: Oxford University Press.

Mursell, G. (2001). *English Spirituality: From 1700 to the Present*. London: SPCK.

Page, R. (1967). *New Directions in Anglican Theology: A Survey from Temple to Robinson*. London: Mowbray.

Platten, S. and Knight, J. (eds.) (2011). *Comfortable Words: Polity, Piety and the Book of Common Prayer*. London: SCM Press.

Ramsey, A.M. (1936). *The Gospel and the Catholic Church*. London: Macmillan.

Ramsey, A.M. (1960). *From Gore to Temple: The Development of Anglican Theology Between* Lux Mundi *and the Second World War, 1889–1939*. London: Macmillan.

Robinson, J.A.T. (1963). *Honest to God*. London: SCM Press.

Rowell, G., Stevenson, K., and Williams, R. (eds.) (2001). *Love's Redeeming Work: The Anglican Quest for Holiness*. Oxford: Oxford University Press.

Sachs, W.L. (1993). *The Transformation of Anglicanism: From State Church to Global Communion*. Cambridge: Cambridge University Press.

Sachs, W.L. (ed.) (2017). *The Oxford History of Anglicanism, Volume V: Global Anglicanism, c.1910–2000*. Oxford: Oxford University Press.

Sayers, D.L. (1943). *The Man Born to Be King*. London: Gollancz.

Schmidt, R.,.H. (2002). *Glorious Companions: Five Centuries of Anglican Spirituality*. Grand Rapids, MI: Eerdmans.

Sedgwick, P. (2005). Anglican theology. In *The Modern Theologians: An Introduction to Christian Theology Since 1918* (eds. D.F. Ford with R. Muers), pp. 178–194. Oxford: Blackwell.

Spencer, S. (2012). *Anglicanism*. (SCM Study guide). London: SCM Press.

Stancliffe, D. (1991). Is there an Anglican liturgical style? In: *The Identity of Anglican Worship* (eds. K. Stevenson and B. Spinks), 124–133. London: Mowbray.

Stott, J. (1986). *The Cross of Christ*. Leicester: IVP.

Sykes, S. (1978). *The Integrity of Anglicanism*. London: Mowbray.

Sykes, S., Booty, J., and Knight, J. (eds.) (1998). *The Study of Anglicanism*. London: SPCK.

Temple, W. (1942). *Christianity and Social Order*. Harmondsworth: Penguin.

Underhill, E. (1911). *Mysticism*. London: Dutton.

Underhill, E. (1936). *Worship*. London: Dutton.

Varcoe, G. (1995). The Anglican church in [sic] Australia. In: *Our Thanks and Praise: The Eucharist in Anglicanism Today* (ed. D.R. Holeton), 187–192. Toronto: Anglican Book Centre.

Wafula, R.S., Mombo, E., and Wandera, J. (eds.) (2016). *Postcolonial Church: Bible, Theology, Mission*. Alameda, CA: Borderless Press.

Wainwright, G. (ed.) (1988). *Keeping the Faith: Essays to Mark the Centenary of* Lux Mundi. London: SPCK.

Ward, K. (2007). *A History of Global Anglicanism.* Cambridge: Cambridge University Press.

Wells, S. (2011). *What Anglicans Believe: An Introduction.* Norwich: Canterbury Press.

Wickeri, J. (ed.) (2000). *No Longer Strangers: Papers of K.H. Ting.* Maryknoll, NY: Orbis.

Wickeri, J. and Wickeri, P. (eds.) (2007). *A Chinese Contribution to Ecumenical Theology: Selected Writings of Bishop K.H. Ting.* Geneva: World Council of Churches.

Wilkinson, A. (1978). *The Church of England in the First World War.* London: SPCK.

Wolf, W. (ed.) (1979). *The Spirit of Anglicanism: Hooker, Maurice, Temple.* Wilton, CT: Morehouse.

Wright, F. (1980). *The Pastoral Nature of the Ministry.* London: SCM Press.

Evelyn Underhill (1875–1941)

Julie Gittoes

Evelyn Underhill is well-known as a prolific and influential writer who, in the midst of the upheavals of the early twentieth century, brought the riches of ancient mystical texts to a wide audience. In our own generation, her insights remain challenging, inspiring, and practical. Her work opens up the meaning of life in communion with God: through honesty about her own struggles and through rekindling an interest in the diverse lives of the mystics.

At the heart of her work is the conviction that God extends an invitation to be loved to every human being: her own quest for God found expression in her vocation to write; to communicate in "plain and untechnical language" how people might participate in and experience the reality of that love (Underhill 1914b, p. 2). One of Underhill's biographers wrote that she believed "mysticism was a way of life, open to all, achieved by the few whose lives were transformed by that which they loved" (Greene 1991, p. 51).

It was this conviction that she shared by means of the written word and as a retreat conductor and broadcaster. The aim of this introduction to Underhill is to place her life and work by rooting it in her wider context, and discerning points of resonance with contemporary perspectives.

Underhill's life spanned the nineteenth and twentieth centuries: a period that saw significant changes in the lives of women but which was also shaped by the impact of two world wars. This social and political context will frame an exploration of her distinctive contribution to Christian theology, including her understanding of pacifism.

Underhill began writing as a poet and novelist and became an accomplished inter-disciplinary scholar. The things that attracted her to the ordinary and extraordinary lives of saints and mystics was their passion, intelligence, and authority. Though her work, what was awakened in her is disseminated to us: not just transformed lives, but the power of the love divine provoking such transformation. Her own passion, intelligence,

Twentieth Century Anglican Theologians: From Evelyn Underhill to Esther Mombo, First Edition.
Edited by Stephen Burns, Bryan Cones, and James Tengatenga.
© 2021 John Wiley & Sons Ltd. Published 2021 by John Wiley & Sons Ltd.

and authority finds its focus on the life of prayer and adoration. That, as well as her emphasis on both liturgy and service, makes her a figure of enduring influence within the Anglican Communion. This is perhaps best summed up in a line from one of her (handwritten) books of private prayers: "Let us ask for a closer communion with our God" (Wrigley-Carr 2018, p. 11).

Pioneer

Born in 1875, Evelyn Underhill grew up in the final decades of the nineteenth century; and her life (and theology) was shaped both by positive changes to the lives of women, but also the impact of conflict. She was undoubtedly a pioneer as a woman studying mysticism and spirituality, becoming an authority on theology and prayer. As Ann Loades notes, she had "no qualifications and no institutional position such as a job in a church or university which might have been hers had she been a man" (Loades 1997, p. xi).

Over her lifetime, in Great Britain, there were significant changes to the lives of women in terms of legal rights, access to education, and the campaign for universal suffrage. Her accomplishments as a scholar and spiritual director are to be set against this backdrop of changing status. In 1867 the National Society for Women's Suffrage was formed. Following shortly after the Married Women's Property Act (1870) came into effect, which allowed married women to own property. It was not until 1918 that women over thirty (and men over twenty-one) were granted the right to vote by the Representation of the People Act. A decade later women over the age of twenty-one were given equal voting rights with men. These changes in law and suffrage were significant in themselves and also signaled something important in terms of intellectual freedom and educational equality. In the 1860s the Taunton Commission said that men and women had the same mental capacity. There were incremental shifts in access to education over the course of the nineteenth century, although gender and class continued to be limiting factors.

However, Underhill was well placed to take advantage of the growing possibilities. The daughter of a barrister, she had been educated at home and spent a spell at a private school. In addition, traveling to Europe nurtured her fluency in and capacity for languages. The opening of a Ladies' Department at King's College, London (KCL) was a significant opportunity for her. She read history and botany but it was her aptitude for languages along with the opportunity to engage with philosophical thought that was to shape her approach to scholarship.

Against this backdrop, her legacy in major works alone is significant: from the impact of *Mysticism* published in 1911 through to *Worship*, published toward the end of her life in 1936.[1] Among other noteworthy "firsts," in 1921 she was the first woman invited to give a series of lectures in religion at Oxford.[2] In 1927, her *alma mater* welcomed her as their first woman Fellow; in 1938 she received an honorary Doctor of Divinity from the University of Aberdeen. That a married, lay Anglican woman had become an authoritative voice on spiritual life and mysticism was a significant accomplishment. It was one which Underhill embraced "quietly and without fuss," in the words of A. M. Allchin (himself a priest and theologian who echoed Underhill's sensibilities) (Allchin 1993, p. 2).

As well as being a pioneer, she was also a pilgrim. As we will explore in the next section, she was influenced by both Roman Catholic and Anglican thinkers. Her own teaching, writing, and direction reflected the breadth and generosity of the ecumenical spirit. The personal is echoed in the wider context. In 1942 the British Council of Churches (now known as Churches Together in Britain and Ireland) was formed to foster interdenominational cooperation.

Allchin himself vividly describes his experience at an Evelyn Underhill festival held in Washington, DC: speakers from the Episcopal, Russian Orthodox, and Roman Catholic traditions – lay and ordained – talked about the way in which her work sustained, liberated and reshaped them.[3] What he summarizes as her clarity, intensity, simplicity, and humor continues to be a gift to Anglicanism and other churches too. She was careful to weave together and engage with the different strands that shape what we have come to know as Anglican theology: "she herself became a notable exponent of the Anglican way with its respect for tradition and its openness to change, its sense of belonging to a Catholic whole which is more than simply English, yet which has its rootedness in the history and experience of a particular people" (Allchin 1993, p. 5).

In terms of shifts in Evelyn Underhill's own thought, one of the most marked was directly related to the seismic impact of two world wars. The context is made explicit in the Preface of *Practical Mysticism*. She considered postponing the publication of "this little book, written during the last months of peace, [that] goes to press in the first weeks of the great war" because it might be felt that in "a time of conflict and horror, when only the most ignorant, disloyal, or apathetic can hope for quietness of mind, a book which deals with that which is called the 'contemplative' attitude to existence is wholly out of place" (Underhill [1914b], p. 1).

Her rationale for going ahead is rooted in a seriousness about "practical" mysticism that cannot be a fair-weather habit. Rather she sees in the lives of mystics – including Joan of Arc and Florence Nightingale – an intense spiritual vision in opposition to suffering and disharmony. She wrote that "it becomes part of true patriotism to keep the spiritual life, both of the individual citizen and the social group, active and vigorous" (Underhill [1914b], p. 2). Hope, beauty, and charity lay beyond violence and ruthlessness. Underhill herself worked at the Admiralty (naval intelligence department), but her views changed. In 1939 she adopted a Christian pacifist stance, joining the Anglican Pacifist Fellowship – writing a pamphlet entitled *The Church and War* in 1940. This sacrificial understanding of pacifism is related to her developments in understanding the doctrine of the incarnation.

Pilgrim

Evelyn Underhill's pioneering work was rooted in her journey of faith as well as her impressive learning, which included psychology, philosophy, theology, liturgy, and languages. Best known for *Mysticism* (1911) and *Worship* (1936) these texts reveal the scope of her thinking and depth of her scholarship as well as shifts in her thinking.

Beyond these major texts, which in a sense "bookend" her life and work, Underhill was exceptionally prolific in producing articles, addresses, essays, and letters as well as other books. There are many substantial biographies of, or introductions to, Underhill (e.g., Armstrong 1975; Greene 1991; Loades 1997). The purpose of this section is to note the figures who shaped Underhill's own exploration of religion. Through the lens of her personal life, we see something of the shifts in her thinking, but also the depth and scope of learning that opened up the lives of the saints to those seeking to find life in communion with God.

In 1907, Evelyn Underhill married one of her childhood friends, Hubert Moore. By that point, her scholarship was being established through her work on *Mysticism;* and her journey of faith had begun to intensify and find focus as she considered converting to Roman Catholicism. Although she had been confirmed at boarding school, her parents and husband were surprised by her conviction. Evelyn herself vividly describes this shift: having thought herself to be an atheist she "was driven nearer and nearer to Christianity, half wishing it were true, and half resisting violently" (Williams 1944, p. 38).

Although drawn to Catholicism, in the end she became a devout anglo-catholic. Loades notes that Underhill's husband was concerned about her relationship with a priest as confessor. However, it was also the support of such spiritual advisors that helped nurture and shape her vocation as a guide to others (both in conducting retreats and in spiritual direction). The Catholic layman Friedrich von Hügel was a particularly significant influence – enabling her to move from an abstract spiritual quest toward an experience of Christ. In her own words, Underhill says: "I owe him my whole spiritual life" (Williams 1944, p. 196). In the introduction to *Evelyn Underhill's Prayer Book*, Robyn Wrigley-Carr describes the way in which von Hügel sought "to balance her intellectual focus with the institutional: care for the poor, church attendance, partaking in the Eucharist" (Wrigley-Carr 2018, p. 5).

Von Hügel's influence on Underhill's ministry can be traced in her correspondence and writings, but also in her choice of texts used in her *Prayer Book*.[4] Wrigley-Carr carefully re-presents this collection – including prayers from the twelfth to the twentieth centuries, across all Christian traditions and including those written by Evelyn herself. Augustine's *Confessions* and *The Imitation of Christ* were important to von Hügel and included by Underhill: their words and their lives continuing to shape the lives of directees and retreatants.

It was in 1922 that Underhill made her first retreat to Pleshey and three years later, she conducted her first retreat there. At first, the was alarmed at the idea of silence; "the mysterious peace and light distilled by it"; and also her distress when it ended and the "clatter began" (Cropper 2003, p. 124). Underhill treasured the light and life of Pleshey, distilled by generations of prayer. It was a place where she was both pilgrim and pioneer – as a woman retreat conductor. Through her meditations, addresses, and offering focal points around her overarching theme/metaphor she was able to support and guide the spiritual life of those who attended Pleshey (and other retreat houses).[5]

Underhill's theological writings leave us a legacy that reveals her own spiritual pilgrimage and also inspired others to immerse themselves in the writings of the mystics. By drawing on the diverse patterns of their lives – rooted in the primary commitment to prayer and adoration – she explores what it means to be grasped and transformed by God's love, manifested in acts of service in the world. The inner spiritual life was not an alternative to or escape from the practical; but the very source revitalized it and made it worthwhile. It was both personal and social. Her work reflects a relational and practical appreciation of the "great cloud of witnesses" who surround the individual pilgrim (and corporate body of the church).

Those witnesses are drawn from across the span of historical and cultural contexts. Some of them lived their faith in domestic settings, others in religious community, and others in solitude. Many of them were also practical, engaged in the realities of their world. As Loades puts it: "she found inspiration in poets, preachers, politicians, soldiers, monastics, mothers and fathers because they spoke with passionate intelligence, enthusiasm and imagination about their experiences of God" (Loades 1997, p. xii). We find Augustine in the company of Joan of Arc; Wordsworth with Blake; St. John of the Cross with Catherine of Siena William Law and Jane Lead.

Allchin's summary of distinctive aspects of Underhill's teaching notes both her awareness of how unattractive the church as an institution can look at times; but he also celebrates her as an exponent of the Anglican tradition (in its diversity and within the wider tradition and her ecumenical context). Just as her exploration of the spiritual life moved from the abstract to the person of Christ, so she also embraced the (often challenging) reality that commitment to the inner life cannot be abstracted the life of the "particular" of people and place. He quotes her saying:

> when we think of pews and the Parish Magazine, we tend to rebel . . . It seems far too stiff and institutional . . . Yet there it is; the Christian sequence is God-Christ-Spirit-Church-Eternal life . . . The incarnation of the Holy in the world is social (Allchin 1993, p. 5).

Theological Themes

Over the course of her life, Evelyn Underhill's writing evolved in relation to her own journey of faith, and the fostering of her vocation as a spiritual director. The theological themes echo the shifts in her personal pilgrimage: from a psychological and historical interest in mysticism to an increasingly explicit focus on Christ, the sacramental life of the church, and Christian doctrine. Through some of her key texts, we get an impression of her distinctive contribution and the way in which she developed her focus on mysticism and prayer over her life time.

As we will see, Underhill's exploration of mysticism places an emphasis on the hunger for love; but she gives space to the importance of the active life of service. As a spiritual pilgrim and guide, she talks about the place of prayer and art, symbol and sacrament within the journey of faith; she takes seriously the lived life of the institutional church and, as the discovery of her prayer books show, was sensitive to seasons of life (personal and ecclesial). Her deepening appreciation of Christian doctrine – manifested in the scriptures and the creeds – includes a focus on the Holy Spirit in relation to Christology, Trinity, and soteriology. We also see the way in which such engagement shapes her practice – particularly, having avoided making public commitment on social issues, in relation to pacifism.

In *Mysticism,* Underhill draws on her study of psychology and history (and from traditions beyond the Christian religion) to argue for the possibility of awareness of God, and the potential for transformation. The book is in two parts: the first introduces the general subject of mysticism; the second contains a more detailed study of the development of spiritual or mystical consciousness. In the Preface to the first edition, she states that mysticism is one of the most abused words of the English language: used in mutually exclusive ways; and claimed as an excuse for, and criticism of, "every kind of occultism, for dilute transcendentalism, vapid symbolism, religious or aesthetic sentimentality, and bad metaphysics" (Underhill 1911, p. 13).

Instead she understands it to be "the expression of the innate tendency the human spirit towards complete harmony with the transcendental order; whatever the theological formula under which it is understood . . . this tendency, in great mystics . . . dominates their life and, in the experience of 'mystical union' attains its end" (Underhill 1911, p. 13). She regards religion, pain, and beauty as the three "authoritative areas of perception and experience" (Loades 1997, p. 17). She describes mystics as "heroic examples of the life of the spirit"; who apprehend "the Absolute, Pure Being, the utterly Transcendent . . . the life of the All, vivid, flowing and changing, and the changeless, conditionless life of the One" (Underhill 1911, pp. 45, 47).

This epic work of curiosity and scholarship is shot through with a deep yearning for love: she draws on the life and words of Augustine and Julian of Norwich, Richard Rolle, and Teresa of Avila. In this rich company she explores symbolism, on the cusp of her own discovery of the power of the sacraments to renew life. In addition, she notes that in order to reflect on their experience, mystics rely on some form of creedal framework. She traces the stages of awakening of the self from purgation/repentance, illumination/assurance of knowing oneself as loved by God and self-surrender/spiritual union.

Underhill ultimately draws us to the garden of "Divine Fecundity" through cross and tomb to resurrection. She says, like the story of the Cross, so too the story of the human spirit ends in a garden: in a place of birth and fruitfulness, of beautiful and natural things: "it ends with the coming forth of divine humanity, never again to leave us: living in us, and with us, a pilgrim, a worker, a guest at our table, a sharer at all hazards in life (Underhill 1911, p. 460).

This is the story to which the lives of the mystics bear witness – echoing her prayer for a closer communion with God.

In the Preface to the Twelfth Edition (in 1930), Underhill notes the shifts within this field of study – from being regarded as a "byway of religion" to "in its intensive form the essential religious experience." Although her final positions remain unchanged, she notes the increasing stress on divine transcendence and of the place of grace, welcoming the work of Karl Barth and Rudolf Otto. She also notes the "disentangling" of mysticism from psycho-physical activity.

It is in *The Mystic Way* that we see an explicitly Christian focus: and here we see the way in which she approaches the doctrine of incarnation. She begins with the first events reported in all three synoptic gospels: the preaching of John the Baptist and Jesus' baptism. Underhill describes the moment of the Spirit descending on Jesus as a "crucial moment": "the strange, new life latent in Jesus of Nazareth, suddenly flooded his human consciousness . . . suddenly became aware of Reality" (Underhill 1914a, p. 87).

She dwells on the imagery of the dove – with all it creative power – and developed her understanding of Jesus' "sonship" as the only human metaphor that expresses "a sudden and irrevocable knowledge of identity with that Source" (Underhill 1914a, p. 88). Freed from sin or separation from God, Jesus still faces temptation: the choice between power and love in the solitude and trials of the wilderness.

It is in *Mysticism* that Underhill articulates her understanding of "Divine Fecundity," communicated in Jesus' preaching and the good news of the Kingdom; but it is in her engagement with the Last Supper and Jesus' death and resurrection that this "vivifying force" is related to a new way of life opened to us in peace and hope. Jesus "exhibited Reality by being it. He is Himself the poem, the symphony, which expresses His unique vision of truth" and Underhill charts the way in which the impulse of new life though him was carried forward in the Pauline and Johannine traditions into the early church (Underhill 1914b, p. 149).

In *Abba*, the nature of the incarnation is explored with reference to seven clauses of the Lord's Prayer. She speaks of Christ's earthly life as "both a correction and completion of human life" and who in teaching us to pray enabled us to "lay hold on the Eternal and experience another level of life" beyond the griefs and limitations of the world (Underhill 1940, p. 3). She leads us from the concern for God's glory and harmony with God's creative will, to our earthly limitations and the ways in which we bring before God our burdens and needs. She explores our physical and spiritual hungers and the symbolism of food leading us to the eucharist as "the crest of a great wave; a total sacramental disclosure of the dealings of the Transcendent God with men" (Underhill 1940, p. 58). For her, the mystery of the incarnation is this constant encounter with God in the ordinary "stuff" of life, and the nature of creaturely dependence in prayer.

We now turn to Underhill's other major work. She begins her Preface to *Worship* by saying that she is not liturgical expert; but her aim "has been rather to explore those primary realities of man's relation to God which our devotional action is intended to express" (Underhill 1936, p. xi). She focuses on the deepest sense of worship – our human response to the Eternal. The first section of this work looks at the characteristics of Christian worship – in what she calls its theocentric yet incarnational temper: moving through reflection on ritual and sacrifice to focus on the eucharistic action itself in its collective and personal aspects. The second section is comprised of descriptive and historic studies intended to illustrate those principles and "show from various angles the response of man to God as it comes to flower within Christianity" (Underhill 1936, p. xi).

This text is born not only out of scholarly interest, but also a personal commitment to participate in the diversity of worship across Christian denominations. We see too a profound reflection on the life of Christ in relation to her understanding of sacrament and sacrifice. This latter category she sees as fundamental to his understanding of his life, ministry, and death. Though him, God and humanity are drawn into communion: "in many and for man, by an entire self-offering, the Divine Logos redeems creation, atones for man's sinfulness, and fulfils man's supreme obligation to God" (Underhill 1936, p. 55).

For Underhill, Christian worship is more than "a supernatural action"; it is "a supernatural life" understood as the creaturely response to divine charity: "a response in which man moves out towards Reality, sheds self-occupation, and finds the true basis of his life" (Underhill 1936, p. 339). Her desire for communion, for a return to the loving heart of God, radiates beyond its ritual expression "penetrating and transforming all the actions of humanity" (Underhill 1936, p. 341). She expresses a rich and audacious vision of life thus "entinctured by the Incarnate Life, and in virtue of this given absolute worth" (Underhill 1936, p. 341).

In prayer, adoration, and contemplation; in loving action that strives for the healing of the world the church responds to God and rises to the fullest meaning of her vocation. Underhill calls this path both evangelical and eucharistic – perhaps prefiguring the challenges we face in holding together the churches call to worship and to mission.[6] This pattern of life is active and creative as it seeks to give "concrete and social expression to the Eucharistic ideal," which completes our adoration (Underhill 1936, p. 342).

Throughout Underhill's writings we see a deepening attentiveness to Christ and an outworking of the mystery of the incarnation. This underpins the prayers of the individual pilgrim and the corporate life of the church; and as we have seen adoration and contemplation flow out into the world in social expression. However, one of the most marked shifts in her thinking was in relation to pacifism. As we noted, in *Practical Mysticism* she acknowledged the impact of conflict on the task ahead she was embarking upon in encouraging others to discover the art of union with "Reality." Life that is more real, is not abstract but practical and affirmative; it is costly and makes demands on loyalty, trust, and self-sacrifice (Underhill 1914b, p. 31).

For Underhill, one response to Christ's sacrifice was intercessory prayer: standing before the love of God with the needs and cries of the world on your heart. Prayers also orientate us to the future; of a world transformed; a world without war. Such prayer is rooted in hope. She writes "to look with real desire for the coming of the Kingdom means crossing over to God's side; dedicating our powers, whatever they may be, to the triumph of His purpose" (Underhill 1940, p. 35).

Here we see the way in which her approach to prayer is full of practical responsibility and action. If our prayer is for the "wide-spreading love transfiguring the whole texture of life," then "money, time and position, the politics we support and the papers we read" must reflect that (Underhill 1940, p. 33). Indeed, radical social reform rests not only on "the most complete dethronement of privilege" but also on the recognition that "peace and joy in the Holy Spirit can only come to us by the free gift of the Transcendent" (Underhill 1940, p. 33).

Her vision of hope and dependence on God and alignment with God's will was such that her response to the looming conflict in the late 1930s turned her to pacifism. The crisis was such that only acceptance of the cross would resolve it. As Loades notes, in "the months before her death she was more and more sure that Christianity and war were incompatible" (Loades 1997, p. 57). The hope and love she had discovered, taught, and practiced, drew on the cross – in its agony and in the peace of absolute abandonment to God. She died before the scale of World War II was evident – but her legacy is one of profound challenge and uncompromising conviction. Underhill wrote that "the true pacifist is a redeemer, and must accept with joy the redeemer's lot. He too is self-ordered, without conditions, for the peace of the world" (cited by Loades 1997, p. 58).

A Distinctive Legacy and an Enduring Influence

The distinctiveness of Underhill's contribution is shaped by her context and the influences that led her to emerge as a prominent and popular thinker. It can be recognized quantitively in the scope, range, and number of publications. However, the qualitative assessment of her legacy reveals the multiple impact of *Mysticism*. It was a publishing success – and opened the field for further scholarship – and the twelfth preface sets out the theological shifts Underhill herself made over two decades of continued work, particularly in relation to grace, service, and pacifism.

Her work made a significant contribution to understanding the human condition (spiritually and psychologically). As her agenda turned toward the development of Christian doctrine, we see a legacy that reflects on both cross and altar as an expression of sacrifice, hope, love, and peace. Evelyn sought to communicate across a range of media: she engaged in scholarly work, shaping the field of mysticism; she wrote books aimed at those outside the academy (and indeed outside the church); she worked with individuals as a spiritual guide and director; she was also a broadcaster, whose talks on *The Spiritual Life* were later published (Underhill 1937). Her vocation as a pioneer and pilgrim ought to encourage us to deploy all forms of communication we have to give an account of the hope that is in us.

As a pioneer and pilgrim, perhaps Underhill also stands as an exemplar for those seeking to bridge the gap between liturgy and theology and the range of social and bio-medical sciences, those working in the arenas of artificial intelligence and climate science. For we do need people like her whose own curiosity and prayerfulness can teach us and help us sustain hope. She raises challenges about whose voices are missing from our theological and ecclesial life; and she asks demanding questions about what sort of community we will be. Evelyn unapologetically and passionately reminds us that adoration of God is the priority.

In that sense, for the wider life of the Anglican Communion, her present influence is summed up in her quest for a closer communion with God: that is, her profound commitment to the life of prayer. It was, as we have seen, a commitment worked out in her pioneering work and her personal pilgrimage. It was a commitment that drew her into deep engagement with the lives of the saints; and which saw her devote herself to exercising her vocation as a spiritual guide and retreat conductor. Institutional life and social engagement flowed from this rootedness in prayer.

The priority she gives to the life of prayer and adoration, encourages and challenges our generation to fix our attention on God as "the main thing." Archbishop Justin Welby has made prayer and the renewal of religious life a priority. He writes that through prayer we establish our true identity: "there has never been a renewal of the spiritual life of the church – which means all Christians, you and me – without a renewal of prayer. That's why I've made it the highest priority of my ministry."[7] It is appropriate then to rediscover the contribution of Evelyn Underhill to this calling. A previous archbishop, Michael Ramsey, wrote that she helped people to "grasp the priority of prayer in the Christian life and the place of the contemplative element within it" (Ramsey 1975, p. x).

In her work we see an interdisciplinary engagement with the journey of faith, reflected in the diversity of the lives of Christian mystics. Her ecumenical engagement remains significant for the Anglican Communion – as she teaches us to attend to and appreciate the different contributions of diverse groups, denominations, and traditions. Her work continues to challenge and inspire the church in a number of areas, including: the value we place of art and how we cultivate practices of popular devotion; the place of liturgy in learning who Christ is; what we mean by "sacrifice" in liturgy and service; and, importantly, how we value differences between us. Let us make Evelyn Underhill's prayer our own: Let us ask for a closer communion with our Lord.

Notes

1   Underhill 2015 [1911] and Underhill 1958 [1936].
2   The Upton Lectures were given at Manchester College and Underhill published them in 1922 under the title *The Life of the Spirit and the Life of Today*.
3   Allchin (1993, pp. 5–6).
4   Biographers and scholars of Underhill refer to the books of prayers Underhill had collected and which she used on retreats; but it had been assumed that they had been lost. Robyn Wrigley-Carr describes the story of their rediscovery – and the way in which she began to copy out the prayers. Her work has enabled them to bless a new generation – the lives and prayers of the saints continuing to shape our lives.
5   Wrigley-Carr's introduction to *Evelyn Underhill's Prayer Book* gives a helpful overview to the way in which she shaped retreats and the place of prayer and spiritual direction within them.
6   For example, Hardy (2001) and Gittoes, Green, and James (2012).
7   https://www.archbishopofcanterbury.org/prayer-partnership-god (accessed July 21, 2020).

References

Allchin, A.M. (1993). Introduction. In: *Daily Readings with a Modern Mystic: Selections from the Writings of Evelyn Underhill* (ed. D. Oberg). Mystic, CT: Twenty-Third Publications.

Armstrong, C.J.R. (1975). *Evelyn Underhill (1875–1941): An Introduction to Her Life and Writings*. London: Mowbray.

Cropper, M. (2003). *The Life of Evelyn Underhill*. Woodstock, CT: Skylight Paths Publishing.

Gittoes, J., Green, B., and Heard, J. (eds.) (2012). *Generous Ecclesiology: Church, World and the Kingdom of God*. London: SCM Press.

Greene, D. (1991). *Evelyn Underhill: Artist of the Infinite Life*. London: Mowbray.

Hardy, D.W. (2001). *Finding the Church: The Dynamic Truth of Anglicanism*. London: SCM Press.

Loades, A. (1997). *Evelyn Underhill*. London: Fount.

Ramsey, M. (1975). Foreword. In: *Evelyn Underhill (1875–1941): An Introduction to Her Life and Writings* (ed. C.J.R. Armstrong), ix–x. London: Mowbray.

Underhill, E. (1911). *Mysticism: A Study in Nature and Development of Spiritual Consciousness*. London: Methuen (Republished by Andras M. Nagy Publications: 2015.).

Underhill, E. (1914a). *The Mystic Way: A Psychological Study in Christian Origins.* London: E.P. Dutton.

Underhill, E. (1914b). *Practical Mysticism: A Little Book for Normal People.* London: Dent (republished by http://RareBooksClub.com. in 2012).

Underhill, E. (1922). *The Life of the Spirit and the Life of Today.* New York, NY: Dutton (Republished by Mowbray in 1995).

Underhill, E. (1936 [1958]). *Worship*, 12e. Welwyn, UK: James Nisbet.

Underhill, E. (1937). *The Spiritual Life: Four Broadcast Talks.* London: Hodder & Stoughton (Reprinted by Martino Publishing in 2013.).

Underhill, E. (1940). *Abba.* London: Longmans, Green and Co.

Williams, C. (ed.) (1944). *The Letters of Evelyn Underhill*, 2e. London: Longmans, Green and Co.

Wrigley-Carr, R. (ed.) (2018). *Evelyn Underhill's Prayer Book.* London: SPCK.

William Temple (1881–1944)

Matthew Peter Cadwell

Among the most significant Anglican theologians of the twentieth century was William Temple (1881–1944), successively Bishop of Manchester, Archbishop of York, and Archbishop of Canterbury. Temple is remembered for his work in philosophical and systematic theology, social advocacy, and leadership within the Church of England and the ecumenical movement into World War II.

It was written that William Temple was the most significant Anglican churchman of the first half of the twentieth century. By the sheer power of his mind, the depth of his faith, seeming tirelessness of his vitality, and the force of his personality, he dominated the Church of England. No comparable figure has arisen since his death to eclipse him either within his own church or as a religious spokesman in the wider world (Carmichael and Goodwin 1963, p. v).

That statement, while dated, provides insight into the esteem with which Temple was held, especially in the last century.

Temple's was a critical voice in twentieth century Anglican theology – because of his role as archbishop during a period of world unrest, and because he wrote at a pivotal moment in theological development. Inheriting a rich theological legacy from such figures F. D. Maurice, B. F. Westcott, and Charles Gore, he prepared Anglican theology for the new insights of philosophical, process, and even liberation theologies.

Biography and Context

William Temple's life and leadership in church and society was as significant (if not more from some perspectives) as his contributions to theology and philosophy. He was born on October 15, 1881 at the height of the British Empire. He was the second

Twentieth Century Anglican Theologians: From Evelyn Underhill to Esther Mombo, First Edition.
Edited by Stephen Burns, Bryan Cones, and James Tengatenga.
© 2021 John Wiley & Sons Ltd. Published 2021 by John Wiley & Sons Ltd.

son of Frederick Temple (1821–1902) and Beatrice Lascelles (1844–1915). Frederick Temple was successively Bishop of Exeter, London, and Archbishop of Canterbury. The senior Temple had been attracted to the "Liberal Oxford Movement" as a young man and was a contributor to the controversial *Essays and Reviews* (1860) with the essay "Education and the World." As Archbishop of Canterbury he officiated at the coronation of King Edward VI in 1902. William's mother descended from British nobility through both grandfathers. Her father was a member of parliament, and held a position in the royal household.

Despite extraordinary privilege, William Temple experienced a difficult childhood. He developed gout at the age of two, was often ill, always overweight, and suffered poor eyesight (Fletcher 1963, p. 244). He was never interested in sports. However, he had many friends, enjoyed music, and was an exceptional student. As a boy he often "played church," desiring to be a priest like his father. He also loved literature. Favorites were Robert Browning, Dorothy Sayers, Shakespeare, and George Bernard Shaw. He went on to study classics as an Oxford undergraduate. While there, he was elected president of the Oxford Union debating society. His "parlor trick" was an ability to present divergent views and concerns, bringing them into consensus and reconciliation, a skill he would develop throughout his life (Fletcher 1963, p. 246). Upon graduation, he accepted a post as lecturer and fellow of Queen's College, Oxford, in philosophy. He studied classical and English philosophers, while time in Germany led him to study with Adolf von Harnack.

At Oxford, Temple developed an enduring, lifelong interest in justice for working people, leading to participation in socialist meetings and work to help London's poor. Like F. D. Maurice in the previous century, Temple wanted to challenge both the "unsocial Christians" and the "unchristian Socialists." In 1908 he became president of the Workers' Educational Association, founded by Maurice. While evangelicals were focused on issues of personal salvation and anglo-catholics on the study of patristics, Temple believed, like Maurice before him, that the power of gospel should lead to societal transformation (Fletcher 1963, p. 247).

Although son of the late archbishop, in 1906 Temple was denied ordination by Oxford's bishop Francis Paget because he was "only inclined, very tentatively" to accept the virgin birth and bodily resurrection (Fletcher 1963, p. 249). Eventually he was ordained deacon by Archbishop Randall Davidson in 1908 and priest a year later. The experience led Temple to the view that in Anglicanism fundamentalism took the form of creedal orthodoxy, rather than biblical (Fletcher 1963, p. 249).

Through a growing friendship with Charles Gore, Paget's successor in Oxford, Temple moved toward a more orthodox position; though, he and Gore never fully agreed.[1] By the time Temple reached his own theological maturity his earlier doubts had been set aside as he embraced a strongly incarnational and even Johannine faith.

In 1913 Temple was appointed to St. James, Piccadilly (London's West End), his only parochial cure. He found himself not especially gifted or interested in pastoral work. Fletcher suggests, "The emotional and the intimate are not his element" (Fletcher 1963, p. 252). However, his skill in the pulpit lead to significant speaking invitations across the United Kingdom and in North America. It was while at St. James that Temple served as president of the Christian Social Union (CSU), founded in 1889 and inspired by the Christian socialism of Maurice. Earlier leaders had included Gore, B. F. Westcott, and Henry Scott Holland. In 1916, while president, Temple married Frances Anson, the CSU's secretary.

Temple resigned from St. James in 1918 to take leadership in the "Life and Liberty Movement." Determined to win self-management for the church, even at the cost of disestablishment, he and others sought to ensure that the church could preach with a clear conscience. He traveled the country speaking on behalf of the movement's proposals, including self-governance through a church assembly, the adoption a new prayer book to reflect better the spirituality of the age, more equitable clergy salaries, and securing the vote for women in ecclesiastical matters (Fletcher 1963, p. 259).

Temple believed as well that women should be ordained to the priesthood, but he never pressed the point. In 1916 he wrote:

> Personally I want . . . to see women ordained to the priesthood. But still more do I want to see both real advance toward the reunion of Christendom, and the general emancipation of women. To win admission now would put back the former and to moot it would put back the latter (Iremonger 1948, p. 452).[2]

Temple accepted a canonry at Westminster Abbey in 1918. He stayed two years, until named Bishop of Manchester. It was a Protestant and conservative diocese; Temple was a liberal-catholic. But the diocese appreciated his larger than life leadership in church and society. It was said that he had a "natural inability to do anything badly" (cited in Fletcher 1963, p. 260).

In 1924 he was named chairman of the "Conference on Politics, Economics, and Citizenship" (COPEC). The beginning of the ecumenical movement, it attracted 1500 delegates from 80 countries uniting various denominations and traditions for a common purpose: "to seek the will and purpose of God in political, social, and industrial life" (Thomas 1979, p. 106). Temple believed that social witness was the strongest basis for church unity. COPEC ultimately led to the Oxford Life and Work Meeting (1937) and the Edinburgh Conference on Faith and Order (1937). Temple took a leading role in both. From them, eventually, was born the World Council of Churches.

In 1926 churches were called to negotiate a coal miners' strike following years of economic ills and owner–miner antagonism. Temple, then Bishop of Manchester, met with Prime Minister Stanley Baldwin to help resolve the matter, arguing that miners had made concessions, but the owners none. Baldwin refused action, suggesting that church leaders were interfering and prolonging the conflict. Temple, however, maintained that the church has both the right and the responsibility to be engaged in social issues, especially concerning the livelihoods of the nation's people. Although failing in this conflict, the interaction made Temple a national figure in support of working people. His views on the coal strike were published as *Essays in Christian Politics* (Temple 1927).

Despite their tense relationship, in 1929 Temple was nominated Archbishop of York by Baldwin. Regarded the "people's archbishop," he served 13 years – his longest tenure in any position. It was at York that Temple's leadership, theology and social radicalism came to maturity (Fletcher 1963, p. 267). He chaired the council of the BBC, was appointed member of the Privy Council, preached at the disarmament conference of 1932, chaired the Lambeth Conference of 1938 (due to the Archbishop of Canterbury's illness), and advocated for the League of Nations. He authored a total of 12 books while at York, including his philosophical treatise *Nature, Man, and God,* originally delivered as the 1932–1933 Gifford Lectures at the University of Glasgow (Temple 1951).

In 1922 Temple was appointed member and later chaired the Church of England's Doctrine Commission (1922–1938). Called to help resolve differences in belief and practice (on the virgin birth, resurrection, theologies and practices of the eucharist, etc.), the commission studied the breadth of belief and practice in English Anglicanism. Consistent with Temple's concern to draw Christians together the final report, *Doctrine in the Church of England* (Lampe and the Church of England 1938), avoided attempts to enforce particular doctrinal positions and instead articulated the range of Anglican thought and practice. This generated scorn among some for a seeming lack of orthodoxy. Ultimately, the tense international situation limited the report's influence as attention turned toward war.

Temple was promoted to Archbishop of Canterbury in April 1942 at the height of World War II. He was the choice of his predecessor, Cosmo Gordon Lang. Winston Churchill disliked Temple's outspoken political positions, but acquiesced to Lang's view that Temple enjoyed such national stature that he was the only choice. Upon learning of the appointment George Bernard Shaw remarked: "An Archbishop of Temple's enlightenment is a realized impossibility" (Thomas 1979, p. 111). As pastor to the nation Temple visited the armed forces, conducted prayer services in industrial plants, and visited bombed communities on Sundays. His sermons were broadcast to troops on ships, in the African desert, and in northern Italy. Hearing him people remarked: "Now we understand for the first time what Christianity really is" (Fletcher 1963, p. 283). Increasingly concerned with the plight of Europe's Jewish population, he was a co-founder of the Council for Christians and Jews in 1942. He urged the British government to provide aid and asylum for the Jewish victims of Nazism, speaking forcefully in the House of Lords (Spencer 2015, p. xviii). He also worked behind the scenes for a negotiated peace, opposing the Allies' policies of unconditional surrender.

While Temple was Archbishop of Canterbury Lambeth Palace was bombed, leaving only a small flat and office habitable. The Temples continued to reside amid the rubble, earning the respect of their neighbors and those living in similarly dangerous circumstances. His robust schedule and output belied the fact that he continued to suffer from ill health throughout his tenure, especially the painful gout that had afflicted him since his childhood. He died of a heart attack on October 26, 1944. Temple's body was cremated and interred in a Canterbury Cathedral garden.

Temple's Theology

Temple stated: "The whole of my theology is an attempt to understand and verify the words: 'He that hath seen me hath seen the Father'" (Iremonger 1948, p. 155). Thus, his theological focus is the exploration of the incarnation. This is a theme that runs throughout Anglican theology, particularly in the nineteenth and early twentieth centuries, in the work of Maurice, Westcott, Gore, and the liberal catholics. Temple stands firmly in this tradition, even as he offers a unique voice.

Philosophical Idealism

Temple described his own task as "Theological Philosophy" (Temple 1951, p. 44), rooting his theology in the British Idealism prevalent in the nineteenth and early twentieth centuries. While varied in their beliefs, the idealists were influenced by Kant and Hegel and saw nature and history as dynamic and progressive expressions or manifestations of the Absolute. Some idealists (the monists) argued that all finite things are aspects of this one Absolute, sometimes described as Spirit, while others (personal idealists) see ultimate reality in a community of loving spirits (Wilkinson 2010, p. 14).

In Temple's project the idealists' concepts are combined, with God the unifying principle or absolute, "who sustains the universe; but value is realised in community" (Wilkinson 2010, p. 14). For Temple, reality is a succession of grades, which include successively: matter, life, mind, and spirit. Each grade experiences fulfillment when it is possessed by the higher grade, and each uses the lower for its expression. He writes: "The lower grades . . . only attain to the fullness of their own being so far as they are indwelt and dominated by those above them. They exist, then, ultimately, to embody or symbolize what is more than themselves. The universe is sacramental" (Temple 1930, p. 16). In other words, everything in the universe is in a constant state of intercourse with higher and lower forms to find its full expression. For him, this process leads to Christ and the incarnation, with God acting through the matter and historical processes of humanity to reveal the truth of Godself, while simultaneously presenting us a true image and example of humanity in Christ.

Revelation

Temple argues that there are two dimensions to this revelation: divine self-disclosure and human perception. Revelation, at its most profound, is the coincidence of event (God's action) and appreciation (human perception) (Temple 1951, p. 315). The theological task is discovering, trusting, and understanding God's self-disclosure.

Revelation is not static, but a dynamic process, just as creation is an ongoing, dynamic process. Offered to us in revelation are not, therefore, "eternal truths" about God, but opportunities for relationship with the living God through God's action in history, and our subsequent interpretation of its meaning (Ramsey 1960, p. 152). As such, the work of theology is ever new as we seek in each new age to understand God's revelation in relation to our life and context.

Dogma and doctrine follow as the church reflects on the meaning and impact of God's revelatory events. However, doctrine is always secondary to the true and authentic life of faith and relationship with God. Temple writes,

> faith is not the holding of correct doctrines, but personal fellowship with the living God . . . I do not believe in any creed, but I use certain creeds to express, to conserve, and to deepen my belief in God. *What is offered to man's apprehension in any specific Revelation is not truth concerning God but the living God Himself* (Temple 1951, p. 322, italics in original).

Incarnation

For Temple, the ultimate revelation is God's incarnation in Christ. He understood the incarnation as the central principal of the universe and the logical culmination of reality (the Absolute in the idealist framework). Temple believed that the whole of the universe is sacramental, with Christ – the ultimate sacrament – at the center of all. In one of his best-known passages he wrote:

> It may safely be said that the one ground for the hope of Christianity that it may make its claim to be the true faith lies in the fact that it is the most avowedly materialist of all the great religions. . . Its most central saying is: "The Word was made flesh," where the last term was, no doubt, chosen because of its specially materialistic associations. By the very nature of its central doctrine Christianity is committed to a belief in the ultimate significance of the historical process, and in the reality of matter and its place in the divine scheme (Temple 1951, p. 478).

Here Temple was stressing the centrality of material substance in God's sacramental revelation, culminating in the incarnation. For Temple, this has profound meaning and impact, touching every aspect of human life. Through Christ, nothing is beyond redemption and all matter has the potential to mediate God's life and love, chiefly and most especially humanity.

For Temple it is important to state that God not only became *a* human in the incarnation, but rather took on humanity as a whole, mediating divinity and humanity, transforming our being, and uniting us to God (Temple 1930, p. 151). This approach is shared with previous Anglicans, such as Maurice, who said repeatedly that "Christ is the Head of every man" (Maurice 1884, p. 155). Temple quotes own father writing that by his incarnation Christ raised "our humanity to an entirely higher level, to a level with His own" (Temple 1930, p. 152). Christ is, therefore, a "Second Adam" (Temple 1930, p. 152), recreating humanity. Temple writes: "Christ is not only a man; He is Man" (Temple 1930, p. 153).

This unity of God and humanity in Christ is accomplished through a spiritual process of love – a love which is ever deepening over time and through history. However, in any particular moment this process of divine–human union is incomplete, and will remain so until the final consummation in the eschaton (Temple 1930, p. 153).

Even God is in some measure in process, through the reality and experience of the incarnation. Temple argues:

> God eternally is what we see in Christ; but temporally the Incarnation, the taking of Manhood into God, was a real enrichment of the Divine Life. God loved before; but love (at least as we know it) becomes fully real only in its activity, which is sacrifice (Temple 1930, p. 280).[3]

His understanding of the enrichment of the divine life will be questioned by those who are concerned to preserve God's immutability. However for Temple it seems to be a consequence of his philosophical framework, as well as his genuine understanding of God's love.

A notable feature of Temple's Christology is his rejection of the concept of "kenosis" (God's self-emptying) in the incarnation. The kenotic view, first promoted in the Anglican theological tradition by Charles Gore in his *Lux Mundi* essay (Gore 1921, p. 264), was an impossibility for Temple as it seemed to suggest that during the period of Jesus' earthly life God had self-emptied to the point of having no being except in Jesus, even while an infant (Temple 1930, pp. 142–143). He calls this idea "intolerable."

Further, Temple is concerned that the kenotic theory makes the incarnation a mere episode in the life of God, after which God is freed from the real human pains endured while incarnate (Temple 1930, p. 144). Instead, he wants to preserve the incarnation as central to the divine life, not a temporary episode of debasement. He writes, "the limitations are the means whereby the Eternal Son, remaining always in the bosom of the Father, lays bare to us the very heart of Godhead, in doing this, moreover, the Son of God has made our condition matter of His own experience" (Temple 1930, p. 144).

Atonement

This leads to Temple's understanding of redemption and atonement. For Temple, the atonement is integral to the meaning of the incarnation, "the mode of the Deity of God" (Temple 1930, p. 255). While his theological outlook is profoundly hopeful and positive, he does not entirely fail to recognize that evil and sin are real, and that they alienate us from God. He writes, "Our whole position is threatened with ruin by the fact of Evil" (Temple 1930, p. 253). However, he is only willing to go so far, arguing that evil has positive value when it leads to higher forms of good, and even can become "constituent elements of the absolute good" (Temple 1930, p. 254). The crucifixion may be the prime example of evil becoming a constituent element of absolute good, demonstrating the love of God.

In similar fashion Temple acknowledges humanity's self-centeredness, but does not consign us to that aspect. He writes:

> Man is self-centered; but he always carries with him abundant proof that this is not the real truth of his nature . . . The image of God – the image of holiness and love – is still there, though defaced (Temple 1976 [1942], p. 65).

Temple defines personal sin as "the wrong direction of my will" (Temple 1930, p. 258). That will is not something external to oneself; rather, he argues, it *is* oneself. This means that God's atoning work is not about preventing the punishment of sin. Its purpose is to "abolish sinners by winning them out of their sin into the loyalty and love of children in their Father's home" (Temple 1930, p. 259).

Thus, he argued against ransom, satisfaction, and substitutionary atonement theories in favor of one that focuses on the force and power of God's love in transforming the world and human lives. The cross and resurrection are focal points of the atonement brought in and by the incarnation. He writes:

We plead His Passion, not as a transferred penalty, but as an act of self-sacrifice which remakes us in its own likeness. Its work in us is not yet perfect. We still misuse God's grace; our prayer is still languid and our faith dim. But Christ will perfect His work in us, and we ask our heavenly Father to regard us (as he Himself wills to regard us) not as the prodigals that we are but as the true brethren of Christ that we are becoming (Temple 1930, p. 264).

Ultimately, for Temple, the atonement is not only about "soul saving" (though it has that aspect, as each person's sinful self is transformed). It is more fundamentally about "world saving" and the transformation of evil to good (Temple 1930, p. 270).

Societal Transformation

In a well-known passage in *Nature, Man, and God*, Temple writes, "It is in the sacramental view of the universe, both of its material and of its spiritual elements, that there is given hope of making human both politics and economics and of making effectual both faith and love" (Temple 1951, p. 486). Thus, he believes that the world can be transformed into something better, something redeemed.

The church, in particular, has a critical role as an extension of the incarnation in the ongoing transformation of society. Temple argues that God uses us to spread the divine reign (understood as a process, always developing and coming into being) through love rather than force, with Christianity aiming "not at Salvation of individuals one by one, but at that perfect individual and social welfare which is called the Kingdom of God" (Temple 1927, pp. 30–31). This leads to his passion for social justice, expressed in an abiding concern and commitment for economic justice, employment, education, healthcare, housing, leisure time, etc. (Temple 1942, p. 97). No aspect of human life – personal or social – is divorced from the concern that the church should have for the social welfare. "Love," he writes, "finds its primary expression in Justice" (Temple 1942, p. 79). Temple did not believe that it was the church's place to devise any particular program of reform, but he steadfastly maintained the need for a constant concern for all. He writes, "Respect for the sacredness of Personality in all citizens will lead us to demand that no child shall be condemned to grow to maturity with faculties stunted by malnutrition or by lack of opportunities for full development" (Temple 1942, p. 88). For Temple, his theological convictions were not merely theoretical, they had real consequences in real lives.

Against the charge that his ideals were utopian, Temple responded only in the sense that they could not be achieved immediately. His death prevented him from seeing them advanced in the post-war society. But his faith in God, whose purposes were always being fulfilled in history would surely lead him to believe that their fulfillment is possible and even likely.

Evaluation

William Temple is nearly universally regarded as the most significant Anglican theologian of the first half of the twentieth century, as a founder of the ecumenical movement, and even as the most distinguished of the archbishops of Canterbury since Anselm. Reinhold Neibuhr said of him:

> It is safe to say that not only in public characters but also in private individuals few if any of us have known any person whose life and personality were so completely and successfully integrated around love for Christ as their focus and their crown (cited in Matthews 1946, p. 110).

Temple's hopeful optimism, shared with other Anglican theologians of the era, can be inspiring but also disconcerting in the limited way that it accounts for or wrestles with evil and sin, which sometimes seem to be ancillary to his theological project. Interpreters in the twentieth century and the twenty-first century have questioned whether this Hegelian idealism is adequate in the face of evil and brokenness over the past two centuries (Ramsey 1960, p. 148; Wondra 2007). Temple did moderate his position in later writings, suggesting in 1939 that there was a new task in theology:

> We cannot come to men [sic] of today saying, "You will find all your experience fits together in a harmonious system if you will only look at it in the illumination of the Gospel". . . our task with this world is not to explain it but to convert it. Its needs can be met, not only by the discovery of its own immanent principle in signal manifestation through Jesus Christ, but only by the shattering impact upon its self-sufficiency and arrogance of the Son of God, crucified, risen and ascended, pouring forth that disruptive energy which is the Holy Ghost. . . . [I]n order to fashion true fellowship in such a world as this, and out of such men and women as we are, He must first break up those fellowships with which we have been deluding ourselves. Christ said that the effect of His coming would be to set much at variance. We must expect the movement of His spirit among us to produce sharper divisions as well as deeper unity (cited in Ramsey 1960, pp. 160–161).

While there is a distinct shift in tone, the theological principles are much the same as his larger body of work. In the fullness of time the truth of his position may be made clear. In the present it is harder to discern. Had Temple lived to see the end of World War II and the full extent of the death it brought, perhaps he would have revised his thinking, or reasserted even more strongly his conviction in the love of God and its unconquerable power revealed in the incarnation.

We do know is that his commitment to alleviating social injustice was a direct consequence of his theological and philosophical worldview. Within the Anglican tradition this perspective will lead to a wider embrace of liberation theologies. We see him opening the door as well to process theology with in his engagement with the philosophy of Whitehead. Finally, Temple's theology of the sacramental universe has much to teach the church about God's ongoing presence in its communal life. While Temple's works are of their time and context, they lead us back to earlier strains in Anglican thought and guide us to those that will come.

Notes

1 The following describes some of their differences: "It has been said that Gore was certain about the creed, but struggled with doubt about God's love, while Temple was certain about God's love but struggled with doubts about the creed" (Fletcher 1963, p. 250).

2 Later, as Archbishop of Canterbury, he would criticize the diocese of Hong Kong for ordaining Li Tim-Oi to the priesthood.

3 These and similar ideas would be expanded in later works by process theologians, building on the philosophy of A. N. Whitehead, with whose work Temple grapples with some sympathy. See especially Temple (1951).

References

Carmichael, J.D. and Goodwin, H.S. (1963). *William Temple's Political Legacy: A Critical Assessment*. London: Mowbray.

Fletcher, J. (1963). *William Temple: Twentieth Century Christian*. New York, NY: Seabury Press.

Gore, C.G. (1921). The Holy Spirit and inspiration. In: *Lux Mundi: A Series of Studies in the Religion of the Incarnation*, 15e (ed. C. Gore), 315–362. London: John Murray.

Iremonger, F.A. (1948). *William Temple Archbishop of Canterbury: His Life and Letters*. London: Oxford University Press.

Lampe, G.W.H. and the Church of England (1938). *Doctrine in the Church of England*. London: SPCK.

Matthews, W.R. (1946). *William Temple: An Appreciation*. London: Clark.

Maurice, F.D. (1884). *The Life of Frederick Denison Maurice: Told Chiefly in His Letters*, vol. 1. London: Macmillan.

Ramsey, A.M. (1960). *An Era in Anglican Theology: From Gore to Temple*. New York, NY: Scribers.

Spencer, S. (2001). *William Temple: A Calling to Prophecy*. London: SPCK.

Spencer, S. (ed.) (2015). *Christ in All Things: William Temple and His Writings*. Norwich: Canterbury Press.

Suggate, A.M. (1987). *William Temple and Christian Ethics Today*. Edinburgh: T & T Clark.

Temple, W. (1927). *Essays in Christian Politics and Other Kindred Subjects*. London: Longmans.

Temple, W. (1930). *Christus Veritas*. London: Macmillan.

Temple, W. (1942). *Christianity and the Social Order*. Harmondsworth: Penguin (Also published 1976 London: Shepheard-Walwyn.).

Temple, W. (1951). *Nature, Man, and God*. London: Macmillan.

Temple, F., Williams, R., Baden Powell, R. et al. (1860). *Essays and Reviews*. London: Longman, Green, Longman and Roberts.

Thomas, O.C. (1979). William Temple. In: *The Spirit of Anglicanism* (ed. W.J. Wolf), 101–134. Harrisburg, PA: Morehouse.

Wilkinson, Michael Bernard. (2010). Value and Natural Order in the Philosophy of William Temple, PhD dissertation (University of Surrey).

Wondra, E. (2007). William Temple. In: *Empire and the Christian Tradition* (eds. P.-l. Kwok, D.H. Compier and J. Rieger), 323–335. Minneapolis, MN: Fortress Press.

T. C. Chao (1888–1979)

Chen Yongtao

T. C. Chao (Zhao Zichen, 1888–1979) was a widely known and deeply respected Chinese Christian theologian and religious philosopher, "arguably China's most important modern theologian" (Wickeri 2007, p. 6).[1] He has also been seen as a profound Chinese scholar, a gentle mystic, a productive writer, a poet, a Christian educator, and a sincere patriot. Moreover, he enjoyed great popularity and prestige in the ecumenical movement in his time. Chao was baptized while studying at Dongwu (also known as Soochow) University; thereafter, he was a member of the Methodist Episcopal Church for many years. In 1941, at the age of fifty-three, he joined the Chinese Anglican Church called Chung Hua Sheng Kung Hui. As an Anglican, he was confirmed in Hong Kong by Bishop R. O. Hall (1895–1975); following his confirmation, he was immediately ordained first as *huili* (deacon), and then as *huizhang* (priest). It became a common saying in the Hong Kong Sheng Kung Hui that the three rites were put into effect in one liturgy.

Since the late 1960s, research on T. C. Chao has been steadily growing both in China and abroad. Up to the present day, however, very little attention has been paid to Chao's relation to Anglicanism, either historically or theologically. Consequently, there is hardly any research touching the impact of the Anglican tradition on Chao's theological thinking. As to his later theological reorientation, almost all researchers attribute it to his prison experience and the influence of Karl Barth's neo-orthodoxy. Although Barth's influence on him cannot be denied, the impact of the Anglican tradition on Chao's later theological formation may be even more significant.

In this chapter, I make a preliminary exploration of the idea of theological contextualization in T. C. Chao's thinking, particularly in terms of Chao's relationship as a Chinese theologian with the Anglican tradition that influenced his thought. While recognizing the influence of Anglican thinking on Chao, I emphasize his intent to be

Twentieth Century Anglican Theologians: From Evelyn Underhill to Esther Mombo, First Edition.
Edited by Stephen Burns, Bryan Cones, and James Tengatenga.

above all a Chinese theologian, not a self-consciously Anglican one. In my survey of his thinking, I especially consider his soteriology, particularly in his later theology. But, first, a sketch of his life.

A Sketch of Chao's Life

Chao was born on February 14, 1888, in the town of Xinshi, Deqing County, Zhejiang Province. He died on November 21, 1979, in Beijing. He grew up in a family that had a strong religious atmosphere. From his childhood, he was influenced by Buddhism and folk religion, and his mother was a pious Buddhist before her conversion to Christianity in her later years.

Chao had a solid classical Chinese education. His preliminary education was well-grounded in the Confucian classics. At the age of fifteen there were two choices for him: either entering a Chinese middle school in Hangzhou in order to receive a traditional Chinese education, or entering a foreign missionary school in Soochow to receive a modern Western education. In order to seek guidance in his decision making, he paid a visit to the Buddhist Juehai Monastery on Lingquanshan and consulted with the Bodhisattva Guanyin. Although he was advised to attend a Chinese middle school in Hangzhou, he followed his own will and chose Dongwu instead (Chao 2007a, p. 136; also Glüer 1982, p. 165; Lam 1994, pp. 3–4; West 1976, p. 71).[2] He studied for an initial year in Cuiying School, which is a Presbyterian foundation in Soochow. Then one year later, Chao transferred to the Affiliated Middle School of Dongwu University. He later became a university student at Dongwu. While studying there, he was influenced by Dr. David L. Anderson, the president of the school, by Professor Walter Buckner Nance, and by various other faculty members. As a consequence, Chao began gradually to appreciate Christianity. John Mott's visit at Dongwu University in 1917 impressed Chao profoundly. As a result, in the following year Chao accepted baptism and became a member of the Methodist Episcopal Church.

From 1914 to 1917 he studied at Vanderbilt University in the United States. In succession, he got his master's degree in sociology and his bachelor's degree in theology. In 1917 he came back to Soochow and became a professor at Dongwu, his alma mater. At that time, China was under the heavy influence of the New Culture Movement. "Saving the nation and building up a New China" became the goal of all the intellectuals of that generation. As a Christian intellectual, Chao could not be an exception. From its very beginning, Chao's theological thinking was thus closely linked to his context as a response to the appeal for national reconstruction.

In 1922 Chao attended in Shanghai the foundational assembly of the National Christian Council of China; he was an active member of the preparatory committee of this assembly. The slogan of "Building up an indigenous Chinese church" was first proposed by the organizers and participants of this assembly. In the following decades, Chao and many other Christian intellectuals struggled trying to actualize this vision.

Chao received in 1925 an invitation to teach at Yanjing (Yenching) University in Peking (Beijing), from John Stuart, the university's president. Chao accepted, and taught at Yanjing until 1952. He was the dean of the School of Religion for a long period of time. Because of his contribution to Chinese Christian higher education,

Dongwu University honored Chao by bestowing on him the honorary degree of Doctor of Letters in 1927 (Glüer 1999, p. 39; Nance 1927, p. vii).

From the early 1920s to the late 1940s, Chao was very active both on the national Protestant scene and in international and ecumenical church relations attending major conferences and taking part in organizations such as the National Christian Council of China and the Young Men's Christian Association (YMCA). He participated in the International Missionary Council (IMC) meetings of Jerusalem in 1928 and of Madras in 1938[3] and he took part in the first general assembly of the World Council of Churches (WCC) in Amsterdam in 1948. There he was elected one of the six presidents of the WCC, representing East Asian churches. During the Jerusalem IMC in 1928, Chao was sitting beside the Archbishop of York, William Temple, who later became the Archbishop of Canterbury. There are no documents telling about the content of their communication, but according to a letter by R. O. Hall, the Anglican Bishop of Hong Kong, though, Chao revealed his growing interest in the Anglican tradition, its order, and liturgical legacy.

Notably, from 1932 to 1933 Chao spent one year at Oxford University as a visiting scholar. According to some researchers, it may be during this time that Chao had opportunity to become familiar with Karl Barth's neo-orthodox theology (see Hui 2008, p.42; Lam 1994, p. 214). However, I believe that, in addition to his encounter with neo-orthodoxy, Chao also took time to learn more about Anglicanism. It may be truer to say that Chao's later theology was influenced more by the Anglican tradition than by Barthian neo-orthodoxy.

R. O. Hall indicates in his letter that in 1939 Chao already had an intention to become an Anglican; two years later he became one and was simultaneously ordained as an Anglican priest. According to Hall, Chao met him sometime in early 1939 in Kunming and discussed the possibility of his movement to the Anglican Church. Thereafter, Chao was continuously in contact with Bishop Thomas Scott, the Anglican Bishop of Peking, and with David Paton, an Anglican missionary. His contacts with Scott and Paton strengthened his consciousness of having being received to the Anglican Church. Soon after, during his sabbatical year, Chao went to Kunming and served at the Anglican Wenlin Church for one year. As a Methodist layperson, Chao got a special authorization from the Anglican bishop to serve at the Wenlin Church. The congregation of the church was composed mainly of students, faculty members, and staff of the United University in Southwest China.

On July 20, 1941, Chao was ordained in Hong Kong by Hall in the small chapel of St. Paul's College, in Bishop's House in Hong Kong. In the ordination ceremony, as mentioned above, Chao received confirmation and then was successively ordained as *huili* (deacon) and *huizhang* (priest). By the time he became an Anglican priest he was already widely known in intellectual circles in China and also in international ecumenical circles.

His later work was marked by some controversy. After having a dispute with John Stuart about the size and the direction of development of the School of Religion of Yanjing University in 1946, Chao was removed from his position as dean of the School of Religion (though he shortly returned to the position). Hall then invited Chao to Hong Kong with the purpose of spending his remaining years in comfort while doing research and writing his books. After some inner struggle and consideration, Chao declined Hall's offer (the Hong Kong Sheng Kung Hui, however, kept a job possibility open for Chao [Tang 2010, p. 46]). And in 1952, when a new political movement – the Denounce Movement – was initiated, Chao was accused of too close a relationship with Western missionaries. He was then forced to resign from his position as dean. In addition, his priesthood was revoked and his theology was criticized (Glüer 1999, p. 40). After that, he gradually disappeared from the public view.

Yanjing Union Theological Seminary was established in 1953. Chao was employed by the newly established seminary as a research professor. About 10 years later, Yanjing Union Theological Seminary was merged into Nanjing Union Theological Seminary (NJUTS), and Chao was invited by NJUTS as an honorary professor, but he never went to Nanjing to take up this position.[4] In 1957, the Anti-Rightist Movement attacked Chao, criticizing him as a rightist. During the "Cultural Revolution" of 1966–1976 he was further persecuted. However, Chao never withdrew his support from the Three-Self Movement of the Chinese Protestant church. He did not give up his dream of constructing Chinese Christian theology, although he no longer had voice in the public arena. He began to study Reinhold Niebuhr's theology and wrote a lengthy review of it. However, from the early 1950s, Chao published no more authentic theological writings (Chen 2016, p. 16; Liu 1990, p. 254), and he died at the advanced age of ninety-one on November 21, 1979, in Beijing. Shortly before his death, he experienced the joy of being officially rehabilitated (for more detail, see Chen 2016, pp. 32–43).

Chao as a Chinese Theologian: His Theologizing

During the first half of the twentieth century, Chao devoted himself to the Chinese Protestant church and to constructing Chinese theology. For decades, he made his contribution to both the Chinese church and the church ecumenical. He insisted that Christianity must be relevant to Chinese culture and to Chinese social-political reality (Chao 1984, p. 84; Glüer 1999, p. 11; Lam 1994, pp. 307–324). One of his concerns, especially in his early period, was that the church should be purified institutionally from its denominationalism and doctrinally from its unscientific views. He wanted to relate the Christian faith to Confucianism or, more broadly, to Chinese traditional culture. His high ideal was to create a relevant, contextualized Chinese theology (Glüer 1982, p. 165; Lam 1994, p. 307).[5]

As a Chinese theologian with a great sense of social responsibility, Chao was always affected by the challenges of his time and the destiny of his nation. It was a changing and restless time, and consequently, Chao's theology was in a process of constant change. From the late 1930s on, he began to depart from his early theological stance, which appeared humanistic and liberal in character, and turned toward a theology of revelation. Though his shift can be attributed to new ecumenical theological trends, the change of direction in his theology cannot be separated from the suffering of his disaster-ridden native land. In the face of his people's struggle, Chao gradually gave up his early, theologically liberal stance. In spite of this, his later theology was still solidly based on his effort to create a contextual Chinese theology.

However, Chao did not drink exclusively from his own Chinese well, namely, from the Chinese culture alone. He also drank from Western wells in order to give his theological response to the problems he was facing in his context. Though filled with Chinese culture and national consciousness, he was extensively influenced by the Western philosophies and theologies of his day (Chao 2003, pp. 9, 49; Chen 2016, pp. 56–70).[6] He knew well that his theological mission was to construct a Chinese theology, not to implant any Western theology. As Glüer rightly notes, Chao's approach to Western philosophy and theology was quite pragmatic. From all Western sources, Chao "selects advisable and practicable elements and uses them as stones and bricks to build up his own theological system" (Glüer 1999, p. 77). All Western sources could serve the purpose of his theological indigenization. Therefore, it might be better to label Chao's theology as a Chinese theology rather than to label it with some Western terms, such as liberal theology (his early period), or neo-orthodox theology (his later period). He said in the preface of his first book, "My crucial question is, as a Chinese Christian, what kind of religious insights I can speak and what kind of great *Dao* (Gospel) I can spread to my compatriots both inside and outside of the church" (Chao 2003, p. 7). It is for Chao a crucial question, requiring an indigenous Chinese theology to be achieved by the Sinicization of Christianity. In his article "The Indigenous Church" (1924), Chao said: "We are forced to answer the question whether or not the tree of Christian religion transplanted from the West and still artificially protected under artificial heat and moisture, will continue to live and grow" (Chao 2010, p. 291).

However, Chao's striving for the relevance of Christianity to Chinese society is only one side of the coin. The other side is that a Chinese theology must be built on the Christian universal truths revealed in Jesus Christ. Among these universal truths, for the early Chao, are God's fatherhood, humanity's brotherhood, both the divinity and the humanity of Jesus Christ, the power of the Holy Spirit, God's earth-oriented reign, the universal spiritual communion of believers, and so forth (Chao 2003, p. 193; Chao 2009, p. 177; Chao 2010, p. 290). Even though his theological stance changed in his later period, his effort to construct a Chinese theology remained (Chao 2009, p. 525), enthusiastically integrating religion and ethics.

Chao realized the fact that Christianity in China had a burden from its past. Because of the relationship between Christianity's entrance into China and Western imperialism, there was in Chao's time a popular saying: "One more Christian, one less Chinese." For a patriotic Chinese, becoming a Christian was a problem. In response to this saying, like his contemporary Chinese Christians, Chao had to ask himself, "Can we Chinese become Christians without being Westernized? How can we Chinese have our identity as 'Chinese Christians'?" These were serious questions to which Chinese Christians at that time – and even nowadays – have had to find answers. That was why Chinese Christians were crying out for the indigenization of Christianity. Exactly for this reason, both Christ and China were the inevitable two points of focus in Chao's effort for theological contextualization.

As a Chinese Christian and a child of his own times, Chao tried to seek a new identity for Chinese Christians. For him, a Chinese Christian must be both a true Christian and a true Chinese citizen at the same time. In order to decrease the tension between the two, Chao put forward the concept of "Christian nationalism," which is both nationalism and internationalism (Chao 2009, p. 227). By this formulation, he intended to reconcile Christianity to rising nationalism. He felt that Christian nationalism could succeed in finding the common point between Christ and China (Chao 2009, pp. 216–217). As both the disciple of Jesus Christ and authentic patriot, Christ and China, personal and social gospel, theology and anthropology, are thus inseparable in his thinking (Chao 2007, pp. 120–121; Chao 1940, p. 3).[7]

Chao saw the necessity of a double loyalty to both Christ and China; he had to be a sincere Christian and a sincere Chinese at the same time (Chao 2009, pp. 107–108).[8] This double loyalty can be observed throughout Chao's theological thinking. For this purpose Chao maintained that the Chinese church is both local and universal.[9] When the number of Christians was constantly increasing, Chao was convinced that Christianity should and could have its great role in the social reconstruction of China.

In his treatment of the Christian faith and of traditional Chinese culture, Chao molded himself on the two aspects of the spirit of Jesus, namely both "revolutionary spirit" and "historical spirit" (Chao 2009, p. 178).[10] His position on Chinese culture can be put into the category of "fulfilling, not destroying," as Lam Wing-hung has stated (Lam 1980a, p. 22; Lam 1980b, pp. 109–115). He attempted to make Christianity relevant to the Chinese mind while retaining its essence, contending that "Confucianism may find Christianity as its own source of life, and Christianity may see in Confucianism an agent of its own truth" (Chao 2009, p. 253). Though Chao's attitude to traditional Chinese culture somewhat changed in different periods (Hui 2008, pp. 186–187), he never gave up this stance. In this sense, his later theology is also a theology of indigenization, which aimed at contextualization. However, he understood well that traditional Chinese culture was a human-centered culture, a sort of secular humanism. Chao was aware that traditional Chinese culture lacks the idea of a transcendent God, and that it lacks also a "sense of sin" (Chao 2009, p. 254). He was convinced that Christianity must fulfill the deficiency of traditional Chinese culture. For the sake of theological contextualization, Chao insisted that Christianity must be "both theocentric and anthropocentric" (Chao 2003, p. 74; Chao 2007, p. 421).[11] He several times criticized Confucianism for its emphasizing only human inner transcendence, but overlooking absolute transcendence, seeing humankind, but not God as the highest (Chao 2007b, pp. 408–409, 497, 526).[12] Chao insisted that revival of Christianity in China relied on whether or not it could inject new blood and new life into Chinese culture (Chao 2004, p. 402). Although Chao recognized the great ethical strength in Confucianism, he admitted without hesitation that Confucianism was utterly inadequate to meet the deep spiritual need of the Chinese. Christianity alone could meet this need (Chao 2007b, pp. 253–257).[13]

There were two things that Chao strived for: one was the Christianization (基督化) of China, which was the aim of his efforts, the other was the Sinicization (中国化) of Christianity (Chao 2007, pp. 235–236), which was the method or means of his efforts. In Chao's usage, the term Sinicization has almost the same meaning as that of indigenization. With the former, Chao had a dream of building up a new China. With the latter, Chao appealed for an indigenous Chinese Christianity, expressing Chinese patriotic and religious aspirations and showing Chinese people a reasonable way of personal as well as social salvation. For Chao, salvation was humanization, which was the central orientation of both his early and his later thinking. In his early period, the validity of theology was based less on its doctrinal orthodoxy than on its contribution to the human quest for a better quality of life and social justice. Chao attempted to develop a Christ-centered humanism based on his view of Christianity and Chinese culture, which sets both God and humanity as two foci of his theology (Chao 2007, pp. 462–463).[14] In his later theology, the orientation of humanization remained, but he recognized that only God's grace could let humanization be realized.

The Later Chao: An "Anglican" Theologian?

As mentioned above, Chao became an Anglican in 1941. He wrote ten poems in memory of his ordination ceremony. One of them includes these four lines: "Since long ago, I had an intention to be ordained,/for fourteen years I have kept this wish.// All my life is like a holy sacrament, /the church ordinance has its right and it should be fully respected.//I bowed my head to receive confirmation,/and by ordination I have wholly inherited the apostolic tradition,/having troubled many good friends to get together in the small chapel,/to help and lead me to worship God in front of the altar.//"[15] These lines express Chao's self-understanding when entering the Anglican tradition. Truly, the influence of the Anglican tradition on the later Chao's theology, which concentrates on incarnation and salvation, cannot be undermined (see Ng 2012).[16] According to David Paton, ". . . R.O. Hall knew that T.C. Chao was seeking a profounder and more deeply Chinese understanding of the Christian faith than was currently available, and was proceeding in the Anglican Catholic tradition some way into this mystery" (Paton 1985, p. 103). What Paton observed and said is true.

It is certain that the later Chao was to some extent approaching the Anglican tradition. According to this tradition, the authority or the norm of faith is based on scripture tradition, and reason (Avis 2000, pp. 50–59).[17] The Bible is the central norm of faith, by which the other norms of faith, such as creeds, tradition, and beliefs are judged. The Bible is also the norm of theology and Christian ethics. Reason also occupies a very important place in the life of faith. On the one hand, faith is beyond reason; on the other hand, faith is also in line with reason. The mystery of faith and the rationality of it are not contradictory (McGrath 1993, pp. 74–78). While the early Chao gave human religious experience greater significance, the later Chao's understanding of the relationship between faith and reason is undoubtedly in agreement with this. We can see in Chao's later theology his emphasis on the authority of the Bible, Christian tradition, and reason (Avis 2000, pp. 50–55; McGrath 1993, pp. 86–89). In Chao's later theology we can also observe the four cardinal elements of the Chicago-Lambeth Quadrilateral, namely, the Bible, the creeds (Apostles' and Nicene), sacraments (baptism and eucharist), and episcopacy (Avis 2000, p. 57). Highlighting the doctrine of incarnation, his emphasis on the significance of the church and his respect for episcopacy all may also reveal the influence of the Anglican tradition on Chao's later theology.

From his book *Four Lectures on Theology* (Chao 1948) we can see Chao's understanding of the sequential order of the importance of the Bible, Christian tradition, and reason in his discussion of theological themes and methods. He maintains that the theme of theology is God's revelation, the tool is reason. Reason without revelation is not effective, power comes from revelation. What reason can accomplish is an interpretation of God's revelation in order that we may understand well our faith (Chao 2009, p. 519). God's revelation in Jesus Christ is "recorded in the Bible, demonstrated in the history of the church, and experienced by the saints" (Chao 2009, p. 500). As the Word of God, the Bible is the testimony of God's incarnation. Chao thus put his emphasis on the authority of the Bible and on Christian tradition (Chao 2009, p. 402). In an article written in 1950, Chao emphasized the importance of God's revelation and human reason. He said that the point of departure for a true theologian is the revelation of God; God's revelation must be accepted and obeyed by real theologians with fervent admiration and trust. However, they must neither underestimate reason nor despise scholarship, but attempt to interpret and explain God's revelation by the help of their intelligence (Chao 2009, p. 184).

Moreover, Chao also realized that doing theology in the Chinese context must deal seriously with the historical, cultural, and social-political situation of China. On the one hand, our theological interpretation must get in touch with these realities; and on the other hand, we need to explain the nature of Christianity by the way of complementing the deficiency of Chinese culture – only this way we can meet the need of the Chinese society (Chao 2009, p. 520). This kind of effort defines Chao as a truly Chinese theologian.

Further, Chao's later soteriology indicates his effort at theological contextualization, while it is somewhat influenced by Anglicanism. When Chao expressed his uneasiness with the traditional Western interpretations of atonement, he points out his own theory of redemption (atonement) as *chengzhilun*, literally meaning "a theory of completing God's own will," and *tongyilun*, "a union or identification theory." Both his *chengzhilun* and *tongyilun* were the fruit of his theological contextualization. In Chao's understanding of justification and sanctification we may see influences on him of both the Anglican tradition and his differentiation from other contemporaneous Anglican theologians (Chen 2015, pp. 169–192).

Chao's letter to his diocesan bishop on Good Friday, 1949, indicates Chao's struggle to hold together context and Anglican tradition. In that letter, Chao expressed his wishes to resign from the priesthood, and begged the bishop to suspend permission for him to function as a clergyperson. Chao even considered leaving Chung Hua Sheng Kung Hui completely.[18] The precipitating factor for this letter was his request to administer a service of holy communion for all Christians at the Yenching University Christian Fellowship. An English missionary at the university objected because this was not permitted in Anglican rubrics. So presumably did the bishop. Chao saw this as a conflict between loyalty to the Church, which he loved, and "loyalty to the truth that Christ grants us to see."[19] The issue of intercommunion led Chao to think more broadly about all church constructs inherited from the missionary movement. He was being pressed by Christian students at Yenching University who saw the church increasingly irrelevant to their lives. And so, he began to think again about the reasons behind his own ordination. As Wickeri rightly indicates, Chao was not experiencing a crisis of faith, but a rejection of the narrow denominationalism represented by the Chung Hua Sheng Kung Hui. He saw Anglican opposition to intercommunion with the wider Christian fellowship as absurd and irrelevant, but this was representative of something more basic. T. C. Chao was an expansive thinker who could not be bound by denominationalism. In writing this letter, he was presenting the challenge of contextual theology to missionary Christianity (Wickeri 2016).

It may be true that a change of tone can be noted in his theological writings after his ordination, but this change has mostly to do with his reflections on his own experience in prison, with his appreciation of Karl Barth, and most significantly, with his critical reflections on the Chinese church and on the urgent challenges of the Chinese context. His theology was undeniably dedicated to contextual thinking. He had little intention simply to copy any Western theology, including an Anglican one. Again, according to Wickeri,

> Long before he became a priest in 1941, T.C. Chao's thought embodied the best of what we might call a distinctively Anglican theology. He saw emphasized the connection between creation and redemption in his theology of culture. He saw God in nature and in Chinese culture and he expressed this in his poetry and hymns. He had a sacramental sense of the world, although he wrote very little about the sacraments per se. Like all other Chinese theologians, he wanted the church to be Chinese, and he was certainly drawn to the churchmanship of the Chung Hua Sheng Kung Hui. Anglicans might be tempted to claim him as one of our own, but then Anglican theology has never lived up to its own insights and sensibility. We need to remember that Chao, the greatest Chinese theologian of the 20th century, was broadly ecumenical, thoroughly contextual, and deeply engaged in the issues of society. There is no evidence that that he sought to identify himself as an Anglican thinker. Indeed, he was at home in different cultures and ways of theological thinking, and as a Chinese Christian, beyond the theological traditions that had been inherited from Europe (Wickeri 2016).

Conclusion

T. C. Chao believed that religion and ethics are inseparable. Religion without ethics is dead, ethics without religion is empty. In his later period, as the result of his theological re-orientation, God's special revelation in Jesus Christ became the major source and the norm of Chao's theological thinking. Most probably, Chao found a similarity between the theological approach of *Via Media* in the Anglican tradition and his own theological agenda of the Sinicization of Christianity. For Chao, his original Methodist background and his theological purport caused him no difficulty in becoming an Anglican Christian and priest. In his later soteriology, when discussing the issue of human salvation, Chao both emphasized God's singular grace and gave human moral life its definite place in sanctification. Obviously, the influence of the Anglican tradition could free him both to accept the doctrine of incarnation and give to the progress of a Christian's life a necessary place in his thinking.

However, it would be inappropriate to label the later Chao a self-consciously "Anglican" theologian. As above analysis indicates, the impact of the Anglican tradition on his later thinking cannot be ignored. Nevertheless, his intention and his theological effort concentrated on constructing a Chinese theology for the China of his time, avoiding copying any Western theological model. We may say with confidence that his primary concern was to be a Chinese theologian, but not a Chinese "Anglican" theologian. Chao was, however, the most creative, productive, and thoughtful Chinese theologian of the first half of twentieth century. His theology, without a doubt, belongs to the rich heritage of the Chinese Protestant church. Chen Zemin (1917–2018), a leading contemporary Chinese theologian, maintains:

> Although most writings had been written before the establishment of New China and could not foresee the task of theological reconstruction of the present Chinese church, his writings are alive with a positive and vivid spirit of exploration, the glinting brilliance of faith and wisdom, and full of his love for his motherland, and his longing for a bright future. It is not without benefit for our Chinese church and Chinese Christians today (Chen cited in Chen 2016, p. 43).

Notes

1 Paton (1985, p. 47) even affirms that Chao would be the foundation of a forthcoming Chinese theology. Because of Chao's knowledge of Chinese tradition, Chao was regarded by Paton as a pioneer in undergirding the quest for Chinese theology.

2 West says that this event happened when Chao was fourteen years old. According to Chao, he was then fifteen years. This event may also be regarded as a sign of Chao's intention to break with his old beliefs.

3 This conference is also called the Tambaram Conference, because it met at Tambaram, near Madras.

4 He was also elected as one of the vice chairpersons of the board of the seminary.

5 Lam concludes that Chao's theology is a theology of relevance. Glüer also notes the truly Chinese character of Chao's writings. He indicates that Chao was deeply influenced by Chinese thought, and struggled for most of his life to make the Christian church in China a *Chinese* church.

6 It is obvious that while Chao created his Chinese theology, he was greatly influenced by various Western philosophies and theologies that flourished in his time. However, Chao was not a follower of any Western school particularly, either philosophical or theological. The method that Chao adopted might be called a "principle of taking," *nalai zhuyi*. *Nailai zhuyi* literally means "taking-from-ism" or "borrowing-ism," which was first put forward in 1934 by Lu Xun, a modern Chinese writer. For Lu Xun, this term means that in the process of China's development, Chinese people should take all the good parts of Western civilization for their own purpose. *Nalai zhuyi* is thus a selective taking, but not a blind following. Chao's approach to Western philosophical and theological sources is such a selective taking.

7 According to Chao, Christian religion should be theocentric, and Christian ethics should be human centered. He emphasized then the church's social responsibility ("Gospel dealing with the 'society'"), whereas he gave a place for spiritual life and religious experience. He called also for arousing in the church the true spirit of Jesus Christ while he saw the necessity of Christianity's accommodation to Chinese national character.

8 According to Chao, educated Chinese Christians "are reverent in their attitude toward the Bible, loyal to their Savior Jesus Christ, and earnest in their desire to serve God by serving China and by assisting in the reconstruction of the Chinese social order."

9 Chao, "The Relation of the Chinese Church to the Church Universal" (1923) (Chao 2009, p. 121).

10 According to Chao, with these two spirits, Jesus both criticized and preserved tradition at the same time. In Chao's treatment of traditional Chinese culture and Christian tradition, he himself also had both a "revolutionary spirit" and a "historical spirit," critiquing and preserving tradition at the same time.

11 Chao believed that Christianity could provide a principle for Chinese ethics, which is the relationship between God and humanity. While concluding that on the ethical and aesthetic level, Christianity is in line with Chinese culture, Chao saw clearly the weakness of Chinese culture, in which its ethical foundation rests on its theory of the cosmos. For this reason, Chao advocated that a sixth relationship – the relationship between humanity and God, which would become the basis of a new ethics – must be added to the traditional Chinese five cardinal relations. With this addition, the other five relationships would gain inner strength to practice human relations.

12 According to Chao, the Confucian proposition that "man can glorify the *Tao*, but the *Tao* does not glorify man" degrades the role of God in human life while stressing moral laws and moral capacity in human nature.

13 Chao lists several aspects of Christianity's possible contribution to China, including its belief in a personal and loving God as revealed in Jesus the Christ, its deep sense of sin and human inadequacy, its sense of other-worldliness, its mysticism, and its institutions.

14 As Kärkkäinen says, "Asia's struggle for humanization faces enormous challenges. An authentically Asian Christology cannot help but delve into the suffering and wounds of Asian people . . . It is the task of Asian Christology to free Jesus for the common people" (Kärkkäinen 2003, p. 276).

15 Here is its content in Chinese: "蓄意由来久，／持心十四年，／生涯咸圣礼，／教职自尊权。／／坚振低眉受，／纯真托体全，／重劳嘉友集，／导引拜坛前。／／."

16 Ng (2012) may have been the first to discover the possible relation of Chao's theological thinking to the Anglican tradition.

17 Different from the early period in which Chao regarded religious experience as the source and norm of theology, he now disregarded the human experience as the foundation of theology, although he did not deny the role of experience in the process of theologizing. As McGrath points out, although regarding human experience as the foundation of theology has a certain attraction, it also brings some difficulty. Therefore, McGrath introduces an alternative method to deal with the relationship between human experience and theology: that theology interprets experience. For him, what theology should do is to narrate experience, interpret experience, and then transcend and transform experience. See McGrath (1993, pp. 86–98).

18 He says, "I beg you to suspend your permission to me to function as a clergyman in the Church. Ultimately, it may become necessary for me to leave the Chung Hua Sheng Kung Hui, completely. I hate to think of such a step, but when it becomes inevitable, I shall not hesitate to take the step at all. I am thinking that when I take that step, I shall not ask for membership in any other Church but shall remain Churchless to the end of my days. Every broken member of the Body of Church, i.e. every so-called Church is built upon indefensible presuppositions which I cannot accept. If, in accordance with the teachings of St. Augustine and others, a person cannot see salvation outside the Church, I shall remain outside, for now there is not the Church anywhere existing."

19 Later letters suggest that he continued to celebrate the Anglican eucharist at the Yenching University Fellowship and other interdenominational settings, with or without Bishop Scott's permission.

References

Avis, P. (2000). *The Anglican Understanding of the Church: An Introduction.* London: SPCK.

Chao, T.C. (1940). Christian faith for a new time. In: *Christianity and New China* (ed. Y.T. Wu). Shanghai: Youth Association Press.

Chao, T.C. (1947). *A Further Interpretation of Christianity*. Shanghai: Youth Association Press.

Chao, T.C. (1948). *Four Lectures on Christian Theology*. Shanghai: Youth Association Press.

Chao, S. (1984). A Chinese church and theology: a discussion. *East Asian Journal of Theology* 2 (1): 82–89.

Chao, T.C. (2003). *The Collected Works of T. C. Chao*, vol. 1. Beijing: The Commercial Press.

Chao, T.C. (2007). *The Collected Works of T. C. Chao*, vol. 3. Beijing: The Commercial Press.

Chao, T.C. (2009). *The Collected Works of T. C. Chao*, vol. 2. Beijing: The Commercial Press.

Chao, T.C. (2009). *The Collected Works of T. C. Chao*, vol. 5. Beijing: The Commercial Press.

Chao, T.C. (2010). *The Collected Works of T. C. Chao*, vol. 4. Beijing: The Commercial Press.

Chen, Y. (2015). T.C. Chao and the Sheng Kung Hui: with particular emphasis on theology, as exemplified by his soteriology. In: *Christian Encounters with Chinese Culture: Essays on Anglican and Episcopal History in China* (ed. P.L. Wickeri), 169–192. Hong Kong: Hong Kong University Press.

Chen, Y. (2016). *The Chinese Christology of T. C. Chao*. Leiden: Brill.

Glüer, W. (1982). The legacy of T. C. Chao. *International Bulletin of Missionary Research* 6 (4): 165–169.

Glüer, W. (1999). *The Theological Thought of T. C. Chao* (originally in German, translated into Chinese by Deng Zhaoming). Shanghai: China Christian Council.

Hui, Hoiming. (2008). A Study of T. C. Chao's Christology in the Social Context of China, 1920 to 1949. PhD dissertation (University of Birmingham).

Kärkkäinen, V.-M. (2003). *Christology: A Global Introduction*. Grand Rapids, MI: Baker Academic.

Lam, W.-h. (1980a). *Chinese Theology in Construction*. Hong Kong: Tien Dao Publishing House.

Lam, W.-h. (1980b). Patterns of Chinese Theology. *Occasional Bulletin of Missionary Research* 4 (1): 20–24.

Lam, W.-h. (1994). *Too High to Be Popular: T. C. Chao's Life and Theology (in Chinese)*. Hong Kong: China Alliance Press.

Liu, Q. (1990). A short biography of T. C. Chao. In: *The Literary and Historical Material of Yenching University*. Yenching: Yenching University Press.

McGrath, A. (1993). *The Renewal of Anglicanism*. London: SPCK.

Nance, W.B. (1927). Soochow University Confers Degrees. *Mission Voice* X: vii.

Ng, T. (2012). *Chinese Christianity: An Interplay Between Global and Local Perspectives*. Leiden: Brill.

Paton, D.M. (1985). *R. O. Hall: The Life and Times of Bishop Ronald Hall of Hong Kong*. Macao: Diocese of Hong Kong and the Hong Kong Diocesan Association.

Tang, X. (2010). The Ambition of A Nighthawk: T. C. Chao after 1949. In: *The Ambition of a Nighthawk: The Collected Works of the "T. C. Chao and the Sino-Western Exchange of Thought" Conference* (eds. X. Tang and X. Xiao). Beijing: Zongjiao Wenhua Chubanshe.

West, P. (1976). *Yenching University and Sino-Western Relations, 1916–1952*. Cambridge, MA: Harvard University Press.

Wickeri, P. (2007). *Reconstructing Christianity in China: K. H. Ting and the Chinese Church*. Maryknoll, NY: Orbis.

Wickeri, Philip L. (2016). Was T. C. Chao an "Anglican" Theologian? Unpublished essay, Hong Kong.

Sadhu Sundar Singh (1889–1929)

C.I. David Joy

The participation of Sadhu Sundar Singh's in the mission and ecclesiology of the Anglican church in India in particular and Anglican Communion in general can only be assessed by understanding the inner dynamics of the Empire and British Raj in India. This chapter considers these dynamics before continuing to locate overlooked voices during the era in which Singh lived. At the same time, it will consider significant ecclesial movements that influenced the origin and growth of the church in India.

Singh's theological and mission strategy was mainly centered around liturgy and preaching. Through meaningful and effective preaching Singh was able to propagate the gospel speaking across different regions and different local cultures. Singh's witness was therefore intercultural, and, indeed, intercultural hermeneutics can be developed by studying the contributions of Singh. From the postcolonial contexts of contemporary readers, these insights can prove helpful in analyzing the theological locations of the church.

Social-Political and Religio-Cultural Contexts

The social-political and religio-cultural contexts of Sadhu Sundar Singh were strongly influenced by colonial forces. A focus on such contexts creates the basis of a framework in which to best understand Singh. First, in order to begin to understand the situation then, it is crucial to consider some observations made by theologians and missionaries of the time, for example, K. S. Mcdonald in his 1898 article for *The Indian Evangelical Review*:

Twentieth Century Anglican Theologians: From Evelyn Underhill to Esther Mombo, First Edition.
Edited by Stephen Burns, Bryan Cones, and James Tengatenga.
© 2021 John Wiley & Sons Ltd. Published 2021 by John Wiley & Sons Ltd.

No proof of doctrine of re-incarnation is found in any of the sacred books of the Hindus and Buddhists who are bound to prove the truth of the doctrine as long as they profess to believe in it. It is a baseless theory –without foundation in reason or revelation (Mcdonald 1898, p. 14).

Mcdonald prized the significance and uniqueness of the revelation of God in Jesus Christ and, in doing so, depreciated other religions found in India.

It is important to be alert to the range of other tensions in the region at the time. For example, *Rise and Fulfillment of British Rule in India* by Edward Thompson and G. T. Garratt is an interesting text for gaining a clear picture of Singh's socio-political and religio-cultural scenario. It presents very vivid historical data about British rule in India. Though written from the dominant historiographical framework, privileging western perspectives, the authors present the real conflicts between the British rulers and the native people. In Panjab, during the time of Sadhu Sundar Singh, the situation was extremely tense due to political and social struggles. Panjab was a land of people's movements and farmer's struggles and Edward Thompson and G. T. Garratt describe the situation:

The Sikhs had watched the Company over a period steadily, and often rapidly, advancing. In the Afghan campaign British troops surged across the Panjab, and used it as lines of communication. It could hardly be unknown that British high officers had freely advocated annexation or partition of the Panjab, on grounds of military convenience (Thompson and Garratt 1935, p. 387).

It was exactly because of these military views and such aggression that the native people had developed such a hostile attitude toward the colonial powers – and so also to Christian missionaries. Sadhu Sundar Singh grew up in that hostility. Two major Sikh wars took place before Dalhousie's annexations made the British administration more powerful, with "rulers and the religious [who] lived ultimately off the peasant's surplus produce" (Thompson and Garratt 1935, p. 422). In order to maximize profit for the East India Company, the British Raj introduced many reforms that impacted the life of the peasants and resulted in structural changes to Indian rural society (Cohn 1987, p. 343).

Two outstanding studies – namely A. L. Basham's *The Wonder that was India: A Survey of the History and Culture of the Indian Sub-continent Before the Coming of the Muslims* and Thomas R. Trautmann's edited book *The Aryan Debate* – further explain the significance of Panjab, seeing its significance for modern civilization given centuries of interaction with other cultures and languages (Basham 2004; Trautmann 2005). Both books discuss the significance of Indus valley civilization and Harappa excavations and their shaping of socio-political and religio-cultural developments in the Panjab region. In discussion of the contributions of Sadhu Sundar Singh as an Anglican theologian it is important to remember Singh's roots in the Panjab and the colonial rule of his time. Sadhu Sundar Singh worked as a Christian missionary and theologian worked in the context of the British Raj and its impact in Panjab.

Teresa Hubel makes an interesting further observation in her book *Whose India? The Independence Struggle in British India and Indian Fiction and History* (Hubel 1996). She identifies varied layers of oppression in the Indian society, and considers Pandita Ramabai's writings and studies to make a point about gender:

> In Pandita Ramabai's construction, imperialism emerges as a contract that has been entered into by two parties of men, the British and the Indians, for the purpose of subjugating Hindu women. Although she does not suggest that the oppression of Hindu women is the primary motive behind the imperialist enterprise in India, Pandita demonstrates that women are caught in its trajectory (Hubel 1996, p. 132).

As a result of their Panjabi identity, people like Sadhu Sundar Singh would likely have observed these conflicts between the British Raj and natives. Conflict between the two parties became especially bitter after the massacre of Amritsar in the Panjab region, on April 13, 1919, in which British troops fired on a large crowd of unarmed Indians. The British killed several hundred people and wounded many hundreds. In his 1967 book *British India 1772–1947: A Survey of the Nature and Effects of Alien Rule,* Michael Edwards explains the impact of the massacre of Amritsar:

> It is not difficult to understand the very special place that the massacre of Amirthsar has in the minds of Indians. In British-Indian relations, it was a turning point even more decisive than the Mutiny. Henceforth, the struggle was to permit of little compromise, and the good faith of British concessions was always to be held in doubt (Edwards 1967, p. 202).

A number of agitations and movements to gain freedom from the British Raj also took place in Singh's time. The Khilafat agitation (among Indian Muslims, 1919–1924), the non-cooperation movement (introduced by Mahatma Gandhi, 1920–1920), and boycotts of councils, boycotts of law-courts, and boycotts of schools and colleges were all significant. Sadhu Sundar Singh's message of transformation and salvation was preached to people caught within such conflicts and struggles. The time was also marked by confusion and uncertainly, not least that caused by "the shadow of a grave national calamity, for the great national leader Tilak had passed away on August 1, 1920" (Manjumdar 1962, p. 85).

Some of the confusion introduced by Gandhi via the non-cooperation movement arguably reflected the values of Jesus of Nazareth, and it was not easy for the British Raj to address the non-cooperation movement because many people irrespective of religion supported it, including but by no means only Christians.

The religio-cultural context in Singh's time was dictated by the ideologies of the British Raj. Official organs of religion danced in tune with the British Raj in many ways and religious ideology was used to subjugate native people. The Raj was not only a system of economic and political oppression, but also a system of ideological hegemony. In *Ideologies of the British Raj*, Thomas R. Metcalf argues very strongly how the British Raj created differences in their colonies, including India:

The Victorians set out, in addition, to order and classify India's "difference" in accordance with scientific systems of "knowing". British progress could not be simply a matter of cultural pride . . . Victorian science, like its historicism, thus necessarily if not always consciously, fitted India into a hierarchical relationship with Europe and provided its firm footing of legitimacy which the British sought for Raj (Metcalf 1995, p. 67).

This is the religio-social background, dictated by the British Raj, in which Sadhu Sundar Singh exercised his ministry of preaching and maintained his own clear picture of a spiritual community based on the revelation of God in Christ Jesus.

Theological Scope and Shifts

Sadhu Sundar Singh's contributions remain relevant and significant today because his theological scope and shifts in his perspectives articulate an indigenous theology and faith. Janet Lynch Watson explains:

Sundar's Sikh faith with its emphasis on a personal God and its rejection of the Hindu caste system, prepared the ground for his later Christian conviction. Christianity was not a rejection of his ancestral beliefs but a fulfillment of them (Lynch-Watson 1975, p. 12).

These observations are foundational. Janet Lynch-Watson further identifies, in the work of Sadhu Sundar Singh, that:

The natural world was precious as a revelation of God at work. Time and again he was to draw upon the workings of nature to illustrate a point. The Church needs to be flooded by the power of the Holy Spirit in the way the Indian plains are inundated by the fresh streams flowing from the Himalayas; frequent communion with God is as necessary to the Christian as rising to the surface of the water for air is to some fish (Lynch-Watson 1975, p. 104).

Singh was engaged with the cultural heritage and natural environment of the Panjab people. Joshua Daniel's very interesting but short life history of Sadhu Sundar Singh provides insights that make quite specific some of Singh's sense of fidelity to his context and peers. Daniel – whose book is based on his personal interaction with Singh – notes a deep resistance in Singh to ideas he deemed ill-fitting to his setting:

Sundar's period of education in the neighbouring American Presbyterian School was not happy or peaceful at all. The Bible teaching given in the school made him very restless and unhappy. He found the New Testament to be very unlike his religion's Granth which is the holy book of the Sikhs, the other Hindu sacred books, and the Koran of the Mohammedans. He used to interrupt the Scripture classes in the school with many naughty questions and cause as much disruption as possible, when the Bible was taught. The future saint in the making was – both at school and at home – a turbulent boy, leading a gang of youngsters against the preaching of Christ, in his village and neighbourhood (Daniel n.d., p. 5).

Indeed, it is clear that there are many stories about the involvement of the young Sadhu Sundar Singh in the religious affairs of the time. According to Daniel, Sadhu Sundar Singh was a powerful boy with a vivid understanding of the contemporary society who was able to draw borders between local culture and other cultures, especially focused on religious experiences. A most important legacy of this would be that later, after the conversion experience and vision Sadhu Sundar Singh experienced, he was able to promote a vivid picture of Christ overcoming the British Empire's colonizing image of Christ. Daniel further suggests:

Not very long after his baptism, Sundar Singh set out on a long missionary journey preaching Christ to all who would hear him. His youthfulness and yellow robe immediately gained attention and opened many doors for him. The saffron robe being the hall-mark of Hindu sadhus and sanyasis, he would be taken initially for a Hindu devotee of some standing. But when he proclaimed Christ, the initial interest would turn into surprise, then resentment and finally opposition to his preaching. From village to village he went, sometimes his feet bleeding from the cuts and bruises sustained on the rough Indian roads and bullock cart tracks. He had, however, no baggage to carry; his only possessions being his Bible and his thin shawl which he draped around his shoulders (Daniel n.d., p. 15).

Over the years, there have been a number of monographs published on the life and ministry of Sadhu Sundar Singh. They constitute a significant pool of resources for insight into his life and ministry. For example, Cyril J. Davey's book *The Story of Sadhu Sundar Singh* (Davey 1950) reveals important stations in the life of Sadhu Sundar Singh such as his encounter with a sadhu in the jungle, his vision, his experience of persecution, and his moving to Buddhist strongholds. Davey relates Singh's account own of his vision:

Something did happen. A few minutes ago Jesus came into my room. As I was praying for the last time a bright cloud of light suddenly filled the room – no, it was no trick of the moon – and out of the brightness came the face and figure of Jesus. He spoke to me . . . (Davey 1950, p. 33).

Later Singh affirmed, for example, "I am a Christian. I can serve no one else but Jesus!" (Davey 1950, p. 34). As Singh had earlier opposed Christianity by burning the Bible, he lamented after his vision of Jesus: "These hands did it. I can never cleanse them of that sin 'til I die" (Davey 1950, p. 34). This episode was itself followed by severe persecution. As Davey describes, Singh:

was found talking seriously with the very Christian teachers whom, a few days previously, he had been mocking, and consorting with some of the little Christian community in the bazaar, and his conversation became the subject of ribald or angry talk throughout Rampur, and almost at once persecution broke out (Davey 1950, p. 37).

These episodes are just some of the most significant turning points in his life, to be set alongside continuities like unbroken respect for his culture.

Movingly, Sadhu Sundar Singh was known as "the apostle of the bleeding feet" because "his feet without sandals to protect them, were cut and bruised, leaving a trail of bloody footprints along the village street" (Davey 1950, p. 52). With dedicated Christian missionary zeal and enthusiasm, he traveled the Himalayas and other remote places preaching the gospel with a highly vivid understanding of God's revelation in Jesus Christ, shaped not least by his own personal vision of Jesus. Along the way, he established a strong relationship with contemporary church leaders and theologians and began to travel the world promoting gospel values. It was in conversations with his friend C. F. Andrews – the Anglican priest and missionary to India who became friends not only with Singh but also with Rabindranath Tagore and Mahatma Gandhi – that Singh related consciously to the Anglican Church, realizing that both he and Andrews shared an Anglican doctrine of the church. T. E. Riddle supports this view of Andrew's significance for Singh in his account of Singh's travel to England where he addressed many gatherings. These travels meant that Singh was able to gain status among Anglicans in England as well as across Europe. Riddle wrote:

During his tour he was probably the most talked of man in Europe. The impression he made was very deep, and thousands were brought back to a realization that Christ lives, and that He is our peace (Riddle 1987, p 63).

Yet as Riddle goes on immediately to note, "At the same time there was much criticism of him, of his expressions, of his visions and his teachings." His Indian idioms, personal vision, and teachings that distinguished the authority of Christ from that of The Raj were all controversial. Yet I suggest that people around the Anglican Communion can even now draw insights from Singh for contemporary spirituality, not least by learning from Singh's approach to prayer, defined in a quite unique manner:

I have special posture for prayer. I may sit, or kneel, or stand. I use no words. I think only of those things that I have been reading, of the things that I have been doing or intend to do, of the people I know of myself and of Jesus – such thought is prayer. And in such prayer God speaks, not man (Davey 1950, p. 98).

He also engaged, as a Christian, in forms of meditation with his strong Indian heritage, as A. J. Appasamy reveals in his *Sundar Singh: A Biography*:

At Oxford Sundar Singh told us that in addition to all this study of the sacred scriptures of India he learnt to practice yoga, which has been followed as an effective method of meditation in India through the ages. He even attained mastery of the Yoga technique and became oblivious of the external world for short spells (Appasamy 1958, p. 19).

There is also much to learn from Singh's faith. According to my evaluation, the most legitimate and reliable book about Sadhu Sundar Singh, is C. F. Andrews' 1934 book *Sadhu Sundar Singh: A Personal Memoir* (Andrews 1934). This assessment is made on the basis of their long association in ministry – even an attempt to form a Christian ashram – as well as their partnership in theological conversations. While Andrews presents Singh's life in a systematic way by narrating his vision, discipleship, ministry in Tibet, understanding of the way of the cross, work of the Spirit, and his unique witness, Andrews narrative also conveys the depth of Singh's faith:

> He would seek to share the baptism wherewith Christ had been baptized, and to drink the cup which he had drunk. Deep down in his heart was the thought – almost the hope – that he would meet his death on this last journey (Andrews 1934, p. 179).

Singh's preaching is also full of insight. On this, Perumalla Surya Prakash's evaluation of Singh's sermons – in a book based on his doctoral thesis, *The Preaching of Sadhu Sundar Singh: A Homiletic Analysis of Independent Preaching and Personal Christianity* (Prakash 1991) – is important. After theological and exegetical analysis of over 120 sermons preached by Singh, Prakash concludes that the main themes in the sermons are life in Christ, prayer, Christian witness, salvation, and the coming of Christ (Prakash 1991, p. 156). From roots in the Panjab, these found voice – and hearers – around the world and still may.

Key Themes

In his preaching and in his life, Sadhu Sundar Singh courageously and vividly presented a picture of Jesus Christ as the source of life. According to R. James:

> There is only one source of Life – an Infinite and Almighty Life, whose creative power gave life to all living things. All creatures live in him and in him will they remain forever. Again this Life created innumerable other lives, different in kind, and in the stages of their progress man is one of these, created in God's own image that he might ever remain happy in his holy presence (James 2012, p. 14).

This vision of life in Christ invites disciples to affirm both their own journeys and those of their neighbors – important in his hearers' context of conflict and confusion and in light of their conversion. The series of visions Singh articulated through his short life strengthened his fellow Christians in their lives, and emboldened them for the next, as James describes:

> When the souls of men arrive in the world of spirits, the good at once separate from the evil. In this world all are mixed together, but it is not so in the

spiritual world. I have many times seen that when the spirits of the good – the sons of light – enter into the world of spirits, they first bathe in the intangible air-like waters of a crystal-clear ocean, and in this they find an intense and exhilarating refreshment. Within these miraculous waters they move about as if in open air, neither are they drowned beneath them, nor do the waters wet them, but, wonderfully cleansed and refreshed and fully purified, they enter into the world of glory and light, where they will ever remain in the presence of their dear Lord, and in the fellowship of innumerable saints and angels (James 2012, p. 22).

He claimed those visions were from the true God, shaped as they often were by his reading of the book of Revelation.

Even in his own times, Singh's ecumenical vision made an impact in the life of Anglican churches, as Archbishop of Canterbury Randall Davidson acknowledged (Lynch-Watson 1975, p. 121). For along with colonial missionary activities, the sin of denominationalism was thrust upon colonized people, including in India. Instead of being focused on the true nature of Christ, as Singh would have wished, many native communities were aggressively oriented within denominational boundaries that reflected ecclesial lines in Europe. These practices both distorted encounter with Christ and minimized the potential liberative element of the Christian gospel. And though many native communities felt uncomfortable about this situation, it took powerful prophets like Singh to challenge the walls of denominationalism. Singh accepted invitations to speak to audiences comprised of people from many denominations and challenged the borders of ecclesial traditions and orientations when he did so.

Sadhu Sundar Singh's legacy has many dimensions and has left strong legacies. On the one hand, as Janet Lynch-Watson states, "Sundar's influence upon Indian theology is to be seen in the work of theologians like his friend Aiyadurai Jesudason Appasamy," an important voice in Indian theology – and Anglican theology – in the next generation. One the other hand, as Lynch-Watson continues, "Indeed Robin Boys goes so far as to suggest, 'it might even prove ultimately that in the history of the Indian Church and its thought Sundar Singh was actually more important for his theology and his method than his ascetic way of life and his success as an evangelist'," (Lynch-Watson 1975, p. 154), his theology is founded on his vision of Christ overcoming both Empire and denominationalism, kept close in prayer, trusted for the future, and endlessly respectful to the Indian heritage of Singh's own life and the struggles of his times. In my view, assent to Lynch-Watsons statement is a solid reason to consider Sadhu Sundar Singh to be one of the very most influential Indian Christian theologians. He was able to propose fresh and creative ways to practice the values of the reign of God based on the life and ministry of Christ while maintaining an attractive vision of Christ. His foundational arguments are mainly based on two elements: the living Christ, and how witness to this Christ must be manifest in order to reflect and be true. Friedrich Heiler summarizes key aspects of Singh's convictions:

In Christ, the personal Saviour, the Redeemer who has become man, we are able to grasp this deep mystery of eternal Love. In Christ the infinite comes down to the level of his needy creature; in Him He turns His face towards seeking humanity, and this Face is a human face full of gentleness and kindness, glorified always by a smile of love (Heiler 1989, p. 143).

Even more succinctly, Appasamy says of Singh: "there was a constant background, which he described thus: 'Christ on His Throne is always in the centre'" (Appasamy 1958, p. 147).

Divine Incarnation in Christ Jesus

It is important to note that various Anglican writers have taken an interest in Sadhu Sundar Singh because of the impact of his life and ministry, in India specifically but also more widely across the globe. For example, Singh's life was portrayed by E. Sanders and Ethelred Judah in *Sadhu Sundar Singh: The Lion-Hearted Warrior* (Sanders and Judah 1923) – and as it was published by SPCK it implies some level of endorsement by the Church of England. Yet it is crucial to note that the book clearly reveals the partial – by no means complete – collaboration between Singh and the British missionaries of his day. Clear differences emerged between them, including differences between many missionaries and Singh over the understanding of the divine incarnation in Jesus Christ.

Before his own conversion, Singh approached the missionaries with suspicion because he blamed missionaries who had "come here to spoil our homeland" (Sanders and Judah 1923, p. 20). He confronted the missionaries aggressively. His own desire to find the true God remained unmet until he had his vision of Jesus. After his vision of Jesus the major focus of his teaching became the full revelation of God in Jesus Christ. He lifted up a Christian discipleship that could endure suffering, because, as Sanders and Judah state:

> Jesus said that the peace-makers shall be called the children of God, and we know that children generally bear some resemblance to their father in their outward appearance. Need we be surprised then that whenever Sundar goes men feel that he is just like their ideas of Christ? Most of us remember the thought that flashed across our minds the first time we saw him, "How like Jesus!" (Sanders and Judah 1923, p. 93).

He was never aligned or ever seen to be aligned with British missionaries. Yet this notwithstanding, Sadhu Sundar Singh did influence the British missionaries of his time, and in many ways. C. F. Andrews' work is just one important example, and Singh's wider influence is clear in *Sadhu Sundar Singh: Called by God* (Parker 1920), written by the spouse of LMS missionary Arthur Parker.

Sundar Singh and the Contemporary Anglican Communion

Given that churches in the Anglican Communion now so readily encounter stress around issues such as migration and refugees, as well as crisis in faith, the vision of Sadhu Sundar Singh seems to me to be very important in directing the church in what we might call a direction of faith. Moreover, discussions on religious pluralism and what the message of Jesus Christ means within it could be helpfully guided by the theological understanding of Singh as he touched theological dimensions of the person and work of Christ, while always speaking from and often to non-Western settings. His pattern of respectful interaction with people of other faiths provides a clear model that can be followed by Anglicans living in multicultural and multifaith contexts.

References

Andrews, C.F. (1934). *Sadhu Sundar Singh: A Personal Memoir.* London: Harper and Brothers Publishers.

Appasamy, A.J. (1958). *Sundar Singh: A Biography.* London: Lutterworth Press.

Basham, A.L. (2004). *The Wonder that Was India: A Survey of the History and Culture of the Indian Sub-Continent before the Coming of the Muslims.* London: Picador.

Cohn, B.S. (1987). *An Anthropologist among the Historians and Other Essays.* Delhi: Oxford University Press.

Daniel, J. (n.d.). *Sadhu Sundar Singh: A Biography,.* http://www.akademijavjecnog-proljeca.org/sundar_eng.html

Davey, C.J. (1950). *The Story of Sadhu Sundar Singh.* Chicago: Moody Press.

Edwards, M. (1967). *British India 1772–1947: A Survey of the Nature and Effects of Alien Rule.* Delhi: Rupa and Co.

Heiler, F. (1989). *The Gospel of Sadhu Sundar Singh.* Delhi: ISPCK.

Hubel, T. (1996). *Whose India? The Independence Struggle in British India and Indian Fiction and History.* London: Duke University Press.

James, R. (2012). *The Life and Visions of Sadhu Sundar Singh.* Knoxville, TN: Brother James Publications.

Lynch-Watson, J. (1975). *The Saffron Robe: A life of Sadhu Sundar Singh.* London: Hodder and Stoughton.

Manjumdar, R.C. (1962). *History of the Freedom Movement in India.* Calcutta: Firma K.L. Mukhopadhyay.

Mcdonald, K.S. (1898). Indian Christianity. *The Indian Evangelical Review*: 14.

Metcalf, T.R. (1995). *Ideologies of the British Raj.* Cambridge: Cambridge University Press.

Parker, "Mrs. Arthur." (1920). *Sadhu Sundar Singh: Called God.* Madras: CLS.

Prakash, P.S. (1991). *The Preaching of Sadhu Sundar Singh: A Homiletic Analysis of Independent Preaching and Personal Christianity.* Bangalore: Word Makers.

Riddle, T.E. (1987). *The Vision and the Call: A Life of Sadhu Sundar Singh.* Delhi: ISPCK.

Sanders, E. and Judah, E. (1923). *Sadhu Sundar Singh: The Lion-Hearted Warrior.* London: SPCK.

Thompson, E. and Garratt, G.T. (1935). *Rise and Fulfilment of British Rule in India.* London: Macmillan and Co.

Trautmann, T.R. (ed.) (2005). *The Aryan Debate.* Oxford: Oxford University Press.

Dorothy L. Sayers (1893–1957)

Stephen Burns

Dorothy L. Sayers is best known for her many works of crime fiction (see Martin 2019), often centered around the exploits of her characters Peter Wimsey and Harriet Vane. *Whose Body?* was published in 1923 and made Sayers famous, and a dozen more best-selling novels followed over the next fifteen years. Her main genre then turned to stage plays for cathedral spaces – *The Zeal of Thy House* (1937) for Canterbury Cathedral, to be the first of several – and also radio dramas, the most notable of which is her *The Man Born to Be King* (Sayers 1943), broadcast on the BBC in wartime. Later work involved translation into English of Dante's *Divine Comedy*, the first two volumes of which – and lion's share of the third – she completed before her death in 1957. Sayers also produced more conventional (albeit sometimes highly creative) works of theology, though not from any official position in either church or academy but from her situation as a public figure. These writings range from papers on Dante's theology – two collections, *Introductory Papers on Dante* (1954) and *Further Papers on Dante* (Sayers 1957) – through to what she herself termed "popular theology," with this latter mode emerging as a response to warm reception of her letter to *The Times* newspaper in 1939, on the question "What do we believe?"

While her novels were value laden, not shy of depicting the faith-thinking of her characters – even occasionally inflecting her appreciation for the ways in which, in her view, anglo-catholic worship could open up vistas of transcendence – she balked at any suggestion that she was a "Christian novelist." She was also sometimes uncertain of her voice as a theologian. For though *The Man Born to Be King* is a distinctive engagement with the gospels, calling itself a "play-cycle on the life of our Lord and Saviour Jesus Christ," and her cathedral plays deal with Christian themes or narratives – *The Zeal of Thy House*, for example, being about the rebuilding of the cathedral choir at Canterbury in 1174 – she found reason to decline William Temple's offer of a Lambeth Doctor of Divinity (DD) degree – the Archbishop of Canterbury's

Twentieth Century Anglican Theologians: From Evelyn Underhill to Esther Mombo, First Edition.
Edited by Stephen Burns, Bryan Cones, and James Tengatenga.
© 2021 John Wiley & Sons Ltd. Published 2021 by John Wiley & Sons Ltd.

honorary award, evoked by what others thought her "fine . . . evangelism" (Reynolds 1993, p. 328). She stated that if it had been a Doctor of Letters (DLitt), not in divinity, she might have received it. And she confided in friends that she did not wish to hold an ecclesial award if it would in any way constrain her voice. Only later – in 1950 – did she accept an honorary doctorate, when Durham University presented her with a DLitt.

Sayers' work is more diverse than many other twentieth century Anglican theologians; and given her fame for more than her explicit theology, she also stands out as one unusual among theologians for being the subject of biography and the kinds of curiosity that involves. There are more available sources to consider in relation to Sayers than there are for most theologians, and the relationship of her thinking and her life circumstances are more evident than is the case with many others. Barbara Reynolds (1914–2015), Sayers' god-daughter, who completed the translation of Dante that Sayers began, produced the major biography *Dorothy L. Sayers: Her Life and Soul* in 1993, the year that marked the centenary of Sayers' birth. In that book, Reynolds narrates Sayers' work in a rich picture of life over time; and in addition to her biography, Reynolds also edited five volumes of Sayers' letters, as well as writing about Sayers' "encounter with Dante" in *The Passionate Intellect* (Reynolds 1989). Reynolds notes that Dante's phrase "the mind in love" (from *Paradise*, Canto XXVII) is aptly applied to Sayers in her turn (Reynolds 1993, p. 368).

Biography of Sayers provides illuming insight into Sayers' thinking. She wrote in one of her letters, for example, that "Christianity is as plain and as common as bread. The simplest person and the youngest child can be a Christian, by faith and baptism. The faith is faith in a Person; the baptism is baptism into His Body" (cited in Reynolds 1993, p. 369) – yet when she wrote to William Temple to refuse his offer of a DD she said she was aware that she was not "a more convincing kind of Christian" (Reynolds 1993, p. 329). Because of biographies about her, we may see in her more than in others what she described for herself (in another letter, to the vicar of All Saints, Margaret Street, London) as a struggle manifest in being "a great deal stronger on doctrine than on practice" (Reynolds 1993, p. 331). Of particular importance in her biography may be the fact that she gave birth to John Anthony, born in January 1924, her "love child" with a man, Bill White, with whom she had had an affair on the rebound from a broken relationship with another man whom she wished to marry, John Cournos. On finding that she was pregnant, Sayers hid her pregnancy by eating herself fat, made excuses to be absent from work, gave birth in secret, and arranged for her boy to be brought up by her cousin, Ivy, who fostered children at her home near Bournemouth. Sayers' secret was kept from all but Sayers' future husband, becoming public knowledge only long after her death, in 1975. Sayers married Oswald Arthur (known as Mac) Fleming, in 1926, when he was a recent divorcee, writing to her parents "I am getting married on Tuesday . . .." This was the first they had heard of Mac, and they were not invited to the registry office, and neither was anyone else. While Dorothy and Mac's marriage was happy for a time, it deteriorated around his severe alcoholism, through which Dorothy decided to remain married, despite the strain. Biographers may speculate as to whether Sayers' decline of a Lambeth DD was related to the "illegitimacy" of her son (Howatch 1994, p. ix), a protection of Anthony, or was something to do with the tensions of her domestic life with Mac, as they also ponder ways in which Sayers' writings – such as her nativity play *He That Should Come* (Sayers 1939) – might have "enable[ed] women, placed as was Dorothy Sayers, to express their tenderness for their children, no matter what the circumstances of their conception" (Loades 1993, p. 16).

Dorothy L. Sayers was herself born in 1893 in Oxford, England, where her father was headmaster of Christchurch (Oxford Cathedral) Choir School. So Dorothy spent her first years of life in the university city to which she would later return as a student – and as one of the very first women to graduate from it in 1920. Her father was an ordained minister in the Church of England and when Dorothy was four, her family (mother, father, and their only child) moved to the fens of East Anglia: to Bluntisham-cum-Earith, near Huntingdon. When she returned to Oxford as a student she had already been taught at home to read French, German and Latin – and so she displayed early in life a verve with language that would manifest in many ways – but she was not at that time known for engagement with Christian institutions, and particularly not with fervent groups that could be found in the university. She had not enjoyed the evangelical version of Anglican tradition she had encountered in her time as a boarding student when a teenager. But she did, however, apparently express a devotional life through this time, keeping a crucifix, for example – a hint, perhaps, of the path toward the anglo-catholic strand of the Church of England in which she would later settle (and serve, becoming churchwarden at St. Anne's, Soho, London, for instance). Insight into her earlier feelings about church might be found in one of her first publishing ventures – for after working for the publisher, Blackwell, and not liking it, and dropping such work, in 1918 she put out a book of poetry, *Catholic Tales and Christian Songs* (Sayers 1918). That book, though not "successful" as her novels would soon be, suggests a somewhat cynical take on church in which Christ is mocked daily by ecclesial wrangling, sentimentality, penchant for war, patronizing clericalism, and facile thinking. So this nascent work can be seen in retrospect as setting the tone for several concerns that surface forcefully later on.

Trinity

A remarkable feature of Sayers' mature "popular theology" is its headlong encounter with Christian doctrine, the Trinity and incarnation above all. When in 1937 she was commissioned by Canterbury Cathedral to produce a play for its third Festival of the Arts (the two previous ones were T. S. Eliot's *Murder in the Cathedral* and Charles Williams' *Thomas Cranmer of Canterbury*), she turned out *The Zeal of Thy House*, a lavish production (with "gigantic angelic figures, . . . fantastic design . . ." [Reynolds 1993, p. 277]) that engaged with the cathedral festival's theme of artists and craftspeople. This play represents a major turning-point for Sayers, marking a shift to explicitly theological themes. Clear from the start that she would not produce a drama that "mug[ed] up the history of kings and archbishops" (Reynolds 1993, p. 274) her telling of the rebuilding of the choir after fire in 1174 turned on the memoir of one of the protagonists, the monk Gervase, who said: "Either the vengeance of God or the envy of the Devil, wreaked itself on him alone" (Reynolds 1993, p. 276).

Notably, the play includes the germ that becomes the central idea for *The Mind of the Maker* in 1941, which elaborates on words that the play puts into the mouth of the Archangel Michael at the very climax of the last act:

> Praise Him that He hath made man in His own image, a maker and craftsman like Himself, a little mirror of His triune majesty. For every work of creation is threefold, an earthly trinity to match the heavenly. First: there is the Creative Idea; passionless, timeless, beholding the whole enterprise complete at once, the end in the beginning; and this is the image of the Father. Second: there is the Creative Energy, begotten of that Idea, working in time from the beginning to the end, with sweat and passion, being incarnate in the bonds of matter; and this is the image of the Word. Third: there is the Creative Power, the meaning of the work and its response in the lively soul; and this is the image of the indwelling Spirit. And these three are one, each equally itself the whole work, whereof none can exist without other; and this is the image of the Trinity (Loades 1993, p. 63).

The Mind of the Maker (Sayers 1941) was to become perhaps her most significant work, and it develops Archangel Michael's speech from *The Zeal of Thy House* to draw out in her own voice what she sees as the relationship between the Trinity and the human act of creation. As she put it: there are always three "books" simultaneously: the Book as You Think it, the Book as You Write it, and the Book as You and They Read it. The process of creating a piece of work is akin to the divine Trinity, in which three persons, each distinctive, exist at once as part of one activity. In making her argument, she insisted that the Christian doctrine of the Trinity is not metaphor, but analogue.

Between *The Zeal of Thy House* and *The Mind of the Maker*, Sayers had made some initial forays into prose writing for newspapers and magazines, with "The Greatest Drama Ever Staged" commissioned by the *Sunday Times* for its Passion Sunday 1938 edition. That same newspaper followed with another commission on the basis of the first one's appreciation by readers. So she produced "The Triumph of Easter" for Easter Sunday. A companion to the first article (though published in a different place – *St. Martin's Review*) was another, "The Dogma is the Drama." This parodied the lack of Trinitarian imagination which her own contribution in *The Mind of the Maker*, nascent in the Archangel Michael's words in *The Zeal of Thy House*, would seek to remedy. Her amusing lampoon includes this dialogue:

Q: What does the Church think of God the Father?
A: He is omnipotent and holy. He created the world and imposed on man conditions impossible for fulfillment; He is very angry if these are not carried out. He sometimes interferes by means of arbitrary judgments and miracles, distributed with a good deal of favoritism. He . . . is always ready to pound on anybody who trips up over a difficulty in the Law, or is having a bit of fun. He is rather like a dictator, only larger and more arbitrary.
Q: What does the Church think of God the Son?
A: He is in some way to be identified with Jesus of Nazareth. It is not His fault that the world was made like this, and, unlike God the Father, he is friendly to man

and did His best to reconcile man to God (see Atonement). He has a good deal of influence with God, and if you want anything done, it is best to apply to Him.

Q: What does the Church think about God the Holy Spirit?

A: I don't know exactly. He was never seen or heard of until Pentecost. There is a sin against Him which damns you forever, but nobody knows what it is.

Q: What is the doctrine of the Trinity?

A: "The Father incomprehensible, the Son incomprehensible, and the whole thing incomprehensible." It's something put in by theologians to make it more difficult – it's got nothing to do with daily life or ethics (cited in Simmons 2005, pp. 65–66).[1]

Despite the fact that Sayers' initial attempt to follow up her newspaper pieces with a book (*Begin Here*, an invitation from the publisher Victor Gollancz to write a "message for the nation") was the nearest thing she ever did to a flop, she went on to publish her essays in later collections, *Unpopular Opinions* (Sayers 1946a) and *Creed or Chaos?* (Sayers 1947).

It might be that her trinitarian thinking, and her discernment of "scalene" – faulty – trinitarian thought, also in *The Mind of the Maker*, has not even yet had the influence on the theological academy that it deserves, but the novelist Susan Howatch, when selecting a small number of texts for the "Library of Anglican Spirituality" in the late 1990s, was one to recognize the significance of *The Mind of the Maker*. She praised its vivid showing forth of how doctrine "attempt[s] to describe living truths," and because in her view writing about creation often lacks insight – especially from the arts – about "the creative process," and for its foreshadowing of interdisciplinary studies. Howarth also praised it for showing how literature and theology illumine one another (Howatch 1994, p. x) in processes about which Howarth holds that Sayers could speak with "complete authority" (Howatch 1994, p. x).

For her own part, Sayers more likely saw authority in the doctrines she proclaimed. From the outbreak of war on, she was quite clear in her own mind that she need do nothing to dramatize the Christian message (i.e., as if to spruce up something dull), because "the dogma is the drama." And the doctrine of the Trinity was not the only doctrine that she saw as far from being boring, but interesting, exciting (see Loades 1993, pp. 115–118), about daily life and ethics.

Incarnation

In 1938, Sayers was commissioned by the BBC to write a nativity play for Children's Hour. She produced *He That Should Come* (Sayers 1939), but the BBC thought it was unsuitable for the young, arranging instead for its broadcast as an "adult" play. Centered on Mary and her maternal love (singing lullabies to Jesus, and so on), it caused some upset at the BCC because of Sayers' insistence that "The whole effect and character of the play depend on its being played in an absolutely natural and realistic style." That is, there was to be no "touch of ecclesiastical intonation or of 'religious unction.'" Indeed, it was Sayers' intention for her realistic style to change perceptions of what counts as "reverence," showing that Jesus' "Manhood" (humanity) "was a real manhood, subject to the common realities of daily life; [and] that the men and women surrounding Him were living human beings, not just characters in a story; that, in short, He was born, not into 'the Bible,' but into the world. . ." (from her "Note to Producers"). The resulting dispute with the BBC brought out her resistance to any pressure to present the Christian message as one about "universal kindness" – though for what it is worth Reynolds' biography vividly reveals Sayers' kindness toward numerous persons, including, in wartime, the German woman who had taught her piano as a child, sending her cooking fat, fruit puddings, reels of cotton, and hairpins among many other things (Reynolds 1993, pp. 369–370). In Sayers' view, Christianity is not about kindness because it is uncompromisingly about incarnation. And the BBC foresaw how controversial the way she wanted to convey this would be. In *He That Should Come* Sayers enacted an antidote to problems she had discerned in *Catholic Tales and Christian Songs*, and about which she had also written at other times: for example, that "at the name of Jesus, every voice goes plummy, every gesture becomes pontifical, and a fearful creeping paralysis slows down the pace of the dialogue" (Loades 1993, p. 6). From 1938 on, her central concern became to present an orthodox Christology, yet affirming the incarnation in ways to which she thought her contemporaries could relate in credible ways. Just as she wanted to show how the Trinity might be "as familiar as [a person's] garter" (Loades 1993, p. 79), so she hoped to reveal Christ Jesus.

As a nativity play, *He That Should Come* was a kind of test-run for a more ambitious endeavor to present a dramatic harmonization of the gospels as a whole. This turned out to be her best-known play, *The Man Born to be King*, which was broadcast in 1941 in the same year as her major work of prose *The Mind of the Maker* was published. In her introduction to *The Man Born to be King*, she wrote:

> Jesus Christ is unique – unique among gods and men. There have been incarnate gods a-plenty, and slain-and-resurrected gods not a few; but He is the only God who has a date in history. And plenty of founders of religions have had dates, and some of them have been prophets or avatars of the Divine; but only this one of them was personally God. There is no more astonishing collocation of phrases than that which, in the Nicene Creed, sets these two statements flatly side by side: "Very God of very God . . . He suffered under Pontius Pilate" (Sayers 1943, p. 20).

> Not Herod, not Caiaphas, not Pilate, not Judas ever contrived to fasten upon Jesus Christ the reproach of insipidity; that final indignity was left for pious hands to inflict. To make of His story something that could neither startle, nor shock, nor terrify, not excite, not inspire a living soul is to crucify the Son of God afresh and put Him to an open shame. . . . Let me tell you, good Christian people, an honest writer would be ashamed to treat a nursery tale as you have treated the greatest drama in history (Sayers 1943, p. 36).

The play was broadcast in eight parts, mainly to acclaim, with some at the BBC hailing it "one of the great landmarks of broadcasting" (Reynolds 1993, p. 321). An extract:

LAZARUS: In a world like this, what is there to be merry about? There is much labour and great disquiet, fear, and a little trembling laughter. The most a man can hope for is tranquility, and perhaps even that is too much to expect. I think

> there is a terror at the heart of God's mystery. Is it not so, Rabbi? Is not the fear
> of the Lord the beginning of wisdom?
>
> JESUS (*DREAMILY*): When He established the foundations of the earth, I was with
> Him forming all things, and I was delighted every day, playing before Him, play-
> ing in the world and delighting myself in the sons of men.
>
> JOHN (*A LITTLE STARTLED – IT SOUNDS ALMOST AUTOBIOGRAPHICAL*): Master, of whom is
> that said?
>
> JESUS: Of the Word and Wisdom of God.
>
> LAZARUS: Does joy go so deep as that? To the very foundations of the world?
>
> (Sayers 1943, p. 187.)

But what gladdened some also caused others consternation, as the play involved the shock of "hearing" the "voice" of Jesus, in a way that had never, until recently, been pos- sible – via radio: so she broke a taboo. And she made shock-waves, too, because the characters in her renditions of gospel stories speak in then-contemporary British idioms and with regional accents, a jolt to listeners used to reading and hearing read the Authorized Version of the Bible. *The Man Born to be King* was, as it were from here and now. The Lord's Day Observance Society and the Protestant Truth Society both opposed the play, and the refusal of the BCC to curtail the production was even blamed for the fall of Singapore to Japan on account of this "blasphemy" (Reynolds 1993, p. 327).

Also, in 1941, Sayers was involved with the archbishop William Temple in the Malvern Conference. She was in fact the only woman to speak to its concern with the rebuilding of Britain after the war. Part of her unfolding contribution to Christian social thinking became to develop a theology of work through the trinitarian ana- logue she had already articulated, and which she turned to underline the graced nature of work (see Loades 1993, pp. 131–143; also Smith 2013). Another contribu- tion that she made to society around this time was to argue fiercely for gender equal- ity. In 1938 she had made one such address and in 1941 she made another, in "Are Women Human?" and "The Human-Not-Quite-Human," respectively. These are gathered into her collection *Unpopular Opinions* (Sayers 1946a), which also includes focus on the creeds, and so she set her reflection on divine incarnation right alongside that on women. The latter of her essays on women argues that

> Perhaps it is no wonder that the women were first at the Cradle and last at the Cross.
> They had never known a man like this Man – there never has been such another. A
> prophet and a teacher who never nagged at them, never flattered or coaxed or
> patronized; who never made arch jokes about them, never treated them either as
> "The women, God help us!" or "The ladies, God bless them!"; who rebuked with-
> out querulousness and praised without condescension; who took their questions
> and arguments seriously; who never mapped out their sphere for them, never urged
> them to be feminine or jeered at them for being female; who had no axe to grind
> and no uneasy male dignity to defend; who took them as he found them and was
> completely unselfconscious. There is no act, no sermon, no parable in the whole
> Gospel that borrows its pungency from female perversity; nobody could guess from
> the words and deeds of Jesus that there was anything "funny" about women
> (Sayers 1946a, p. 122).

But, she added, the church did not always seem to believe this, "though one rose from the dead." Though Sayers resisted the label "feminist" (and did not support the ordination of women on the basis of it being, she thought, a "barrier with the rest of Catholic Christendom" [Reynolds 1993, p. 358]), her thinking on women was related to that on work, as seen in her insistence on particularizing the question of whether "a women is as good as a man" by asking the further question, "at doing what?" As Ann Loades distils Sayers' argument, "Poets should not 'entangle themselves with engines' and mechanically-minded persons should not 'issue booklets of bad verse'. The elephant 'would make a poor showing in the Derby', and a racehorse would be speedily eclipsed by an elephant 'when it comes to hauling logs.'" So "jobs need to be done by the persons who do them best" (Loades 1995, p. 24), with questions of, in Sayers' phrase, "sex-equality" being meaningless until the kind of work that women might do is identified (Loades 1995, p. 26). At the very least, Sayers' essays on "women" hint at some ways Sayers' took herself and her own skills seriously, just as in Dante she found another high estimation of women.

Encounter with Dante

Through the war years, Sayers read Dante Alighieri's (1265–1321) *Hell* while ensconced in air-raid shelters under London streets, as bombs dropped. She related her own context to Dante's inferno (see Loades 2011). She was introduced to Dante's work by Charles Williams, whose own play preceded *The Zeal of Thy House* at Canterbury Cathedral - Williams having recommended Sayers to follow him as the next cathedral playwright, and who had also himself written a book on Dante in 1943. A first fruit of Sayers' engagement on Dante was another of her cathedral plays, this time for the Midlands city, Lichfield, in 1946. *The Just Vengeance* (the title of which draws from *Purgatory*, Canto XXI) is what she called a "miracle play of Man's insufficiently and God's redemptive act," vividly set in a contemporary war-torn context. It centers on the death of a pilot shot from the sky in a bomber:

> . . . Let go.
> It is no use now clinging to the controls.
> Let some one else take over. Take, then, take . . .
> There, that is done . . . into Thy hand, O God (Sayers 1946b, p. 348).

This play deals with the doctrine of atonement, as distilled in her pressing together of two New Testament texts (Romans 8.22 and Colossians 1.24): "Whoso will carry the Cross, the Cross will carry him" (Sayers 1946b, p. 91). The distillation is key to what she finds in Dante's opus.

Over time, Sayers set about translating the entire *Divine Comedy* into English – publishing *Hell* in 1949 (Sayers 1949), and *Purgatory* in 1955 – and then two books about Dante, in 1954 and 1957. The figure of Dante's childhood sweetheart, Beatrice, is one of Sayers' foci, as it was for Charles Williams. Beatrice's presence conveying grace to Dante is a major preoccupation for Sayers' reading. Just as the act of creation served as analogue for the Trinity in her earlier work, in her reading of Dante Beatrice is an analogue of the eucharist – a sacramental person, one in whom, for Dante, "Heaven's glory [walks] the earth bodily" (Sayers 1947, p. 67). What Sayers seems most to have imbibed about Beatrice is Dante's sense that her greeting (*salute*, a word that can be rendered both "salutation" and "salvation") left him feeling that "there was no enemy left to me; rather there smite into me a flame of charity, which made me forgive every person who had ever injured me; and if at that moment anybody had put a question to me about anything whatsoever, my answer would have been simply 'Love', with a countenance clothed in humility" (quoting Dante's *Vita Nouva* in her Introduction to the first volume on *Hell* [cited in Loades 1993, p. 166]). Sayers saw this as, among other things, an affirmation of the female, a corrective to so much of the Christian tradition that had not affirmed the capacity of women (bar Mary, maybe) to mediate grace. On the contrary, Dante's witness is to being "transhumanzied" (i.e., transformed almost beyond words) by Beatrice who "makes it possible for him to become God's lover" (Loades 1995, p. 137), wells up a fountain of happiness in his heart, and gives him a taste for the joy of heaven. Whatever was going on in Dante's imagination, Sayers' reads his and Beatrice's exchange as pointing to a dimension of human life which – like work and the creation of things – puts human beings in touch with God, such that they may find "the manifestation of the Divine glory in whatsoever beloved thing becomes to every man his own particular sacramental experience" (Sayers 1957, pp. 192–193).

Sayers had not completed the third volume of the *Comedy*, *Paradise*, when she died out and about in London Christmas shopping in late 1957. While leaving some thirteen Cantos unfinished – work that would be picked up by Barbara Reynolds[2] – Sayers had made a translation of the crescendo at the very end of the trilogy, because she sent those lines to friends as her Christmas card in 1949. They depict "the love that moves the sun and other stars" as three spheres, one of which is "limned with our image" – Trinity and incarnation beheld, as they had been in so much of own her life's work.

Notes

1 "The Dogmas is the Drama" (1938) was written for *St Martin's Review* (Reynolds 1993, p. 289) and collected into Dorothy L. Sayers, *Creed or Chaos? and Other Essays in Popular Theology* (Sayers 1947).

2 The volume on heaven, *Paradiso*, was published by Penguin in 1962, five years after Sayers' death.

References

Howatch, S. (ed.) (1994). Introduction. In *The Mind of the Maker* (D.L. Sayers). London: Cassell.

Loades, A. (ed.) (1993). *Dorothy L. Sayers: Spiritual Writings*. London: SPCK.

Loades, A. (1995). Are women human? Dorothy L. Sayers as a feminist reader of Dante's Beatrice. *Feminist Theology* 8: 121–138.

Loades, A. (2011). Dorothy L. Sayers: war and redemption. In: *C.S. Lewis and Friends: Faith and the Power of Imagination* (eds. D. Hein and E. Henderson), 53–72. London: SPCK.

Martin, J. (2019). Dorothy L. Sayers (1893–1957): God and the detective. In: *Anglican Women Novelists: from Charlotte Bronte to P.D. James* (eds. J. Maltby and A. Shell), 87–102. London: Bloomsbury.

Reynolds, B. (1989). *The Passionate Intellect: Dorothy L. Sayers' Encounter with Dante.* Kent, OH: Kent State University.

Reynolds, B. (1993). *Dorothy L. Sayers: Her Life and Soul.* London: Hodder and Stoughton.

Sayers, D.L. (1918). *Catholic Tales and Christian Songs.* Oxford: B. H. Blackwell.

Sayers, D.L. (1937). *The Zeal of Thy House.* London: Victor Gollancz.

Sayers, D.L. (1939). *He that Should Come.* London: Methuen.

Sayers, D.L. (1941). *The Mind of the Maker.* London: Mowbray.

Sayers, D.L. (1943). *The Man Born to Be King.* London: Gollancz.

Sayers, D.L. (1946a). *Unpopular Opinions.* London: Gollancz.

Sayers, D.L. (1946b). *The Just Vengeance.* London: Victor Gollancz.

Sayers, D.L. (1947). *Creed or Chaos? And Other Essays in Popular Theology.* London: Methuen.

Sayers, D.L. (translator) (1949). *Dante: The Divine Comedy: Hell.* Harmondsworth: Penguin.

Sayers, D.L. (1954). *Introductory Papers on Dante.* London: Methuen.

Sayers, D.L. (1957). *Further Papers on Dante.* London: Methuen.

Sayers, D.L. (1962). *Paradiso.* Harmondsworth: Penguin.

Simmons, L.K. (2005). *Creed without Chaos: Exploring Theology in the Writings of Dorothy L. Sayers.* Grand Rapids, MI: Eerdmans.

Smith, C.M. (2013). *The Artist and the Trinity: Dorothy L. Sayers' Theology of Work.* Eugene, OR: Wipf & Stock.

Austin Farrer (1904–1968)

Robert MacSwain

In September 2011, while still Archbishop of Canterbury, Rowan Williams gave a lecture at Lambeth Palace to an audience of Roman Catholic bishops committed to the ecumenical and interfaith Focolare Movement. Titled "The Word of God in Anglican Tradition," the concluding paragraph is built around a passage by Austin Farrer, whom Williams simply introduces as "the greatest Anglican intellect of the last century."[1] Given Williams' own stature in contemporary Anglican theology, as well as the high-profile ecumenical context of this evaluation, one might expect Farrer to be a major source of inspiration and influence within Anglicanism since his death 50 years ago – but this is not the case. The significance of his legacy, and why he has been surprisingly neglected, will be the topic of this chapter.

First it is important to place him in context. As will be described in more detail in the subsequent section, Farrer was English, born in 1904 to a Baptist family, and converted to the Church of England as an Oxford undergraduate in 1924. His nationality, date of birth, and education meant that Farrer belonged to the generation of British scholars who were too young to fight in World War I, too old to fight in World War II, but who lived through both. As Ann Loades explains in the introduction to an anthology of Farrer's work,

> Farrer was fortunate to have been born on a date which kept him clear of service in the appalling conditions the First World War battlefields, although only the most privileged in Britain escaped the privations inescapable in wartime in respect of fuel and food. Comparable privations were to continue during the period after the war, with a General Strike in the UK and the economic slump that followed it. Europe was to be in turmoil for much of his life, with the Russian Revolution and the advent of Communist governments, and the almost indescribable menace of the rise of National Socialism and Fascism. To follow

Twentieth Century Anglican Theologians: From Evelyn Underhill to Esther Mombo, First Edition.
Edited by Stephen Burns, Bryan Cones, and James Tengatenga.
© 2021 John Wiley & Sons Ltd. Published 2021 by John Wiley & Sons Ltd.

were the horrors of the Second World War, with systematic mass murder, aerial bombing of civilians, including the saturation bombing of German cities by the Allies, and a tragic culmination in the atomic bombing of Hiroshima and Nagasaki in the Far East (Loades and MacSwain 2006, p. ix).

Loades continues that although Farrer served as a college chaplain in Oxford during World War II, the university "was anything but isolated from what was going on, as the terrible war memorials in its college chapels vividly remind us." She further observes that although these social and political events were not Farrer's primary focus in either his academic or pastoral writings, they are nevertheless the actual background against which he worked, thought, and wrote (Loades and MacSwain 2006, pp. ix, x; Loades, 1998, pp. 120–123).

Farrer's career basically spanned 1930–1970. He thus ministered as a priest during the archiepiscopal reigns of Cosmo Gordon Lang, William Temple, Geoffrey Fisher, and Michael Ramsey. Temple and Ramsey are also featured in this volume, and Ramsey was a personal friend: he and Farrer went to theological college together and embraced anglo-catholicism during its high tide in the Church of England. The years 1930 to 1970 were also a period of great ferment in British philosophy, theology, and biblical studies, and these intellectual developments preoccupied Farrer far more than the social and political events mentioned above (see Chadwick 1990, pp. 31, 34, 46, 51, 69, 97).[2]

Biography

Austin Marsden Farrer was born in London on October 1, 1904.[3] His father Augustine (1872–1954) was a Baptist minister who taught at Regent's Park College, first in its original location in London and then also when it moved to Oxford. The Farrers were a serious and devout Non-conformist family, but not in sympathy with the more conservative forms of English Baptist theology that were prevalent at the time, so they found it difficult to find a congenial worshipping community. Young Austin's experience of several congregational schisms and awareness of his father's intellectual isolation from his co-religionists contributed to Austin's eventual decision to be baptized in the Church of England instead. In a series of letters to Augustine he explained that he valued Anglicanism's liturgical, sacramental, historical, and intellectual heritage (MacSwain 2006, 2012).

In 1923 Farrer went up from St. Paul's School in London to Balliol College, Oxford, where he studied classics, philosophy, and theology, and then trained for ordained ministry at Cuddesdon Theological College, just outside Oxford. He was ordained a deacon in 1928 and a priest in 1929, and served his curacy in Dewsbury, Yorkshire.

In 1931 Farrer returned to Oxford where he spent the rest of his life in teaching, writing, pastoral ministry, and administration. In a general survey of religion in Oxford from 1914 to 1970, historian F. M. Turner states, "More than any figure of his generation in the University, Farrer embodied the highest ideal of the college chaplain-theologian" (Turner 1994, p. 309). He was Chaplain and Tutor at St. Edmund Hall

(1931–1935), Fellow and Chaplain of Trinity College (1935–1960), and finally the Warden of Keble College (1960–1968). While at Trinity he married Katharine Newton, an Oxford graduate and the daughter of an Anglican clergyman. They had one child, a daughter named Caroline.

Farrer delivered the Bampton Lectures (Oxford) in 1948, the Edward Cadbury Lectures (Birmingham) in 1953–1954, the Gifford Lectures (Edinburgh) in 1957, the Nathaniel Taylor Lectures (Yale) in 1961, and the Deems Lectures (New York University) in 1964. A good friend of C. S. Lewis (1898–1963) and a regular participant in Lewis' Socratic Club for Oxford undergraduates, Farrer was also a leading – if comparatively moderate – figure in the anglo-catholic wing of the Church of England in the mid-twentieth century, closely associated with such luminaries as Kenneth Kirk (1886–1954), Gregory Dix (1901–1952), Michael Ramsey (1904–1988), and Eric Mascall (1905–1993). Farrer died at the age of sixty-four on December 29, 1968 (nineteen days after Karl Barth); earlier that year he had been elected as a Fellow of the British Academy.

Major Themes

In the preface to his Bampton Lectures – published by Dacre Press in 1948 as *The Glass of Vision* – Farrer wrote: "Scripture and metaphysics are equally my study, and poetry is my pleasure. These three things rubbing against one another in my mind, seem to kindle one another, and so I am moved to ask how this happens" (MacSwain 2013a, p. 12). In terms of his total output, however, it is clear that Farrer's "study" also included Christian doctrine. For the most part, poetry remained a personal "pleasure" and yet one that informed and infused his whole intellectual perspective. Farrer contributed to more than one academic discipline, and this thematic section will therefore focus on scripture, metaphysics, and doctrine, with primary attention to metaphysics and doctrine.[4]

Scripture

Farrer's work as a New Testament scholar falls into three categories: (1) his argument against the so-called "Q" source, augmented by the accompanying "Farrer hypothesis" regarding the literary dependence between the three Synoptic Gospels; (2) his studies of Mark and Matthew; and (3) his studies of the Book of Revelation. In all three cases he argued against dominant and still influential paradigms of thought.

Category (1) is expressed classically in Farrer's essay "On Dispensing With Q" (see Nineham 1955). Farrer argues that if Mark is primary, and if Matthew read Mark, and if Luke read both Mark and Matthew, then that sequence combined with Matthew's and Luke's own material is sufficient to explain the complex relationships among the Synoptics without positing an additional missing "source." This is perhaps Farrer's most influential contribution to current biblical studies (Poirier and Petersen 2015).

The second category begins in the final chapter of *The Glass of Vision*, "The Poetry of the New Testament," with Farrer's purely literary argument that Mark 16.8 ("for they were afraid") was the original conclusion to the Gospel, and then continues in *A Study in St Mark* (Farrer 1951) and *St Matthew and St Mark* (Farrer [1954] 1966). Farrer's arguments here, based largely on alleged prefiguring typological allusions to other biblical texts, perhaps received more attention from secular literary critics than from biblical scholars: for example, they were criticized by Helen Gardner and defended by Frank Kermode.

Category (3) consists of two related studies, *A Rebirth of Images: The Making of St John's Apocalypse* (Farrer 1949) and *The Revelation of St John the Divine: A Commentary on the English Text* (Farrer 1964b). As with his work on the Gospels, Farrer applied a creative literary analysis to the symbolic structures and prophetic poetry of the Apocalypse, finding hidden patterns and imaginative allusions that have intrigued and baffled most readers almost as much as the original. But even when other scholars are dubious about his details, these texts continue to be read by those grappling with the Book of Revelation.

More broadly, Farrer is recognized as one of the first to apply the methods of literary criticism to biblical texts. In addition to his technical studies described above, Farrer is also noted for his theory of divine inspiration and revelation, but that topic will be treated in the section on doctrine (see Titley 2010).

Metaphysics

According to the philosopher Ian Crombie, "Farrer had as penetrating a philosophical mind as anyone of his generation, though the truth of this – which puts him on a par with such practitioners as J. L. Austin and Gilbert Ryle – was not apparent outside the relatively small circle of those who engaged in philosophical discussion with him. His especial genius lay in his ability to penetrate through the cloud of detail to the essential structure of a problem or the essential features of some doctrine" (Crombie 2004, p. 121). Educated in the 1920s, Farrer's philosophical formation occurred before the rise of logical positivism in the 1930s and the professionalization of English philosophy in the 1940s. Nevertheless, as an original philosopher he took account of these two developments, albeit in varying ways.

Negatively, Farrer reacted against A. J. Ayer's 1936 positivist manifesto, *Language, Truth, and Logic*, in which Ayer famously wrote that the "metaphysical question concerning 'substance' [that is, a fundamental reality behind or beneath empirical observation] is ruled out by our [verifiability] criterion as spurious" (Ayer [1936] 1946), pp. 40, 42–45). For logical positivists, if a statement was not tautological or could not be verified empirically then it was meaningless, which ruled out not only metaphysics but also ethics and theology. By contrast, in his first major volume, *Finite and Infinite: A Philosophical Essay* (Farrer [1943] 1959), Farrer observed that it is "generally recognised that there are some metaphysical questions which must be settled if we are to vindicate the significance of any theological statements whatever of the traditional type" (Farrer [1943] 1959, p. v). And, as Farrer saw it then, the concept of substance was chief among those metaphysical questions that require such vindication: not just the one infinite substance we call "God," but also the many finite substances that make up everything else, including human beings. Indeed, in 1943 Farrer explicitly claimed that "finite substance has to be vindicated if theism is to be upheld" and thus devoted most of *Finite and Infinite* to achieving that goal by restating "the doctrine of the analogy of being in a credible form" (Farrer [1943] 1959, pp. 21 and vi).

In 1959, Farrer admitted that when he wrote *Finite and Infinite* he was "possessed by the Thomist vision, and could not think it false" (Farrer revised preface in latter edition of [1943] 1959, p. ix). Thus, in 1943 he was reacting not just against Ayer's rejection of substance but also Karl Barth's equally famous rejection of the analogy of being, memorably expressed as "the invention of the Anti-Christ" in the Preface to *Church Dogmatics* I/1 – a volume Farrer reviewed in *Theology* XXXIII (Farrer 1936). In short, Farrer's attempt to defend a reformulated Thomistic doctrine of substance was meant to respond simultaneously to Ayer's philosophical critique and Barth's theological critique. As an anglo-catholic, Farrer rejected both Ayer and Barth: against Ayer, Farrer did not think that ethical, metaphysical, and theological beliefs were meaningless, and tried to show this through purely philosophical argument; against Barth, Farrer thought that natural knowledge of God was not contrary to God's will but part of the divine condescension toward us.

Nevertheless, unlike French Thomists such as Étienne Gilson and Jacques Maritain or Farrer's fellow anglo-catholic Eric Mascall, Farrer distinctively sought to repair Thomism with the resources of contemporary British philosophy. So, while he responded negatively to the excesses of logical positivism, he responded more positively to at least some forms of what eventually came to be known as analytic philosophy (for a relevant discussion, see Harris and Insole 2005.) According to Basil Mitchell, Farrer shared with early analytic philosophy "its suspicion of obscurity and pretentiousness and its concern for clarity and precision of statement" (Mitchell 1983, p. 452; also Mitchell 1957, to which Farrer contributed two essays). Thus, Farrer's second major work of metaphysics – his 1957 Gifford Lectures published as *The Freedom of the Will* (Farrer 1958) – defended libertarian free will against determinism (an unusual move at the time) through arguments that drew more directly on contemporary British philosophy rather than traditional Thomism.

As indicated above, Farrer's thought on these matters continued to evolve, and his final book *Faith and Speculation: An Essay in Philosophical Theology* (Farrer 1967) sought to clarify both continuity and development in his metaphysical reasoning. While many scholars focus on Farrer's important defense of divine agency in that volume (e.g., Hebblethwaite and Henderson 1990), a crucial shift in Farrer's understanding occurred in the 1950s when he began to emphasize what we might call "causal interaction" over "contemplative apprehension." "Contemplative apprehension" refers to Farrer's early conviction that God's metaphysical uniqueness means that, while we cannot validly *infer* divine existence at the end of a chain of propositional reasoning, we can still adopt a contemplative attitude toward finite reality that will gradually lead us to *apprehend* divine reality as well. While not necessarily abandoning such contemplative apprehension, Farrer later came to stress that God is not an inert object that we contemplate passively, but rather an active reality with which we are intimately engaged on the most profound level of our life (see MacSwain 2013b).

Doctrine

Farrer's contribution to Christian doctrine – and thus specifically to twentieth century Anglican theology – is more diffuse than his work in either scripture or metaphysics and so will be expressed more through summary descriptions (Sedgwick 2005, pp. 183–184; also Williams, 2003b, p. 242). To begin with, as an anglo-catholic Farrer was formally committed to creedal orthodoxy and thus unsympathetic to liberal or revisionist strains of thought, particularly those that began to emerge toward the end of his life – such as, for example, John A. T. Robinson's *Honest to God* (1963) in England and Thomas J. J. Altizer's *The Gospel of Christian Atheism* (1966) in the United States.[5] And yet, as even those who disagreed with him observed, there was nothing defensive or reactionary about him, and thus even his conservatism was expressed in fresh and creative ways.

Second, as already mentioned in the biographical section, Farrer's theological vision was shaped by the specific community of anglo-catholic scholars to which he belonged: Kirk (moral theology), Dix (liturgy), Ramsey (biblical and doctrinal theology), and Mascall (historical, philosophical, and doctrinal theology). Within that collective division of labor, Farrer did indeed focus mostly on "Scripture and metaphysics" rather than Christian doctrine, and his work in this third area was expressed primarily through essays, sermons, and comparatively minor (but still substantial) books such as *Saving Belief: A Discussion of Essentials* (Farrer 1964a). In short, Farrer was not a "systematic theologian."

Rowan Williams has reflected on both of these aspects of Farrer's doctrinal work, namely its communal context and its occasional nature. In an essay on Robinson's *Honest to God*, Williams observes that in the 1940s Dix, Farrer, and Mascall "had all produced work that represented an amazingly creative reworking of classical themes," and yet "if the immediate postwar period produced such an explosion of first-class Anglican doctrinal reflection, still fresh and suggestive more than fifty years later, it rather looks as through the 1950s had forgotten why any of this mattered" (Williams 2003a, pp. 109–110; also Shortt 2005, pp. 13–14). While Williams does not provide any detailed explanation for this development, he notes the postwar changes that swept through English church and society in the 1950s, changes that led to the yet more radically transformed cultural landscape of the 1960s. In this new setting, "amazingly creative reworking of classical themes" did not generate much interest, while being "honest to God" did. Farrer thus wrote somewhat defiantly in the preface to *Saving Belief*: "There is nothing in these pages about nuclear bombs, artificial insemination, free love, world government, Church reunion, or the restyling of public worship. Those who seek after news may save their pains" (Farrer, 1964a, p. 6).

In another context, Williams said:

Farrer to me is exemplary not so much because of a work like *Finite and Infinite*, which is a great systematic essay, but because of his willingness to start again. After he'd finished it, it's almost as if he said, "It's a good idea, but it's not quite the way to do it," and increasingly he wrote in a sort of essayist style. His short pieces, collected posthumously, are often of the greatest possible value. I find that in six pages on the Incarnation he can say a great deal more than anybody else in a book on the subject. The same applies to his sermons; he's another person who theologizes through his sermons. And he's a man who cares intensely how things are said (Breyfogle 1995, p. 310).

For Williams, texts such as *The Glass of Vision* (a series of eight "lecture sermons"; Farrer 1948) and Farrer's essay and sermon collections are thus of enormous contemporary value.

Williams' provocative claim that "in six pages on the Incarnation [Farrer] can say a great deal more than anybody else in a book on the subject" is interestingly corroborated by the US Episcopal theologian Mark A. McIntosh in his study of the Christology of Hans Urs von Balthasar, one of the greatest Roman Catholic theologians of the twentieth century. In the introduction McIntosh sets out a key Balthasarian theme and then says: "Because this line of thought is absolutely central to von Balthasar's Christology, it is worth illustrating it here, even at some length, in the lucid words of the Anglican Thomist Austin Farrer, who develops an exactly parallel argument in his own works, stated in this instance more comprehensively than in any single place in von Balthasar" (McIntosh 1996, p. 6). McIntosh then quotes the following passage:

> If Jesus was God, it seems he could have no soul to save, no lessons to learn, no destiny to make, no surprises to meet, no temptations to resist; and without such experiences, he would not be a man at all. Whereas, if he was fully human in all these ways, then what can be meant by saying that he was God? . . . The trouble is, that we have taken a false starting-point. We cannot understand Jesus as simply the God-who-was-man. We have left out an essential factor, the sonship. Jesus is not simply God manifest as man; he is the divine Son coming into manhood. What was expressed in human terms here below was not bare deity; it was divine sonship. God cannot live an identically godlike life in eternity and in a human story. But the divine Son can make an identical response to his Father, whether in the love of the blessed Trinity or in the fulfillment of an earthly ministry. All the conditions of action are different on the two levels; the filial response is the one. Above, the appropriate response is a cooperation in sovereignty and an interchange of eternal joys. . . . Below, in the incarnate life, the appropriate response is an obedience to inspiration, a waiting for direction, an acceptance of suffering, a rectitude of choice, a resistance to temptation, a willingness to die. For such things are the stuff of our human existence; and it was in this very stuff that Christ worked out the theme of heavenly sonship, proving himself on earth the very thing he was in heaven; that is, a continuous perfect act of filial love (Conti 1975, p. 20).[6]

Farrer's Christological reflections have found an appreciative response in contemporary Anglican theologians such as Williams, McIntosh, Brian Hebblethwaite, and David Brown.[7] However, while Farrer was formally committed to orthodox Trinitarianism, and while his liturgical and spiritual mediations on the Trinity are sound enough (and often quite moving), in his attempts at theoretical doctrinal expression he occasionally slipped into a functional binitarianism – a lapse that has produced some consternation among his admirers.[8]

Given the characteristic Anglican emphasis on the incarnation it was fitting to dwell at some length on Farrer's reflections on this theme. However, Farrer's contribution to the doctrine of divine revelation in holy scripture is of equal significance. In brief, against the typical polarity of seeing such inspired revelation – what Farrer called "the form of divine truth in the human mind" – in terms of either *propositions* or *events*, Farrer proposed a distinctive theory of revelation through *images*, or more precisely through the "interplay" of image and event.[9] This is one of Farrer's most fertile doctrinal ideas and his "non-verbal" or "symbolic" theory of divinely inspired human thought has been developed further by others, both inside and outside the Anglican tradition.[10]

Conclusion

I have already noted Rowan Williams' genuine puzzlement over the eclipse of Farrer and his whole generation of anglo-catholic theologians in the 1950s and 1960s. The liberal, skeptical, and revisionist trend continued from *Honest to God* through *The Myth of God Incarnate* (1977), the work of scholars such as Maurice Wiles (1923–2005) who were overtly deistic and unitarian, and finally reached its apogee in the "Christian non-realism" of Don Cupitt (*b.* 1934). Although there were important precursors such as Donald MacKinnon (1913–1994) and Stephen Sykes (1939–2014), the theological tide in the Church of England arguably began to turn in the late 1970s/early 1980s with the work of Williams himself (*b.* 1950), advocating a re-engagement with classical categories. This shift continues in the "post-liberalism" of David F. Ford (*b.* 1948), the "Radical Orthodoxy" of John Milbank (*b.* 1952) and his associates, what I have elsewhere called the "Critical Catholicism" of David Brown (b. 1948), the "*théologie totale*" of Sarah Coakley (b. 1951), and others.[11] But of these theologians, only Williams and Brown have made any notable use of Farrer.

In the United States the theological reception of Farrer radiated out first from Yale Divinity School through Julian Hartt (1911–2010) and Hans Frei (1922–1988) and secondarily from Princeton Theological Seminary through Diogenes Allen (1932–2013) – a student of Hartt and Frei as well as of Farrer himself. For example, Frei commends understanding theology as "first of all the contemplative and devotional habit of the mindform of the knowledge and love of God, and second, the use of the trained intellect in penetrating that abiding mystery" and then adds parenthetically: "Austin Farrer's Bampton Lectures, *The Glass of Vision*, come to mind."[12] Likewise, Stanley Hauerwas (*b.* 1940), the leading American theological ethicist of his generation, testifies to the metaphysical influence of Farrer during his studies at Yale in the 1960s, and engages with Farrer in recent work.[13]

But, the significant British and US figures cited above notwithstanding, Farrer is still remarkably neglected in contemporary Anglican theology – in the United Kingdom, the United States, and throughout the world. It may be that he is simply too much a product of mid-twentieth century Oxford philosophy, theology, and college chapel life to be transplanted easily and fruitfully outside that now-vanished intellectual–ecclesial context. However, in addition to Farrer's lack of attention to social and political issues (although he is hardly unique in this respect!), I suggest that the greater challenges for wider contemporary reception are his interdisciplinary explorations, self-revisionist tendencies, and the occasional nature of his doctrinal reflections. Farrer thus presents a difficult, protean, and elusive subject, but certainly merits further study and engagement.

Notes

1 For the address see http://rowanwilliams. archbishopofcanterbury.org/articles. php/2282/the-word-of-god-in-anglican-tradition-archbishop-addresses-focolare-bishops (accessed July 13, 2020). Williams cites the Farrer quotation from Rowell, Stevenson, and Williams (2001, p. 661). For the full text, see Farrer's essay, "The Inspiration of the Bible" (Farrer 1976).

2 Ramsey and Farrer were exact contemporaries, both born in 1904, but Ramsey outlived Farrer by twenty years. Chadwick's book is thus an excellent source of information for the Church of England and British society during Farrer's shorter life as well.

3 This biographical material is condensed from MacSwain (2013b, pp. 91–93). For a full-length memoir, see Curtis (1985).

4 The discussion of Farrer's New Testament scholarship will be brief, as it falls outside both my own area of expertise and the primary concern of this volume. It is, however, indispensable for a full understanding of Farrer's mind.

5 For Farrer's reaction to Robinson, see MacSwain (2013b, p. 175); and for his response to Altizer, see Farrer (1968).

6 Originally preached in Keble College Chapel in 1961. McIntosh notes the parallel with John Henry Newman's sermon "The Humiliation of the Eternal Son" (1836) (McIntosh 1996, p. 152 note 11).

7 For Williams, in addition to the texts noted above, see especially his recent Williams (2018). For Hebblethwaite, see Hebblethwaite (1987, pp. 112–124). For Brown, see Brown (2011), pp. 209–10 and 256.

8 The most egregious passage is Farrer (1964a, pp. 127–129). See also Farrer's letters to David Attfield in Appendix 1 of Conti (1995, pp. 261–264). For an analysis and critique, see Hebblethwaite (2007, pp. 107–115). See also Williams (2007, p. 125 and p. 146 ft 118), and Williams (2002, p. 107).

9 For details see MacSwain (2013a), including pp. 1–8 and then essays in Part II by David Brown, Ingolf Dalferth, Hans Haugh, Douglas Hedley, David Jasper, and Gerard Loughlin. For Rowan Williams' joint review of MacSwain 2013b – important as a statement of his appreciation for and understanding of Farrer – see *Journal of Theological Studies*, 66.1 (2015): pp. 504–507.

10 See, for example, Dulles (1992), Law (2001), and Brown (2006).

11 In addition to Sedgwick's chapter cited above, see King et al. (2012). For Brown's "Critical Catholicism," see MacSwain (2016), pp. vii–x.

12 Frei (1992, p. 120). Frei's collected essays and letters contain several appreciative comments about Farrer's significance for his own work.

13 See Hauerwas (2010, p. 52); and Hauerwas (2015, pp. 70–89).

References

Ayer, A.J. [1936] (1946). *Language, Truth and Logic*. London: Victor Gollancz.

Breyfogle, T. (1995). Time and transformation: a conversation with rowan Williams. *Cross Currents* 45: 293–311.

Brown, D. (2006). The role of images in theological reflection. In: *The Human Person in God's World: Studies to Commemorate the Austin Farrer Centenary* (eds. D. Headley and B. Hebblethwaite), 85–105. London: SCM Press.

Brown, D. (2011). *Divine Humanity: Kenosis and the Construction of a Christian Theology.* Waco, TX: Baylor University Press.

Chadwick, O. (1990). *Michael Ramsey: A Life.* Oxford: Oxford University Press.

Conti, C. (ed.) (1975). *The Brink of Mystery.* London: SPCK.

Conti, C. (1995). *Metaphysical Personalism: An Analysis of Austin Farrer's Theistic Metaphysics.* Oxford: Clarendon Press.

Crombie, I.M. (2004). Austin Marsden Farrer (1904-1968). In: *Oxford Dictionary of National Biography*, vol. 19 (eds. H.C.G. Matthew and B. Harrison), 121–123. Oxford: Oxford University Press.

Curtis, P. (1985). *A Hawk Among Sparrows: A Biography of Austin Farrer.* London: SPCK.

Dulles, A. (1992). *Models of Revelation.* Maryknoll, NY: Orbis Books.

Farrer, A. (1936). *Review of Karl Barth, The Doctrine of the Word of God/God in Action*, 370–373. XXXIII: Theology.

Farrer, A. (1948). *The Glass of Vision.* London: Dacre Press.

Farrer, A. (1959 [1943]). *Finite and Infinite: A Philosophical Essay.* Westminster: Dacre Press.

Farrer, A. (1949). *A Rebirth of Images: The Making of St John's Apocalypse.* Westminster: Dacre Press.

Farrer, A. (1951). *A Study in St Mark.* Westminster: Dacre Press.

Farrer, A. (1966 [1954]). *St Matthew and St Mark.* Westminster: Dacre Press.

Farrer, A. (1955). 'On Dispensing with Q". In: *Studies in the Gospels in Memory of R. H. Lightfoot* (ed. D.E. Nineham), 55–88. Oxford: Blackwell.

Farrer, A. (1958). *The Freedom of the Will.* London: A&C Black.

Farrer, A. (1967). *Faith and Speculation: An Essay in Philosophical Theology.* Edinburgh: T & T Clark.

Farrer, A. (1964a). *Saving Belief: A Discussion of Essentials.* London: Hodder and Stoughton.

Farrer, A. (1964b). *The Revelation of St John the Divine: A Commentary on the English Text.* Oxford: Oxford University Press.

Farrer, A. (1968). Review of Thomas J. J. Altizer, *The Gospel of Christian Atheism* (1966). *Journal of Theological Studies* XIX: 422–423.

Farrer, A. (1976). The inspiration of the Bible. In: *Interpretation and Belief* (ed. C.C. Conti), 9–13. London: SPCK.

Frei, H.W. (1992). *Types of Christian Theology.* New Haven, CT: Yale University Press.

Harris, H.A. and Insole, C.J. (2005). *Faith and Philosophical Analysis: The Impact of Analytical Philosophy on the Philosophy of Religion.* Aldershot: Ashgate.

Hauerwas, S. (2010). *Hannah's Child: A Theologian's Memoir.* Grand Rapids, MI: Eerdmans.

Hauerwas, S. (2015). *The Work of Theology.* Grand Rapids, MI: Eerdmans.

Hebblethwaite, B. (1987). *The Incarnation: Collected Essays in Christology.* Cambridge: Cambridge University Press.

Hebblethwaite, B. (2007). *The Philosophical Theology of Austin Farrer.* Leuven: Peeters.

Hebblethwaite, B. and Henderson, E. (eds.) (1990). *Divine Action: Studies Inspired by the Philosophical Theology of Austin Farrer.* Edinburgh: T&T Clark.

King, B.K., MacSwain, R., and Fout, J.A. (2012). Contemporary Anglican systematic theology: three examples in David Brown, Sarah Coakley, and David F. Ford. *Anglican Theological Review* 94: 319–334.

Law, D.R. (2001). *Inspiration.* London and New York: Continuum.

Loades, A. (1998). Austin Marsden Farrer. In: *The SPCK Handbook of Anglican Theologians* (ed. A.E. McGrath), 120–123. London: SPCK.

Loades, A. and MacSwain, R. (eds.) (2006). *The Truth-Seeking Heart: Austin Farrer and His Writings.* Norwich: Canterbury Press.

MacSwain, R. (2006). Above, beside, within: the Anglican theology of Austin Farrer. *Journal of Anglican Studies* 4: 33–57.

MacSwain, R. (2012). Documentation and correspondence related to Austin Farrer's baptism in the Church of England on 14 May 1924. *Anglican and Episcopal History* 81: 241–276.

MacSwain, R. (ed.) (2013a). *Scripture, Metaphysics, and Poetry: Austin Farrer's the Glass of Vision with Critical Commentary.* Farnham: Ashgate.

MacSwain, R. (2013b). *Solved by Sacrifice: Austin Farrer, Fideism, and the Evidence of Faith.* Leuven: Peeters.

MacSwain, R. (2016). Editor's introduction. In: *God in a Single Vision: Integrating Philosophy and Theology* (David Brown; eds. C.R. Brewer and R. MacSwain), vii–x. London: Routledge.

McIntosh, M.A. (1996). *Christology from within: Spirituality and Incarnation in Hans Urs von Balthasar*. Notre Dame, IN: University of Notre Dame Press.

Mitchell, B. (ed.) (1957). *Faith and Logic: Oxford Essays in Philosophical Theology*. London: Allen and Unwin.

Mitchell, B. (1983). Austin Farrer: the philosopher. *New Fire 7*: 452–456.

Poirier, J.C. and Peterson, J. (eds.) (2015). *Marcan Priority without Q: Explorations in the Farrer Hypothesis*. London: Bloomsbury T&T Clark.

Rowell, G., Stevenson, K., and Williams, R. (eds.) (2001). *Love's Redeeming Work: The Anglican Quest for Holiness*. Oxford: Oxford University Press.

Sedgwick, Peter. (2005). Anglican theology. In *The Modern Theologians: An Introduction to Christian Theology since 1918* (eds. D.F. Ford with R. Muers), pp. 178–193. Oxford: Blackwell.

Shortt, R. (ed.) (2005). *God's Advocates: Christian Thinkers in Conversation*. London: DLT.

Titley, R. (2010). *A Poetic Discontent: Austin Farrer and the Gospel of Mark*. London: T & T Clark International.

Turner, F.M. (1994). Religion. In: *The History of the University of Oxford. Volume VIII: The Twentieth Century* (ed. B. Harrison), 293–316. Oxford: Clarendon Press.

Williams, R. (2002). *On Christian Theology*. Oxford: Blackwell.

Williams, R. (2003a). *Anglican Identities*. London: DLT.

Williams, R. (2003b). Theology in the twentieth century. In: *A Century of Theological and Religious Studies in Britain* (ed. E. Nicholson), 237–252. Oxford: Oxford University Press.

Williams, R. (2007). *Wrestling with angels: Conversations in Modern Theology* (ed. M. Higton). London: SCM Press.

Williams, R. (2018). *Christ the Heart of Creation*. London: Bloomsbury.

Arthur Michael Ramsey (1904–1988)

Lizette Larson Miller

Arthur Michael Ramsey, the one-hundredth Archbishop of Canterbury, was an important and influential theologian of the twentieth century. His place in that arena is not simply because of his dates, nor is it only because of his position as Archbishop of Canterbury. Michael Ramsey was an Anglican theologian and ecumenist who made important and lasting contributions. He was, in the classification of theological type by John Macquarrie, "thoroughly Anglican," nourishing his imagination and theological interpretations from the triad of scripture, tradition, and reason.[1] He was also an ecumenist, seeing the lack of response to the dominical call to be one a scandal, and worked through his offices as tutor, priest, bishop, and then archbishop, to bring to fruition his conviction for the unity of the Church founded on Jesus Christ. He felt that being Anglican was to turn naturally to ecumenism, because Anglicanism was itself born of so many forces and directions and therefore had, at its best, the gift of comprehension necessary to name the essentials of unity. But beyond this lifelong commitment to ecumenical dialogue, Ramsey also focused on and lifted up particular theological issues that became central to his life of faith and prayer, to his ministry, and to his teaching and study. Drinking deeply from the wells of early and eastern Christianity in particular, the dual theological allure of the glorification of Christ and our divinization through that became for him the antidote to what he perceived as an overemphasis in ecclesial circles on political and cultural answers to current issues. It was not that he was uninterested or unaware of the important issues in the world, particularly in the profound cultural changes of the 1960s and 1970s, but rather that he saw the inspired contribution of the church in the articulation of theology. It was in keeping Christ at the heart of everything that the dynamism of transformation to which each Christian as well as the church catholic was called would bear fruit and by which "paradosis" would be most faithfully practiced. For Ramsey, this "paradosis," or handing on the riches of the church, was very much focused on the ongoing implications

Twentieth Century Anglican Theologians: From Evelyn Underhill to Esther Mombo, First Edition.
Edited by Stephen Burns, Bryan Cones, and James Tengatenga.

of divine revelation and incarnation. These related foundations developed and influenced much of his theological writing as well as his pastoral initiatives in his service as archbishop and beyond and remain at the heart of why Archbishop Ramsey's work is so important for the Anglican Communion today.

Biography

The outline of Michael Ramsey's life is readily available in many encyclopedia and online articles today. What follows is a summary of his life in the interwoven spheres of academia, church, and personal life, the latter particularly centered on several turning points, which we know from external facts as well as Ramsey's own reflection on those events.

The Right Reverend and Right Honorable Arthur Michael Ramsey was born on November 14, 1904, in Cambridge, England. While his mother Mary Agnes (Wilson) was Anglican, his father was Non-conformist, or congregationalist, which meant an early introduction to the breadth of Christian ecumenism. His father, Arthur Stanley Ramsey, was a mathematics don at Cambridge University who became president of Magdalene College in 1915, remaining so until 1952. Both of Michael Ramsey's parents were highly educated, his mother in modern history, and that academic breadth rooted the lives of their family, Michael, his brother Frank, and sisters Bridget and Margaret. It is particularly in the relationship with his brother Frank, a mathematician and philosopher who brought those twin backgrounds to a teaching career in economics at Trinity College, that a good deal of academic inspiration and theological articulation were worked out in Michael's own study.

Michael Ramsey moved through Magdalene College, beginning in 1922, with obvious skills in political leadership before turning to a growing interest in theology. Much speculation has been written whether his beloved older brother Frank, who professed to be an atheist, was part of the inspiration, and that challenge may have contributed to the changed focus, but by 1926, there were other influences working on Ramsey, including anglo-catholic worship and social justice as presented to him through Fr. Conrad Noel (a follower of F. D. Maurice), as well as Ramsey's own reading of William Temple and Charles Gore. In 1927 Ramsey made the commitment toward holy orders and entered Cuddesdon College, Oxford. His entry into seminary was temporarily set aside, however, with the death of his mother in an automobile accident. The ensuing depression resulted in a leave of absence from Cuddesdon and an embrace of the fairly new field of psychotherapy, which he would support for years to come as a legitimate process for believing Christians to engage with, even while the stigma of depression and mental illness remained in larger ecclesial circles.

Ramsey returned to Cuddesdon a term later, was ordained a deacon in 1928 and went to serve, for two years, at the Church of Our Lady and St. Nicholas near the Liverpool docks, in a world far removed from Cambridge academia. He was ordained a priest on September 22, 1929 and accepted a call to go to Lincoln Theological College as sub-warden, lecturing in theology and beginning a long career in theological writing (his first book, *The Gospel and the Catholic Church* [Ramsey 1936], was published while at Lincoln). Another tragedy hit soon after beginning at Lincoln.

Michael's brother Frank died in 1930 at the age of twenty-six following complications from abdominal surgery in London. From that point on, a clear determination to focus on the work of writing and teaching to raise up what Ramsey felt was a better direction for the Church of England to pursue, moved Ramsey from Lincoln to Boston Parish Church to St. Benedict's Church, Cambridge, and in 1939 to Durham Cathedral as canon and professor of divinity at Durham University. In 1942 Ramsey married Joan Hamilton, a marriage that endured until his death in 1988. Lady Ramsey died in 1995 and is buried next to him in the gardens of Canterbury Cathedral. There were no children from the marriage.

Ramsey served the church and academy at Durham for ten years, during which time his second and third books were published (*The Resurrection of Christ* [Ramsey 1945] and *The Glory of God and the Transfiguration of Christ* [Ramsey 1949]). Many biographies point to the development of Ramsey's interest in Eastern Christianity during this time, and while that interest is evident in his writing, it did not begin in Durham. While a student at Cuddesdon, Ramsey came to know Derwas Chitty, an Anglican with a deep knowledge and love of Eastern Orthodoxy, who introduced Ramsey to the world of Eastern monasticism and theology, and to the Fellowship of St. Alban and St. Sergius, established in 1927. The larger platform of Durham did afford Ramsey an opportunity to share his belief that in Eastern Christianity one could find a centering of primary theological emphases that the Church of England would benefit from adopting.

In 1950 Ramsey was appointed Regius Professor of Divinity at Cambridge and a Fellow of Magdalene College. Returning to where his academic career began would have seemed the beginning of a long and stable academic life, but only two years later he was asked to permit his name to be submitted for Bishop of Durham. He was consecrated bishop in 1952, and also named Lord Ramsey as the see came with a seat in the House of Lords. At the heart of his time in Durham, Ramsey continued to expand his academic and theological interests, building on both his growing sense of the rightness of anglo-catholic theology and the gifts of Eastern Orthodoxy. During this time his fourth book was published (*F. D. Maurice and the Conflicts of Modern Theology* [Ramsey 1951]). Being Bishop of Durham afforded him an opportunity to be part of the larger stage of ecumenical conversation at the 1954 meeting of the World Council of Churches in Illinois (USA).

In 1956 Ramsey became primate of England and the ninety-second Archbishop of York, remaining in that position for five years. With increasing obligations to travel and speak for the broader church, Ramsey deepened connections particularly with Roman Catholicism in England and elsewhere and published a review of a half century of Anglican theological development in *From Gore to Temple* (Ramsey 1960) in which he criticized several directions in Anglican theology. In June 1961, Ramsey was enthroned as the one-hundredth Archbishop of Canterbury, a position he would hold until he retired in 1974. His tenure as archbishop was a busy one, within the Church of England he oversaw the institution of the General Synod, and changes around clergy appointments, ecumenically he was the president of the World Council of Churches (WCC) from 1961 to 1968 and worked for the uniting of the Church of England with the Methodist Church. During this time he developed close relationships with the Pope (Paul VI) and several patriarchs (Athenagoras and Alexius), continuing his interest in ongoing conversation toward unity with Roman Catholicism and Eastern Orthodoxy. He also continued writing and publishing, including *Introducing the Christian Faith* (Ramsey 1961/1964a), *Image Old and New* (Ramsey 1963), *Canterbury Essays and Addresses* (Ramsey 1964b), *Sacred and Secular* (Ramsey 1965), *God, Christ and the World* (Ramsey 1969), *The Future of the Christian Church* (Ramsey with Cardinal Suenens 1971), *The Christian Priest Today* (Ramsey 1972), and *Canterbury Pilgrim* (Ramsey 1974).

Upon retirement at the mandatory age of seventy, Ramsey and his wife lived in several different places (Cuddesdon, Durham, Bishopthorpe, and Cowley), and he remained engaged through his honorary fellowships of Magdalene and Selwyn Colleges, Cambridge, Merton, Keble, and St. Cross Colleges, Oxford, in addition to other trustee and honorary fellowship appointments. His students reported the delight he took in spending several terms spent at Nashotah House, an Episcopal seminary in Wisconsin in the United States. In addition to traveling and lecturing, Ramsey completed four more books during retirement: *Holy Spirit* (Ramsey 1977), *Jesus and the Living Past* (Ramsey 1980), *Be Still and Know* (Ramsey 1982), *The Anglican Spirit* (Ramsey and Coleman 2004).

Arthur Michael Ramsey died on April 23, 1988 at St. John's Home attached to the All Saints' Sisters in Cowley, Oxford. His funeral was held in Canterbury Cathedral on May 3, and he was cremated with his ashes buried in the cloister garden at the cathedral, where his wife Joan, is also buried. His memorial stone contains words from St. Irenaeus "the Glory of God is the living man; and the life of man is the vision of God." Memorials to him are found from Canterbury Cathedral to the distant chapel of Nashotah House Seminary.

Some Theological Emphases

As with any writer and thinker in the broad arena of theology, Michael Ramsey's thinking developed and shifted over a long career of publishing and speaking, as well as responding to various "real-time" situations that influenced his perspective.[2] While the themes of "glory" and "transfiguration" or "transformation" are usually the key words one associates with Ramsey's theology, it might perhaps be more accurate to begin with the theological foundation on which these theological points (as well as Christology, trinitarian theology, incarnation, redemption, ecclesiology, and ecumenism) are built, and that is *kenosis*. Again and again, Ramsey returned to the source of self-giving, self-sacrifice, self-emptying as the shape of being for Christian churches, for the church catholic, and for Christian individuals because it is the model of Christ and of the triune God. It is a center consistent with Ramsey's focus on the cross and the passion of Christ as truth and response to the turmoil of the 1960s and beyond, and ties together the various points of focus throughout Ramsey's theological career, pastoral and academic. But first the focus on glory by Ramsey himself and his biographers and followers.

The association of the theology of glory with Michael Ramsey's legacy is perhaps most notable in the flurry of writing and lectures around the major celebration of Ramsey's birth. In 2003 (in anticipation of the 2004 centenary), *Glory: The Spiritual Theology of Michael Ramsey* was published (Dales 2003), followed in 2005 by *Glory Descending: Michael Ramsey and His Writings* (Dales et al. 2005). Ramsey himself wrote in 1949 (and republished in 1967 in an updated edition) *The Glory of God and the Transfiguration of Christ* (Ramsey 1949) in his Durham days, when the influence of Eastern Christianity was becoming more prominent in his writing. The book was originally written as a reflection on the theme of glory in scripture, but it is a reality at the interface of much of Ramsey's theology, not isolated within biblical theology. Glory "expresses in a remarkable way the unity of the doctrines of Creation, the Incarnation, the Cross, the Spirit, the Church and the World-to-Come" (Ramsey 1949, p. 5). As with any complex theological idea, "glory" can mean many things, but as Ramsey developed it throughout his life, from the scriptural analysis of his 1949 book to his post-retirement lectures at Nashotah House, glory more and more was done and seen through the kenotic actions of Jesus the Christ.

For Christians, glory has been entirely transfigured in Christ. The central message of Christ's life, passion, death, and resurrection is that true glory, the glory which is that of God's own self, is not what humans would normally term as glory, it does not have what we could call honor or radiance. Rather, Christ reveals to us what glory truly is. Christ reveals the true nature of the glory of God (Cramer 2010, p. 24).

This true nature is about love in action, *caritas,* love that is self-giving. "When Jesus dies we see the glory which is God's in all eternity, the glory of the self-giving love of the Triune God" (Ramsey 1970, p. 26). This definition of glory – not one of triumph (at least not yet) nor great honor – is the lens through which a number of Ramsey's theological articulations can be viewed.

Glory in humility and often in suffering is not an exaltation of suffering itself. Suffering reveals something of the nature of God, which is itself glory. Ramsey turned to William Temple for a clarification about a suffering God and human suffering; "It is truer to say that there is suffering in God than that God suffers [because] the suffering is an element in the joy of triumphant sacrifice."[3] Having borrowed and incorporated that important distinction, Ramsey's trajectory is summarized by Rowan Williams in returning attention to the centrality of the cross for the church's theology. "It is Jesus on the cross that reveals the deepest truth about humanity, that God is revealed in loving obedience and giving up of oneself, inaugurating a new humanity that is new because it is according to God's original purposes" (cited in Cramer 2010, p. 20).

This is really about Ramsey's understanding of glory and humility and transformation in the love of the Trinity for all creation, especially for humanity. The self-offering love of Christ for the Father, continued in the work of the Spirit, is a glimpse of the Triune God engaged in interdependence and submission that changes everything:

> The doctrine of the Trinity is the affirmation that self-giving is characteristic of Being, that mutuality of self-giving love belongs to God's perfection: and the self-giving of God toward his creatures is possible because of the glory that the Father has with the Son in the love of the Spirit eternally (Ramsey 1969, p. 99).

If kenosis is the fullest revelation of what it means to be God in Ramsey's theology of glory, these Christological and Trinitarian perspectives are also about transformation, or what this kenotic theology of glory leads into. Here Michael Ramsey's incarnational theology is central, as it is for many Anglican theologians. Ramsey follows closely on the heels of the more catholic Anglican voices of the previous generation as well as his own, looking at a number of theologians in the early church and next door to recapture the definition of "catholic." He writes that "the essence of

Catholicism" is not in a particular individualistic piety or sectarianism but is to be found "in the unbreakable life to which the sacraments, scriptures, creeds and ministry have never ceased to bear witness" (Ramsey 1936, p. 174). In the midst of this interwoven web sits the incarnation, because the sacramental theology of Ramsey's "catholicism" emphasizes not the "gulf between God and the sinful and broken world of the human and natural order" found in some of the Protestant Reformation theology, but rather the "spirituality of participation: the material – water, bread and wine, the human person – as signs or medium of divine presence." These latter material vehicles for the presence of God are themselves rooted in God become flesh, marking a "coherence between creation and redemption in the Incarnate Christ" (Griffiss 1995, p. 41). Ramsey felt that in the incarnation, the engagement of God with humanity reaches an apex, or the point of extraordinary self-emptying and unity.

> Thus it is in Jesus that we see man becoming his true self, in that giving away of self which happens when man is possessed by God. The meaning of what it is to be man appears when man is the place where deity fulfils himself, and the glory of the one is the glory of the other (Ramsey 1969, p. 100).

"Christmas is as costly as Good Friday" (Cramer 2010, p. 22) and this mode of the incarnation that demonstrates the self-emptying kenosis of God in the person of Jesus, is "an act of perpetual self-restraint and self-giving that runs like a golden thread throughout the whole gospel story until his death on Calvary" (Cramer 2010, p. 14). Rowan Williams on Ramsey writes that "we must hear the gospel of the Incarnation as a summons to self-abandonment before all else, not as a reassuring endorsement of the best we can humanly do" (Williams 2004, p. 90).

This "golden thread" leads to the transformation of humanity as the economy of God moves through the passion, death, and resurrection of Christ. The incarnation is salvific, as is the cross, and a balance is maintained through all of them by drawing on the broader theology of the early church. Here Ramsey's rooting (and his claims for Anglicanism's rooting) in patristics is an antidote against the narrower focus of some reformed Christian conversations. But it is also a contributor to the eschatological tension of the full impact of the resurrection for the church.

Michael Ramsey's ecclesiology was shaped by many factors, but it was articulated against the cultural and political cooption of the Church of England at various times in its history. "First, the church was not something outside scripture, but was itself rooted in the dying and rising of Christ" (Leech 1995, p. 103). It is "a gift from God to humanity and its very existence is nothing less than the proclamation that God has entered humanity with the hope of reconciling all people to God and one another through Jesus Christ" (Cramer 2010, p. xiii). Here again, the church is both "the extension of the Incarnation and the passion of Christ" in which Ramsey develops the earlier writing of Charles Gore (Leech 1995, p. 103). While not blind to the human failings of the church, historically and contemporarily, Ramsey saw both the structure of the church and its expression in the eucharist as essential to its divine founding: "Its order has its deepest significance not in terms of legal validity but in terms of the Body and the Cross; its Eucharist proclaims God creator and redeemer; and its confessional is the place where man sees that in wounding Christ sin wounds his body and where by learning of the Body they learn of Christ . . ." (Ramsey 1936, pp. 179–180).

Ramsey also initially began to discuss the church as a transformative agent in the larger culture, "a new social organism" (Leech 1995, p. 105) with the potential to change hearts, rather than be solely transformed by cultural mores.

Finally, the kenotic underpinning of Ramsey's theology of glory through Christology, Trinitarian theology, incarnation, redemption, and ecclesiology carried over into his advocacy for ecumenical unity. If the dominical call to "be one" is taken seriously, then the reconciliation of all peoples must be a priority of the church catholic. But, each part of the body of Christ is lacking "unless it is united with the whole church" (Cramer 2010, p. xvii) including in holy orders, where "all orders are deficient until the church is united" (Ramsey 1972[1985], p. 33). This ecclesial humility extends to each individual ecclesial community and each denominational entity, especially in the episcopacy that is meant to signify the unity of the Church. "All that is Anglican or Roman or Greek or partial or local in any way must share by an agonizing death to its own pride" (cited in Cramer 2010, p. 69). Even the doctrine of apostolic tradition shares in this humble approach to incompleteness. Ramsey was clear that Anglican claims to apostolic tradition are not an occasion of self-commendation but are rather to be used "as a symbol of our nothingness qua ourselves and of our dependence upon the universal church and upon Jesus in the flesh" (Ramsey 1936, p. 217). Because, in Ramsey's take on St. Augustine, "the church is a mixed community of sinners called to be saints" (Ramsey 1964a, p. 70), we need each other, through the ages and in the present, to learn how to love each other.

Theological Legacy

As many authors in many essays have pointed out, some of Ramsey's language and ideas are bound up with the cultural changes of the 1960s and 1970s as well as culturally bound to particular theological and political issues in the Church of England. But in the past decade, particularly around the renewed interest occasioned by the centenary of Ramsey's birth, a clearly growing perception is that Ramsey might contribute to bridging the gap between evangelicals and catholics within the Anglican Communion, or between liberals and conservatives, or between biblicists and humanists, all of which, for Ramsey and many others, are false dichotomies. The newer generations, with sympathy for the liberal-catholic political activism represented by Michael Ramsey, along with the centrality of core theological beliefs (such as the resurrection of the body, the virgin birth, and other doctrines "out of touch" for many liberal Protestants), are well represented in the resurgence of interest in Ramsey's reconciling of East and West, evangelical and catholic, activism and contemplation.

The collections of essays gathered by students who met and championed Michael Ramsey in his later years are an interesting statement of the power of his personality perhaps, but also the image of a saint reapplied to its author. If a saint "is someone who makes God real," Michael Ramsey seemed to have had that effect. Can the effect continue without firsthand knowledge of the personality and prayerfulness of this notable Christian disciple? In the reintroduction of his writings, his work and challenge to the World Council of Churches and the Anglican Communion, and continued systematization of his theology, Arthur Michael Ramsey will have an ongoing impact on Anglican theology in the twenty-first century.

Notes

1 http://anglicanhistory.org/amramsey/macquarrie1990.html (accessed July 13, 2020).

2 The most notable theological debate was how (and whether) the church should "update" itself to accommodate theologically contemporary social and political shifts or hold with tradition presented afresh. The argument was shaped by the publication of *Honest to God* in 1963 by John A. T. Robinson and countered by Michael Ramsey in Temple 1963 (Ramsey 1963).

3 Ramsey cites Temple in Ramsey (1960). He further summarizes Temple's thinking in Ramsey (1991, p. 100).

References

Cramer, J.C. (2010). *Safeguarded by Glory: Michael Ramsey's Ecclesiology and the Struggles of Contemporary Anglicanism*. Lanham, MD: Lexington Books.

Dales, D. (2003). *Glory: The Spiritual Theology of Michael Ramsey*. Norwich: Canterbury Press.

Dales, D., Habgood, J., Rowell, G., and Williams, R. (eds.) (2005). *Glory Descending: Michael Ramsey and His Writings*. Grand Rapids, MI: Eerdmans.

Griffiss, J.E. (1995). Michael Ramsey: Catholic theologian. In: *Michael Ramsey as Theologian* (eds. R. Gill and L. Kendall), 29–46. London: SPCK.

Leech, K. (1995). The social theology of Michael Ramsey. In: *Michael Ramsey as Theologian* (eds. R. Gill and L. Kendall), 101–123. London: SPCK.

Ramsay, A.M. and Coleman, D. (2004). *The Anglican Spirit*. New York, NY: Church Publishing.

Ramsey, A.M. (1936). *The Gospel and the Catholic Church*. London: Longmans, Green.

Ramsey, A.M. (1945). *The Resurrection of Christ*. London: Geoffrey Bles.

Ramsey, A.M. (1949). *The Glory of God and the Transfiguration of Christ*. London: Longmans, Green and Co.

Ramsey, A.M. (1951). *F. D. Maurice and the Conflicts of Modern Theology*. Oxford: Oxford University Press.

Ramsey, A.M. (1960). *An Era in Anglican Theology from Gore to Temple: The Development of Anglican Theology between 'Lux Mundi' and the Second World War 1889–1939*. London: Longmans, Green.

Ramsey, A.M. (1963). *Image Old and New*. London: SCM Press.

Ramsey, A.M. (1964a). *Introducing the Christian Faith*. London: SCM Press. 1961/

Ramsey, A.M. (1964b). *Canterbury Essays and Addresses*. London: SPCK.

Ramsey, A.M. (1965). *Sacred and Secular*. London: Longmans.

Ramsey, A.M. (1969). *God, Christ and the World*. London: SCM Press.

Ramsey, A.M. (1970). *Freedom, Faith, and Future*. London: SPCK.

Ramsey, A.M. (1972[1985]). *The Christian Priest Today*. London: SPCK Published in the US 1985 Cambridge MA:Cowley.

Ramsey, A.M. (1974). *Canterbury Pilgrim*. London: SPCK.

Ramsey, A.M. (1977). *Holy Spirit*. London: SPCK.

Ramsey, A.M. (1980). *Jesus and the Living Past*. Oxford: Oxford University Press.

Ramsey, A.M. (1982). *Be Still and Know*. London: Fount.

Ramsey, A.M. (1991). William Temple. In: *The Anglican Spirit* (ed. D. Coleman), 95–106. London: SPCK.

Ramsey, A.M. with Suenens, L.J. (1971). *The Future of the Christian Church*. London: SCM Press.

Williams, R. (2004). *Anglican Identities*. London: DLT.

Donald M. MacKinnon
(1913–1994)

John C. McDowell

Fergus Kerr regards Donald MacKinnon as having been "by far the most influential British theologian of the twentieth century" (Kerr 2004, p. 266). Yet while a list of those who have learned directly from him reads like a theological "Who's Who" of late twentieth century British philosophers and theologians (not least Nicholas Lash, Rowan Williams, and Iris Murdoch), he still remains both relatively little read and little studied.[1] When his name is mentioned it is more often in conjunction with the weird and wonderful folklore depicting him as an eccentrically larger-than-life character. Fortunately, however, there are now signs that this scholarly ignoring of his work is changing. Not only is he beginning to be read more geographically widely by a younger generation (in North America and Australia) in the early twenty-first century, but many of his out-of-print papers are in process of being collected and republished.

One of the reasons why MacKinnon has not gained an audience the quality of his writing deserves may well have to do with the manner of his publication outputs. He had a distinct preference for the densely arranged and allusively written essay, the occasional paper, and the book review over the monograph or book. This more condensed writing vehicle was more than the expression of a quirk of character – rather it suited an unsystematic approach to intellectual engagement, and it can be particularly demanding. Readers encounter his eclectic appeal to a range of thought resources from the likes of Lenin and later Marxist thinkers, Plato, Aristotle, and Immanuel Kant, high Attic tragic dramatists, Williams Shakespeare, Arnold Schoenberg, Teilhard de Chardin, Joseph Conrad and other fiction, P. T. Forsyth, Hans Urs von Balthasar, and Karl Barth, among many others.

Where the erudite MacKinnon continues to have an impact on theological work is through what Rowan Williams names his "style" and "mood," an occasionalist form of writing that offers deep and penetrating interrogations of many cherished

Twentieth Century Anglican Theologians: From Evelyn Underhill to Esther Mombo, First Edition.
Edited by Stephen Burns, Bryan Cones, and James Tengatenga.
© 2021 John Wiley & Sons Ltd. Published 2021 by John Wiley & Sons Ltd.

theological and philosophical assumptions. MacKinnon's writings stylistically perform MacKinnon's refusal to provide simplistic responses to complex problems or the tome-like impression of the last word on any and every issue.[2] That mood MacKinnon spoke of as being a "deliberate cultivation of an interrogative . . . mentality", in fact "profoundly interrogative" (MacKinnon 1966, p. 94; Surin 1989, p. ix).

> [P]aying attention to his writing might still yield discovery of a method of inquiry that sharpens one's own intellectual investigation and encourages the kind of intellectual reasoning and conversation that many find all too rarely occur in the contemporary West with the increasing particularization and professionalization of discourses, and the reduction of public discourse to the banal, trivial and shallow (McDowell 2011, p. viii).

Brief Biography

Donald Mackenzie MacKinnon was born on August 27, 1913 in Oban in the Scottish Highlands, and was educated in schools in Edinburgh and Winchester. During his time in England, he became a communicant member of the Anglican Church, and this, according to Stewart Sutherland, gave him a "liturgical discipline which was the context for most of his intellectual work" (Sutherland 1998, p. 382). Yet being a lay Scottish Episcopalian enabled MacKinnon to retain a critical insight into the theological politics of Anglican ecclesiastical order south of the border. His university training began in philosophy at the University of Oxford's New College, and was sufficiently impressive for Isaiah Berlin to comment on MacKinnon's aptitude as a "very rare thing – a natural philosopher" (Berlin, cited in Muller 2010, p. 27). His first academic post involved a year's teaching moral philosophy (1936–1937) at the University of Aberdeen working with A. E. Taylor. A Fellowship at Keble College, Oxford, followed, and between 1945 and 1947 he was a lecturer in philosophy at Balliol College, Oxford. In 1947 he was appointed as Regius Chair of Moral Philosophy at the University of Aberdeen, and much of his work during this period was devoted to engaging Utilitarian and Kantian forms of moral reasoning.

In 1960, MacKinnon was persuaded to move into a position more congenial to philosophical engagement with theology – the Norris-Hulse Chair of Divinity at the University of Cambridge, from which he retired to the city of Aberdeen in 1978. At this time Logical Positivism's empiricism, influentially introduced to Britain by A. J. Ayer, was in the philosophical ascendancy and theology was under pressure to verify the veracity of its claims. At Cambridge this pressure led to the lecture series to which MacKinnon contributed, which was published under the title of *Objections to Christian Belief*. Even so, MacKinnon was ill-disposed to philosophical attempts to shore up theological claims if that activity involved failing to attend to the complex particularities of the claims themselves, and providing what he calls an "apologetic eagerness" that produces a cheap or dishonest victory (MacKinnon 1974, p. 124). It was during his time in the Norris-Hulse Chair that he delivered the Gifford Lectures in 1965–1966 on "The Problems of Metaphysics."

Two Key Themes

The title of a little-known paper of 1966, "Can a Divinity Professor Be Honest?" indicates a question lying at the heart of MacKinnon's sense of his own place in the church (MacKinnon 1966). Whether or not the pressure MacKinnon places on the theologian, here, reflects the sensibility of a lay Scottish Episcopalian intellectual whose ecclesial responsibilities are potentially more "free" in a clergy-dominated Anglican setting, it certainly has to do with his commitment to the discipline of theological integrity, to the theologian's engagement in truth telling. What he most personally struggles with is how to be true to his academic "calling" that necessitates "follow[ing] the argument whithersoever it leads," while remaining a person of the church even when he has to be "particularly alert to the clerical bias which almost inevitably on occasion threatens objectivity of judgment" (MacKinnon 1966, pp. 95, 96).

There are at least two highly significant themes that identify and explicate MacKinnon's disruptive sensibility with regard to the church: kenosis and the tragic. These both exhibit an "almost tortured sense of honesty" (McDowell 2011, p. viii) required for making theological claims, exposing to view trivializing shortcuts and premature solutions, and providing therapy for the complacency and sentimentality of church performance. As Nicholas Lash argues, theology is to contribute to "weaning us from our idolatry" (Lash 2008, p. 102) or according to Rowan Williams, "The theologian's job may be less the speaking of truth . . . than the patient diagnosis of untruths, and the reminding of the community where its attention begins" (Williams 2000, p. 196). Yet while this set of concerns is discernible throughout MacKinnon's career, his *critical* ecclesial *responsibility* is particularly apparent in the mid-to-late 1960s, a few years after his arrival as Norris-Hulse Professor (1960) and the controversy over John Robinson's *Honest to God* (1963).

Kenosis and Establishment: Christ Versus Caesar

Two years after his 1966 lecture MacKinnon delivered the Gore Memorial Lecture at Westminster Abbey, a bastion of Anglican power and British monarchical sovereignty. In it he identifies a temptation that disrupts the church's ability to enact its life as the people of *God*. This is "only one primary instance of the way in which those involved in ecclesiastical structures cling obstinately to the fading memory of a position they once enjoyed" (MacKinnon 2016, pp. 169–170). The problem that concerns him is the power of the *established* church. Two things emerge even in his introduction to the published collection in which his lecture was originally the opening chapter: that this situation fails "altogether to meet the realities of a post-Constantinian situation," a cultural post-war upheaval that MacKinnon regards as appropriately able to subject the conservative church to merciless satire and public contempt by the likes of the BBC; and, that this way of establishment deflects ecclesial performance away from the performance of God's humiliating expression of being God with the world in Jesus (MacKinnon 2016, p. 170). Bringing these themes together he argues in a later paper:

> Jesus, in the reality of his self-giving, in the mystery of God's self-giving in him, in his movement from Galilee to Jerusalem to Galilee, in his life, death, and

resurrection, remains the only valid *raison d'être* of his Church . . . But we crave security: we flee from the reality of crucifixion-resurrection, impatient of the indirection of Christ's resurrection, wishing that he had come down from the Cross that so we might have believed by a faith finally corrupted by its object's betrayal of his mission . . . [Instead] it is to Jesus, author and finisher of our faith, that we must look and look again (MacKinnon 2011, pp. 274–275).

The first thing the lecture does, then, is to identify the way that the constitutional power of the Anglican establishment operates. For this he uses the shorthand "Constantinianism." The reference is, of course, to the first Christian emperor of the Roman Empire, and from this MacKinnon declares that "Constantine's so-called conversion in all its consequences . . . [is] arguably the greatest single disaster in the history of the Christian Church" (MacKinnon 1987, p. 142). His sense of the problem lies not so much with any historical concern over Constantine's temperament and even with his religious motivations for professing conversion and Christian commitment. While MacKinnon refuses to disregard "the achievements of Christendom," he does admit that these were bought at a particularly "terrible price" (MacKinnon 2016, p. 170). Most notably, the argument draws on a number of images from the Gospels:

> From Caesar, the church of Christ learned to speak with the accents of Caiaphas, learned how often it was expedient that one man should die for the people, how often it was a luxury to be indulged only by the irresponsible to leave the ninety nine sheep in eager quest for the wayward stray (MacKinnon 2016, p. 170).

Moreover, even when the church did avoid Caiaphas' accent, once it was aligned with the state in imperial patronage "it deliberately abdicated from the task of criticizing the methods adopted by allegedly responsible human authorities" (MacKinnon 2016, p. 170), quiescently accepting rather protesting, obeying rather than revolting. After all, he continues, tacitly even when not explicitly, it was assumed that "the ways of government were the ways of God" (MacKinnon 2016, p. 170).

The second dimension of the lecture's argument provides the theological perspective for offering critical purchase on ecclesial performance as one of "a long history of compromise and betrayal" (MacKinnon 2016, p. 175). This is the kenotic or self-emptying work of God in Jesus Christ. Here MacKinnon has to provide a significant clarification. Firstly, the concept functions as an indictment of those MacKinnon accuses of an "obstinate, ecclesiological fundamentalism" while having little sense of the relevancy of the historical foundations of their faith to the substance of the church (MacKinnon 2016, p. 171). Secondly, MacKinnon challenges its grounding in problematic assumptions to which even Charles "Gore remained in bondage throughout his life," and those associated with the nineteenth-century theological faculties at Tübingen and Giessen who used it to provide a certain kind of metaphysical explanation (MacKinnon 2016, p. 175). The intellectual problem among the dominant German kenotic tradition had been how to relate divine and human in the incarnation, and "kenosis" was regarding as being the conceptual bridge that supposedly solved this philosophical conundrum. Yet this is not how MacKinnon employs this term from Philippians 2. In fact, he suggests elsewhere that this perspective actually generates difficulties for making the presence of God in Christ continuous with God's being in God's self, as it were "depotentiating" the Logos incarnate. If God has to *give up* or *give away* certain attributes (omniscience, omnipresence, impassibility, etc.) then Jesus lacks qualities that supposedly makes God God. What is *divine* about Jesus, then, and what it is that Jesus reflects of God in his life, become thorny questions.

MacKinnon construes the term theologically rather than metaphysically. It says something ontologically about the plenitude of God's own life of gift and responsive receptivity rather than the metaphysics of what God dispenses with in the Logos' becoming incarnate. That means that the incarnation does not involve a lack but is rather the expression of the very fullness of love that God is essentially – *in se*, in God's self. It is a manifestation of the God who is constant in God's actions *in se* and *ad extra*. Here MacKinnon finds help in the Swiss Roman Catholic theologian Hans Urs von Balthasar since he sees in the latter the kenosis as a trinitarian act of the divine humility of "eternal relatedness" the logic of which is manifest in the incarnation (MacKinnon 1979, p. 159). Consequently, the concept of kenosis, being bound up with the passion of the Son of God, operates as an uncompromising measure of the adequacy of any attempt to witness to the God of Jesus Christ. What is meant by "God" and the attributes of divine power and knowledge have to be learned precisely at this point and therefore beyond the "always perilously suffused with anthropomorphic suggestions of a consummate mastery of the world" (MacKinnon 1979, p. 155). Accordingly, it is only the concept of kenosis that enables us to treat the ministry and work of Jesus Christ as "the very standard by which we must test the adequacy of every attempt to articulate to ourselves the concept of God" (MacKinnon 1975, p. 5). The "agony and dereliction of the cross is the only measure" of the adequacy of our talk of God (MacKinnon 1975, p. 4).

Christ's kenotic life shapes not only what is meant by divine power, but also what is meant by its proper reflection on performance. Approvingly citing von Balthasar, MacKinnon claims that "For authentically Christian faith and belief there is no passing-by the *via dolorosa*, no escaping the sheer surd-element of Good Friday" (MacKinnon 1975, p. 8). For MacKinnon, the beginning and end of creaturely life takes place in the divine economy, and that economy is one irreducibly bound up with the "authentic manner of his sovereign dominion," the "self-disregard" concretely exhibited in the history of Gethsemane and Golgotha (MacKinnon 1975, p. 8). Accordingly, creaturely life has its shape and form only as it appropriates divine purposefulness for "our proper humanity," "the true pattern of our humanity" (MacKinnon 2011, pp. 16, 26). Given that God bodily self-demonstrated or incarnated in Jesus Christ, the way of God's people (those called to embody the shape of God's economy as witness to all things) is to be a kenotic one.[3] This, however, MacKinnon finds to be disrupted in the theology of Establishment, marked as it is by a relation to power that embeds a "grasping" rather than a kenotic "giving." As he complains in his critique of the practice of a certain kind of power seen in a triumphalist church, "the Christian God [has been] endowed imaginatively with the attributes of a human Caesar" (MacKinnon 2011, p. 266). The image the church embodies is the image of "a transcendent Caesar" rather than the disruptive image of God embodied in the "vulnerable Nazarene" (MacKinnon 2011, p. 266). The uncompromising criticism here is that a church that has such a relationship with temporal governmental power loses its counter-cultural urgency, slips into complacency, and actually misconstrues its own God. Yet while the voice of MacKinnon's paper is interrogative, the underlying drive is to witness the critically transformative testimony of the ecclesial body of the crucified:

> To live as a Christian in the world today is necessarily to live an exposed life; it is to be stripped of the kind of security of that tradition, whether ecclesiological or institutional, easily bestows (MacKinnon 2011, p. 190).

Theology and Tragedy: Being Exposed in the Borderlands of Theology

Engaging in this critical work in service of the gospel involves MacKinnon in listening to a wide range of voices. These voices do not for him speak imposingly from "outside" in a form of "cultural theology," but, as he observes in an article review of the Jewish Marxist philosopher Ernst Bloch's *The Principle of Hope*, they constitute a reminder of suppressed (and thus forgotten) critical insights proper to the gospel itself (MacKinnon 1988, pp. 247–252). They occur in what MacKinnon calls "the border-lands of theology." Citing just such a broad range of dialogue partners, MacKinnon argues that

> A radical Christian should be among the first to insist that many existing religious beliefs, institutions and *performances* . . . are fair target not only for disciplined academic criticism but for the kind of merciless satire on TV and radio which has caused so much indignation among the *bien-pensants* (MacKinnon 1966, p. 96).

In other words, Christian theology, for the sake of its own health (hearing the world's judgment upon itself) and for the sake of God's world (the environment of the now fallen-but-still-graced-creation), has to be in the business of conversing widely. "God", Williams declares, "is to be sought and listened for in all occasions" (Williams 2000, p. 6). Theological "integrity can be recovered" "from any crass ideological bondage," Williams announces, to the extent that it can show itself "capable of conversation" and can turn on itself in the most rigorous self-examination (Williams 2000, p. 4).

One particular series of conversations that MacKinnon fruitfully had was with tragic dramas. Sophocles and Shakespeare, or at least Shakespeare as the author of *Hamlet* and *King Lear*, stand alongside the likes of Aristotle, Kant, von Balthasar, and Barth in MacKinnon's list of important educators and thinkers on the nature of human knowing and living without comforting illusions. Handling theology and the tragic together is particularly perilous. MacKinnon is aware of D. Daiches Raphael's claim that "there is no place for tragedy in the Judeo-Christian worldview" (MacKinnon 2016, p. 203). Moreover, MacKinnon recognizes the influence on Western thought of Plato's banishment of the tragedians from his *Republic*. Nonetheless, he laments the lack of courage to read the gospels in the light of "tragedy," and of their consequent following Plato's sense of "the certainty of a 'happy ending'" (MacKinnon 2016, p. 193). Something significant has been lost theologically when sensitivity to the tragic is anesthetized. Intractable problems with suffering and evil cannot be met by comforting justifications of that evil (theodicies) or by eschatological optimisms that postulate what George Steiner calls "a compensating heaven" (Steiner 1961, p. 129) or Reinhold Niebuhr describes as "the resolution of tragedy" (Niebuhr 1938, p. 155). While MacKinnon announces that the "belief that Jesus was raised from the dead . . . is a *prius* of my whole argument," the theologian has to be careful how that is worked out in relation to matters of evil and suffering (MacKinnon 1968, p. 95). What is more appropriate is "a certain reverent agnosticism" (MacKinnon 1968, p. 186). Indeed, "all our hopes," MacKinnon articulates, "are set" in "the descent of Christ into the tomb" (MacKinnon 2011, p. 260).[4] So without eternalizing some "tragic sense of life," MacKinnon claims that there is nonetheless an irreducibly tragic element in the Christian faith, as is particularly evidenced in the cross and is not silenced by the gospels' "extremely complex and elusive resurrection narratives" (de Unamuno 1972, cited by MacKinnon 1979, p. 195). Indeed, he goes so far as to say that it is "of central importance" (MacKinnon 1968, p. 94). So, if MacKinnon appears to be asking questions that are alien to a Christian mood he provides several series of brief, impressionistically sweeping but no less profound, meditative readings of Jesus' ministry in a tragic mode. In that regard, it is the very texture of the gospels themselves that press to be read in some sense in terms of "the tragic."

Firstly, as far as the realization of Jesus' eschatological hopes for Israel was concerned, his ministry was something of a "failure." Secondly, for MacKinnon it is in the figure of Judas that Jesus' failure is focused, since it is here that the "tragedy" of the cross is ineradicably exposed. "The light has shone in the darkness, which has failed to overcome it; but the darkness still remains, and of the end of the traitor there is no record" (MacKinnon 1968, pp. 91–92). Thirdly, MacKinnon observes about the "appalling *sequelae*" that the open-ended horror of anti-Semitism is "the terrible sequel to the story of the cross," as well as the fact that Jesus appeared to abdicate any responsibility for influencing the arrest of the Jewish move to self-destruction in 70 CE (MacKinnon 1975, p. 4; MacKinnon 1968, p. 103). So in his review of Teilhard's *Le Milieu Divin*, MacKinnon declares that "any essay [in theology] must be condemned as ultimately frivolous, which does not reckon with the reality of Auschwitz . . . [W]e have to assure ourselves that . . . we do not forget that the age in which we live is that which has seen the Holocaust, and is marked indelibly by its consequences" (MacKinnon 1983, p. 53).

Fourthly, "victories" in conflicts are not free from the tragic qualities of waste and destruction. Accordingly, MacKinnon draws attention to the fact that in "the acclamation of *Christus Victor*" "[t]he character of that victory is a paradox. Its trophy is a scaffold" (McDowell et al. 2016, p. 47). Although Christians believe they know how Jesus' incarnate story "ends," they cannot allow this to obliterate the memory of the catastrophe, scandal, and failure of the preceding events. The passion remains an "unstaunched wound" (MacKinnon 1975, p. 4). So, the resurrection cannot be properly conceived of as a descent from the cross postponed for thirty-six hours, a sudden dramatic Hollywood happy ending, or a reversal, all of which obliterate the memory of the preceding catastrophic events. By way of support, MacKinnon notes how the risen Christ retains the marks of his execution. Moreover, Jesus' post-Easter commerce with the disciples is elusive and restricted, as if to guard them against the mistake of supposing that they were witnesses of a reversal, and not a vindication, of those things that had happened. As the Father's "Amen" to the life of Christ, if the resurrection does anything it drives one back to find the secret of the order of the world in Christ's words and deeds, and the healing of its continuing bitterness in the place of his endurance. Fifthly, and finally, moral planning exhibits a tragic texture so that in his warning against *hubris* MacKinnon can claim that "our greatest achievements bear within them the seeds of tragic disorder as well as the promise of a new heaven and a new earth" (MacKinnon 1979, p. 4).

Notes

1 Muller (2010) may begin to address that problem.
2 In their own way they are testimonies of a sort to the prevention of "the frozen certitudes of the dogmatic, the inertia of the canonic," to adapt George Steiner's description of Søren Kierkegaard's style (Steiner 1996, p. 253).
3 MacKinnon hopes that the church will overcome its urge to self-securing and turn its "energies again to serious engagement with the ethical problems raised by war" (MacKinnon 2016, p. 189).
4 Language of "descending," however, suggests an activity whereas, as Alan E. Lewis reminds, the grave was a void, a place of desolation and the inactivity of the dead (Lewis 2001, p. 3).

References

Kerr, F. (2004). Remembering Donald MacKinnon. *New Blackfriars* 85: 265–269.

Lash, N. (2008). *Theology for Pilgrims*. London: DLT.

Lewis, A.E. (2001). *Between Cross and Resurrection: A Theology of Holy Saturday*. Grand Rapids, MI: Eerdmans.

McDowell, J.C. (2011). Editor's introduction. In: *Philosophy and thee Burden of Theological Honesty: A Donald MacKinnon Reader* (ed. J.C. McDowell), vii–xiv. London: T&T Clark.

MacKinnon, D.M. (1966). Can a divinity professor be honest? *The Cambridge Review* (November 12): 94–96.

MacKinnon, D.M. (1968). *Borderlands of Theology and Other Essays*. London: Lutterworth Press.

MacKinnon, D.M. (1974). *The Problem of Metaphysics*. Cambridge: Cambridge University Press.

MacKinnon, D.M. (1975). A master in Israel: Hans Urs von Balthasar. In: *Hans Urs von Balthasar, Engagement with God*, (trans. J. Halliburton), 1–16. London: SPCK.

MacKinnon, D.M. (1979). *Explorations in Theology*. London: SCM Press.

MacKinnon, D.M. (1983). Re-review of Pierre Teilhard de Chardin's *Le Milieu Divin*. *Modern Churchman* 25: 189–195.

MacKinnon, D.M. (1987). *Themes in theology: the three-fold cord*. In: *Essays in Philosophy, Politics and Theology*. Edinburgh: T&T Clark.

MacKinnon, D.M. (1988). Article review: *The Principle of Hope*, by Ernst Bloch. *Scottish Journal of Theology* 41: 247–252.

MacKinnon, D.M. (2011). *Philosophy and the Burden of Theological Honesty: A Donald MacKinnon Reader* (ed. J.C. McDowell). London: Continuum/T&T Clark.

MacKinnon, D.M. (2016). *Kenotic Ecclesiology: Select Writings of Donald M. MacKinnon* (eds. J.C. McDowell, S. Kirkland and A.J. Moyse). Minneapolis: Fortress Press.

Muller, Andre. (2010). Donald M. MacKinnon: The True Service of the Particular, 1913–1959. PhD dissertation (University of Otago).

Niebuhr, R. (1938). *Beyond Tragedy: Essays on the Christian Interpretation of History.* London: Nisbet and Co. Ltd.

Robinson, J. (1963). *Honest to God.* London: SCM Press.

Steiner, G. (1961). *The Death of Tragedy.* Oxford: Oxford University Press.

Steiner, G. (1996). *No Passion Spent: Essays 1978–1996.* London: Faber and Faber.

Surin, K. (1989). Donald MacKinnon. In: *Christ, Ethics and Tragedy: Essays in Honour of Donald MacKinnon* (ed. K. Surin), ix–xi. Cambridge: Cambridge University Press.

Sutherland, S.R. (1998). Donald MacKenzie MacKinnon, 1913-94. *Proceedings of the British Academy* 97: 381–389.

De Unamuno, M. (1972). *The Tragic Sense of Life in Men and Nations.* Princeton, NJ: Princeton University Press.

Williams, R. (2000). *On Christian Theology.* Oxford: Blackwell.

Leon Morris (1914–2006)

Neil Bach

Leon Lamb Morris grew up in Australia, then a nation of just over five million people. He was born in Lithgow, New South Wales in 1914, an area once inhabited by the Wiradjuri aborigines. By his time settlers had taken over, largely connected to the iron and steel industry. The mining town abutted a rural setting. The immediate society was substantially Anglo-Saxon with a strong Church of England influence.

His early life was marked by steady family life. Even World War I did not interrupt his upbringing. His father was required to stay in town to work in industry, and Leon was too young to absorb much of the war's impact. Apart from his emerging intelligence and losing the sight of one eye in a stick-throwing incident, his childhood was normal. Influences included strong parental involvement in the Church of England, his father's entrepreneurial skill running a small independent foundry and the family leaning toward the value of education. The Depression of the 1930s, and a young lady named Mildred Dann were further significant influences.

Upon leaving home for Sydney with partial family sponsorship for university studies, and just before the Depression took full hold, he carried a new future and responsibility. The 1930s eclipse of Lithgow's mining power, combined with the full impact of the Depression produced the collapse of the family business. These events made Morris more indebted for his privileges and marked his psyche, intensifying his predisposition to work hard and get the best from himself.

His studies for a science degree were normal and he confessed that he was scared to try for honors. More remarkable was his spiritual development where he came under the helpful guidance of All Souls Church of England, Leichhardt. The Rev. R. B. Robinson and his wife nurtured him through these years, with two young men of the church and others at university also being influential. The Robinsons were evangelical, evangelistic, generous in spirit, lovers of all sorts of people, and committed to social action.

Twentieth Century Anglican Theologians: From Evelyn Underhill to Esther Mombo, First Edition.
Edited by Stephen Burns, Bryan Cones, and James Tengatenga.
© 2021 John Wiley & Sons Ltd. Published 2021 by John Wiley & Sons Ltd.

Morris appropriated the Christian faith for himself while still living in Sydney, building on the faith of his father and mother. He discerned a call to the Anglican ministry and not long after received unmistakable guidance from God to serve with the Bush Church Aid Society in outback Australia.

He possessed a logical mind and sequential memory, an ability to identify important information from data, a photographic recall of information bearing on a question or position, and an ability to reject complicating or confusing information. He was able to use simple language to explain complexities without losing depth. He possessed a discipline in study seldom seen when combined with rare concentration. His humility and faith trusted God's revelation and that it made sense.

Theological Beginnings

Morris' research caused a shift in theological history for all those in the conservative stream. He was elected the first Australian member of the Society for New Testament Studies and holds the mantle of Australia's most significant New Testament scholar and pastor. All this is remarkable as he was the first member of his family to ever to get near a university and was an independent theological student never attending a theological college. He eventually influenced Christian leaders on five continents through two million books, the training of priests, and teaching visits.

Scholarly Contribution

George Eldon Ladd surprised Morris in 1960 by exclaiming that Leon Morris had re-established evangelical scholarship in the twentieth century. Today this has been widely acknowledged. Morris' trajectory began within evangelical Anglican scholarship and then moved to worldwide Christian scholarship after 1955. Early scholarly writing led to additional writings more accessible for the Christians of his Anglican Church and Christians worldwide.

A largely self-taught theologian he adopted the method of writing straight out of his head. He then went back to read other scholarly views with the intention of correcting any errors he uncovered in his thinking. His scientific background gave him helpful objectivity about evidence, allowing that all people hold presuppositions. His mantra was that "if there is no evidence, the theory is no good" (Treloar 1999, pp. 25–26). Rather than opting for rigid literalism or a sea of relatively for meanings, he chose to carry out robust intelligent research.

Theological Themes

Scriptural Revelation

Morris was acutely aware that the pendulum of twentieth century thinking had swung from respect for authority, to the view that what is embraced personally matters. He linked this change of loss of respect for authority to a loss of respect for the view that God had revealed truth to us.

In a technical presentation in Boston in 1966, he argued for the Bible's view of its own authority (Morris 1967). Against the view that the Bible's words explained some God "events," with the words themselves not that important, Morris argued that the words used in the Old Testament were not just explanations of revelatory events. Rather, God had put these exact words in the prophets' mouths, and therefore these words were important and inspired. If the written message was from the commandment of God (e.g., 1 Corinthians 14 : 37) and the oral preaching was from God (e.g., 1 Corinthians 2 : 4; cf. 1 Thess. 1 : 5), it is hard to see on what grounds we should deny that those writings that embody the message are the very word of God. He recognized problem passages. For example, Jesus says in Mark 14 : 22 (RSV; Revised Standard Version), "This is my body" and in Luke 22 : 19 (RSV), "This is my body which is given for you." It is legitimate to say that the differences are unimportant, but does this discount biblical authority?

He concluded: firstly, that the Bible does not come to us as a bare word and nothing more. God's Spirit still witnesses and applies the word to the devout reader's need. Final authority is not just paper and ink. God uses his word to affect his purpose. Second, the Bible's witness to itself must be taken with full seriousness. The difficulty is that the Bible's writers did not use our categories, never speaking in terms of inerrancy and seldom of inspiration. They were not concerned that all their statements were obviously consistent, yet they regarded what they had written as fully authoritative. Third, we need a way of looking at the Bible that holds it to be fully authoritative but is not distracted over minor points. The Bible writers do not speak of inerrancy. Our concern is not to prove inerrancy by lining up every statement in harmony; our concern is to show the Bible is eminently trustworthy.

Morris suggested that Christ's quotation of his own words in John's Gospel was a clue. In no case is the quotation verbally identical with the original. In no case is the sense distorted. We cannot look for more than the Bible writers give us, or settle for less. We must not impose an inerrancy of our own making on the Bible. The inerrancy the Bible teaches is compatible with variant reports of the words used on a given occasion. So the Bible is reliable. It will not lead us astray. As we accept it, it gives us true knowledge of God. In the 1970s Morris wrote *I Believe in Revelation* (Morris 1976) where he championed the authority of scripture. It sold some twelve-thousand copies and was then translated into Chinese, Korean, Spanish, German, and Swedish.

In the 1980s he disagreed with some Christian scholars' views that the collection of books we call the Bible is no different to any other collection of old books. A talk expressed his view (Morris 1980). In it he defended the Bible for Christians, and rebutted what he took to be loose thinking in the scholarly world on the nature of the Bible as holy scripture. He argued that Jesus emphasized the place of the Bible and so should his followers; revelation is basic. He also illustrated his points, for example: several times in Exodus we see, "the Lord said to Moses." It is not easy to see that the writer wants us to think that this was a bright idea that Moses had thought up. Similarly, "the word that came to Jeremiah from the Lord" (Jeremiah 7:1) scarcely reads like the reflection of the prophet. Morris noted Jesus regarded the Old Testament as the utterance of God.

The New Testament is not inferior to the Old Testament, as declared in 2 Corinthians 3:7–11. By inference the New Testament's writings are not inferior. Morris noted that Jesus speaking, "My words shall not pass away" implies that his teaching is of divine origin. Jesus gave authoritative directions on an equal footing with scripture – "You have heard that it was said . . . of old . . . but I say to you." He also noted instances where words from God himself were recorded in the New Testament as well as passages affirming the divine origin of the Christian message. Furthermore, Paul viewed scripture's authority in terms of divinely given sufficiency and claimed his message was from God or of God.

Christianity also depends on what God has made known; as an historical religion a record must exist of the basic historical events; there has never been a Christianity without a Bible; any religion may develop, but this must be in accord with its essential basis; Christianity's basis is the Bible. He said, "Why throw away a belief in revelation that all Christians had held as basic for centuries?"

God's Love

Morris expressed deep satisfaction in his book *Testaments of Love: A Study of Love in the Bible* (Morris 1981). He thought that many scholars' theologies of the Old and even New Testament did not give adequate weight to the love of God. His book combined earlier and later research.[1] He maintained that "God is love" in asserting that "this means more than that God is loving, it means that love is of the essence of his being" (Morris 1981, p. 136). He cited statements in the Johannine literature, and Paul's use of *agape* to establish that for Paul, God, and love are closely related and that *agape* is the expression of God's nature.

Morris maintained that God's essential character was love. To see God's love and the depth of the love of God for us we also had to appreciate the nature of humankind, the nature of the cross, and the nature of the problem in the relationship between God and us. And also appreciate how markedly different the biblical view is from that of modern western society.

God's love is given to us irrespective of our merit and without a desire to possess us. God's love pervades the New Testament and the events of the cross. Morris' belief in the God of love, and his experience of that love seen at the cross, helps understand how he accepted the unpalatable aspect of God's settled anger toward our sinfulness. He maintained that without the cross we would never have known what *agape* is, let alone experienced it. The action of the Son of God in laying down his perfect life for sinners and dying for us without merit is *agape* (Morris 1981, p. 143).

The Atonement Through the Cross

Morris held that the cross is central to the New Testament. Its central theological importance became his lifelong work. He argued that each Gospel leads to the cross, giving prominence to its impact for our salvation. Matthew concentrates a third of his writing on the last week and death of Christ. When Jesus dies, the curtain of the temple is torn in two, the earth shook, the rocks split, and the tombs broke open. The bodies of many holy people were raised to life (cf. Matthew 27:51). The Apostle Paul tells us "we preach Christ crucified" (1 Corinthians 1:23). In Revelation, we are saved, "by the blood of the Lamb" (Revelation 7:14). When a person is baptized it is a baptism into Christ's death (Romans 6:3). In taking holy communion we proclaim the Lord's death until he comes (1 Corinthians 11:26).

Secondly, the cross is central because of the fact of sin. People want to believe that the problems within the human person are a lack of education, or resources, or whatever. The Bible consistently reminds us that we are all sinners (Romans 3:23) The consequences of sin are more serious than earthly dilemmas. "We must give account of ourselves to God" (Romans 14:12). Thirdly, the cross is central because there we see the love of God. God loves us continuously because he is love (1 John 4:8,16). His love brings salvation for sinners in Christ's death (Romans 5:8). God's forgiveness is in the cross and not divorced from it.

Finally, the cross is central because when a person repents God graciously forgives, based on what Christ's death has accomplished. To say that no atoning act is needed is to give us a non-Christian view.

Morris used a word study approach to biblical theology, resting in the stream of theologians like Gerhard Kittel. He explained how key biblical words express central and constant theological themes (see Adam 2007). His linguistic skills complemented his brilliant scholarship.

Some were amused that Morris often counted the number of times a word was used in the Bible, suggesting that it indicated the strength of the idea for the author. And that it might carry weight for meaning. Equally he just liked counting words. Perhaps it was a reaction to his average ability at cricket? If he scored three he regarded that as success, but in counting words he could get into the hundreds.

He rigorously placed meaning within scriptural context. He embraced what was true of previous historical views of the atonement while focusing more closely on unexplored aspects. Thus he clarified and sometimes sought to correct other views on the meaning of the cross. So while agreeing with much of C. H. Dodd's analysis, he diverged in his understanding on the wrath of God, maintaining that Dodd seriously misinterpreted some evidence. Rather, Morris refused to sift out unpleasant ideas of God's rightful displeasure at sin. God was not an irrational ancient deity but had a settled opposition to that which could destroy his creatures. Morris likened it to a parent that rescues a child. The parent deeply loves the child but is rightly upset when the child willfully wanders near a moving car. And the parent rescues the child.

Illustrative of his word studies is his study of redemption (see further word studies in Morris, 1955; Morris 1983; Bach 2015). He argued that the early Christians used this word because the non-religious world already understood the importance of redemption in other spheres of their life. To capture the original meaning of redemption, one begins with the basic word of the word group, "ransom." Originally the word meant "loosing," "releasing," or "freeing" – for example, when releasing prisoners of war in exchange for a payment. Morris' research found that the meaning of "ransom" changed to the "payment for loosing," a ransom price. He argued that this idea of payment is the basis of release, which is the reason for the existence of the whole word group. Other words were available to denote simple release (Morris 1955, p. 12). He then explored the compound word "redemption," found in non-biblical literature with its roots in the word "ransom." Outside the New Testament, he found only ten uses of the word, and "in every passage, without exception, there is a payment of a ransom price to secure the desired release" (Morris 1955, p. 18). In the Old Testament he considered the verb *lutrow* and its derivatives *g'l, pdh* and then the related noun *kopher* – again the idea surfaced of a ransom price paid to gain release from a death sentence (Exodus 30:12). A ransom price was not required in the Old Testament when God is the subject: God is not required to pay us a ransom price. He noted that even when God is the subject, his effort is equivalent to a ransom price. Ransom and its derived words are properly applied to redemption by payment of price. He found references in rabbinic writings were generally used in much the same way.

What of the New Testament? Morris found "ransom" in only one saying in Mark 10:45 and Matthew 20:28 that he took as authentic. He concluded that the intended meaning of the ransom reference was that Jesus gave his life as a payment price instead of us, or in exchange for us having to do so.

What of related words "redeem" and "redemption" (for example, *lutrow* and *lutrosis*) in the New Testament? Morris looked at important passages like Titus 2:14, where Christ "gave himself for us, that he might redeem us from all iniquity" (KJV; King James Version), as they referred to a ransom and pointed in the direction of substitution. Jesus not only proved his obedience to God and that it benefits sinners, but his death ransoms them.

The most typical word for redemption used in the New Testament is *apolutrosis*. Morris located ten occurrences. The three clearest passages are Romans 3:24, Ephesians 1:7, and Hebrews 9:15. This compound word is used in a particular way in the New Testament, perhaps pointing to the unusual nature of Christ's redemption. Further, a redemption price was mentioned in each case. With regards to the other occurrences of "redemption," such as future redemption, he observed that redemption, even without a price specifically mentioned, directly looks back to a price that was paid.

Early Christians therefore understood the atonement as a process of ransoming. The New Testament idea of "ransom" focuses on one aspect of the atonement: the payment of a price, and the price is the death of Christ. Instead of our death, there is his: a substitution. Thus Morris was able to critique and clarify muddled views of redemption.

We compare this to today. Australian swimming champion Kieren Perkins competed in the 1996 Atlanta Olympics swimming 1500 m with his reputation in the pool sinking. Having swum his heat he limped into the final in eighth place. The gun sounded and Perkins led throughout. Delighted viewers stood on chairs as Perkins claimed his second Olympic gold. He pumped his arms, having redeemed his reputation in his own strength. Many apply self-earned redemption to religion; Morris reminded us that the cross shows that only God's love can redeem.

Morris identified three aspects of the process of atonement:

1   The state of sin: our situation is likened to slavery, a captivity where we cannot redeem ourselves.
2   The price that is paid: the terminology used means that Christ has paid the adequate price of our redemption; he took what we should have paid and paid it.
3   The resultant state of the believer: we who are redeemed are brought into a state of real freedom to do the will of God.

Continuing Atonement Issues

Atonement debates often concern the nature of God, and how the cross touches God, Christ, our sin, and us.

An academic in philosophy wrote to Morris arguing that the idea that an innocent Christ could bear the consequences of our sin is contradictory and impossible (McCullagh 1988). He objected that God's anger could be compatible with God's love; that righteous anger can punish rather than reform and that reconciliation needs satisfaction. He stated that God should forgive just as we do, proposing that the cross is about the Father and the Son convincing people of their willingness to suffer for their sins, even suffer death and yet love them. The cross does not make possible God's forgiveness of our sins, for that was always part of his love for us. We simply need faith in that forgiveness. The cross removes the barrier of disbelief within us. He said this answered Morris' question "If Christ's death did nothing to bring about our forgiveness, then exactly why did Christ die?" But Morris had trouble with a statement that the cross was only an act to help God and Christ convince us of their love. He rejected a purely subjective impact within sinners and still asked, "If His death did nothing to bring about our forgiveness, then exactly why did Christ die?" He accepted that a barrier can lie in us but asserted that the barrier does not lie primarily in us. There is something objective about the Father's view that Jesus paid a price to ransom sinners from Satan, and the Reformers' view that Jesus endured the penalty sinners had incurred, and Gustav Aulen's view that Jesus won the victory. The cross did something, quite apart from its effect on the sinner. Morris suggested that "the soul that sins shall die," plus other ideas are more than subjective. Redemption has objective consequences of release. The New Testament deals with the objective plight of the sinner. This exchange about God's nature and scriptural teaching revealed Morris holding to evidence that contained uncomfortable, and to some, unpalatable ideas.

Morris' Continued Relevance: Some Issues

Many have simply denied the emphasis on atonement Morris gave in his day, and today some evangelicals dislike the idea of a God of love expressing righteous anger, and go to extraordinary lengths to dismiss it. Some charge that twentieth century evangelicals began with an assumption that retributive judgment was a given, and developed their teaching from that supposition. But the charge belittles earlier scholars' ability to know their own assumptions, and current treatments can be weak in doctrines of human depravity and of God's holiness. While theologians say all sorts of things, Morris would suggest that it comes down to the best grasp of the evidence of the New Testament.

Morris knew of the "New Perspective on Paul" that has been part of later twentieth-century biblical studies. Morris and the New Perspective theologians were not that far apart on issues such as justification. However, some New Perspective views (Wright 2016), supporting an overarching narrative about God's covenant people, can unfairly minimize impact of the cross.[2] Ignoring New Testament evidence marginalizes truths, like Christ as our substitute undergoing God's punishment for sin on behalf of sinners, and God's wrath being dealt at the cross. Morris' teaching in these matters was far more nuanced and careful than the selective treatment sometimes offered of earlier views. Thus it is possible to even see moves away from the full impact of the cross in books on the crucifixion. Exegetes of Romans 3:21–26, for example, can deny the specifics of the textual evidence to make overarching claims.

The place of women in ministry remains divisive in some forms of Anglicanism, not least Australia. Morris came from a world where men led and "headship" was assumed. In the 1970s he revisited the matter. He wrote more expansively as time went on that the New Testament evidence could be interpreted favorably toward including women in all forms of ministry. He employed women on that basis. He recognized other scholars might see the evidence differently. Yet he saw enough evidence of the treatment and inclusion of women in ministry in the New Testament against the culture of the first century to himself be a gentle supporter of women in ministry. So, he supported women who lectured and preached at Ridley College and continued as they made their way into church leadership. His influence enabled changes across the Australian Anglican church that otherwise would have taken many more years.

Morris influenced the Diocese of Melbourne. At one point he had trained half of its clergy. He took his place on various local and national Anglican bodies over the years, liturgical and doctrinal, and contributed his wisdom. He advised Anglican Church leaders seeking counsel. He influenced thinking Christians and academics worldwide with his writings and teachings on the New Testament and cross. He was also socially active expressing God's love for everyone. He and his wife Mildred helped many "down and outs" who called on him for help, and he was instrumental with others in forming the TEAR (The Evangelical Alliance Relief) Fund in Australia. Morris would not have described himself as living out incarnational theology, but his practice demonstrated the same locally involved expression of servanthood. Finally, an important trajectory in Morris' ministry was his commitment to evangelism. He saw the cross and its offer of new life as leading directly to the churches' ministry of evangelism. With earlier divines he believed that there was no greater work than the conversion of a soul. He believed that evangelism transcended theological nit-picking and supported others of varying belief in individual, congregational, and combined evangelistic activity. Notably, he went out of his way to support Billy Graham, the international evangelist of his day.

Notes

1   An early treatment based on his research and sermons in the 1940s–1950s is in "The Love of God," Leon Morris, Conference notes Church Missionary Society Spring School, Christchurch, New Zealand, in August 1954. Later material, e.g., sixteen varying papers on God's love, is archived at Ridley College, Melbourne, Australia.

2   Consider the dismissal of some credible evangelical views in Wright (2016).

References

Adam, P. (2007). Morris, Leon Lamb. In: *Dictionary of Major Biblical Interpreters*, 2e (ed. D.K. McKim), 751–755. IVP: Nottingham.

Bach, N. (2015). *Leon Morris: One Man's Fight for Love and Truth*. Milton Keynes: Authentic Media.

McCullagh, C.B. (1988). Theology of atonement. *Theology* 91: 392–400.

Morris, L. (1955). *The Apostolic Preaching of the Cross.* Grand Rapids, MI: Eerdmans.

Morris, L. (1967). Biblical authority and the concept of inerrancy. *The Churchman* 81: 22–38.

Morris, L. (1976). *I Believe in Revelation.* Grand Rapids, MI: Eerdmans.

Morris, L. (1980). *The Authority and Relevance of the Bible in the Modern World: The Oliver Beguin Lecture.* Canberra: Bible Society in Australia.

Morris, L. (1981). *Testaments of Love: A Study of Love in the Bible.* Grand Rapids, MI: Eerdmans.

Morris, L. (1983). *The Atonement: Its Meaning and Significance.* Milton Keynes: Paternoster.

Treloar, G. (1999). Interview with Leon Morris. *Lucas: An Evangelical History Review* 25&26: 201.

Wright, N.T. (2016). *The Day the Revolution Began: Reconsidering the Meaning of Jesus's Crucifixion.* San Francisco, CA: Harper One.

K. H. Ting
(1915–2014)

Philip Wickeri

When Bishop K. H. Ting died in November 2014 most commentators focused on his political role as the preeminent Chinese Christian leader during the period of "Reform and Openness" that began in 1979. Of less interest was his role as a theologian, let alone an Anglican thinker, except insofar as this was related to "theological reconstruction."

Anglicans all over the world have seen Bishop K. H. Ting as part of the communion and have used his writings to interpret Christianity in China. In this chapter, I offer an interpretation of Bishop Ting's theology and intellectual outlook as a modern and "post-denominational" Christian leader in order to determine how he can be considered an Anglican theologian.

Life and Times

Born in 1915, K. H. Ting lived through the turbulent history of twentieth century China. Protestant missionaries from Europe and North America came to China in the early nineteenth century, and over the next one-hundred-and-fifty years, they built churches, hospitals, and educational institutions all over the country. The missionaries came under attack for being agents of imperialism after the establishment of the People's Republic in 1949, and within a few years, they were all gone. The churches and institutions they had established entered a period of decline. Chinese Christians were criticized for being "semi-foreign." In the early 1950s, church leaders associated with the Chinese Christian Three-Self Patriotic Movement (TSPM) sought to reconstruct a *Chinese* Christianity free from foreign control, but their efforts were subsequently overtaken by the political movements of the times. Churches all but

Twentieth Century Anglican Theologians: From Evelyn Underhill to Esther Mombo, First Edition.
Edited by Stephen Burns, Bryan Cones, and James Tengatenga.
© 2021 John Wiley & Sons Ltd. Published 2021 by John Wiley & Sons Ltd.

ceased to exist during the Cultural Revolution era (1966–1976), and many observers concluded that Christianity in China would eventually disappear.

In the late 1970s, however, religious life slowly reemerged, and churches began to be reopened. Since then, there has been a resurgence of religious life in China, with various ups and downs. Over the past four decades, Chinese Christianity has enjoyed an unprecedented period of growth and development. But it is a fragile community, beset by problems on all sides: continuing pressures from local government officials; an inadequate number of trained leaders; underdeveloped and insecure institutions; problems with sectarianism and heterodoxy, particularly in rural areas. K. H. Ting presided over the church in China during three decades of growth and development as he attempted to address the problems the church faced from within and without.

Raised in a middle-class family in cosmopolitan Shanghai, which was the center of Protestant missionary activity, K. H. Ting grew up in the Anglican church and studied for the priesthood. His experience as a YMCA (Young Men's Christian Association) student worker and priest in a city under Japanese occupation (1937–1945) convinced him of the need to be involved in the struggle for national salvation and freedom from foreign domination. But he was also committed to the ecumenical movement, and after the war he went with his wife Kuo Siu-may to Canada, where he was appointed mission secretary for the Student Christian Movement. He later moved to New York, to study at the Union Theological Seminary and Columbia University, and from there to Geneva, where he worked for the World Students' Christian Federation (WSCF).

In 1951, against the advice of many friends and colleagues, the Tings returned to China with their young son. They were committed to work for social change in the People's Republic of China, and Ting became associated with the newly established TSPM. He subsequently moved to Nanjing where he became principal of the newly established Nanjing Union Theological Seminary. In 1955, he became the Bishop of the Zhejiang Diocese. He was seen as a trusted and well-known interpreter of the Chinese revolution in the West. All denominations ceased to exist in 1958, and worship services were unified. With the intensification of political movements in the late 1950s, Ting was drawn to the "ultra-leftist" line. He was removed from all his church and political posts at the start of the Cultural Revolution and only came back into public view in the early 1970s.

In the late 1970s, K. H. Ting became China's preeminent Protestant Christian leader, heading the newly organized China Christian Council (CCC) and the reestablished TSPM. He also rose in the ranks of national government bodies. Ting worked for the reopening of churches, seminaries, and other religious institutions, the printing of the Bible and religious literature, and increasing contacts with churches in other parts of the world. As the church's best-known theologian, his intellectual focus shifted to love as God's primary attribute, and the importance for Christians to practice love in their ethical witness in society. By the time of his retirement in 1996, Ting had become the most significant voice in China for the interests of the church, making use of his important government positions and personal prestige to enhance religious freedom and give attention to reforming church structures. His interest in "theological reconstruction" became the culmination of a lifelong effort to the promote reconstruction and renewal in Chinese Christianity.[1]

K. H. Ting's life and thought has been an ongoing dialogue with the church and the politics of modern and contemporary China. Even in retirement, Ting continued to be a prominent figure in China and an internationally respected ecumenical leader, up until a few years before his death in 2014.

The Sources of K. H. Ting's Theology

In 2000, four years after his retirement and two years after the beginning of the "theological reconstruction" initiative, K. H. Ting published a special issue of the *Nanjing Theological Review* containing the entire text of Tang Zhongmo, *A Modern View of the Bible* (Zhongmo 2000).[2] The booklet was originally published in 1936, and was one that he himself had first read as a student of theology at St. John's University. By 2000, Tang Zhongmo's ideas were long out of date in their approach to biblical scholarship, but they challenged the fundamentalist interpretation of the Bible that was still current in China. Tang was a traditional Chinese Anglican, and his study was a mixture of modernist biblical criticism and Anglican piety. Ting's insistence on having this book published illustrated that he had not strayed far from the Anglican-Episcopal tradition that he had grown up with and had studied at St. John's.

K. H. Ting's theological approach did not change a great deal from the 1930s to the 1990s. He was religiously formed through family devotions, led by his mother, and in the life of St. Peter's Episcopal Church. His theology was Anglican and Episcopal, and emphasized social engagement and theological liberalism. It was also ecumenical and was a theology in dialogue with the times, and with people both inside and outside the church. Besides his religious upbringing, the sources of Ting's theology were: the theological education he received at St. John's University; participation in the Shanghai Christian Student Movement; and his ecumenical involvement both in Shanghai and overseas.

The theology K. H. Ting learned at St. Johns was Anglican and Episcopal. The Chung Hua Sheng Kung Hui (CHSKH) in Shanghai was affiliated with the American Church Mission, and at St. John's, all of the professors were either American or Chinese who had studied in the United States. Their theology was modern, insofar as they accepted the historical critical approach to the Bible and Christian engagement with modern culture, but not modernist. According to Michael Ramsey, all Anglican theology during this period emphasized "the Incarnation, the striving after synthesis between theology and contemporary culture which the term 'liberal' broadly denotes, [and] the frequent shift of interest from dogma to apologetics" (Ramsey 1960, p. vii). Contemporary trends in secular thought, including evolution and socialism, were regarded not as "enemies to be fought but as friends who can provide new illuminations of the truth that is in Christ" (Ramsey 1960, p. 3). The best theology written during this time was ready "to risk untidiness and rough edges and apparently insecure fences" for it is "in and through the intellectual turmoil of the time – and not aloofness from it – that that the Church teaches the catholic faith" (Ramsey 1960, p. 89; see also Wickeri 2007, p. 49).

St. John's Theological Seminary was not known for its great theologians, but the Chinese who taught there were in touch with the broader cultural developments in Shanghai and their interests were not confined to the world of the Church.

The CHSKH was not really touched by the Fundamentalist-Modernist controversy, which largely affected Presbyterians, Baptists, and independents. Theology in the CHSKH was not as important as it was for other continental and American Protestant transplants. The CHSKH followed a tolerant *via media*. Attentive to the centrality of liturgy and the life of prayer, it was evangelical, liberal (and therefore modern), and catholic (or traditional).

In later years, Ting criticized theological education at St. John's as of "the Thirty-nine Articles" type, meaning it was not very relevant for the Chinese situation. Still, many if not most of the theological ideas that he developed were from his upbringing in the CHSKH and his studies at St. John's: the centrality of the Incarnation and the Trinity; the connection between creation and redemption; an historical and critical approach to the Bible; love as God's primary attribute; dialogue between Christianity and contemporary culture; openness to society and to those not part of the Church; the importance of catholicity and Christian unity. K. H. Ting wrote his BD thesis – which I have never been able to locate – on the Oxford Movement. Whether he selected this topic because of a concern for the catholicity of the church or for some other reason is difficult to say. The subject was far removed from the concerns of the Shanghai Student Movement and his emerging social and political consciousness, which was a second source of Ting's modern theology.

K. H. Ting's involvement with the Shanghai Student Movement gave his theology an activist bent. As a university student, he did not have a strong interest in traditional Chinese culture, but rather in modern writers (especially Lu Xun) and the broader movement for social change. He had been a student leader in his university days, associated with the "Shanghai Christian Student Union." After graduation, he began work for the YMCA that was part of the broader student union. By this time, he had put aside his theological studies, to work with students in the movement for national salvation and resistance efforts against Japan. In his earliest writings, his theological concern was to relate Christian faith to society, rather than encourage students to relate more closely to the church. His involvement with students and the YMCA continued even after his return to seminary studies and his ordination to the priesthood in 1942. He became pastor of Community Church in occupied Shanghai, which served the foreign Christian community, and worked with the "Student Church," which involved activist students, whether Christian or not. It was during this time that he came into contact with underground Communist Party members. His interest was to relate enduring theological themes to the social situation in which Christians lived. Like many intellectuals and young people of his generation, Ting's involvement with the national salvation movement and subsequently the resistance movement against Japan, emphasized a social commitment.

Ting's ecumenical involvement, the third source of his theological formation, was already evident in his work with the student movement. The five years he spent overseas helped to open him to the wider world. His intellectual interests had never been confined to the Church and its priestly ministry. His work, studies, and writings overseas reveal a commitment to the issues of church and society embraced by the ecumenical movement, including of course the WSCF. Ting was never as "Anglican" as many of his overseas admirers liked to say in his later years. Or to put it in a different way, he was an ecumenical Anglican, like his friends Luther Tucker, David Paton, and John Coleman, none of whom had strong interests in the narrow concerns associated with the Anglican communion as distinct from world Christianity, or with the search for "Anglican identity" rather than social change. In his year at Union Theological Seminary (1947–1948), Ting took no courses in Anglicanism, and in fact, most of his courses there were in education and psychology rather than theology. These were more important for his interest in Chinese social concerns. At the WSCF, he became committed to developing a new missiology, and this put him in touch with a new generation of Christian leaders in other parts of the world with interests similar to his own.

It should be noted that theology for Ting and for his contemporaries, both in China and in the ecumenical movement, was more than a question of ideas. It had to do with how theology would situate itself, and how Christian beliefs could be reflected in practice as well as in written work. Theology was more than just a matter of writing books and articles. It was reflected in teaching, preaching, in daily life, and in the choice of what issues to focus on.

By the time he returned to China in 1951, the cultural and social aspects of Ting's theology were already in place. Politically, his support for the "New China" was clear, but he had been overseas during the Civil War and had not been directly involved in the changes that were taking place in church and society. Shortly after his return to China, he became the principal of the newly established Nanjing Union Theological Seminary (1952). This was a newly formed theological institution, and Ting had spoken of the need to embark on a new path in theological education in the meetings leading up to the formation of the seminary.

Ting was modern, but not a modernist. Nevertheless, he was cast as a typical "modernist" by Fundamentalist leader Wang Mingdao in the mid-1950s. I disagree. I have argued previously that "theirs was not really a theological debate but a highly charged polemic shaped by the struggles of the times" (Wickeri 2007, p. 121). I see no reason to revise this judgment. In the 1950s, up until the Anti-Rightist Movement, K. H. Ting never surrendered his theology to a political agenda, although he did strongly identify himself with the patriotic, anti-imperialist political of the TSPM and the leadership of the Communist Party. Several of the theological essays he wrote during this time elaborated the theological viewpoint he had taken decades earlier. His "On Christian Theism," in which we can detect his Anglican roots, was a Christian apologetic and was not particularly "political." As an Anglican modern, there was no contradiction between Ting's theology and his politics in the 1950s.

K. H. Ting as a Modern Chinese Theologian: The 1980s and 1990s

The basic themes of K. H. Ting's theology have been discussed and analyzed many times over the past three decades, and there is no need to add to what has already been written.[3] His theological writings have stressed the continuity between creation and redemption; the Cosmic Christ who presides over human history, and who was in China before the missionaries came; Love as God's major attribute; the importance of constructive Christian participation in society; human beings as "half finished products" who participate in God's work of creation and redemption; not overstressing the divide between Christian faith and non-believers; and (after 1998) a de-emphasis on "justification by faith," all of which became prominent in his personal promotion of "Theological Reconstruction" in his retirement years.

I want to suggest that K. H. Ting's position as a theologian is important not so much in terms of content and ideas, but in terms of structure and method. By structure I mean the way in which theology is ordered and conceived. This is a fluid definition that would include both traditional and contextual theological approaches. The structure of his areas of theological interest formed the basis on which he did theology. The ideas mentioned above were not only written but acted upon, and not only in his work as a theologian, but in his role as church leader and political figure. The *theological modern*, in Ting's understanding, is the primary structure (and not simply the content) of Ting's thought and practice – ecclesiastically, ecumenically, politically, socially, and culturally.

K. H. Ting became China's preeminent Christian leader during the period of reform and openness, the Deng Xiaoping era of modern China. From the late 1970s until his retirement in 1996, he was the leading voice in Chinese theology. He never would see himself as an "Anglican" theologian, but we can discover many Anglican ideas in his theology. After 1996, he edited what became his collected works, and introduced the initiative for "theological reconstruction" that continues to this day. As he had always done, he wrote theological essays in response to the times, but it was a theology rooted in the Bible and Christian tradition. He was developing what might be called a theology of "reform and openness," although he himself never would have used this term. What is distinctive is that his theology was attempting to be modern in many different ways at once.

Given China's modernizing political context, what was important about the structure of K. H. Ting's theology? In the 1980s and 1990s, he was attempting to create a theology that he believed could be accepted by the conservative majority of Chinese Christians. Modernization emphasized unity for the sake of reform and K. H. Ting emphasized unity as the structure for reform in the Christian community. It was on his initiative that the China Christian Council (CCC) was created in 1980 in an attempt to win over Christians who were alienated from the TSPM. The CCC was a *church* structure for unity and reform. Also in 1980, *Tian Feng* republished the essays that Ting had originally written for seminary students in the 1950s, and now collected as *How to Study the Bible*. For the unity of the Church, this was written in a devotional style and was a generally orthodox approach to Bible Study. One of the terms he coined for church unity and reform was "running the Church well," which was a movement from an emphasis on "Three-Self" to an emphasis on church-building. His idea of the church was typically broad church Anglican

Throughout the 1980s and into the 1990s, Ting was writing theological essays as a church leader, and his theology was designed to encourage Christians and show that he respected their religious feelings. He did not promote a particular kind of theology, but he did emphasize the need for a "theological reorientation," which meant, "daring to think, daring to blaze new trails, daring to enable theological thinking to open its doors to the reality of the world. . ." (Wickeri 2000, p. 102; for background on the 1950s, see Wickeri 2000, pp. 137–150; also, Wickeri 1988, pp. 258–261, and Wickeri and Wickeri 2002 for his thinking over time). In addition, his defense of home worship gatherings and his desire to win over evangelicals underscored his promotion of Christian unity and reform. In the late 1980s, he even spoke of the TSPM as a temporary structure, which there would be no need for after the Church was established. This was a radical idea that was opposed by other leaders in the TSPM and the CCC. In the 1990s he continually emphasized "running the church well" as an important focus of his theology. All of this was related to what I term the *church modern*.

Part of Ting's theological and church agenda in the 1980s was reestablishing international ecumenical relationships. From 1979 onward, he led many delegations to churches and ecumenical meetings around the world. Some of the essays in his collected works were originally delivered in English, and in these essays he developed theological ideas that stress the international involvement of the TSPM and the CCC. "Self-isolation is not is not one of our three selves," he liked to say. Reestablishing international relationships was not only important for diplomatic reasons, but for the Chinese Church to reach out, learn from Christians overseas, and reform. Ting felt most at home in Anglican and Episcopal settings, but he tried to balance relationships with other churches so as to be ecumenical. This I term the *world modern*.

Christian unity was related to national unity, and so it was important for Ting and other Christian leaders that theology should be patriotic. And so, in the 1980s, an emphasis on Three-Self patriotism became the political structure for Ting's modern theology. There would be no attempt to return to the pre-1949 past, and there would be no substantial criticism of the TSPM from the 1950s. Especially important in this regard was the reform of religious policy, and to remove the stigma of "religion as an opiate" from government descriptions of religion (Wickeri 1993). Ting accepted the definition of modernization advanced by the Communist Party as the political context for patriotism and reform in the Christian community. He believed this was a responsible position for Chinese Christians, one that in no way went against Christian beliefs. There were, of course, many who disagreed with him, and so there were conflicting approaches to what I term the *political modern*.

Theology, was a matter of actions as well as words. Ting encouraged Christians to involve themselves in society, to contribute to reform, and do good works. Christians were still a tiny minority in China. In the 1980s and 1990s, most people knew little about Christianity, and there was the legacy of the past to live down. He did not want Christians to close themselves off in their churches, but to reach out to society. In 1985, the Amity Foundation was founded in order to contribute to modernization, make Christian participation more widely known, and serve as a channel for the international sharing of resources. One aspect of Amity was its outreach to the world. Indeed, Ting's modern theology involved openness to the outside world as he redeveloped international relationships and worked to bring theology up to date. Amity became an important structure for Christian involvement in Chinese society. To be sure, there were many other ways in which Christians were involved in society, and as civil society expanded, there would be other structures for the *social modern*.

Once religion was no longer seen as opium, and therefore inherently destructive, it could be understood as a legitimate part of culture. As early as the mid-1980s, many

Chinese scholars outside the church became interested in religious studies, and particularly in the study of Christianity. By the early 1990s, programs of Christian studies had begun in many universities and research centers. It was termed the study of "Christian Culture," for the government did not want to be seen as promoting religion, but as studying culture. K. H. Ting termed these scholars interested in the study of Christianity "Culture Christians," as a way of affirming what they were trying to do. In 1994, the Amity Foundation and the Institute of World Religions of the Chinese Academy of Social Sciences cohosted the first international academic consultation on Christianity in Beijing, under the theme of "Christianity and Modernization" (Wickeri and Cole 1995). K. H. Ting had been encouraging more dialogue between Christians and Chinese intellectuals even before this. He had started an art department at Nanjing Seminary to show the importance of art for theological education. He was involved in dialogue with Chinese intellectuals about the reform process, and wrote several essays on subjects far removed from theology. He said that Christianity should be more pluralistic and contribute to culture. This may be termed his interest in the *cultural modern*.

After he stepped down as leader of the CCC/TSPM, K. H. Ting began to select and edit the sermons, speeches, and essays he had written over the past decades. In 1998, these were published as *The Collected Works of K.H. Ting (Ding Guangxun wenji)* (Ting 1998). By then, he was already 84 years old, not the time of life to begin something new. All but four of the papers in this volume were written between 1979 and 1998. K. H. Ting intended the *Collected Works* to be his intellectual and theological legacy. In an afterword to the volume, he writes that his work should be interpreted in light of efforts to strengthen "socialist spiritual civilization":

> The "Resolution on Several Important Issues in Strengthening Socialist Spiritual Civilization" passed by the Party Central Committee of the Chinese Communist Party on 10 December 1996 states: "Socialism and communist thinking and morality should be conscientiously promoted throughout the whole of society. At the same time, advanced and wide-ranging ideas should be brought together to encourage support of all thinking and morality beneficial to liberating and developing the forces of socialist production, national unity, ethnic unity and social progress, and the pursuit of truth, goodness and beauty, while resisting falsehood and evil, and popularizing upright thinking and morality. . ." With this encouragement, I have selected and edited the contents of this book (Ting 1998, p. 512).

This is an important paragraph in considering Ting's approach to the socialist modern. The *Collected Works* constitutes the basis of what might be called Ting's theology of "reform and openness" corresponding to the "reform and openness" of the Deng Xiaoping and Jiang Zemin periods in society as a whole.

In November 1998, theological reconstruction was taken up as an important task by the TSPM/CCC.[4] This was an initiative from above, not below. The government endorsed theological reconstruction, for it fitted with the broader agenda of the adaptation of Christianity to socialism. Theological reconstruction shifted Ting's emphasis to the reform of theological thinking and a critique of fundamentalist theology. He wanted theology to be more ethically responsible. Especially controversial was his idea of downplaying the doctrine of justification by faith. Ting felt that this doctrine diluted the ethical element in Chinese Christianity and had assumed an importance far beyond what was originally attended by St. Paul. Critics charged that in so doing, he wanted to remove what was distinctive about Christianity, but they forget that he continued to speak of love as God's primary attribute. By and large, the effort to encourage greater openness to theological thinking has helped churches and seminaries become more open to new ideas.

Conclusion

K. H. Ting's theological legacy must be seen in the context of his whole life, and not just in his collected works or in theological reconstruction. There is no evidence that he set out to establish a particular school of theology. He was a "doer" as much as he was a "thinker." His theological ideas were not, for the most part, particularly innovative or new. Many of the themes he discussed (the Cosmic Christ, the connection between redemption and creation, the ethical content of theology) had been developed more fully by others, both in China and abroad. Indeed, K. H. Ting had neither the time nor the inclination to develop his own theological thought in great depth, given his role as a church leader and political figure.

Like other contextual theologians, K. H. Ting did theology in response to the times. What was unique about his contribution is that in the 1980s and 1990s, he wrote as the preeminent leader of one of the fastest growing Christian communities in the world, in a society undergoing rapid political and social change. He was working on many different fronts at once: church unity and reform; openness to the outside world; political change, especially affecting religious policy; social participation and involvement; Christianity and culture. These challenges shaped the ideas out of which the modern structure of Ting's theology emerged.

K. H. Ting's theology – ecclesiastically, ecumenically, politically, socially, and culturally – was a comprehensive approach to church renewal, openness, and reform. It is a theology grounded in the Bible, tradition, experience, and reason. It is a typically Anglican theology, of a certain type). He was concerned in the years after the Cultural Revolution to promote unity in church and society, with due attention to the "religious feelings" of Christians at the grassroots. To do this effectively, he had to reestablish and help "normalize" international church relations. He also had to give attention to the politics of the time, especially the policy of religious freedom and the critique of dogmatic "Leftist" thinking. He also had to make the Christian contribution to modernization and reform more widely recognized, and so there had to be a theology and a practice of social reform (hence, the Amity Foundation). This gave his theology a social-ethical orientation, similar to the theologies of his predecessors in the 1930s and 1940s, notably T. C. Chao and Y. T. Wu. Neither of them, however, had a theological structure similar to that of K. H. Ting. Christian theology for Ting had to be involved in a dialogue with culture, an ad hoc correlation of Christian faith in dialogue with modernity.

The theological alternative to Ting in the 1980s was the premodern or anti-modern theologies of the Christian fundamentalists and other sectarians. In the 1990s and beyond various kinds of post-modern or post-colonial theologies would challenge the theological modern, especially among liberal intellectuals. Ting's structuring of theology in a way that concretely addressed the issues of church and society steered a middle path between the pre- and post-modern, a *via media* of sorts. He would be seen as a "modernist" by the former and as somewhat old fashioned by the latter. Yet Ting saw the need for theology to address, in particular ways, a variety of issues all at once, in a time of restoration and rebuilding after years of chaos and turmoil.

K. H. Ting did not touch on many key theological issues, Anglican or otherwise, but then he was not a systematizer. And yet, it is unlikely that his achievement will be duplicated anytime soon. This is partly due to his personal charisma and the position of respect he held in church and society, nationally and internationally. But it also has to do with his vision and individual sense of purpose. By structuring a theology that would make a lasting contribution to church building, international church relations, reform of religious policy, the involvement of Christians in society, and cultural dialogue with the intellectual world, almost all at once, he set the stage for what would follow.

So was he an Anglican? The answer must be affirmative, and not only because he remained a duly consecrated bishop until his dying day. When they first met, Archbishop of Canterbury Robert Runcie said that Bishop Ting was an Anglican Bishop *plus* something, not *minus* anything. His was an enhanced Anglicanism, not a diminished Anglicanism (Wickeri 2007, p. 240). Ting presided over a post-denominational church. He may be called a "post-denominational Anglican," if that is not a contradiction in terms. K. nH. Ting's theology is grounded in China's post-denominationalism, but its personal and ecclesiological roots are Anglican and episcopal, enhanced by ecumenical commitment and political participation. His was a particular variety of an Anglican modern theology, comprehensive in scope and focused on its context.

Notes

1 This biographical information is from Wickeri 2007. Parts of this chapter draw on an unpublished conference paper, "K.H. Ting as a 'Modern' Theologian," Eighth International Symposium on the History of Christianity in Modern China, Hong Kong Baptist University, June 14–15, 2013.

2 This was also published as a separate pamphlet in Shanghai: The China Christian Council, 2000 (July).

3 My own discussion of Ting's theology may be found at different places in Wickeri 2007 and other writings. A recent study of Ting's theology is Chow 2013, in which chapter 4 discusses K. H. Ting's Cosmic Christ.

4 The term "theological reconstruction" or "the reconstruction of theological thought" is an English rendering of *shenxue sixiang jianshe*. The translation of the term as "theological reconstruction" is in the same spirit as the translation of the name of the former Chinese periodical *Zhongguo Jianshe* (*China Reconstructs*) a publication in which K. H. Ting published several essays in the 1950s. About the same time that Ting's *Selected Works* was published, political essays in China were using the term "ideological construction" (*sixiang zhengzhi jianshi*) to speak of the need to develop ideology and morality in the spirit of Jiang Zemin's vision

of socialism. As Ting writes in the afterword to the *Collected Works* (Ting 1998) he is offering a Christian theological contribution to this same overall effort. Some people now prefer the English term "theological renewal." It has a softer ring to it. My response is that had he wanted to speak of renewal, there were other perfectly acceptable Chinese terms he could have used.

References

Chow, A. (2013). *Theosis, Sino-Christian Theology and the Second Chinese Enlightenment: Heaven and Humanity in Unity.* New York, NY: Palgrave/Macmillan.

Ramsey, M. (1960). *From Gore to Temple: The Development of Anglican Theology Between Lux Mundi and the Second World War, 1889–1939.* London: Longman.

Ting, K.H. (1998). *Collected Works of K. H. Ting (Ding Guangxun Wenji).* Nanjing: Yilin Press.

Ting, K.H. (2000). *Love Never Ends: Papers by K. H. Ting* (ed. P. Wickeri). Nanjing: Yilin Press.

Wickeri, P.L. (1993). Reinterpreting Religion in China. *China News Analysis* 1485 (15 May): 1–9.

Wickeri, P.L. (1988). *Seeking the Common Ground: Protestant Christianity, the Three-Self Movement and China's United Front.* Maryknoll: Orbis Books.

Wickeri, P.L. (2007). *Reconstructing Christianity in China: K. H. Ting and the Chinese Church.* Maryknoll: Orbis Books.

Wickeri, P.L. and Cole, L. (eds.) (1995). *Christianity and Modernization: A Chinese Debate.* Hong Kong: Daga Press.

Wickeri, P.L. and Wickeri, J.K. (eds.) (2002). *A Chinese Contribution to Ecumenical Theology: Selected Writings of K. H. Ting.* Geneva: World Council of Churches.

Zhongmo, T. (2000). *A Modern View of the Bible (Chinese). Nanjing Theological Review* (October).

John A. T. Robinson (1919–1983)

Natalie K. Watson and Ian C. Browne

In this chapter we will discuss John Robinson's work as a theologian in the Anglican tradition. After a brief biographical sketch outlining the major milestones of Robinson's life, we will look at Robinson's work in the three main areas to which he made a substantial contribution to the life of the Church of England and to theological scholarship; we will look at Robinson as a biblical scholar and at his – perhaps less known – contribution to the development of worship and liturgy, before finally evaluating the ongoing value of the theological legacy of Robinson and his best-known work, *Honest to God*.

Life

John Arthur Thomas was born in Canterbury on June 15, 1919 as the first child of Arthur Robinson, a priest, and his wife Beatrice, nee Moore, a former nurse. He spent his early childhood in the Precincts of Canterbury Cathedral, where his father was one of the residentiary canons.

His father died in 1928, when John was already at prep school at Broadstairs. Following his father's death, the family's means were significantly reduced, and John had to move to a different and less expensive prep school before winning a scholarship for sons of the clergy to attend Marlborough. It was at Marlborough that his interest in theology and in a vocation to ordained ministry first emerged. In 1938, at the time of the Munich conference, he went up to Jesus College Cambridge to read divinity. In Cambridge, he joined the Student Christian Movement, and at its 1939 summer conference at Swanwick encountered the work of the German theologians that was to be profoundly influential for him.

Twentieth Century Anglican Theologians: From Evelyn Underhill to Esther Mombo, First Edition.
Edited by Stephen Burns, Bryan Cones, and James Tengatenga.
© 2021 John Wiley & Sons Ltd. Published 2021 by John Wiley & Sons Ltd.

As war was looming, he had to register for National Service, but as a candidate for ordination he was declared exempt. In Cambridge, John became a member of the Cloister Group, a regular gathering of pacifists and non-pacifists led by Charles Raven and William Temple. Temple, soon to be Archbishop of Canterbury until his untimely death in 1943, was a profound influence on the young ordinand.

Following graduation, Robinson was already showing promise as an academic theologian – he had completed his doctoral thesis on Buber's *I and Thou* – and was offered an academic position in the United States, which he declined. On the advice of George Bell, then Dean of Canterbury and a friend of the family, John decided to pursue ordination. His encounter with Mervyn Stockwood led to his curacy at St. Matthew's, Moorfields in Bristol, a poor area of the city, inhabited by low-skilled and low-paid working-class people. He was ordained deacon at Michaelmas 1945.

Following his curacy John took up the post of Chaplain at Wells Theological College, and in 1951 he returned to Cambridge to follow C. F. D. Moule as Dean of Clare College.

Robinson's former training incumbent and mentor Mervyn Stockwood was vicar of Great St. Mary's in Cambridge, and, when he became Bishop of Southwark, Stockwood invited Robinson to join him as Suffragan Bishop of Woolwich. The case for a young man of forty to become a bishop had to be argued with the Archbishop of Canterbury who thought Robinson's theological talents should be allowed to flourish for a few more years before preferment could be considered. Yet, it was precisely because of Robinson's theological mind that Stockwood wanted him as his suffragan. Stockwood eventually persuaded the Archbishop (and Robinson) to change his mind, and Robinson was consecrated at Michaelmas 1959.

One of Robinson's most important achievements during his time in the Southwark diocese was the development of the Southwark Ordination Scheme, a "theological college without walls," where young men continued to work in their professions during the day and followed a program of theological study and ministerial formation in the evenings and weekends. For Robinson, this came out of his experience as chaplain at Wells Theological College, where students frequently saw training for ordination as a way of retreating from the challenges of living in the world. In many ways, the Southwark Ordination Scheme was ahead of its time and anticipated later developments of non-residential training in the Church of England.

In 1969, Robinson returned to Cambridge to succeed H. A. Williams as Dean of Chapel. Robinson died from cancer in 1983.

There has been much speculation about why he was never invited to follow the path of the diocesan scholar–bishop of other Cambridge New Testament scholars like Lightfoot and Westcott, but instead resumed his academic career, and this is not the place to add to it, as we are primarily concerned with Robinson's achievements as a theologian for which his career in Church and academia provides the framework.

Biblical Scholar

For the greater part of his working life John Robinson was a diligent scholar and teacher of the New Testament. He came from a clerical dynasty, his father being a Canon of Canterbury, and his uncle, Joseph Armitage Robinson was a distinguished scholar of New Testament and Patristic texts. Like them, he was educated at Cambridge, and he saw himself as an exponent of a living tradition of careful scholarship that dated back over a century. He upheld the work of Joseph Lightfoot, B.F. Westcott, and Fenton Hort, who addressed the challenges posed by the arrival of biblical criticism from Germany. The Quest for the Historical Jesus, the Synoptic Problem, and the rejection of the traditionally accepted authorship and dates of New Testament texts came as a shock to the English-speaking world. Much of this criticism was perceived as destructive of faith. It marked a growing separation of academic theology and religious practice that would lead to the rejection of all criticism and the growth of an unquestioning fundamentalism. The response of these Cambridge scholars was not to reject all criticism but to use it in a carefully calibrated way to answer some of the questions raised by continental scholarship. The Revised Version of the Bible (1881) followed Westcott and Hort's scholarly Greek Testament text. Lightfoot defended the New Testament canon and the provenance of Paul's epistles and St. John. In so doing, they questioned the assumptions and rejected many of the more sensational assertions of German critics. In turn, they provided a defense of traditional authorship and dating of the texts based upon reasoned criticism rather than an unquestioning acceptance of tradition. Hoskyns and Davey's *The Riddle of the New Testament* (1931) and *The Fourth Gospel* (1940) maintained this theological culture in the early twentieth century. These were the scholars that John Robinson recommended to his pupils because he himself had been inspired so much by them. Of his contemporaries, he valued the works of C. H. Dodd: the *New English Bible* and his *Historical Tradition and the Fourth Gospel* and Joachim Jeremias for his careful work of the recovery of the figure and teaching of Jesus.

Robinson published biblical writings span a range of material reflecting his role as a parish priest and an academic theologian. His early works included *In the End God* (Robinson 1968) and *Jesus and His Coming* (1957) where he examined the *Parousia*. While these were studies for theologians he would also publish titles for a wider public. He never wrote a commentary but tackled the most influential of Paul's letters in, *Wrestling with Romans* (Robinson 1979). It contains a university lecture series produced in the form of what he termed a "conducted tour." Likewise *Can we trust the New Testament?* (Robinson 1977) contains the key ideas from *Redating the New Testament* (Robinson 1976) his most ambitious work.

It may come as a surprise to many that one who is chiefly known as a radical theologian from the 1960s should have produced a work that questioned the assured results of modern scholarship. Why did he question the theological status quo on the New Testament? While he certainly enjoyed himself outflanking conservative evangelical writers by advocating earlier dates and provenances for certain book than they this was not part of his purpose. In the introduction to *Redating the New Testament* (Robinson 1976) he describes the impact of radio-carbon dating upon the chronologies of ancient history and archeology. This new scientific method had shown that many of the assumptions used for dating remains and artifacts were inadequate and untested. The impact of Darwin's *Origin of Species* spread far beyond biology, so that evolution over time became a mode of explanation that dominated many disciplines: history, geography, geology, and political theory. The Liberal Protestant higher criticism adopted these ideas and assumed that complex theological ideas could only develop when primitive Christianity changed through the adoption of Hellenistic modes of thinking. Implicit in this was the historical Jesus who became the Christ of faith, early Christian statements of faith were simple and that the complex Christology belonged to later centuries. Once such ideas became the accepted norms, few people investigated them, and no one challenged them. This prompted him to open the whole question afresh and showed him being true to the academic traditions of the Cambridge scholars who were such a big influence upon him.

Robinson suggested that the destruction of the Temple in Jerusalem in 70 CE was one of the defining moments in the history of Christianity. Paul's genuine letters predate this, but the Gospels posed a more difficult problem because only Mark was generally dated before 70 CE. The discussion of the relationship between the Synoptic Gospels allowed for the transmission of Mark to later Jewish and Gentile communities resulting in the Gospels of Matthew and Luke. These were placed in the period of 75–85 CE. John's work was often titled the Fourth Gospel, which removed the name John and placed the work well into the second century. Robinson placed all three Synoptic Gospels within the 40–60 CE and thought there was little evidence for the destruction of the Jewish Temple. If Jesus had seen himself as the fulfillment of the Temple and sacrificial system, early Christians would have been able to portray the end of the temple as a vindication of their beliefs. No such claims are to be found in the Gospels. Robinson built upon the work of Dodd to show that the Gospel of John contains considerable historical detail. It is the only Gospel that provided an account of Jesus' several visits to Jerusalem. Its "high Christology," like that of the Letter to the Hebrews, has every indication of being of an early date. In a later book, *The Priority of John* (Robinson and Coakley 1984) completed by a research student J. F. Coakley, he developed the argument for John's early date and independent provenance.

In the New Testament he discovered a presentation of Jesus: "a faithful portrait – full of faith to be sure, but true also to fact" (Robinson 1977, p. 8).

Worship and Liturgy

Less known today than Robinson's work on the New Testament or his contribution to theology in the Church of England is his thought on worship and liturgy,[1] which was a major part of his work as college chaplain in Cambridge, both at Clare and later at Trinity:

> Worship is an expression of what we believe and we want to put it into our own language, not one that is far away from us. If we cannot put it into the same sort of language as that in which we live the rest of our lives, it compartmentalizes religion. We want in worship to be taken out of ourselves, but not into another culture (James 1987, p. 207).

Robinson's views on liturgy are most clearly expressed in his book *Liturgy Coming to Life*, in which the by-now Bishop of Woolwich reflects on the liturgical experiment at Clare College. He believed that genuine liturgical reform could only come "from the bottom upwards" and that a liturgical experiment in the local worshipping community is vital to the health of the Body of Christ (Robinson 1960, p. 15).

It seeks to describe how liturgy can come to life in both senses, so that Holy Communion may occupy its central and creative position in the common life of a community (Robinson 1960, Preface).

Robinson begins by admitting that "liturgy is not 'my line'" (Robinson 1960, p. 9) and by reminiscing about his own experience in theological college, where "there was no subject that seemed to be so remote from any living concern for the Gospel and its relevance to the modern world" than liturgiology. What was taught was "deduced entirely by precedent and pedigree, and there was no need to stop to ask whether it bore any relation to what the Spirit might be saying to the churches to-day" (Robinson 1960, p. 9). His own approach was then influenced by his experience as curate of a parish shaped by the Parish Communion movement where he began to see "the essential connection between liturgy and evangelism" (Robinson 1960, p. 10), and he later concludes: "It is in the Holy Communion supremely that the Gospel is shown forth: liturgy is the heart of evangelism" (Robinson 1960, p. 11). The eucharist is for Robinson the center of the gospel in action: it "is the crucible of the new creation, in which God's new world is continually being fashioned out of the old, as ordinary men and women are renewed and sent out as the carriers of Christ's risen life" (Robinson 1960, p. 22).

He rejected the "clericalization of the Eucharist" and argued that the body of Christ takes shape in the gathering of the eucharistic community, which is the action of the whole body of Christ, not of the celebrant or president alone: "There can be no communion without community, without *that* community" (Robinson 1960, p. 35).

His liturgical experiment was in fact closely connected with his fundamental theological project of making the Christian faith accessible to the secular world: "But we shall never break the thought-barrier between the Eucharist and the secular world, and so liberate the powers of the Eucharist into the secular world, until we have first removed that barrier *in church*" (Robinson 1960, p. 39): "For liturgy is nothing less than the gospel of the Word made flesh in action, Christ through his body about his saving work, taking the things of this world, and through the power of his sacrifice, leaving *none* of them untouched" (Robinson 1960, p. 44).

"It was a witness to the fact that the action of the Eucharist (. . .) is not something that can possibly stop in church. As it begins, in the offertory, with the thrust of the secular into the heart of the sacred, so it ends with the releasing of the sacred into the midst of the secular" (Robinson 1960, p. 77).

Theologian

John Robinson's first theological book was published in 1950, while he was chaplain at Wells Theological College. It was entitled *In the End, God . . .: A Study of the Christian Doctrine of the Last Things* (Robinson 1968). In it he identifies the starting point for most of his later theological work by identifying the chasm between established orthodox theological thought, imagery, and language and the world of modern "secular" human beings. His attempt to overcome and identify this chasm originates in his experience as a curate in Bristol, a world away from his sheltered Cathedral

Close and public-school upbringing, and his work at Wells Theological College, where he sought to engage students who thought they had come for a time of withdrawal to prepare for preaching the kingdom of God in a world beset with problems and essentially little interest in the Church.

It is not possible, in the space of this short chapter, to discuss in detail all of Robinson's theological books. Therefore I would like to focus on the work for which he is best known and remembered today, his 1963 *Honest to God* (Robinson 1963), which was to become one of the most sold and most widely discussed works of theology in the English language. Never before, and rarely thereafter, was a book on theology going to hit the headlines of the national newspapers. In *Honest to God* Robinson reflects on Christian doctrine, sexual ethics, and pastoral methods as they are encountered by the people of his time whose lifeworld is shaped by modern science. Robinson is convinced that Christianity has by no means had its day, but that it needs to rethink how it expresses itself:

> My sole concern is to question whether the doctrine must necessarily be expressed in certain images and categories which might have the effect for many of our generation to make it unreal (James 1987, p. 122).

> I want God to be as real for our modern secular scientific world as it was for the "ages of faith" (James 1987, p. 118).

While the actual content of the book like most of Robinson's work is of its time, we cannot underestimate the fact that Robinson as a bishop and therefore a representative of the established Church was prepared to write theology for his time and for the people of his time. It was probably not so much the content of the book itself but the fact that a bishop of the Church of England was giving people permission to think critically and to explore ways in which the Christian faith and the ethical teaching of the Church could be credible to the people of a modern secular society.

In terms of its content, *Honest to God* is a piece of ephemeral theological reflection that could easily have disappeared among many others, had it not been written by a bishop of the established Church. It is a piece of contextual theology with little in it that is new or original. Robinson essentially remains orthodox in his theology and conventional in his radicalism.[2] The author reflects on the work of three German theologians, who had only relatively recently come to the attention of an English-speaking audience. It is interesting to note that, while, as a biblical scholar, Robinson is rather critical of the work emerging out of nineteenth-century Germany, three German theologians, only recently published in England, Rudolf Bultmann, Paul Tillich, and Dietrich Bonhoeffer, make his theological project possible. In teaching theology to students today, it can be difficult to communicate the impact of these writers, whose work may appear somewhat dated now, and the thought worlds against which they reacted. What is significant is that Robinson writes what he writes, not as an academic theologian (though like Bultmann he was a noted New Testament scholar) nor as an outsider from the margins of the Church (not from prison like Bonhoeffer or from exile like Tillich) but from the very heart of an institution the days of which he sees as numbered, ecclesial establishment.

I would therefore like to suggest that we need to engage with *Honest to God* not so much in terms of its content but in terms of the history of its reception. At regular intervals, there have been commemorations of the publication of *Honest to God*, some of which homed in on the limitations and shortcomings of this short book, while others indulged in nostalgically looking back to the days of Southbank religion. Since its publication in 1963, *Honest to God* has been in print continually, and the range of readers it has attracted is rivaled by few, if any, theological books. We need to ask what constitutes the attractiveness of what is essentially a "tract for its time," and I would like to suggest that it is the question of the credibility of the Christian faith and of how the Church presents this faith that is at its heart. Although the issues that exercised the Church of Robinson's time may have been different from those of our day, the question of the integrity and the identity of the Church remains. Robinson's world was shaped by the Cold War, the Cuban Missile Crisis, the perceived threat of Communism and its rejection of religion, or even the raw memory of World War II and the Holocaust, while today's Anglican theologians find themselves in contexts that are shaped by complex relationships of different faith narratives and religions. In the 1960s, the established Church was beginning to discover that it could no longer take its privileged position for granted, something Bonhoeffer anticipated in the 1940s. It had to learn to engage with the "Other," the secular world, where Christianity was no longer the dominant narrative, though perhaps still part of collective residual memory, if only as the object of rejection. Our context in the twenty-first century is a different one: for many, Christianity or any religion has never been part of their lifeworld, while at the same time, some of the major conflicts in today's world are fought in the name of conflicting religious narratives. While Robinson's understanding of the secular and of religion are perhaps no longer of use for today's world, his question of the credibility, integrity, and identity of the Church is one that we need to ask in our own time.

Robinson and *Honest to God* have retained their place in the English theological imagination, and well beyond the Church of England. While this short book could so easily have been a flash in the pan of religious publishing, there are those who say that they owe their ability to continue to believe in God to it and its author. While *The Observer* announced its publication with the headline "Our image of God must go," it was certainly an attempt to engage with the idea that God himself had gone and that faith was no longer relevant. *Honest to God* and what followed may not have had the profundity of the challenge to do "theology after Auschwitz" of Moltmann and others, nor did it indulge in the language of mission, evangelism, and fresh expressions of church prevalent today, but it is perhaps a reminder of the lost art of theology in the public square, and thus a chapter on Robinson in a book on Anglican theologians is appropriate.

Notes

1   I would like to thank the Revd. Prof. Paul Ballard, a Baptist, for drawing my attention to this by telling me about his encounters with Robinson at Cambridge. Robinson writes that "Free Churchmen (sic.) must be made to feel that it is also their Chapel. Its liturgy and its clergy, indeed, are Anglican, but I am convinced from experience that it is also possible to go a very long way toward integrating them in a genuinely ecumenical

community, alike in worship and in witness." (Robinson 1960, p. 14).

2 Robinson anticipated such criticism in the Preface to *Honest to God*: "What I have tried to say, in a tentative and exploratory way, may seem to be radical and doubtless to many heretical. The one thing of which I am fairly sure is that, in retrospect, it will be seen to have erred in not being radical enough." (Robinson 1963, p. 10).

References

James, E. (1987). *A Life of Bishop John A. T. Robinson: Scholar, Pastor, Prophet.* London: SPCK.

Robinson, J.A.T. (1957). *Jesus and His Coming: The Emergence of a Doctrine.* London: SCM Press.

Robinson, J.A.T. (1960). *Liturgy Coming to Life.* London: A. R. Mowbray & Co.

Robinson, J.A.T. (1963). *Honest to God.* London: SCM Press.

Robinson, J.A.T. (1968). *In the End, God. . ..* London: Fontana.

Robinson, J.A.T. (1976). *Redating the New Testament.* London: SCM Press.

Robinson, J.A.T. (1977). *Can We Trust the New Testament?* London: Mowbrays.

Robinson, J.A.T. (1979). *Wrestling with Romans.* London: SCM Press.

Robinson, J.A.T. (1985). *The Priority of John.* London: SCM Press.

Robinson, J.A.T. and Coakley, J.F. (1984). *The Priority of John.* London: SCM Press.

John Macquarrie (1919–2007)

Ryan Kuratko

Is it so very difficult to entertain more than one idea at a time? Has Anglicanism, traditionally the *via media*, something to teach the other branches of the Christian Church on these matters?

(Macquarrie 1993, p. 142)

The Celt and Anglican: The Context of Macquarrie's Work

John Macquarrie begins his autobiographical reflection on his life and theology with a chapter-length sketch of the history and culture of the Celtic peoples before and after the birth of Christ (Macquarrie 1999, pp. 1–10). While this detour might seem an odd beginning to a brief, academically focused autobiography of a Scottish man born in 1919, the reflection is in character and on point for Macquarrie. A chorus of voices shapes every idea and life, and Macquarrie's theology listens and operates by weighing the importance of the voices that shape Christian doctrines. Reading his theology is like following a master composer who always begins composing with the harmony parts rather than with the theme; Macquarrie singles out the various voices that shape the polyphony around the doctrine before clarifying his chosen melody. In a text devoted to describing the relationship between his life and writings, he looks back thousands of years to search the topic first for the background sounds and noises out of which the tune of his life's work emerges.

Out of this Celtic background, Macquarrie believed that he gained his sense that all humanity shares a spiritual sensitivity to God's immanence in the world (Macquarrie et al. 1986, p. xi). This sense of immanence underlies Macquarrie's theology, both in his systematic and in his more practical texts. From this Celtic background, Macquarrie also learns to hear from more than one source at a time, to hear as a whole the

Twentieth Century Anglican Theologians: From Evelyn Underhill to Esther Mombo, First Edition.
Edited by Stephen Burns, Bryan Cones, and James Tengatenga.

discordant chorus of voices of Christian teaching. Much as early Celtic Christians could combine ancient practices with new ones, bringing old sacred stones into new church buildings, Macquarrie incorporates diverse expressions of faith in each construction of doctrine. His theology emerges at each stage from this cacophony of voices, and much as the stories of Brigid the saint incorporate the prestigious tales of Brigitta the Celtic goddess and turn them to Christian purpose, Macquarrie draws contemporary philosophy, ancient Christian formulations, and scripture into new kinds of harmony.

This defining quality, writing theology as a composition from a chorus of voices, is essential for understanding Macquarrie's context as a theologian. Macquarrie is shaped by a profound curiosity as much as by a sense of God's immanent presence in every dimension of the world, and he was able within his scholarly context to pursue these ends in systematic theology throughout his career.

His physical locations, primarily in Glasgow, New York, and Oxford, suggest a perspective of privilege, but a fuller picture of his life suggests a more complex context. Undoubtedly, his location granted him access to the leading theorists of the century, especially in existentialist philosophy and academic theology. Measured by influence and innovation, Macquarrie was one of the most important systematic theologians of the twentieth century in any denomination, and that success shaped his freedom to write from his position within an academic stronghold. Yet, this privilege belies other aspects of his context – a working-class upbringing, a disabled child, and military service as a chaplain for prisoners of war are all biographical details that point toward a more nuanced experience of human life than his prominent tenure at Oxford suggests.

Macquarrie was a prolific writer, and he strongly shaped his writing for each work's intended audience. Macquarrie often wrote for the church, articulating a language for faith that could be believable and of use to both philosophers and lay practitioners. With his early roots in the Church of Scotland, and longer tenures in the American Episcopal Church and Church of England, Macquarrie writes in ways shaped by these intended audiences. He responded to the worries of the church in these locations from the 1950s through the 2000s, influenced by such diverse topics as increased secularization, the ordination of women, the death of God movement, hippies, and a renewed focus on liturgy and the sacraments.

His writer's ear was also attuned to feedback from the church beyond the Anglican tradition and to the discipline of philosophy. He frequently quotes the responses of ecumenical and interreligious dialogue partners to his theology, and he clearly paid close attention to his reception in religious communities beyond the church. He also wrote for and remained open to critique from philosophers. He believed that theology has a role to play within the academy, as a deeper investigation into the metaphysics arising in philosophical reflection and as a phenomenological examination of the spiritual dimension of human life.

"I Learned More About Human Nature" (Macquarrie 1990, p. 14): Macquarrie's Biography and Writings

Macquarrie grew up in Renfrew, Scotland, a village near Glasgow and the River Clyde. On full scholarship, he studied at the University of Glasgow, finding his courses in mental philosophy far more satisfying than the study of theology. Nonetheless, he persisted in theology in part through the support of the woman who became his life-long wife, Jenny. He continued with ordination in the Church of Scotland and military service during World War II as a chaplain. His knowledge of German proved felicitous as he came to organize and administrate thirty German clergy in overseeing worship for German prisoners of war, who were held in camps in the Middle East. The work also introduced him to Islam in Egypt, Libya, and Palestine.

After his chaplaincy service, he returned to Scotland to work as a minister in Brechin, eventually beginning work on his PhD at the University of Glasgow at a distance. His academic work led to his taking a lectureship there in 1953. His early work builds on his German language expertise, and it examines Rudolph Bultmann's theological appropriation of Martin Heidegger's existentialist philosophy as a way to recover and rediscover Paul's theology. Both Bultmann and Heidegger proved lasting conversation partners for Macquarrie's thinking. Macquarrie came to believe that Bultmann's radical demythologizing of the New Testament placed an unsustainable divide between the details of Jesus' life and the fact of his existence, but Macquarrie finds insight in Bultmann's subjecting of revelation to intense inquiry as a way to evaluate Christian doctrine. Heidegger's expansive work in ontology and existentialism, particularly in *Being and Time* (of which Macquarrie was the co-translator into English), influenced Macquarrie's theology in many ways, not least through its thorough-going anthropological approach. While aware of the ethical conflict of engaging Heidegger's work (Heidegger remained in Germany during the Third Reich, and the ways his thought could be understood as a subtle support of Nazism has always dogged Heidegger's philosophy), Macquarrie seems to have believed Heidegger's work was insightful more than problematic. Heidegger's phenomenological method and particular insights remained influential on Macquarrie throughout his life, and Macquarrie continued to pair Heidegger's existentialism with other philosophical approaches as well as with close readings of Christian sources.

In 1962 Macquarrie moved to the Union Theological Seminary in New York as Professor of Systematic Theology. During this time, he was much influenced by a developing friendship with the New Testament scholar John Knox, who was ordained into the Episcopal Church not long after Macquarrie's relocation. Macquarrie developed a relationship with a diverse parish on the edge of Harlem (St. Mary's), and was ultimately ordained in the Episcopal Church by Bishop Horace Donegan in 1965. During his tenure at Union, Macquarrie wrote the first edition of *Principles of Christian Theology* (1966, revised as Macquarrie 1977). Other important writings include a survey of *Twentieth Century Religious Thought* (Macquarrie 1963) and a collection of essays on Christian existentialism. He also wrote a series of books responding to both cultural and academic problems of the time. *God-Talk* (Macquarrie 1967b) examines the nature of religious language as coherent and truth bearing rather than only emotive; *God and Secularity* (Macquarrie 1967a) responds to the "death of God" movement as well as secularism more broadly; and *Three Issues in Ethics* (Macquarrie 1970) responds to situational ethics and works to develop a clearer picture of the role of theology in ethics.

Theology must be systematic, Macquarrie argues, because its whole must be reasonable (rather than reduced to reason or entirely divorced from inquiry). The role of reason is not to construct metaphysical truths out of whole cloth, an approach that he sees as fruitless and discredited in the modern era, but nor is it simply to acquiesce to biblical stories whose scaffolding, myths, and constructions it can easily see. Rather, reason has the role of faith seeking understanding, always working to unpack the details and realities of faith in light of present conditions and ideas.

Macquarrie returned to the England in 1970 as the Lady Margaret Professor of Divinity at Oxford and Canon of Christ Church. He retired in 1986 and remained in Oxford, traveling for lectures and writing until the end of his life in 2007. His main works while at Oxford include systematic works and a number of bridging texts that connect theology with other voices and concerns. These include *Existentialism* (Macquarrie 1972a), an overview and evaluation of existentialist thought; *The Faith of the People of God: A Lay Theology* (Macquarrie 1972b) a way of doing theology that incorporates and replies to more academic treatments of doctrine with an approach styled more for and by people engaged in the diverse world; and *Paths in Spirituality* (Macquarrie 1973) that bridges more academic expressions of theology with practical piety and spirituality. *In Search of Deity* (Macquarrie 1984) emerged from Macquarrie's giving of the Gifford Lectures in 1983–1984 and argues for the doing of natural theology as a human phenomenon, and together with *In Search of Humanity* (Macquarrie 1982) and *Jesus Christ in Modern Thought* (Macquarrie 1990) was intended as a three-volume systematic approach to Christology. He also released several collections of essays during this period, including *Thinking about God* (Macquarrie 1975), which reflects on the nature and purpose of contemporary theology.

He was a prolific writer and continued writing after his retirement, turning toward completing some themes and texts begun at Oxford. Several are on Christology, which is the focus of *Jesus Christ in Modern Thought*, an extended treatment that begins with a historical examination of the elements of the doctrine of the incarnation, as well as *Christology Revisited* (Macquarrie 1998), which continues on themes begun in his earlier Christology. He also continued to write on areas of ecumenical and interreligious concern, like Mariology (Macquarrie 1991), sacraments (Macquarrie 1997), religious pluralism, and mysticism.

Macquarrie's later texts turn toward particular religious practices. He writes on the sacraments, contemplative practices, and more ecumenical themes. This last turn in his texts is notable because it draws out one of the full implications of his dual focus on existential and ontological concerns, or on subjective and objective elements of theological inquiry. Macquarrie insisted on the importance of both perspectives – theology must study something real in the ontological makeup of the world but also must be attentive to the ways that subjects are affected by that reality. Nowhere is this commitment clearer than in his last writings, where the self-consciously subjective approach to theology with its attendant methodological language blends cleanly into the practices that form the primary experience of most practicing Christians.

These late writings also make clearer the importance of community in Macquarrie's thought, a theme to which Macquarrie frequently returned. Macquarrie is clear that to be a subject is always already to be enmeshed and engaged in community. Faith must be, even in an individual life, about more than the individual. As important as this aspect is in Macquarrie's work, it remains in need of further development. While he argues that community holds a foundational role in spirituality, that the spiritual dimension of human life must always be inflected by and respond to the world and culture in which it finds itself, and that sacraments reflect the sacramental character of all creation (especially shaped by Jesus and Christian tradition), he never quite addresses the ways that the radical diversity within Christian communities might affect the legibility of sacraments in a profound way.

Holy Being and Relating to Christ: Central Themes in Macquarrie's Thought

The quantity and breadth of Macquarrie's writing as a theologian makes identifying only a few distinctive themes difficult. As an avowedly systematic theologian who argued that Christian doctrine must make sense as a whole, and that each part of theology must be seen in its relationship to the other parts and to the experience of human life, Macquarrie covers much ground. This brief treatment will not come close to touching on every interesting corner of his thought. The focus here is on two main themes that are determinative for this thought and because he intentionally worked systematically, these central themes turn up throughout his writing. These two central themes are: his understanding of God as Holy Being, and his emphasis in Christology on the need for relationship.

Holy Being, God, and Natural Theology

Macquarrie characterizes God as Holy Being, an understanding of God that he describes as akin to panentheism. God is not like a being in the world, subject to limit and duration in space and time. Rather, God interpenetrates all of Being. This formulation takes an element of Heidegger's philosophy, his analysis of Being, and consciously evolves it in a new direction, much as Macquarrie argues that Thomas Aquinas seeks to do with Aristotle's metaphysics.

Macquarrie argues for thinking of God as Holy Being as a way to balance a variety of different concerns in theology. Caution, however, is in order, as the word "Being" in English can give the misleading sense that Being (capital "B," Being as such) is treated as another being in the world (which defeats the insight of Macquarrie's argument). In one sense, Being itself does not "exist" (like an object in the world); rather, Being is the foundation, process, performance space and actors, and actual dynamism of existence. Literally nothing "is" outside it. Being is as much process and evolution as substance, and as much possibility as it is actuality. Precisely these distinctive markers of Being are part of what Macquarrie hopes to capture with the term Holy Being, namely, the way in which God is infinitely present and active in all aspects of creation and yet not reducible to them. Being is understood as the mystery that anything "is" at all and the creativity in which we live and move and have our individual beings.

Macquarrie sees panentheism as striking a middle way between pantheism, the sense that God is simply the immanent spirit of the world, and a more radically transcendent understanding of God that places divinity utterly beyond our created reality.

With a panentheistic view, we explore a paradox open to our reason, one which holds the tension of God's complete immanence and transcendence.

The qualifier "holy" in Holy Being indicates something learned in revelation (and not only Christian revelation), the disclosing or unveiling by Being of its own nature. Being is not neutral, a happenstance with no value to us or in itself, but is distinctive in the strength of its goodness, its awe-inducing loveliness, its pervasive uniqueness. Being is holy. Those things that move us into un-being, which denature ourselves and deny our full growth and capacities, are of sin, a fact available to any conscious being through serious reflection but given clearest shape in Christ. Those things that enable us to live in the full richness of Being are characteristic of love, which also finds its ultimate expression in Christ. Love, God's, and thus Holy Being's identity as disclosed in Christian revelation, has the character of "letting-be." Love "lets-be" not as we might imagine when we are influenced by sin, in the sense of leaving utterly alone. Rather, love "lets-be" in the same way God in the book of Genesis "lets-be" light, creatively, encouraging, and supporting each thing growing into itself in ever-growing and evolving relationship to everything else. Love literally makes us who are and who we become. Love is Holy Being.

Thinking of God as Holy Being has the benefit for Macquarrie of making sense of other religious lives and practices beyond Christianity. If Being itself is holy, then to participate in Being in any way is to share in a spiritual reality. Human beings have access to that spiritual reality in a different way than other parts of creation due to our consciousness, and so we have some capacity to respond and a richer existential need to be consciously shaped by God. Every human life has a spiritual dimension, and we should be unsurprised that the generosity of Holy Being appears in other religious traditions. At the same time, every religion may present its insights in radically different, even conflicting ways – history, as the unfolding of the possibilities of Being, is always particular and results in diversity as a mark of its success and not its failure. That difference continues to matter because each is a real enactment of Being.

Natural theology (or philosophical theology) is not for Macquarrie an academic construction of metaphysical first principles designed to engender belief but rather one of the most natural human phenomena. Natural theology is descriptive, a way of attempting to make sense of the spiritual dimension of beings within Being in a way accessible to reason. This way of approaching natural theology opens up systematic theology to particularly insightful descriptions of human life in any discipline, tradition, or history, in order to see how these ideas might further open up the possibilities of Being, but it also serves as a hermeneutic for rereading historic Christian doctrines, creeds, and writers. Every voice of the tradition has something to contribute when read in the right way.

While this present collection on Anglican theologians acknowledges the ambiguity and disagreement inherent in finding a "core" in Anglican theology, my sense is that one of its distinctive markers is this aspect of Macquarrie's thought: every voice, rightly heard, speaks of God, and the task of theology is finding hermeneutic methods that uncover God's gift in every voice. This principle invariably makes Anglican theology seem less distinctive – it unabashedly draws voices from outside itself, from history, and from other disciplines. Nonetheless, this drawing is distinctively Anglican, and Macquarrie exemplifies it well.

Christology and Relationship

Although Macquarrie writes extensively on Christology in different sets of categories (person and work, atonement, from above and below), the guiding concern throughout is the question of relationship: in what way can we come to know Christ, and what difference does that knowing make? Where, for Macquarrie, philosophical theology offers an entryway for reason into the spiritual dimension of Being, Christology, as symbolic theology (his preferred term rather than the older "dogmatic theology"), is fundamentally a process of clarifying a vision handed down through past doctrine, practices, and the Christian community. Christology uncovers the particular revelation of Jesus and is not, by contrast, a theoretical analysis of the conditions that would make possible the incarnation.

Because Christology responds to the particular occasion of Christ, it has a therapeutic character because it needs to respond to current human culture, concepts, and language, and the ways that these categories reveal or disguise Jesus as the Christ. Macquarrie worries that the primary impediment in the twentieth century is too strong a focus on Jesus' divinity and transcendence. Because of this diagnosis, much of his Christology attempts to unpack how we as human beings might see the humanity of Christ.

Macquarrie is sometimes criticized for too strong a focus on the humanity of Christ, or even of adoptionism, but the pattern of his whole thought reflects a concern not with, for example, whether the Chalcedonian formula has worth (it surely does in Macquarrie's thought), but what we contemporary human beings – influenced by the sciences, biblical criticism, and new understandings of history – can say about Jesus that reflects an authentic and life-changing relationship. Bare recitation of Chalcedon's "one person, two natures" is useless (or worse) if our conceptual categories have shifted such that it no longer opens up relationship to Jesus; we need new ways to speak old truths. Although Macquarrie's Christology evolves throughout his life, the thematic consistency is his concern for genuine, transforming relationship with the real person of Jesus, and cultivating language that clarifies and makes available Christ in our own day.

Because of this emphasis on Christ in our own day, his approach to Christology is divided between attempts to understand Christ in scripture and historical doctrines, and analyses of what difference Christ makes for us. As elsewhere in his thought, Macquarrie distinguishes in his systematic thought between ontological and existential differences. Christ brings God's redeeming grace into the world in a definitive way, a way that forever alters the nexus of beings, but as modern people, we need ways to conceive this shift that are not magical or mythical. Jesus reveals the deepest character of Holy Being as well as full human life, "empowers a change of direction, [and] brings the dynamic activity of God into the midst of human society" (Macquarrie 1977, p. 321). Jesus makes the crucial difference in the world. The story of Being is reinvigorated from the inside through the highest focus of Being into the full human life of Jesus, and this is an ontological shift.

Existentially, however, we must connect to this story for it to make actual differences within our lives. Macquarrie considers many ways that we build this relationship, including contemplative practices and scripture, but two in particular receive his strong attention. First, we relate to Jesus in the sacraments, symbols through which the whole of Being is made present. Mirroring the focus or thickness of Being in Christ, which shows the way in which full humanity can display the fullness of Being, the sacraments distribute the ontological change throughout time; they, too, can become an encounter with the fullness of Being. Macquarrie's own piety and autobiography turned at different points on the eucharist, and he frequently emphasizes the way that sacraments offer powerful occasions for relating to God through Jesus by re-presenting Jesus to the community. Second, Macquarrie argues that we meet Jesus in Christian community. Through encounters with other people who are themselves affected by relationships with Jesus, we ourselves come to see the effects of and come to know the freedom and grace that comes from relationship with Jesus.

In Macquarrie's therapeutic responses to Christological concerns, we see that the aim of Christology is not to have the right idea about Jesus but, by holding various thoughts in tension, experience a change of life and mind through relationship with God in Christ.

More than One Idea: Ongoing Engagement

Macquarrie's work continues to be influential in studies of natural theology and appropriations of German idealism, although anecdotally, I would note that many clergy I have met over the years remember his work much more fondly for his impassioned analyses of the sacraments and prayer than his more explicitly doctrinal work. In both the natural and sacramental theology, Macquarrie's reasoned defense of a spiritual dimension inherent to human experience remains a lively resource.

Also, in nearly all of his texts, Macquarrie reflects on the ways Christians should understand people of other religious traditions. His perspective evolves over time from his first encounters with Islam during his military service, to the simplistic typology of *Principles*, to the more considered approach of *The Mediators* (Macquarrie 1995).

While he shares the twentieth century's growing awareness of religious plurality and its tensions, Macquarrie is striking in his understanding that these other religious communities and their ideas belong in *theology*, rather than simply ethics or apologetics. The need for this type of engagement has become more pressing than in Macquarrie's context – increasingly, Christians are more self-aware about the multiplicity of cultures we share, even within each person. Our actual beliefs and practices often mix, and likely always have mixed, a variety of religious practices and ideas. *Vipassana* meditation and yoga mingle with doctrines of sin and prayer.

Macquarrie's direct forays into comparative theology, by, for example, attempting to distill a common theology of mediation from the world religions in *Mediators*, are not as promising for ongoing engagement as his more general theological method. One of Macquarrie's key insights for comparative theology is his method for working with ideas from different sources. The quotation heading this chapter, which comes from an exasperated reflection on the need think about spirituality in a holistic way, is deeply revelatory of Macquarrie's overall method in writing theology. In working to find a *via media*, Macquarrie insists that what theology needs is the ability to entertain multiple visions at the same time. This is true when working with Heidegger's philosophy, the council of Chalcedon, and biblical scholarship, but it is also true in Macquarrie's thought upon encountering other religious communities and ideas.

Where his method continues to show promise is in the insight derived from entertaining more than one idea at a time. The mechanics of this work are clearest in his self-consciously ecumenical work, particularly with the Roman Catholic Church, where dialogue with Catholic theology informs his own writing without making Catholic theology immune to criticism. This method is essentially the same as Macquarrie's approach to Heidegger's philosophy. He holds different ideas at once, shaping dialogue to the benefit of the reader without reducing real and distinctive differences. This same approach shows promise in comparative theology, where Christian theology can gain by learning from its neighbors. Rather than a single system to understand each idea, or the self-deception of double-thinking, Macquarrie's generous way of holding more than one idea at a time remains a fruitful resource for building dialogue and theology reflective of a diverse world, concerns that fueled Macquarrie's writing throughout his life.

References

Macquarrie, J. (1963). *Twentieth Century Religious Thought*. London: SCM Press.

Macquarrie, J. (1973). *Paths in Spirituality*. New York: Harper Row.

Macquarrie, J. (1967a). *God and Secularity*. London: Lutterworth.

Macquarrie, J. (1967b). *God-Talk: An Examination of the Language and Logic of Theology*. London: SCM Press.

Macquarrie, J. (1970). *Three Issues in Ethics*. San Francisco, CA: HarperCollins.

Macquarrie, J. (1972a). *Existentialism: Theological Resources*. London: SCM Press.

Macquarrie, J. (1972b). *The Faith of the People of God: A Theology of the Laity*. London: SCM Press.

Macquarrie, J. (1975). *Thinking About God*. London: SCM Press.

Macquarrie, J. (1977). *Principles of Christian Theology*. London: SCM Press.

Macquarrie, J. (1982). *In Search of Humanity: A Theological and Philosophical Approach*. London: SCM Press.

Macquarrie, J. (1984). *In Search of Deity: An Essay in Dialectical Theism*. London: SCM Press.

Macquarrie, J., Kee, A., and Long, E.T. (1986). *Being and Truth: Essays in Honour of John Macquarrie*. London: SCM Press.

Macquarrie, J. (1990). *Jesus Christ in Modern Thought*. London: SCM Press.

Macquarrie, J. (1991). *Mary for All Christians*. London: Fount.

Macquarrie, J. (1993). *Paths in Spirituality*. London: SCM Press.

Macquarrie, J. (1995). *The Mediators*. London: SCM Press.

Macquarrie, J. (1997). *A Guide to the Sacraments*. London: SCM Press.

Macquarrie, J. (1998). *Christology Revisited*. London: SCM Press.

Macquarrie, J. (1999). *On Being a Theologian: Reflections at Eighty*. London: SCM Press.

John Stott (1921–2011)

Mark Meynell

John Stott might be described as an anomaly for several reasons, but one is beyond doubt. He was an *Anglican* anomaly. This is not to suggest that he recoiled from his Anglicanism. Far from it, since he often took great pains to explain his commitment to the Church of England. It is simply because nobody else made a comparable impact on global Anglicanism while following such an unusual career path.

Ordained deacon when aged twenty-four, Stott only ever ministered in one parish: All Souls, Langham Place, at the affluent heart of central London. In fact, he spent almost his entire life there, having been first taken with his family at the age of two and remaining a member until his retirement to St. Barnabas College aged eighty-six. He became Rector at All Souls at twenty-nine, yet never attained higher ecclesiastical office, nor was he ever elected to General Synod (or its predecessor, the General Assembly). He wrote prolifically and widely, was awarded three honorary doctorates and a Lambeth DD, yet never held a prestigious academic post. Finally, his global reputation rests firmly on his commitment to a consensual evangelicalism – he has been grouped together in an incongruous triumvirate of twentieth century, anglophone evangelicalism's most formative influences (the others being Billy Graham and C. S. Lewis, despite the latter not adhering to classic features of evangelicalism[1]) – yet of the three, Stott arguably had the greatest impact in the Majority World. Michael Cromartie once described his friend to the renowned *New York Times* columnist David Brooks, with a tongue not far removed from his cheek, "If evangelicals could elect a pope, Stott is the person they would likely choose" (Brooks 2004, p. 30). Stott would jokingly rebuke Cromartie for such flippancy but Brooks' article certainly brought him to wider attention. In the very next year he was astonished to be numbered in the "2005 Time 100" of the world's most influential people, with an endorsement by none other than Billy Graham (Graham 2005). That list rarely includes religious leaders, especially those from outside the United States, unless a conclave has elected them to the Throne

Twentieth Century Anglican Theologians: From Evelyn Underhill to Esther Mombo, First Edition.
Edited by Stephen Burns, Bryan Cones, and James Tengatenga.
© 2021 John Wiley & Sons Ltd. Published 2021 by John Wiley & Sons Ltd.

of St. Peter (Pope Francis has appeared five times, to date, Benedict XVI three times). For it to happen to a British parish incumbent seems almost absurd.

Yet, for many around the world, Stott's churchmanship was unexpected and even problematic. Within both the Church of England as well as within the looser networks of evangelicalism, his theological commitments were often seen as incongruous if not incompatible with contemporary Anglicanism. For some, he was too evangelical, for others too Anglican. This tension lay sometimes in parallel, sometimes in convergence, with his interlocutors from the liberal and conservative wings within Anglicanism. On this, he wrote:

> Some on the right wing have already dismissed me as a quasi-liberal . . ., while others to the left of me regard as much too conservative for their liking. I often find myself caught in the cross-fire between these groupings (Edwards and Stott 1988, p. 34).

As someone who doggedly pursued broad consensus around the confessional core of what he took to be Reformation, and therefore historic, biblical, Christianity, this may well have reassured him. Stott certainly did not see a contradiction between his theology and his ordination. Quite why and how will be the focus of this chapter.

Evangelical Influences: Stott in Context

As yet, there has been only one significant scholarly attempt to engage with the significance of Stott's ministry, although of course many others have assessed his legacy in the course of broader histories and analyses (Stanley 2013; also Hastings 2001; more anecdotally, Barclay 1997). Alister Chapman's *Godly Ambition: John Stott and the Evangelical Movement* (Chapman 2014) identifies, with masterly concision and insight, how much Stott both reflected, and yet also challenged, the culture of his era.

In his early years, at least, he exuded British establishment values. Groomed to serve the empire, even in its twilight, through his exclusive private education at Rugby and then Cambridge University, he began with every advantage, and burden of responsibility, associated with his class. His senior military surgeon father expected a career in diplomacy; his conversion at sixteen to evangelical Christianity (through the ministry of E. J. H. Nash, known by friend and foe alike as "Bash") led to lifelong Christian ministry. As he wrote in his teenage diary, "Up till now Christ had been on the circumference and I have but asked Him to guide me instead of giving Him complete control" (Dudley-Smith 1999, p. 96). In those words are the seeds of a dynamic that operated throughout his life. Wherever there might be a tension between the establishment or received opinion and his understanding of a Christ-determined ethic or viewpoint, the latter would trump the former, sometimes at great personal cost. But his new-found beliefs crystallized in what would come to be described by David Bebbington as the evangelical quadrilateral: *conversionism* (the need for all to be changed), *activism* (conversion results in service), *biblicism* (a high view of the Bible), and *crucicentrism* (stress on the centrality of Christ's sacrificial death on the cross)

(Bebbington 2003, pp. 2–3). Throughout his ministry, Stott would preach and write frequently on all four of these themes. Indeed, we might identify at least one of his fifty or more published works for each corner of the quadrilateral:

- *conversionism*: *Confess Your Sins: The Way of Reconciliation* (Stott 1964); also, the university mission talks that became his best-selling *Basic Christianity* (Stott 1958, revised 1991)
- *activism*: *Christian Mission in the Modern World* (Stott 1975, revised 1977)
- *biblicism*: *The Bible: Book for Today* (Stott 1982)
- *crucicentrism*: *The Cross of Christ* (Stott 1986b).

For all the developments and shifts in his thought, he would never be shaken from these priorities. He was a lifelong, unashamed evangelical. Stott himself would frequently defend:

> the contemporary Evangelical emphasis on the Bible and the cross, and on the finality of both. It is not because we are ultra-conservative, or obscurantist, or reactionary or other horrid things we are sometimes said to be. It is because we love Jesus Christ and are determined, God helping us, to bear witness to his unique glory and absolute sufficiency (Stott 1979, p. 32).

Nash's central, if controversial, strategy for restoring evangelicalism's rightful place (as he saw it) at the heart of Anglicanism, was to reach boys in top private schools. Over the decades, hundreds were drawn into the vacation camps at Iwerne Minster, in Dorset. As Rugby's head boy and then a double-first Cambridge student, Stott epitomized the ideal Iwerne man. Iwerne challenged few features of that elite culture apart from the personal appeal to put Christ first. It would probably never even have occurred to Stott to consider ministry in any denomination other than the Church of England.

Stott was to prove entirely willing to resist prevailing mores, however. By the 1939 declaration of war on Nazi Germany, Stott, like Nash, had become a pacifist. With military conscription, at the age of twenty, fast approaching, his only alternatives to fighting were either to register as a conscientious objector (which might possibly lead to imprisonment) or train for ordination (for whom military service was exempted). To his father's fury, he chose the latter, and so moved from Trinity College, Cambridge to the nearby, Ridley Hall. His relationship with his father would never fully recover.

He was also willing to break out of the mold set by his mentors. The Cambridge theology faculty was predominantly liberal and "something of a graveyard for evangelical religion," according to Stott's biographer (Dudley-Smith 1999, p. 181). This undoubtedly contributed to evangelicalism's deep-rooted anti-intellectualism, embodied by Nash himself. They had witnessed too many getting swayed out of their allegedly obscurantist and outmoded beliefs. Where they had to undertake theological studies, many "survived" through fulfilling minimal requirements while essentially ignoring the implications of what was taught. Stott refused to follow suit. As former Archbishop of Canterbury Robert Runcie would reflect years later, "Stott had a brilliant mind, had been taught in the best Cambridge tradition of liberal theology, and had secured a first-class degree . . . The trouble was, he didn't believe it!" (cited in Dudley-Smith 1999, p. 183). Instead, he was committed to a high view of scriptural authority, and therefore had to work exceptionally hard with little help to do justice to the theological bombardment without losing the integrity of his convictions. Far from being obscurantist, however, he was determined to hold only to whatever he had become convinced of. He subsequently described the challenge of reaching such conclusions as resulting in "pain in the mind" (Dudley-Smith 1999, p. 183), but the discipline to persevere in such a process continued throughout his working life. So, for example, he was determined to do justice to the revolution in Pauline studies advanced by E. P. Sanders and others when writing his Romans commentary (for the *Bible Speaks Today* series). He was already in his seventies but worked every hour he could on it.

> I spent all the time I could on Romans. Since it is a storm centre of contemporary controversy, in which old traditions are facing new challenges, I have found my studies at times a painful struggle (Dudley-Smith 2001, p. 411).

Perhaps the aspect of evangelicalism with which non-evangelicals most take issue is the commitment to conversionism. Care to clarify terms is required here. An appeal, say, to "come to Christ to be born again" might seem to many too crude, socially intrusive, or aggressive for an authentically Christian ministry, while for others it is entirely unnecessary (especially where theologies akin to baptismal regeneration are the norm). However, Stott was consistently careful to condemn any evangelistic methodologies that manipulated or cajoled. He was clear that evangelism "is neither to convert people, nor to win them, nor to bring them to Christ, though this is indeed the first goal of evangelism. Evangelism is to preach the gospel" (Stott 1975, p. 39). He was adamant, therefore, that there is a message to declare at the very least, with propositional content, while always recognizing that Christianity is far more than mere propositions. A failure to do so would result in what he frequently termed "Our Guilty Silence" (the title of Stott 1967).

> The gospel is not good advice to men, but good news about Christ; not an invitation to us to do anything, but a declaration of what God has done; not a demand, but an offer (Stott 1967, p. 70).

Once that offer has been made, the onus for a response lies with the individual hearer, under the aegis of the Holy Spirit. Whether it came at a crisis point or over a period mattered little; the crucial point is that, at some point, a person must make the kingdom step of repentance and faith. Stott held to this throughout his ministry. In the early years, his name was especially associated with "mission weeks" to university campuses, initially in the United Kingdom, but eventually all over the world. He led over fifty of these campaigns, and even after declining energy levels and accumulating commitments prevented him from continuing, he never lost his support of them. Few others with his intellectual caliber and leadership ability sustained this kind of passion. Lest any claim that such a commitment was inconsistent with Anglicanism, Stott would happily have appealed to the 1945 report, *Toward the Conversion of England*.

Under the auspices of Archbishop William Temple, and then dedicated to him after his death, Bishop Christopher Chevasse chaired its working group, thus making it explicit that evangelism was a necessary responsibility for Anglicans. The report certainly galvanized the small evangelical presence in the denomination to renewed evangelistic endeavor.

Nevertheless, for all the theological and ecclesiastical assaults that might have undermined him, an Evangelical he remained. The question is, how did its broader commitments square with his Anglicanism?

Anglican Commitments: Stott in Ministry

Stott was clear that he was a Christian first, evangelical second, and Anglican third, only because "the Church of England is the particular historical tradition or denomination to which I belong" (cited in Reid 1986, and used as an appendix in Stott 2008). Denominations could never claim an exclusive purchase of the truth, not least because to do so would be to succumb to the medieval trap of equating the divine kingdom with the visible body. As he wrote, "denominationalism is hard to defend" (Reid 1986, p. 17). Yet it would be a significant error to assume that his "cradle to grave" Anglicanism was the product of inertia or thoughtless acquiescence. To leave something so basic to a mere default would have been entirely out of character, even if in the early years of his ministry he is unlikely to have considered Non-conformity.

The more he evaluated his churchmanship, the more he gained strength from the precedent of his personal hero, Charles Simeon of Cambridge (1759–1836). He would often call himself "a Sim," as Simeon's acolytes called themselves. Simeon had been a lifelong fellow of King's College, Cambridge, but more importantly, influenced generations of Cambridge students through his biblical expository preaching at Holy Trinity church, nearby. In an introductory essay to that ministry, Stott wrote, "Simeon's uncompromising commitment to Scripture captured my imagination and has held it ever since" (Stott 1986a, p. xxvii).

The parallels between the two men are uncanny, despite the separation of two centuries. Gary Jenkins summarizes:

> Two men, both bachelors, both Cambridge-educated, both from upper-middle-class homes . . . Neither was married, neither was promoted to high office, and neither moved from their initial parochial base. Both were the undisputed leaders of the Anglican evangelicals of their day, both were accomplished preachers, and both sought to help, encourage and train a new generation of preachers in the art of preaching a certain kind of sermon (Jenkins 2012, p. 3).

Stott was unabashed about acknowledging his debt to Simeon's model of text-shaped preaching. Yet it is equally clear that Simeon shaped Stott's evangelical approach to committed Anglicanism.

In a lecture on Simeon, former Archbishop Donald Coggan remarked: "He loved the Church of England. He loved its liturgy and he was content to live and die a son of the Church of England, even though within that Church he suffered so much and saw so much that was weak and unworthy in its priests and people" (cited in Carr 2000, p. 160).

Much the same can be said of Stott, although his ordeals were far less overt; he never had to endure, as Simeon had, being regularly pelted with rotten eggs or being locked out of his pulpit by irate church wardens. Furthermore, Paul Carr comments, "It is widely accepted that Simeon, by his loyalty to the Church of England, was instrumental in keeping evangelical Anglicans within the fold rather than following the Dissenters into Non-conformity" (Carr 2000, p. 160). Yet again, where Simeon had blazed before, Stott diligently followed. At least one generation of British evangelicals was convinced to find their home in the Church of England both by Stott's cogent arguments and, even more importantly, by his example.

The challenges afflicting the Church of England in the late eighteenth century were of course different from those of the mid-twentieth century. What they do have in common, however, was the sense of marginalization experienced by many evangelicals. Stott commented about his own experience:

> When I was ordained in 1945, soon after the end of World War II, there were few evangelicals in the Church of England. For over a century Anglo-Catholic thought had predominated, though weakened by liberal theology . . . There were no evangelical bishops and no evangelical theological teachers in any university. The few evangelical clergy there were fought bravely, but had their backs to the wall. The evangelical movement was despised and rejected (Dudley-Smith 1999, p. 217).

That this was far from the case half a century later is in large part due to Stott's influence.

But what of his ecclesiology? Evangelicals in general have occasionally been chastised for an apparently weak doctrine of the church. This becomes especially apparent in evangelical Anglicans because of the frequent recourse to the explicitly pragmatic (and therefore sociological) argument that the Church of England, as the established church, is "the best boat to fish from." It is an argument that extends back even to Simeon's day (for example, Grass 2008, p. 99).

It should be noted that when the accusation is made, however, the common objection is not so much a weak ecclesiology as simply a rejection of a more Catholic (in the denominational sense) doctrine. So for Stott, the Oxford movement was an unhelpful, if understandable, attempt to bring renewal to a spiritually lethargic and arid, church. So, in his dialogue with David Edwards, he contrasts his own understanding of catholicity with that of high church theologians.

> If "Catholic" merely describes those who value the Christian tradition as a precious heritage, who have a high view of the Church and its two gospel sacraments, and who find that the externals of architecture and liturgy, as well as the example of the saints, speak helpfully to them, then again I take my place beside you as a Catholic. But would Catholics (whether Anglican or Roman) accept your definition as adequate? Confining myself now to the Anglican Church, the Catholicism which I cannot myself accept, and which is still held by

many, teaches (for example) that the historic episcopate is indispensable to a true Church; that Scripture is neither supreme in its authority nor sufficient for salvation, since it needs to be supplemented by tradition that a baptism is a "christening" since it makes people Christian irrespective of their repentance and faith; that the "inner reality" of the bread and wine is changed into Christ's body and blood, and therefore Christ is in some sense contained and localised in the consecrated elements; and that in the Eucharist we share in the sacrifice of Christ, meaning not that we share in its benefits and offer ourselves in humble gratitude (our sacrifice being a response to his), but that we share in the actual offering of it (our sacrifice blending with his). Such things cannot be proved from Scripture; Evangelicals believe that Scripture rather excludes them (Edwards and Stott 1988, p. 38).

With such statements, Stott barely diverts from the Church of England's reformed roots as they coalesced in the Elizabethan Settlement, nor indeed, from the Lambeth Quadrilateral of 1888.[2] He would be explicit about this reformation heritage, even regularly preaching from the 39 Articles at All Souls. To curious US friends, he would often explain his denominational allegiance as grounded in "a commitment to history and a commitment to geography," by which he meant being conscious both of standing within the tradition of reformed, confessional Christianity and of ministering within a parish system that bears responsibility for every parishioner regardless of church attendance.

Yet he was quite prepared for the denomination to be mixed, accepting the implications of what was termed Anglicanism's "comprehension." In contrast to the extreme responses to being in a mixed denomination (that of separation in the pursuit of doctrinal purity or compromise through a passive resignation to differences) he advocated this better way. This sought to "pursue truth and unity simultaneously, that is to pursue the kind of unity commended by Jesus Christ and his apostles, namely unity in truth" (Chartres 2011, p. 13). Here he resorts to Alec Vidler's helpful summary:

The principle of comprehension is that a church ought to hold the fundamentals of the faith, and at the same time allow for differences of opinion and interpretation in secondary matters, especially rites and ceremonies . . . (cited in Chartres 2011, p. 15).

Stott sought to put this principle into practice. He regarded that "the way of the Holy Spirit with the institutional church is more the way of patient biblical reform than of impatient rejection" (Stott 1977, p. 163). He stood out from contemporary evangelicals both because of his willingness to reflect theologically with some sophistication, but also because he combined this intellect with an innate political nous. This resulted in the formation of many influential organizations, several of which outlasted him. Many had a specific Anglican focus. For example, he revived the Eclectics Society in 1955, first inaugurated by John Newton in 1783 as a forum for friendship and mutual encouragement among young evangelical clergy. Stott limited membership to those under forty to keep numbers sufficiently small to foster trusted relationships, but this simply meant various offshoots were established around the country (Dudley-Smith 1999, pp. 305–308). In contrast to that closed (and perhaps occasionally cliquey) society,

Stott was instrumental in inaugurating both the Church of England Evangelical Council (CEEC) in 1960 and the Evangelical Fellowship of the Anglican Communion (EFAC) in 1961.

The concern frequently articulated, however, both by free church evangelicals and more conservative Anglicans, was whether or not comprehension came at the expense of too much compromise. The dramatic events of two national conferences are instructive.

In October 1966, the Non-conformist minister of Westminster Chapel, Martyn Lloyd-Jones, presented an address to the Evangelical Alliance's National Assembly of Evangelicals. John Stott was in the chair. Despite being over twenty years Lloyd-Jones' junior, the two men shared a great mutual respect, so much so that earlier that year, Lloyd-Jones made a stunning offer: "I would like you to be my successor at Westminster Chapel." Stott was astonished. "While I am greatly honoured, I have no sense of calling to leave All Souls', or indeed the Church of England" (Steer 2009, p. 131). This private commitment was given a public airing just months later.

Lloyd-Jones had given some warning to the conference committee about his intended message. While expressing concern for Christianity's cultural decline in Britain, he criticized those who were "content to be an evangelical wing of a territorial church, hoping to infiltrate and show others they are wrong." His intended target was not hard to discern. So without detailing what he envisaged, Lloyd-Jones called for "something new," "a fellowship or association of evangelical churches" (Chapman 2014, p. 93).[3] Immediately after the end of the address, Stott took the unusual step of commenting on what had just been said.

> I believe history is against what Dr Lloyd-Jones has said . . . Scripture is against him, the remnant was within the church not outside it. I hope no one will act precipitately . . . We are all concerned with the same ultimate issues and with the glory of God (Murray 1990, p. 525).

This action marked a turning point. It steeled the resolve of many Anglicans evangelicals unsettled by the furore caused by the publication of Bishop John Robinson's *Honest to God* three years earlier, and Archbishop of Canterbury, Michael Ramsey's "Common Declaration" with Pope Paul VI in Rome six months earlier.

In April 1967, a thousand delegates assembled at Keele University for the National Evangelical Anglican Congress. This was very much a product of Stott's various initiatives. The CEEC organized it, while undergirding its preparations and leadership were the Eclectics, which Stott subsequently described as "the driving force behind" both the 1967 congress and its follow up in Nottingham in 1977 (Dudley-Smith 1999, p. 308). According to Chapman, Stott had anticipated a CEEC-orchestrated event, with speakers merely directing delegates to agreed policies or strategies. Ironically, it was younger clergy from the Eclectics (Stott was by now too old for membership) who argued strongly for more public debate (Chapman 2014, pp. 95–96). A sign of the times, perhaps, so this was conceded, and many worked with Stott overnight to draft a congress statement. The most significant consequence of Stott's appeal to leave the comfortable, evangelical "ghetto" was a reinvigorated evangelical confidence about entering into the denominational structures. Stott's commitment to

Anglicanism could not have been clearer. Unfortunately, many ties with those in the free churches were impaired, broken perhaps for a generation, by their perception of denominational unity taking precedence over theological unity. Within global Anglicanism, it laid the ground for growing influence, especially among Evangelical Anglicans in North America and Australasia.

After such relentless activity and widespread influence within global Anglicanism, it is perhaps surprising that Stott was never raised to the episcopate. Opinions vary, with some suggesting that he would have declined, others that he was disappointed not to be approached. There is little doubt that Ramsey (as both Archbishop of York and subsequently of Canterbury) was reluctant to promote evangelicals. He remarked to the then Prime Minister, Harold Macmillan, that "while evangelicals had their part in the Church he did not think that on the whole they had the qualities suitable for being bishops" (Dudley-Smith 2001, p. 43). Nevertheless, as more evangelicals were appointed to higher office in the subsequent decades, Stott's efforts had surely laid the groundwork (Dudley-Smith 2001, p. 461, note 95). Furthermore, Stott's global influence would surely have been severely restricted had he been burdened with relentless diocesan duties. Perhaps unsurprisingly, the more his itinerant ministry grew, the less influence he had on his home turf in Britain. In the 1980s and 1990s, a generation of Evangelical Anglicans rose up without the loyalty to Stott shared by their predecessors.

We have noted how Stott frequently articulated his evangelical theology in reformation terms, thus aligning himself with the historic beliefs of Anglicanism. He was tireless in his efforts to develop new generations of evangelical leaders across the world, but especially in the Church of England and the Anglican Communion. But there is one aspect of Stott's ministry that proves him to be the most Anglican of all. Its roots are no doubt complex, perhaps influenced by German thought for one thing (he read French and German at Cambridge). His thought process invariably resorted to the classic Hegelian dialectical approach, with its goal of a synthesis from initial thesis and its antithesis. He would frequently appeal for what he called BBC (in a winking reference to All Souls' neighbor in Broadcasting House), or "Balanced Biblical Christianity." The danger of course is that the proponent invariably locates his or her case as the neatly correct one with an inevitability that was perhaps not so evident previously. It would also frustrate those over the years who felt that this desire for consensus prevented him from taking decisive action where that might be required.

There were of course tensions and developments along the way. A particularly painful example occurred when an All Souls curate, Michael Harper, was one of the first Anglicans in Britain to have what previously had been most associated with Pentecostalism, a "baptism in the Spirit." While Stott was prepared to learn more despite initial skepticism, it did lead to a rupture, and Harper left to become one of the founders in 1964 of the Fountain Trust which sought charismatic renewal in "the historic churches." Much of contemporary Anglicanism, certainly in England, sustains more of a general charismatic flavor than it does of Stott's more cerebral approach. Another All Souls curate in the 1960s, the New Zealander Ted Schroder challenged Stott in another direction, this time with more success. He pushed Stott to engage with the social and cultural issues of the day in his preaching, thus setting him on a trajectory that led to his significant contribution to the Lausanne Congress in 1974 and beyond. At the congress, he urged the convenor Billy Graham to allow for a mission commitment that was much broader than simply evangelism and discipleship, especially because of the testimonies of African and Latin American leaders seeking to reach societies enduring turmoil and dictatorships. Much of his thinking on the subject would be encapsulated in his 1992 book, *The Contemporary Christian* (Stott 1992).

For all the shifts and developments, however, Stott never moved from his Evangelical moorings. He was always careful to listen to differing viewpoints, and meticulous in his desire to do them justice especially when countering them in public. This is not to say that he would then resort to the midpoint between two poles – he would relish the paradoxes of a both/and position which he regarded as central to the Bible's method. But there is something quintessentially Anglican about this *via media* approach, derived no doubt from the challenge of working within a comprehensive and mixed church. The fact that he did with such grace, humility, and generosity of spirit is the reason why he was so respected and even loved.

Notes

1 See for example https://religionandpolitics. org/2012/05/01/john-stott-c-s-lewis-j-r-r-tolkien-why-american-evangelicals-love-the-british (accessed July 15, 2020); and an account of the one occasion on which all three met: Mark Meynell, *To Have Been A Fly On the Wall*, https://www.markmeynell. net/2009/10/20/to-have-been-a-fly-on-the-wall-graham-stott-lewis-in-1955 (accessed July 15, 2020).

2 While he regarded episcopacy as perfectly compatible with the biblical theology, he firmly rejected the insistence on it "as a condition of union with other churches" (Stott 2013, p. 79).

3 Chapman (2014, p. 93).

References

Barclay, O. (1997). *Evangelicalism in Britain 1935–1995: A Personal Sketch*. Leicester: IVP.

Bebbington, D. (2003). *Evangelicalism in Modern Britain: A History from the 1730s to the 1980s*. London: Routledge.

Brooks, David. (2004). Who is John Stott? *New York Times*, November 30.

Carr, P.A. (2000). Are the priorities and concerns of Charles Simeon relevant for today? *Churchman* 114. https://churchsociety.org/docs/churchman/114/Cman_114_2_Carr.pdf.

Chapman, A. (2014). *Godly Ambition: John Stott and the Evangelical Movement*. Oxford: Oxford University Press.

Chartres, C. (ed.) (2011). *Why I am Still an Anglican*. London: Continuum.

Dudley-Smith, T. (1999). *John Stott Vol. 1: The Making of a Leader*. Leicester: IVP.

Dudley-Smith, T. (2001). *John Stott Vol. 2: A Global Ministry*. Leicester: IVP.

Edwards, D. and Stott, J. (1988). *Essentials: A Liberal-Evangelical Dialogue*. London: Hodder and Stoughton.

Graham, Billy. (2005). Builders and Icons: John Stott. *Time Magazine*, April 18.

Grass, T. (2008). *Modern Church History*. London: SCM Press.

Hastings, A. (2001). *A History of English Christianity 1920–2000*. London: SCM Press.

Jenkins, G. (2012). *A Tale of Two Preachers: Preaching in the Simeon-Stott Tradition*. Cambridge: Grove Books.

Murray, I. (1990). *D. Martyn Lloyd-Jones: The Fight of Faith 1939–1981*. London: Banner of Truth.

Reid, G. (ed.) (1986). *Hope for the Church of England*. Eastbourne: Kingsway.

Stanley, B. (2013). *The Global Diffusion of Evangelicalism: The Age of Billy Graham and John Stott*. Leicester: IVP.

Steer, R. (2009). *Inside Story: The Life of John Stott*. Leicester: IVP.

Stott, J. (1958). *Basic Christianity*. Grand Rapids, MI: Eerdmans.

Stott, J. (1964). *Confess Your Sins: The Way of Reconciliation*. Waco, TX: Word Books.

Stott, J. (1967). *Our Guilty Silence*. London: Hodder and Stoughton.

Stott, J. (1975). *Christian Mission in the Modern World*. London: Falcon.

Stott, J. (1977). The sovereign god and the church. In: *Our Sovereign God* (ed. J.M. Boice). Grand Rapids, MI: Baker.

Stott, J. (1979). *Focus on Christ*. London: Collins.

Stott, J. (1982). *The Bible*. Leicester: IVP.

Stott, J. (1986a). Charles Simeon: a personal appreciation. In: *Evangelical Preaching: An Anthology of Sermons by Charles Simeon* (ed. J. Houston). Colorado Springs, CO: Multnomah.

Stott, J. (1986b). *The Cross of Christ*. Leicester: IVP.

Stott, J. (1992). *The Contemporary Christian*. Leicester: IVP.

Stott, J. (2008). *The Living Church*. Leicester: IVP.

Stott, J. (2013). *'But I Say to You' – Christ the Controversialist*. Leicester: IVP.

William Stringfellow (1928–1985)

James Walters

William Stringfellow is an unusual addition to a collection of twentieth century Anglican theologians for a number of reasons. He was an unconventional, even eccentric, Christian writer/activist and to tell the story of his life is by no means a mere preamble to expounding his theological writings. He viewed each human life as a parable of the Word of God (Stringfellow 1982, pp. 15–23)[1] and the oddities of his own biography inform his significant contribution to contemporary Anglican thought. Thus, three respects in which he is uncharacteristic of Anglican theologians will be highlighted in the course of a brief biographical sketch before elaborating on his major theological themes.

First and most obviously, Anglican theologians of the modern era (the men at least) have tended to be clergy or professional academics. Stringfellow was more than content to be neither. He was born in Rhode Island in the United States in 1928 and grew up in a working-class Episcopalian family. He describes himself as a "religiously precocious" (Stringfellow 1970, p. 80) child for whom the liturgical life and fellowship of the church was central to his upbringing. Yet, at the age of fourteen he rejected what he viewed as coercive pressure to enter the priesthood and developed an early anger at the implicit clericalism he encountered: "I would not be a priest and, moreover, I would spend my life refuting any who suppose that to be serious about the Christian faith required ordination" (Stringfellow 1970, p. 82).

Stringfellow won a scholarship to attend Bates College in Maine to study politics and economics in 1945, going on to obtain a Rotary scholarship for study at the London School of Economics (LSE) in 1949. His student life was dominated by an extraordinary commitment to Christian organizations and ecumenical activities. He was on the council of the Student Christian Movement in America and president of the United Student Christian Council, which he represented at the World Conference

Twentieth Century Anglican Theologians: From Evelyn Underhill to Esther Mombo, First Edition.
Edited by Stephen Burns, Bryan Cones, and James Tengatenga.
© 2021 John Wiley & Sons Ltd. Published 2021 by John Wiley & Sons Ltd.

of Christian Youth in Oslo in 1947. He also attended the inaugural assembly of the World Council of Churches in Amsterdam in 1948 aged twenty. In his reference to the LSE the Dean of Bates College wrote: "I continue to be amazed that Mr Stringfellow is able to be a straight A student and do so many other things, and do them well, while at the same time he is now and then away from the campus on his church youth movements for days at a time."[2]

Stringfellow later describes this zealousness as "pharisaic" and a different kind of "professionalizing" of Christian faith in response to his rejection of priesthood. In London he seems to have had some kind of liberation – almost a conversion experience – that freed him, not just from priesthood and the hyperactivity of the "super-Christian" he had become, but from ambition and success of any kind, including the obvious alternative career of politics:

> I had elected to pursue *no* career. To put it theologically, I died to the idea of career and to the whole typical array of mundane calculations, grandiose goals, and appropriate schemes to reach them. I renounced simultaneously, the embellishments – like money, power, success – associated with careers in American culture, along with the ethics requisite to obtaining such condiments. I do not say this haughtily; this was an aspect of my conversion to the gospel, so, in fact, I say it humbly (Stringfellow 1982, p. 125).

Following a period of military service in which we are told he read the Bible rapaciously "in order to keep my sanity" (Boak Slocum 1997, p. 4), Stringfellow went on to train as a lawyer at Harvard Law School (1953–1956). But, on graduating, he did not pursue the kind of lucrative and prestigious professional life such an education made possible. Instead he moved to East Harlem, a deprived district of New York where he provided legal services to many unable to pay for them, first within the East Harlem Protestant Parish and then setting up his own legal practice. He takes obvious pride in his peers' view of this decision as "idiosyncratic and controversial" and he derides a view of law that "rationalizes a preference for the *laissez faire* interests of commerce as opposed to the freedom, safety, and welfare of human beings, or that asserts a so-called sanctity of property that devalues and demeans human life" (Stringfellow 1982, p. 130). This engagement with those on the margins of society would characterize his subsequent writing and his consideration of the Church's engagement with the "principalities and powers of the world." He continued to write and speak extensively on a range of theological topics, but all focused on the interface of faith and politics. His writing is not, therefore "academic" but it is lucid, interacts with a wider theological discourse as well as current affairs, and conforms to a remarkably consistent theological schema. He famously shared a platform at the University of Chicago in 1962 with Karl Barth who commended his message to the people of the United States and with whom a relationship of mutual admiration appears to have developed. So Stringfellow was a lawyer by profession and a theologian in word and action as his witness to the Word. He describes his vocation, and that of everyone else, as "the vocation of being human, nothing more and nothing less" (Stringfellow 1982, p. 126).

A second unusual and noteworthy characteristic is Stringfellow's sexuality. Given the level of acrimony that continues to plague the Anglican Communion on the issue of same-sex relationships and the consequent side-lining of LGBT voices in the Church, Stringfellow stands out as an unlikely and seemingly contradictory figure. He can by no means be characterized as a "queer theologian" of the kind that has emerged in more recent years,[3] but neither should it be denied that his advocacy for gay people (both in the Law and in the Church), as well as his moving writing about his own "sweet companion of seventeen years," Anthony Towne, is integral to and clearly formative of his theological imagination. In 1965 he addressed a group of gay Christians at Christ Church Cathedral, Hartford, Connecticut on both the legal situation for homosexuals (the sodomy law was not repealed in Connecticut until 1971) and the theological questions at stake for gay Christians. He describes Christian faith as having to do with "that form of self-acceptance which is a gift of God and not something achieved or sustained ascetically, psychiatrically, mystically or pietistically" (Stringfellow 1965).

His own personal journey of self-acceptance is largely undocumented but perhaps alluded to in moments such as the London "conversion" experience and a remarkably rich understanding of the psychology and theology of sex published in *Instead of Death* (Stringfellow 1963, pp. 37–55). His friend Bill Wylie Kellermann describes Stringfellow's moving in with Towne in 1962 as a limited "coming out" to at least "a certain circle" (Wylie Kellermann 1997, pp. 37–55). But the significance of sexual identity in his theological work should not be confined to single moments or biographical detail. A disposition of "queerness" (not a word he uses) and the paradoxes of exclusion and acceptance within societal institutions (the Church, the Law, the Nation) run through his work in many dimensions. He articulates this proto-queer theology in the Hartford lecture, saying that he is "not too much impressed by the mere fact that homosexuals are rejected by society [as a basis for moral condemnation]. After all, the Pioneer of the faith expended His ministry for the whole world by caring for the outcasts – whores and tax collectors, the blind and the idiotic, lepers and insurrectionists, the poor and those possessed by demons" (Stringfellow 1965). More than this, Stringfellow describes his own relationship with Towne as a locus of profound theological learning in the overcoming of fear and fragility, particularly in the face of their respective ill health: "The secret of the relationship of Anthony and myself was not that we were able to affirm each other in defiance of dread, but that we were each enabled to apprehend and mediate to the other the truth that the Word of God alone has the ability to identify and affirm either of us as persons or to offer the same to any other human being" (Stringfellow 1982, p. 50).

Stringfellow and Towne moved from their Manhattan apartment to the relative seclusion of Block Island in the state of Rhode Island in 1967 where their home "Eschaton" was a center of hospitality and retreat for friends and fellow activists. These included the Jesuit priest Daniel Berrigan who, as one of the "Catonsville Nine," was evading imprisonment for destroying draft papers in an act of protest against the Vietnam War. He was apprehended in August 1970, and Stringfellow and Towne were indicted and charged with harboring a fugitive. These events prompted Stringfellow's most significant theological work, *An Ethic for Christians and Other Aliens in a Strange Land* (Stringfellow 1973). Formulated in conversation with Berrigan it takes the biblical images of Jerusalem and Babylon as the basis for a Christian ethic of resistance in the contemporary United States.

An Ethic for Christians exemplifies the third unusual characteristic of Stringfellow as an Anglican theologian, which is that his work is dominated by a theme more associated with the Evangelical Right than liberal Episcopalianism: spiritual warfare. The struggle against death in the world in the form of "principalities and powers" could seem too Manichean or biblically literalist for Anglican sensibilities but it is the consistent theme in Stringfellow's theological vision. Stringfellow argues that dark forces such as racism, exploitation, and capitalist alienation are not merely diseases of the human heart but powers that become embodied in human institutions and systems. He does not shy away from the language of demonic possession to describe this captivity to the power of death.

Stringfellow speaks of death, therefore, as a metaphor for all the malign forces of sin in the world but also deeply literally. The ultimate power of the state is to execute its own citizens and murder others in war. Hiroshima is a symbol of death to which he frequently turns. More than that, the struggle against death was real and longstanding in Stringfellow's own body. Lifelong health problems were seriously compounded in the 1960s when his pancreas failed and had to be surgically removed. Subsequent conditions including an enzyme deficiency and debilitating diabetes pain and frailty were constant realities. "Death," he wrote in this period, "is no abstract idea, nor merely a destination in time, nor just an occasional happening, nor only a reality for human beings, but, both biblically and empirically, death names a moral power claiming sovereignty over all men and all things in history" (Stringfellow 1970, p. 53).

Among their more eccentric interests, Stringfellow and Towne had a shared love of the circus, spending several weeks in the summer of 1966 touring with a circus troupe around New England. The circus was, for Stringfellow, a vision of the eschatological age in its evocation of wonder and joy, its strange and inclusive diversity, but most of all in its defiance of death. Acrobats, lion tamers, sword swallowers, engage in an "open ridicule of death," which "shows the rest of us that the only enemy in life is death and that this enemy confronts everyone, whatever their circumstances, all the time" (Stringfellow 1994, p. 286).

Towne died in 1980, a loss that prompts the pastoral reflections of *Simplicity of Faith*. Stringfellow's death at the age of fifty-six followed on March 2, 1985. Their ashes are interred together on Block Island near a plaque that reads "Near this cottage the remains of William Stringfellow and Anthony Towne await the resurrection."

Principalities and Power

Stringfellow's theology is not without a positive narrative, but the modes in which he feels most at home are those of social, political, or ecclesiastical critique, sometimes to the point of excoriating attack. The few theological influences he acknowledges are those from whom he primarily borrows these prophetic tools of deconstruction. His first book, *A Private and Public Faith* (Stringfellow 1962), launches a characteristically Barthian attack on "the folly of religion" as the trappings of piety and spiritual seeking in contrast to the reality of the Gospel: "Religion is the attempt to satisfy the curiosity of men in this world about God; Jesus Christ is the answer to the curiosity of men in this world about what it means to be truly a man in this world which God created" (Stringfellow 1962, p. 15). Similarly, this work references the theologian and Christian anarchist Jacques Ellul (with whom Stringfellow enjoyed a long friendship), adopting Ellul's more Kierkegaardian critique of the complacency and capitulation of liberal Protestantism. Stringfellow rails against clericalism and neglect of the Bible, frustrations he expressed early in his letter of resignation from the Protestant parish in Harlem. "In the congregations of the parish," he wrote, "the Bible was closed; in the group ministry there was even scorn for the Bible as the means through which the Word of God is communicated in contemporary society" (Stringfellow 1964, p. 88).

As his work develops, the language of "principalities and powers" becomes the overarching vehicle for his theological critique of all that replaces or inhibits the Word of God in the world, extending this unmasking of idolatry in multiple directions. While Marxism is itself included among these idols, there is a hint of Marxist critical theory in his identification of reductive ideologies and systems that alienate rather than liberate human life, perhaps an influence attributable to his time at LSE where he attended several lecture courses by the socialist academic Harold Laski (see Walters 2015, pp. 657–664). Marx's concept of ideology seeks to name the diverse elements of our cultural "superstructure" that reinforce and perpetuate destructive and unjust systems and sustain the "false consciousness" that leads people to accept them. Stringfellow's principalities are similarly broad and serve the same function expressed in theological terms. He categorizes principalities as *images* (characteristic of the semiotic direction Marxist cultural theory had taken, with Marilyn Monroe cited as an example), *institutions* such as the modern capitalist corporation, and *ideologies* including both those to which the United States was ostensibly opposed (communism, fascism, racism) and those it considered benevolent (humanism, capitalism, democracy, rationalism) (see Stringfellow 1964, pp. 49–73).

Many of the biblical words that Stringfellow identifies with the principalities are synonyms for Satan ("tempter," "adversary," the enemy"). Just as the biblical understanding of the devil is of a fallen creature rather than an equal and opposite force to God, so Stringfellow characterizes principalities as elements of the world with potential for good (the church is among the principalities) but whose ends have been turned away from human flourishing. In other words, they are fallen and, as such, "falsely – and futilely – claim autonomy from God and dominion over human beings and the rest of creation, thus disrupting and usurping the godly vocation or blaspheming, while repudiating their own vocation" (Stringfellow 1973, p. 80). Stringfellow thus fuses a traditional understanding of idols and their demand for sacrifice with an apparently more Marxist definition of false consciousness that explains the irrationality and godlessness of modern life: "The principality, insinuating itself in the place of God, deceives humans into thinking and acting as if the moral worth or justification of human beings is defined and determined by commitment or surrender – literally, sacrifice – of human life to the survival interest, grandeur, and vanity of the principality" (Stringfellow 1973, p. 81). Whether the principality is the military, the corporation, the sports club, or even the family, it is inclined to present itself as the false god that demands the self-giving and veneration that should only be directed toward God.

The principalities, therefore, exercise demonic power, an agency that Stringfellow describes as ultimately mysterious but which he characterizes as having the effect of eroding moral responsibility and perception. In a chapter in *An Ethic for Christians* on the "Stratagems of the Demonic Powers" he gives a Christian take on a range of contemporary political concerns that perhaps resonate even more strongly in our own age of "fake news" and the digital distortion of truth. The denial of truth is a central strategy of the principalities, not merely in the telling of lies but, more perniciously, in "the premise of the principalities that truth is non-existent . . . that there can be no thorough or fair or comprehensive or detached discovery and chronicle of events and that any handling of facts is ideologically or institutionally or otherwise tainted" (Stringfellow 1973, p. 99). This inattention to the reality of truth is part of a range of strategies and language games that define the modern idolatry of the principalities and powers, from secrecy and surveillance, deception and diversion, through to the use of propaganda and "doublespeak," a term Stringfellow borrows from George Orwell's dystopian novel *1984*. But he sees all of this as an expression of biblical "babel" – the inversion of language and "that species of violence most militant in the present American circumstances" (Stringfellow 1973, p. 106).

The question of what it means to be the church in such circumstances runs through Stringfellow's writings, although again it is fair to say that he is more often clear about the church's failings than he is in articulating a constructive ecclesiology. If the nation state is the "preeminent principality" whose moral authority is founded on death (Stringfellow 1973, p. 107), the church is called to be the holy nation, "the exemplary nation juxtaposed to all other nations," a principality that "transcends the bondage to death in the midst of fallen creation" (Stringfellow 1977, p. 102). The church becomes an idolatrous principality when it colludes with death and submits to the authority of the state through land acquisition, tax privileges or other "Constantinian arrangements." So Stringfellow's ecclesiology is caught in a tension between his politically important insistence that we cannot talk about the church ahistorically as a disembodied entity on the one hand and his concern that the worldly existence of the church is almost irreconcilably compromising on the other. He concludes that the authentic church is first and foremost "an event of the moment . . . episodic in history; the church lives in imminence so that the church has no permanent locale or organization that predicates its authenticity as the church." All is dependent on the church in any time and place "awaiting the second advent of Jesus Christ" (Stringfellow 1977, p. 105).

An Uneasy Anglican?

This eschatological ecclesiology is certainly challenging to the conventional Anglican polity of the likes of Cranmer or Hooker. Furthermore, Stringfellow's almost dualist theology of the Principalities and Powers, and the political conclusions he frequently draws from it, can feel more characteristic of Anabaptist or Mennonite Christianity than Anglicanism, and at times his commitment to the Episcopal Church does seem very ambivalent. His critique of the Constantinianism of contemporary American Christianity is not uniquely directed at the Episcopal Church but sits particularly uneasily with the traditions of Anglican political theology to which he gives little direct consideration. His acerbic criticisms of the Presiding Bishop in 1980 (see Stringfellow 1994, pp. 280–283), his questionable anger at the Church's treatment of

Bishop James Pike,[4] and his frustrations at its equivocation over women's ordination and racial equality can leave you wondering why he remained an Episcopalian at all.

Yet if his worldview takes evil more seriously than the more sanguine incarnational theologies that arose from English Idealism, his response to that is perhaps recognizable as a more dynamic form of Anglican sacramentalism. Anglican thought and practice pervade his writing and an early interest in Archbishop William Temple,[5] though never clearly acknowledged, is detectable in a number of theoretical moves. Most especially, Stringfellow grounds his rigorously biblical political theology in a sustained liturgical practice. In a passage lamenting the disunity of Christians and the lack of communion between denominations, he argues, "At no point in the witness of the church to the world, is its integrity as a reconciled society more radical and more cogent than in the liturgy, the precedent and consummation of that service that the church of Christ and the members of this Body render to the world" (Stringfellow 1966, p. 150). In terms very reminiscent of William Temple's "sanctification of the citizen" (Temple 1940), Stringfellow insists that the laity are not "spectators but participants" in "the normative and conclusive ethical commitment of the Christian people to the world" (Stringfellow 1966, p. 153). Also like Temple (Temple 1941, pp. 101–102), he points to the materiality of eucharistic worship – bread, wine, water, money, cloth, etc. – as a sign of the liturgy's transformation of the real world through worship: "Sacramentally, we have in the liturgy a meal that is basically a real meal and which nourishes those who partake of it as a meal. At the same time, this meal portrays for the rest of the world an image of the Last Supper, of which Christ Himself was Host, and is also a foretaste of the eschatological banquet in which Christ is finally recognized as the Host of all men" (Stringfellow 1966, p. 154).

Through the lens of this liturgical encounter with the Word, Stringfellow develops a distinctively Anglican sacramentalism that allows a narrative of grace and redemption to be brought to bear on the dark forces of the principalities and powers. In his discussion of money, for example – one of the more obvious powers of his age and ours – he recognizes that the Christian's freedom from the idolatry of money is not to renounce it altogether so much as to discover its sacramental use, "as a sign of the restoration of life wrought in this world by Christ" (Stringfellow 1966, p. 45). This is symbolized in the offering of money within the liturgy and practiced in the world through "the freedom to use money, to spend money without worshipping money and thus it means the freedom to do without money, if need be, or, having some, to give it away to anyone who seems to need money to maintain life a while longer." As such it mirrors the liturgy's "specific dramatization of the members of the Body of Christ losing their life in order that the world be given life" (Stringfellow 1966, p. 46).

That is a courageous way to live, one of the many radical challenges that William Stringfellow presents to an Anglican culture often prone to accommodation or even capitulation to the unjust ways of the world. His own courage to practice what he preached – in working among the marginalized after such a prestigious education, in supporting gay Christians before decriminalization, in continuing to live for others and for God in the face of his own debilitating ill health – makes his readable theological corpus all the more compelling. Its radicalism, its lucidity, and its energy have much to contribute to a politically serious Anglican theological discourse in the twenty-first century.

Notes

1 All the volumes by Stringfellow referred to in this chapter have been republished by Wipf and Stock Publishers, Eugene, Oregon. Citations here are taken from these volumes. The dates given are the original publication dates.
2 Reference Letter from Harry W. Rowe dated March 15, 1949, LSE Student Archive.
3 Marcella Althaus-Reid and John J. McNeill SJ, for example, have adopted a biblical hermeneutic and theological method in more explicit dialogue with queer theory.
4 Given Stringfellow's stridently orthodox theology and moral clarity, his defense of the

Bishop of California (1958–1966) is difficult to understand, beyond Pike's advocacy of numerous progressive causes and a clear personal friendship. Pike was subject to heresy procedures throughout the 1960s for the rejection of central Christian beliefs and exploration of the paranormal (see Stringfellow and Towne 1967, 1968).
5 His application to LSE implies that Temple would be the focus of his study although we cannot know how closely he followed this through.

References

Boak Slocum, R. (1997). *Prophet of Justice, Prophet of Life: Essays on William Stringfellow*. Eugene, Oregon: Wipf and Stock.

Dancer, A. (2011). *An Alien in a Strange Land: Theology in the Life of William Stringfellow*. Eugene, Oregon: Wipf and Stock.

Stringfellow, W. ([1962] 1999). *A Private and Public Faith*. Eugene, OR: Wipf and Stock.

Stringfellow, W. ([1963] 2004). *Instead of Death*. Eugene, OR: Wipf and Stock.

Stringfellow, W. ([1964] 2005). *My People Is the Enemy*. Eugene, OR: Wipf and Stock.

Stringfellow, W. ([1964] 2006). *Free in Obedience*. Eugene, OR: Wipf and Stock.

Stringfellow, William. (1965). *The Humanity of Sex*. Available at Stringfellow Archives, Ithaca, NY Cornell University.

Stringfellow, W. ([1966] 2006). *Dissenter in a Great Society*. Eugene, OR: Wipf and Stock.

Stringfellow, W. ([1970] 2005). *A Second Birthday*. Eugene, OR: Wipf and Stock.

Stringfellow, W. ([1973] 2004). *An Ethic for Christians and Other Aliens in a Strange Land*. Eugene, OR: Wipf and Stock.

Stringfellow, W. ([1977] 2004). *Conscience and Obedience*. Eugene, OR: Wipf and Stock.

Stringfellow, W. ([1982] 2005). *A Simplicity of Faith (1982, 2005)*. Eugene, OR: Wipf and Stock.

Stringfellow, W. (1994). *A Keeper of the Word: Selected Writings of William Stringfellow* (ed. B. Wylie Kellermann). Grand Rapids, MI: Eerdmans.

Stringfellow, W. and Towne, A. ([1967] 2007). *The Bishop Pike Affair*. Eugene, OR: Wipf and Stock.

Stringfellow, W. and Towne, A. ([1968] 2007). *The Death and Life of Bishop Pike*. Eugene, OR: Wipf and Stock.

Temple, W. (1940). *The Hope of a New World*. London: SCM Press.

Temple, W. (1941). *Citizen and Churchman*. London: Eyre and Spottiswoode.

Walters, J. (2015). The defiant ringmaster: lessons in Christian leadership from William Stringfellow. *Anglican Theological Review* 97: 657–664.

Wylie Kellermann, B. (1997). 'Listen to this man': A parable before the powers. In: *Prophet of Justice, Prophet of Life: Essays on William Stringfellow* (ed. R. Boak Slocum), 1–16. New York, NY: Church Publishing.

Desmond Tutu (1931–)

Michael Battle

In this chapter on Desmond Tutu, previous Archbishop of the Anglican Church of Southern Africa, I explore how Tutu's spiritual theology exercised influence on contemporary thought and practice of peacemaking. Even though Tutu was the titular head of a major province in the Anglican Communion, many would categorize Tutu merely as a political agent. In this chapter I argue against such constricted classifications. In addition, Tutu's impact is vital to move beyond either the narrow identification of Anglican theology with the western world or with the European construction of systematic theology. In short, not only is Anglican theology difficult to define, so too is the particular figure of Tutu. In fact, in my book, *Tutu, South African Confessor: A Spiritual Biography of Desmond Tutu* (Battle 2021), I argue that Tutu interestingly enough belongs more in the theological genre of Christian mysticism. Before we discuss this further, it may be helpful to display a brief chronological biography of his public witness.

Tutu was born on October 7, 1931 and from an early age was formed by the company of Anglican monks from the Community of the Resurrection (CR) who first went from England to South Africa in 1902. Trevor Huddleston became the most well-known CR monk to influence Tutu to be a major spiritual and political leader. The CR assisted Tutu to study in the United Kingdom in 1962. He returned to South Africa in 1966 to teach at the Federal Theological Seminary in South Africa. He became the Director of the Theological Fund of the World Council of Churches in 1972. Tutu's rise in the institutional Anglican Church was meteoric. In 1975, he served as the first black Dean of St. Mary's Cathedral in Johannesburg and then as Bishop of Lesotho in 1976. From 1978 to 1985 Tutu served as General Secretary of the South African Council of Churches, which brought him international attention to win the Nobel Peace Prize in 1984. He became Bishop of Johannesburg (1985–1986) and Archbishop of Cape Town (1986–1996). He became president of the All Africa Conference of Churches in 1987. In 1996, Nelson Mandela appointed Tutu to be the

Twentieth Century Anglican Theologians: From Evelyn Underhill to Esther Mombo, First Edition.
Edited by Stephen Burns, Bryan Cones, and James Tengatenga.
© 2021 John Wiley & Sons Ltd. Published 2021 by John Wiley & Sons Ltd.

Chair of the Truth and Reconciliation Commission (TRC) (1996–2000) to oversee the transition of South Africa into its first democratic government. In 2007, Tutu became a founding member and Chair of the Elders.[1] In most of these cases of public witness above, Tutu was the first black African to hold the position.

As South African history is perpetually being written, Tutu may be remembered the most because of his leadership in South Africa's TRC, which was an amazing governmental proceeding in which South Africans gathered to hear the truth and seek amnesty to restore a common South Africa capable of containing black, white, colored, and all people without separation. At the end of apartheid in 1994, Mandela appointed Tutu to help South Africa in affect confess its sins as well as offer forgiveness. Of course, such a process was controversial as witnesses who were identified as victims of gross human rights violations may have felt no justice occurred through the TRC. Tutu's response was always that his vision for the TRC was not that of retributive justice; instead, it was for restorative justice to rebuild a nation.

Tutu's Theological Impact

As Tutu navigated profound experiences in South Africa's birth of a nation, his anchor of understanding was unashamedly grounded in his spiritual formation and illumination that the ultimate substance of peace is Jesus. As mentioned above, however, such grounding cannot be easily classified as Tutu states, "I believe Jesus Christ would have liked us Christians to be as Gandhi whose stand was closer to that of Jesus than mine" (Tutu n.d.a). Such a statement would confuse conservative Christians and bewilder his progressive political base. For example, although it is a declension for Christ's standards, Tutu thinks the West was justified in going to war against Hitler. Ugandans were justified in taking up arms against Idi Amin; and Tutu finds himself unable to argue with any conviction that Muslims in Bosnia should not resort to violent resistance against ethnic cleansing.

For Tutu during the apartheid years (1948–1994), the use of force should not be a long-term solution, but it could be last resort for black people pushed against a wall. He often had to say this very strongly to angry whites who protested against an appeal by the Diocesan Council of the Anglican Diocese of Cape Town that all South Africans should give up their personal firearms. One white South African Anglican asked Tutu why he had not appealed to criminals (i.e., black activists) to give up their weapons, the implication here being whites should not disarm because they were defenseless in the face of attack from blacks. In Tutu's wisdom he knew that whites were experiencing the same sort of tension and fear that blacks had lived with for generations.

In Tutu's spiritual theology, he often advocated that God's peace was not merely the absence of conflict; rather, God's peace was substantive. Such substance was displayed primarily for Christians in the revelation of God through the person of Jesus. In the midst of this, Tutu appealed to churches and Christians to demonstrate this revealed substance of peace:

> [The South African Government] doesn't like our work of supporting the families of political prisoners, of those detained in solitary confinement without trial,

of those who are banned to five years of a twilight existence as nonpersons . . . who can't attend a gathering in the presence of more than two people according to the law. . . Thank you for bringing ecclesiology to life for me, for us. It is a tremendous thing to belong to the church of God, to know, to experience almost as a physical thing being upheld, borne up by the care, the concern, the hope, the laughter, the prayers of so many . . . the most touching support was from Sunday school children at St James Church, Madison Ave. New York who sent me what they called passports of love which I pasted on the walls of my office . . . I said this church of God, this Body of Jesus transcends time, space, culture, race, sex, status, etc. It is everything apartheid negates. And it is part of God's movement for His Kingdom, to recover the primordial shalom that was shattered by sin . . . our task as churches was to help create the right moral atmosphere, to make it possible for politicians to take the risk of advocating humane, compassionate policies (Tutu n.d.b).

Tutu's spiritual impact accentuates an anthropological theology based in how Jesus' own humanity opens the opportunity for persons to move through the mystery of becoming a relative of God, a child of God. It is not that Tutu lacks a trinitarian theology with his emphasis upon Jesus; rather, Tutu's theology imprints upon Jesus in order to know how to be human. Herein Tutu becomes well known in his use of Ubuntu as an African concept of how all human beings are interdependent and inextricably linked together (see Battle 2009). In such connectivity, Tutu, is also deeply influenced by the desert tradition and Christian mysticism expressed keenly through the monastic tradition (Battle 2021).

Through the CR and Tutu's theological training he matured in his own habits of prayer and religious community. Although Tutu never became a monk himself, his daily disciplines of praying around seven times a day, conducting regular retreats, regular practices of confession with his spiritual director, and the Anglican daily office and eucharist, made him look almost like a monk. If one got to know Tutu, it would become apparent how Tutu survived as both an anti-apartheid leader and the Chair of the TRC. He not only survived but flourished in leadership during those experiences because of his focus on the divine life and mystery of Jesus' revelation of God.

Spirituality and Politics

Tutu's spirituality, however, was never separated from the political witness against apartheid that in its own way was a kind of spirituality for white South Africans to claim the exclusive presence of God championing their election to control South Africa. White South Africans instituted the law of the land called apartheid in which theological justification was derived to support the legal separation of black, white, and colored races of people.

In an anxious white South African worldview,[2] whites were responding to the similar insecurity above around gun control of no longer being in control of the colonial narrative of European domination. In light of this past they sought to arm themselves to the teeth. Tutu also knew, however, that black communities too were awash with weapons. That is why he said our church, the Anglican Church, has adopted a program of peacemaking under the slogan, "No weapons here." One of the other Anglican bishops, David Beetge, paraphrased it this way, "Anglicans do it without arms." Tutu knew all of this would not get rid of personal firearms; this step must be made as a small step toward a comprehensive campaign that included the creation of a new professional police force. Tutu was also prophetic in wanting a denial of any general right to bear arms in a new constitution: "We don't want to follow the American route in South Africa" (Tutu 1994). Tutu also asked for a timetable for the progressive disarming of all parts of the population after the adoption of South Africa's new constitution on May 8, 1996. Tutu concludes, "As president of the All Africa Conference of Churches, I have already said we want the whole continent to demilitarize as soon as possible. The arms race is particularly obscene amongst poverty-stricken people" (Tutu 1994).

Tutu's interconnectivity of spirituality and politics derived from Jesus' kenosis of sharing personhood with others. In such a worldview, there can be no isolated public policies. For Tutu, South Africa only had two options: Either whites share power or whites hold on to what they have, dig in their heels and refuse to share with everybody else. If they chose the latter then a bloodbath was inevitable. B. J. Vorster, served as the Prime Minister of South Africa from 1966 to 1978 and as the fourth State President of South Africa from 1978 to 1979. Vorster called a bloodbath the alternative too ghastly to contemplate. P. W. Botha was the leader of South Africa from 1978 to 1989, serving as the last Prime Minister from 1978 to 1984 and the first executive State President from 1984 to 1989. Botha spoke of the need to adapt or die. For Tutu, they were saying much the same thing and refusing to share power. As Tutu preached Jesus' substance of peace in public, Tutu in so many words said if South Africa's apartheid government continued down the same course of destructive action, they would lose it all. Instead, Tutu advocated for a more substantial peace and tried to negotiate a settlement with those whom blacks regarded as their authentic leaders and those whites in power. Tutu said, "and you are just being ostrich like if you think you can exclude Oliver Tambo, Nelson Mandela etc. I support no political party. I speak only as realist who has a passionate love for this country, and for all its people and hate to see us going headlong to avoidable disaster" (Tutu n.d.a).

As a result of his spiritual sight, Tutu knew that South Africa's future will be determined ultimately between the Afrikaner and the African – both of whom are Africans. Botha said he wanted time. "We can give him the time if we believe he is determined to dismantle apartheid and wants a non-racial South Africa with a bill of rights guaranteeing individual not group or ethnic rights" (Tutu n.d.a). Tutu advocated for a rule of law in which people will count because they are human beings made in the image of God and not based upon any biological irrelevancies. Tutu concludes: "Time is short, desperately short. But I want to repeat my offer to him. If he will do only 4 things (the same 4 things) with a specific timetable." These four things were:

1 Give a commitment to a common citizenship for all South Africans in an undivided South Africa (for Blacks this is not negotiable);

2 Abolish the Pass Laws, detention without trial and lift all banning orders (or charge the alleged miscreants);
3 Stop immediately all forced population removals; and
4 Establish a uniform educational system.

If Botha facilitated these four items, then he should have a chance to change since at that time he seemed to be talking about real change. For Tutu, "These are not radical demands. They are very reasonable and moderate. Anything else means we are for the birds. God help us" (Tutu n.d.b).

Tutu knew this was a very solemn and critical time for peace after the violence in Pretoria, Maputo, and Bloemfontein and even more shatteringly after three blacks who had thought they were striving for a new kind of South Africa were hanged. Tutu states:

> I myself have said times without number that I am opposed to all forms of violence – that of those who wish to uphold the vicious and unjust and totally immoral evil system of apartheid and those who want to overthrow that system. I have also said that the primary and provocative violence is that of apartheid, the violence of a deliberately inferior educational system intended to prepare our children for perpetual serfdom in the land of their birth, the violence of hunger and malnutrition in their Bantustans deliberately created as ghettoes of poverty and misery, unlimited reservoirs of cheap labor, the violence of forced population removals when over 2 million blacks have been uprooted from their homes and dumped in the poverty stricken Bantustans bereft of their South African citizenship by a violence that has turned them into aliens in their Motherland; we are talking about the violence of the migratory labor system which forces men to live unnatural existence in single-sex hostels, with deleterious consequences for Black Family Life; I refer to the violence of harassing squatters at K.T.C. Camp and Crossroads (Tutu 1983).

Tutu also referred to the legalized violence of detention without trial and of arbitrary banning. He said many times before that this institutionalized structural violence of South Africa is making many blacks desperate as they despair of peaceful change. From 1912 to 1960, black political groups struggled valiantly to bring about change through peaceful means. But the result was a growing intransigence on the part of the white authorities, replying to nonviolent resistance with teargas, police dogs, police bullets, and death. Such a response, often condoned by the Dutch Reformed Church in South Africa, escalated violence that shut out the possibility of peaceful negotiation. Tutu became impatient with the sham political motions in those dangerous times when politicians and church members were biding time using the so-called process of constitutional proposals. Tutu states, "I have warned that when people become desperate, then they will use desperate methods" (Tutu 1983).

Unity is always a crucial matter in the business of the liberation struggle, but never more so than when South Africa was caught in a spiral of violence that often lead inexorably to a bloodbath, the so-called alternative too ghastly to contemplate. In light of this, Tutu also had to address his black community. In this stalemate, Tutu resorted to the prowess of his sense of humor.

> We all know that we blacks, as they say, are slow thinkers . . . but is high time we held such a National Forum worried as we must all have been by the fragmentation of the black community making it easier for the enemy of the struggle to apply the old ploy of divide and rule. We have been bickering amongst ourselves forgetting that the *raison d'etre* of our existence as organizations was not an end in itself but was for the sake of the liberation of the oppressed first and then of the oppressor. I have said it seems we have not yet suffered enough for we indulge ourselves in the luxuries of tiffs in public over ideological and other differences, whilst the oppressors laugh themselves sick that we are making their situation so much easier (Tutu 1983).

Without grounding and discipline, Tutu thought black folk did white folk's dirty work for them, especially by washing dirty linen in public. The internal fighting had to also stop to avoid the inexorable blood bath. What does it really matter whether you say you are an exponent of black consciousness and somebody else is an upholder of the Freedom Charter, whether you are AZAPO (Azanian People's Organization), COSAS (Congress of South Africa Students), or Committee of Ten? For Tutu, the most important thing for the struggle itself was for total liberation and the liberation of all the people of South Africa, black and white to live where the rule of law actually could exist. This would be where all have full citizenship rights and obligations and where all, black and white, have a share in all important decision making. This would be where there would be an equitable distribution of all the resources of country, mineral, land, wealth, education, social, and economic resources. The gut check occurred when Tutu stopped and asked, "Is that not what we are all striving for?"

Herein was the substance of Tutu's peace. It was a peace not made for one side over the other or a peace in which the oppressed came into power only to repeat cycles of abuse. The substance of peace meant that all could be human beings consciously made in the image of God. Like St. Paul's epistles to the struggling churches in Asia Minor, Tutu then coached his black community, "Why then are we so often at one another's throats? Why are we so keen to denigrate one another and impute the worst motives to one another and actually sabotage the liberation struggle by our petty jealousies, wanting to gain credit and credibility at the expense of our fellow blacks, whilst the enemy rolls about in uncontrollable mirth?" (Tutu 1983).

Tutu's substantial peace indeed needed a new start in which the black community needed to be ready to speak only good of one another. He coached them about how to refuse to discuss differences in negative ways in the press and in public before ever trying to sort out those differences privately and amicably. Tutu's spirituality of Ubuntu was the back drop for his worldview a new South Africa: "We must sink and swim together." An injury to one is an injury to all. Good black leadership must draw together all black groups to operate under one umbrella organization – one that could even include white people (Tutu 1983).

Role of Confessor

In a myriad of crises in South Africa in which there were incessant states of emergency and the deadlock on negotiations to end apartheid in the 1980s, spiritual communities were forced into an urgent adjustment of their role in South African society. They could not afford the luxury of just being communities of worship. Tutu was increasingly called upon to articulate the relevance of spirituality among several contexts of political strife. He realizes this as he states, "We come out of this reflection with the conviction that we are faced with a situation which calls on us to return to the type of protest actions on which we were forced to embark before February 2, 1990 [when Mandela was released from prison]" (Allen 1992). And yet Tutu felt that clarity was needed to discern between political practice and the craft of practicing the spiritual life. To be fair to Tutu's arch-bishopric and his leadership in the TRC, his focus was primarily on the theme of the development of a spirituality of transformation for the church and world that would thereby change not only South Africa. In other words, the milieu of apartheid was parasitic to a dysfunctional religious worldview in many areas of the world. But another of Tutu's aims was to address the tensions that arose in the church as a result of his leadership position "in the frontline in the struggle." In many ways I assume that Tutu did this by accepting his official position in history as South Africa's confessor.

In 1992, on the verge of South Africa's democratic election, it was the most dangerous time before the birth of South Africa's real nation. Tutu states:

> Feathers have been ruffled, hurts inflicted by what many have experienced as abrasive and turbulent. I don't think that could be avoided and in any case the gospel is almost always disturbing to comfortable status quos. But I hope we can have a different emphasis: That of seeking to strengthen the inner life of the church, of pouring oil and balm on wounds, of nurturing our people for the tasks of transformation (Allen 1992).

In South Africa's birthing process, Tutu became a spiritual leader meant to facilitate the vehement criticism, even abuse, that was South Africa's history. Tutu's spirituality was complicated in that he often stirred both sides of any South African debate in order for there to be the imagination for how to proceed together. Tutu's call for South Africa to confess the truth grew out of this stirring. Even before the formal process of the TRC, Tutu called on the rest of the world to hold South Africa accountable to the truth. Tutu received severe criticism from both white and his Anglican Church in his call to the world to ban South Africa from the 1992 Summer Olympics in Barcelona, Spain.

A good confessor in Christian spirituality is one who facilitates a vulnerable environment in which the confessee can actually see the truth. When Tutu's spiritual leadership used non-violent means such as boycotts it appears to have brought home to many whites the consequences of their abuse far more effectively than Tutu's impassioned appeals that did not affect the white public as directly. In other words, a good confessor cannot force a confession – it must be revealed to the penitent. Like the prodigal son, Tutu made it clear that he embarked on this course of public leadership reluctantly: "I had hoped those days were behind me," he told his congregation at St. George's Cathedral. Reflecting more on it to a journalist later, Tutu added: "I really don't want to be going back that way. I meant everything I said when I said I was an interim leader and that once the political process became more normal, I would really want to step out of being at center stage. It is only that one sees our country moving so inexorably almost to disaster, when we could in fact make the choice that would mean stability, peace, security, prosperity for all" (Tutu 1993).

Despite these qualifications on the clarity of his own political involvement as a spiritual leader, Tutu vigorously defended the continued right of spiritual communities to become involved in political action in as clear a way as possible while remaining spiritual; for example, he constantly stressed that the church must remain autonomous and, in particular, must have just as much right now and in the future to act independently of political parties. In February 1990, within weeks of the South African President F.W. De Klerk's milestone speech, this was underlined by the Anglican Synod of Bishop's decision banning priests from being members of political parties a well as their call for the African National Congress to abandon the armed struggle.

In conclusion, the lesson learned in Tutu's substance of peace is that there is a need for spiritual leadership that seeks transcendent ways out of political deadlock. Tutu's thought and actions here could not easily be classified in tidy bundle of conservative or liberal and western or eastern. Tutu's spiritual leadership was so effective that he convinced his Anglican Church to do creative stirring of South African society to include all people. He convinced the Anglican Church to be mindful of its call to transform society while at the same time remain distinct as God's church, one that does not need permission to bring peace. For example, when it was put to Tutu that some in the democratic movement were unhappy that he had not consulted them, he responded sharply: "I wasn't looking for backing from anyone. I am speaking, as I always have spoken, on moral and theological grounds. The fact that other people are disagreeing is a good thing in one way: it shows the church doesn't take instructions from anybody. I am not a lacky of political organizations" (Allen 1992). Perhaps Tutu articulated best the reason why spiritual leaders are needed on the "frontline" of politics while remaining spiritual leaders when he told a journalist, "People are angry. People are also sadly becoming despondent and beginning to lose hope that a new dispensation will happen. I am afraid that once people become clearly hopeless then we could easily see the situation degenerate into all-out civil war. And we want to avert that" (Allen 1992).

The current world still teeters on hopelessness. We would learn a great deal from Tutu how to move communities from jumping off the edge. Tutu understood the context of South Africa as derived from the imperatives of Jesus' actions and being and not from dysfunctional political dogma. Because of Jesus Tutu thought the church cannot with integrity remain aloof from socio-political involvement. Jesus teaches us that our relationship with God demands and is authenticated by our relationship with our fellow human beings. God's kind of reign on earth as exemplified in Christian spirituality is not a nebulous, platonic "ideal state" in the hereafter. It is, as Jesus said, among us already, and its signs are tangible, this-worldly effects – where demons are exorcized; where the hungry are fed and the naked clothed; where stigmatizing diseases are cleansed, and the lame made to walk again, the deaf to hear and the blind to see; where sins are forgiven, and the dead are raised to life again. When all are exposed for who they are, and evil is overcome by good; when oppression and exploitation are resisted, even at the cost of freedom and life itself, then we have a real foretaste of the substance of peace.

Notes

1 The Elders is an organization that envisions a world where people live in peace, conscious of their common humanity and their shared responsibilities for each other, for the planet, and for future generations.
2 White South Africans were comprised of Afrikaners (those of Dutch descent) and English (those who benefitted from England's colonial rule of both Afrikaners and Blacks). Afrikaners began to control South Africa in 1948 when they constructed apartheid.

References

Allen, John. (1992). Re-entry of the "Meddlesome Priest". *Sunday Tribune*, June 28.

Battle, M. (2009). *Reconciliation: The Ubuntu Theology of Desmond Tutu*. Cleveland, OH: Pilgrim Press.

Battle, M. (2021). *Tutu—South African Confessor: A Spiritual Biography of Desmond Tutu*. Louiville KY: Westminster John Knox.

Tutu, D. (1983). *Unity and Liberation*. Hammanskraal: National Forum Committee.

Tutu, D. (1993). PostScript: to be human is to be free. In: *Christianity and Democracy in Global Context* (ed. J. Witt Jnr.), 311–320. Boulder, CO: Westview.

Tutu, Desmond. (1994 [1993]). Address to Gandhi Memorial Opening, Durban.

Tutu, Desmond. (n.d.a). Tutu, Is Peaceful Change Still Possible in South Africa? Desmond Tutu Archives, New York, NY.

Tutu, Desmond. (n.d.b). The Issues Facing the Third World in Meeting Basic Needs. Episcopal General Convention, USA, New Orleans, September 5–15.

John Pobee (1937–2020)

Titre Ande Georges

Introduction: His Life

John Samuel Pobee (1937–) is a Ghanaian theologian, ecumenist, missiologist, and church leader. He studied at Cape Coast Government Boys' School (1942–1949), Adisadel College, Cape Coast (1950–1956), University of Ghana (1957–1961), and Selwyn College, University of Cambridge (1961–1966). He had his priestly formation at Westcott House, Cambridge with John S. Mbiti who both, among others like Kwame Bediako, became the pioneers of the African theology. At the University of Ghana, Pobee was Head of Department for the Study of Religions, and Dean of the Faculty of Arts. He later worked at the World Council of Churches in Geneva. He is Emeritus Professor at the University of Ghana. He is married to Martha, a career diplomat of the Ghana Foreign Service. Ordained on the October 23, 1988, he later served as Canon of the Anglican Diocese of Accra and worked as the Vicar General of that diocese (2005–2012). He was a member of Inter-Anglican Doctrinal and Theological Commission from 1981 to 1986 and member of Anglican-Roman Catholic International Commission (1983–1994). Pobee's areas of specialization are in the New Testament (NT), missiology and ecumenics, liturgy and worship. He was once his country's Director of the Ministry of Foreign Affairs, and the Head of Chancery of the Embassy of Ghana in Washington, DC.

Yet another of Africa's unsung heroes, Pobee has been nicknamed "living ancestor" by colleagues and friends, and he undoubtedly deserves much more recognition than he has so far received. His pioneering and continuing scholarship on many aspects of theology, religion, social, and political life in Africa, and his great ecclesiastical engagements, are reflected in a number of his books and essays. The following pages will only present few of his contributions in the area of African theology.

Twentieth Century Anglican Theologians: From Evelyn Underhill to Esther Mombo, First Edition.
Edited by Stephen Burns, Bryan Cones, and James Tengatenga.
© 2021 John Wiley & Sons Ltd. Published 2021 by John Wiley & Sons Ltd.

African Theology

John Vernon Taylor, an Oxford scholar who spent many years as a missionary in Zambia and Uganda, made from his experience a statement that reflected the nature and character of the evangelistic encounter between the missionaries and Africans:

> Christ has been presented as the answer to the question a white man would ask, the solution to the needs the Western man would feel, the Saviour of the world of the European world-view, the object of the adoration and prayer of historic Christendom. But if Christ were to appear as the answer to the questions that Africans are asking, what would he look like? (Taylor 1963, p. 24).

This assertion has provoked many questions regarding theology, teaching, and Christian practices of the missionaries who brought Christianity to the African continent in the seventeenth century. John Pobee was among the earliest African theologians who sought to discover and develop an indigenous theology drawn from and speaking to the African context. He realized that the presentation of Christianity was masked in the models of European cultures and traditions, thus, making Christ a stranger to Africans. This concern has motivated the rise of African theologies. Pobee asserts that "the concern of African theology is to attempt to use African concepts and African ethos as vehicles for communication of the gospel in an African context" (Pobee 1976, p. 82). Even though the attempt to do African theology involves the full scope of Christian doctrine, African *Christology* has gradually become the central issue of theological enterprise on the continent. Pobee emphasized that the form of Christianity brought to Africa was loaded with Anglo-Euro cultural assumptions and has become a major problem for the articulation of an "authentic African Christology" (Pobee 1979, p. 2). Therefore, determination of who Jesus is by Africans for African Christians – using indigenous categories – has become imperative for theological endeavor.

The main methodological question was about the kinds of resources that should be guiding principles for doing theology in Africa. Should they be rooted in indigenous cultural ideas? If so, how indigenous is indigenous or how traditional is traditional? Pobee has always affirmed that African theology should be based on the Bible, understood and interpreted in the light of all the recent advances of historical and literary criticism. Also, theologians need to analyze African religions, approaching them in an unbiased and descriptive way, but at the same time seeking to understand their sacred texts theologically. Then they need to put biblical and traditional sources in confrontation, so as to draw out both their similarities and their divergences. Pobee insists that such theologizing should have the practical aim of serving the needs of the Christian community.

But Pobee is also well aware of the multiplicity of different cultures within Africa and what local cultures mean. He explains that *Homo Africanus* is a multiheaded hydra, in much the same way as "*homo sapiens*" is multiheaded hydra. Also, a *Homo Africanus* of 1976 is different from a *Homo Africanus* of 1876 because of the impact of Westernism expressed through laws, learning, art, and more (Pobee 1979, p. 49). So, culture is understood to be what is happening here and now; it is the result of many different influences, the Western and the missionary influences as well as the result of the earlier traditions, and it is therefore living and contemporary. However, Pobee also notes that, although there is a plethora of African cultures because of their remarkable differences based on tribal background, the Africanness of the culture, religious beliefs and practices must always be recognized (Pobee 1979, p. 30).

For the wholeness or unity of theology and life, academia and church, Pobee warns that African persons should not be treated as museum pieces or anthropological curios, but as persons who grow in stature, mentality, culturally, and in other ways. Consequently, some of the things that may be paraded as African theology may yet speak to others belonging to other ethnic groups (Pobee 1979, p. 31).

In Pobee's view, African theology must be pluralistic, missiological, and ecumenical. By pluralism Pobee points out that African theology concerns and applies to all religions in Africa – African Traditional Religions, Christianity, Islam, and so on – that are "in varying compositions in different parts of Africa" (Pobee 1993, p. 139). For him, African theology is distinguished by its dialogue with culture. It has to be *dialectical and dialogical*, in non-hostile *mutuality*, and with emphasis on the personal level rather than the institutional. Terminologies in the areas of the divinity and the centrality of Christ must be tackled first in anticipation of Islam's monotheism and the acceptability of a "finality and absoluteness" about Christ in plural contexts.

African theology must also be ecumenical to guard against Western factionalism. Pobee notes that theology has been for too long denominational, partly because in the nineteenth century, when much mission in Africa was carried out, theologians and church leaders thought that their denomination was the true church. The younger churches in Africa have been cast as branches of European church organizations.

Also, Africa deals heavily with political issues: human dignity, unrest, ideologies, and slogans both religious and secular, with power being the bottom line. There are politicians "claiming to be the conscience of society" (Pobee 1993, p. 140), usurping the churches' self-appointed role. So, a political ethics touching on value systems must be developed. To do theology in Africa is to tackle poverty, either in the material sense or in forms of marginalization and related realities. Pobee especially points out the areas of ecclesiology and ministry as areas needing the most attention. It is here that the context of power (with which European Christianity was shaped) is most evident but has gone unquestioned in relation to the context of powerlessness in African society. This is why a more relevant hermeneutic of the poor is needed (Pobee 1993, p. 141).

Pobee insists on the necessity of biblical scholarship, which must make an effort to connect with the African worldview, and Africa must itself be able to express biblical theology in a way not alien to it. The existence of the Africa Bible Commentary comes to fulfill such wishes. Contextualization has also been done in the areas of pastoral studies, church history, and Christian education.

African Christology

Who is Jesus Christ? What manner of human being is he? How does he affect my life? Why should an Akan relate to Jesus of Nazareth, who does not belong to his clan, family, tribe, and nation? John Pobee poses such questions because he realized – as noted earlier – that the presentation of Christianity has been masked in the models of European cultures and traditions, thus, making Christ a stranger to Africans. Of course, Africa today has become the locus of an optimistic and numerically strong Christian life. But there was long one-way transfer of theological thinking from Europe to Africa, which for many centuries determined the relationship between the continents. Christianity, including Christology, was still embedded in Anglo-Euro religious cultural categories. Therefore, determination of who Jesus is for African Christians, using indigenous categories has become imperative for theological enterprise. Pobee asserts that "the concern of African theology is to attempt to use African concepts and African ethos as vehicles for communication of the gospel in an African context" (Pobee 1976, p. 82).

Pobee underlines the importance of Christology and points out that "at the heart of the encounter between Christianity and African culture is the subject of Christology (doctrine of the person and work of Christ" (Pobee 1979, p. 81). And the guiding principles of such Christology consist of functionality, concreteness, activity, Akan proverbs, experiences, and culture.

According to Pobee, Christological discussion continues to be much referenced to the Nicene Creed because "it was ratified and expanded by the Council of Constantinople as the plumb line of orthodoxy" (Pobee 1979, p. 81). But the Creed was an attempt of a predominantly Hellenistic society to articulate its belief in Jesus in its own language and concepts. Most of the ideas and idioms of the Nicene Creed are unfamiliar to us today, especially in the context of modern languages and thought forma that have developed since the formulation of the creeds:

> Who today, theologian and philosopher included, normally uses terms such as "substance" or "person" or "hypostasis" in their technical Chalcedonian sense? The Creed was indeed an attempt to "translate" the biblical faith into contemporary language and thoughts forms. In other words, so far as it concerns us, the issue is to get behind the Creed to the biblical faith. And so, whatever we evolve should be tested against the plumb line of the biblical faith (Pobee 1979, p. 82).

For Pobee, the classical theology is heavily dependent on the use of metaphysics for the discussion of Christology (Pobee 1979, p. 82), which comes from the Greco-Roman culture. But Christology in the Bible was expressed in functional terms, expressing impressions of Jesus in terms of his activity (Pobee 1979, p. 82).

> Metaphysical speculation about the relations within the Godhead is absent (in the bible). Even the Fourth Gospel, which declared "The Word was God", nowhere speculates on how the Word was God. Indeed, it soon leaves the heavenlies and comes down to earth with the tremendous affirmation: "The Word became flesh and dwelt among us, full of grace and truth; we beheld this glory" (John 1, 14 Revised Standard Version) (Pobee 1979, p. 82).

For exhibiting concreteness, Pobee finds that the Akan reflect on matters of life in the form of proverbs, which play a very important function in directing human life and interactions. He declares that the use of proverbs even in very serious discussions in the Akan society confirms that functional approach to the discussion of Christology will be the most apt approach to take toward an Akan Christology (Pobee 1979, p. 82). Thus, proverbs must necessarily replace Western philosophical abstraction in the discussion of Christology for Akans.

Pobee identifies two major trends in the NT, namely "Judeo-Christian and Hellenistic-Christian" (Pobee 1979, p. 82). He highlights teachings on the Cosmic Christ as found in the Captivity Epistles and the priestly conceptions found in the Book of Hebrews as examples of these trends, and he welcomes the plurality of Christologies in the NT because theological formulations spring out of people's experiences and culture.

Pleading for a theology rooted in everyday life and for an appropriation to make Jesus Christ "at home," Pobee used biblical sources and African cultural categories with special reference to the ancestral paradigm. He suggests that the direction of such theology may as well start from the African culture.

Fullness of Life and Ancestral Paradigm

Pobee places emphasis on the humanity and the deity of Christ as the starting point for an Akan ancestor-Christology. With reference to Jesus' humanity he asserts, "the humanity of Jesus is one aspect of NT Christology which the attempt to construct a Christology in an African theology cannot skirt" (Pobee 1979, p. 84). According to the Creed, Christ is truly God and truly human, and Pobee expresses Christ's divinity and humanity according to the Akan understanding, in which kinship, circumcision, and baptism are rites of incorporation into a group (Pobee 1979, p. 89). Pobee further purports that Akan humanity expressed through fear of death and finitude of knowledge are also part of Christ's humanity. He states:

> In Akan society the Supreme Being and the ancestors provide the sanctions for the good life and punish evil. And the ancestor holds that authority as minister of the Supreme Being. Our approach would be to look on Jesus as the Great and Greatest Ancestor – in Akan language Nana . . . As Nana he has authority over not only the world of men, but also of all spirit being, namely the cosmic powers and the ancestors (Pobee 1979, p. 90).

According to Pobee – and also to other African theologians such as Bénézet Bujo – life is a participation in God, but hierarchically ordered. It means God is the source of all life, and this divine life can be enjoyed in its fullness when the ancestors are remembered and honored. It is life as unity in its wholeness, for Africa knows no distinction between individual, social, religious, and political life. Although life is always mediated by one standing above the recipient in the hierarchy of being, it is not life merely seen in a biological sense, but it is a metaphysical concept. Ancestors who lived exemplary lives had laid down laws, and established customs, which embodied their own experiences, and which they passed on to their descendants as a precious legacy. The historical Jesus of Nazareth brought life in its fullness, working miracles, healing the sick, opening the eyes of the blind and raising the dead to life. All these qualities and virtues Jesus manifested are those that Africans like to attribute to their ancestors and which lead them to invoke the ancestors in daily life. Therefore, Jesus is the Great and Greatest Ancestor, not in a biological sense, but in an analogical way.

Community: Belonging Together and Mutual Interdependence

Pobee raises also the issue of fullness of life in Christ and Community as a sense of belonging together and of mutual interdependence associated with the recognition of common interests, attitudes, beliefs, and values in the smallest group of the family and within the wider groups. The starting point of Pobee's sense of community is "*Cognatus ergo sum*," which means "I am related by blood, therefore I exist," or more clearly expressed, "I exist because I belong to a family" (Pobee 1979, p. 49). According to Pobee, any action that threatens the sense of belonging together and mutual interdependence of humans in a community is considered a sin. In fact, this idea of the essence of sin as an anti-social act is widespread in Africa. For instance, not to revenge a murdered "sister" or "brother" by another tribe is seen a sin, regardless of the origin or the causes of the fighting.

The church is the community of those who accept the sovereignty of Christ and the identity of the church is intimately related to the identity of Christ in who is the fullness of life. As God is the sovereign ruler of all life, political and socio-economic life cannot be excluded from the sovereignty of God. For Pobee, humans, created in the image of God, are created for community and human life in community is a response to the initiative of God, but it still is relational understanding of human personality. However, Pobee states that the relationship in the human community is possible only because of God. This implies that the well-being of the community depends on God. And this well-being is fullness of life.

According to Pobee, life is the well-being of people in society, while death is anything that weakens the relationships within the community. But life in its fullness is offered to people through Jesus Christ, who is himself the supreme example of life for he is in perfect relationship with others in the human community (Pobee 1986, p. 8). Therefore, the church is the community of those who accept the sovereignty of Christ. However, fullness of life is identified with the well-being of people as they are related to each other in the community. Pobee aims to respond positively to the religious dimension of the cultural context.

But Pobee gives also serious attention to political and economic aspects for well-being is as physical as it is spiritual. As God is the sovereign ruler of all life, political life cannot be excluded from the sovereignty of God. Thus, Christian involvement in politics is non-negotiable, and "where two or three are gathered in connexion [connection] with the society there is politics" (Pobee 1979, p. 25). Pobee from Akan society suggested that, as Christians "we ought to ensure that our affirmation about humans bearing the *imago Dei* and the *sensus communis* as well as the holistic approach to life are fed into political life and the creation of a national ethics in a plural society and world" (Pobee 1986, p. 25). He rejects a complete identification of the church with the political structures, and the government should obtain religious legitimation for its policies. Power can work for life and peace only if it is informed by Christian notions of *imago Dei* and love (Pobee 1986, p. 26). The church has to act as "the conscience of society."

However, it is worth noticing that a wrong conception of sin results in a wrong view of salvation. In ancestral theology, sin is societal. Sin is an anti-social act, and salvation can be procured by satisfying social demands. But according to NT writings on individual sin, salvation is not based on works of kindness (Ephesians 2.8–9), but on God's grace and can be accepted only by faith. Good works follow, but do not precede nor produce salvation. Also, any Christ-centered theology must keep a good balance between Christ as human and Christ as God. To stress the historical Jesus as the Great and Greatest-Ancestor may lead to the risk of considering Jesus as one of the African divinities. Jesus Christ is the historical point of departure for Christianity, and Christian theology is obliged to return to him in the course of its reflection. Care must be taken in using indigenous categories to bring down to earth the reality and mystery of incarnation into the Body of Christ. This will help to meet Pobee's challenge for Africanization to couch "Christian theology in genuinely African terms and categories without losing an iota of authentic and essential Christianity" (Pobee 1979, p. 79).

Contribution to the Anglican Communion and the Worldwide Church

The Anglican Communion has been tested by difficult theological tensions, which in many its parts have not only caused alienation and pain, but have also affected mission in different contexts. There is still continuing deep difference and disrupted relationships in the Anglican Communion. Others even wonder whether the Anglican Communion has the necessary theological, structural, and cultural foundations to sustain the life of the Communion. As ever, the question the Communion is facing is: "Who is Jesus Christ for Anglicans?" The entire Christian faith stands on the person and work of Jesus Christ. The denial of the full deity of Jesus Christ can only lead to a new "Anglican-Christianity," which would be a projection of relativism hiding beneath the language of devotion and piety.

It is true that Africa suffered from a "prefabricated theology," something John Pobee called "the North Atlantic captivity of the church." While there are still signs of Africa's "theological captivity," we must truly aspire to think and live as globally oriented Christians. As the center of Christianity has moved significantly and Western Christians are now in the minority, then we should expect this shift to be reflected in Christian theology as the methodological interpretation of the Christian faith. It should no longer be possible to do Christian theology adequately today without taking into account the reflections and insights of Africans concerning Jesus Christ. John Samuel Pobee has been consultant to three Lambeth Conferences of bishops, in 1978, 1988, and 1998 at which key members of the Anglican Communion began to give consideration to so-called "Third World theologians."

Africans are concerned with the practical effects of belief in Christ. Africans preach a Christ who is a dynamic personal reality in all situations. African Christology is holistic in the way it integrates the person and work of Christ. Its view of the person of Christ is constantly informed by what Christ has accomplished in history and what he continues to do in the world. Christ is seen as no stranger to the practical realities of poverty, illiteracy, ethnic tensions, colonialism, dictatorship, and suffering. This is what John Pobee called "multiheaded hydra." It means African Christology takes seriously the physical, socio-political, cultural, and economic realities of the African context. It is how the person and the work of Christ apply to the whole of African life.

Therefore, for Africans, God as the supreme deity is alone the guarantor of life and coherence in the human community and the cosmos. Cosmos and nature are both taken into consideration. This is why Jesus has a cosmological significance in the relationship of Jesus to creation and redemptive significance in his relationship to humankind. It shows the lordship of Christ. So, Pobee's preference of concreteness of expressions could help some Anglican theologians to avoid theological abstractions or metaphysical speculation so theology is done with commitment in daily life for real life in the church and society.

Concerning the use of cultural categories, we understand that culture is given by God for the sake of human flourishing, but all cultures must take the human fallenness into consideration. The gospel judges and evangelizes the cultures, but also the gospel needs to be inculturated. So, the Christian faith can be exposed brilliantly without compromise if there is inculturation. Inculturation is the process by which the gospel message is incarnated into cultures and local contexts, so that it is meaningful to the members of a given Christian community and is easily understood by those outside it. Hearing the gospel can lead to a purifying of cultures, while different cultural expressions can enrich the proclamation of the Gospel message. Therefore, the gospel can redeem culture as well as individuals.

African emphasis on the Bible should help us to take our responsibility to keep the integrity of the apostolic teaching in its passing on across cultures and down the ages. In doing so, we need to take into account the local and the global in order to remain in communion with others. In his addresses at Lambeth 2008, Rowan Williams warned the gathered bishops that the global horizon of the church matters because churches without this are always in danger of slowly surrendering to the culture around them and losing sight of their calling to challenge that culture.[1] Pobee's experience on his cultural theology could be a good warning to himself and to the Anglican Communion so contextualization of God's Word is done without surrendering blindly to the living culture.

Furthermore, the Anglican Congress of 1963, held in Toronto, Canada, proposed a radical reorientation of mission priorities and stressed mutual responsibility for mission between all Anglican churches as equal partners. It stated:

> In our time the Anglican Communion has come of age. Our professed nature as a worldwide fellowship of national and regional churches has suddenly become a reality . . . The full communion in Christ, which has been our traditional tie, has suddenly taken on a totally new dimension. It is now irrelevant to talk of "giving" and "receiving" churches. The keynotes of our time are equality, interdependence, mutual responsibility.[2]

Unfortunately, as Ian T. Douglas noted, this Congress' vision of Mutual Responsibility and Interdependence in the Body of Christ (MRI) remains a goal to be achieved rather than a reality that is lived. Douglas proposes two reasons of this slow move. Firstly, we are not yet free from the vestiges of colonial power and for new colonial abuses. He states that when the West gives to/or holds back money from "partner churches" in the Southern Hemisphere, based upon its needs and desire, or when brother bishops and archbishops from around the world take it on themselves to set up alternative polity structures in the United States as a means to support "orthodox" believers, these actions run counter to the spirit and commitments of MRI. He concludes that colonialism dies hard. Secondly, Anglicans formed in Enlightenment thought pride themselves on being able to figure things out, to know limits, to be able to define what is right and what is wrong, who is in and who is out (Douglas and Kwok 2000, p. 222).

Pobee's view of community as a sense of belonging together and of mutual interdependence associated with the recognition of common interests, attitudes, beliefs, and values in the smallest group of the family and within the wider groups, fits well with the Anglican vision of MRI. It would make a vital contribution to our relationships within the whole Church of God. It therefore summons our Churches to a deeper commitment to Christ's mission through a wide partnership of prayer, by sharing sacrificially and effectively their manpower and money, and by a readiness to learn from each other as expressed in Resolution 67, Lambeth Conference 1968.[3]

Conclusion

In conclusion, Paul's words in Romans 12.4–5, are apt: "For just as each of us has one body with many members, and these members do not all have the same function, so in Christ we, though many, form one body, and each member belongs to all the others."

Notes

1 The Archbishop of Canterbury, Rowan Williams launched the official program for the Lambeth Conference 2008: Equipping Bishops for Mission, at Lambeth Palace http://aoc2013.brix.fatbeehive.com/articles.php/1331/launch-of-lambeth-conference-2008 (accessed July 15, 2020).
2 http://anglicanhistory.org/canada/toronto_mutual1963.html (accessed July 15, 2020).
3 http://www.anglicancommunion.org/resources/document-library/lambeth-conference/1968/resolution-67-the-role-of-the-anglican-communion-mutual-responsibility?author=Lambeth+Conference&year=1968 (accessed July 15, 2020).

References

Douglas, I.T. and Kwok, P.-l. (eds.) (2000). *Beyond Colonial Anglicanism: The Anglican Communion in the Twenty-First Century.* New York: Church Publishing.
Pobee, S.J. (ed.) (1976). *Religion in a Pluralistic Society.* Leiden: Brill.
Pobee, S.J. (1979). *Towards an African Theology.* Nashville, TN: Abingdon Press.

Pobee, S.J. (1986). Life and peace. In: *Variations in Christian Theology in Africa* (eds. J.S. Pobee and C.F. Hallencreutz), 14–31. Nairobi: Uzima Press.

Pobee, S.J. (1993). African theology revisited. In: *Religious Plurality in Africa: Essays in Honour of John S. Mbiti* (eds. J.K. Olupona and S.S. Nyang), 135–143. Berlin: Lang.

Taylor, J.V. (1963). *Christian Presence amid African Religion*. London: SCM Press.

Ann Loades (1938–)

Stephen Burns

Ann Loades (1938–) was born in Stockport, north-west England, in the year before the outbreak of World War II, and she was sent to boarding school at the early age of three (Brown 2008a, p. 271). It would seem that these aspects of her young life gave contours to her intellectual quest and in turn shaped the contribution to theology that she made toward the end of the century: when interviewed and asked about what she prayed for most, she answered "an end to the scourge of war,"[1] and a distinctive feature of her "enlarged feminism" (Loades 2001a, p. 1) is that while concerned with women's self-determination, so it is no less with their dependents.

Despite her own protestations about not being a professional historian (Loades 1985b, p. vi), Loades' work is marked by a very strong historical consciousness in which habitual recall of contexts of war, and the (by others, often unacknowledged or ignored) shadows that war casts on theological work is just one example. To turn a phrase of Karl Barth – one he penned in the year that Loades went to boarding school – there is no support in her work for theology being done *"as if nothing had happened"* in the wider world (Barth, cited in Leech 1985, p. 386, italics in original).

As well as becoming expert on the work of some of the widely acknowledged luminaries of her own Anglican tradition – C. S. Lewis (e.g., Loades 1989a; Loades 2010b) and Austin Farrer (e.g., Eaton and Loades 1983; Loades and MacSwain 2006), most notably – she has also called attention to the often overlooked contributions of a number of women – Evelyn Underhill (e.g., Loades 1997, 2015, 2019) and Dorothy L. Sayers (e.g., Loades 1993, 1995, 2001a, 2011); and to numerous other women (Loades 2020a). That such women may now not be so sidelined is in part because of Ann Loades' resort to their legacy.

Twentieth Century Anglican Theologians: From Evelyn Underhill to Esther Mombo, First Edition.
Edited by Stephen Burns, Bryan Cones, and James Tengatenga.
© 2021 John Wiley & Sons Ltd. Published 2021 by John Wiley & Sons Ltd.

Under the encouragement of a tutor at boarding school and her teachers at Hulme Grammar School for Girls, Loades went on to study at Durham University, the institution where she herself would teach theology from 1975 to 2003, and in which she became the first woman to be given a personal chair. Between her undergraduate degree and the start of her teaching career, she undertook further studies at McMaster University, Canada, and turned down the option of heading for the University of Chicago in order to return to Durham as College Officer (responsible for admissions, library, and pastoral care of students) at St. Mary's, a women's college, and then Collingwood, Durham's first mixed-sex college. With the support of Professor John Rogerson she completed a Durham doctorate, then competed for her post and moved full-time into Durham's Department of Theology. Her doctorate was on Immanuel Kant, a figure with a recurring presence in Loades' thinking (e.g., Loades 2001b), and the entrée into the focus of her early writing on eighteenth and nineteenth century figures.[2] Her first post in Durham's theology department was in philosophical theology (see e.g., Loades and Rue 1991), and it should be noted that at the time Durham – a university with a strong component of ordinands in its theological cohorts – did not teach courses in Christian doctrine to women: as they could not be ordained, at least as priests in the Church of England. By the time Loades became the first Anglican woman to be made professor of theology in the United Kingdom, in 1995,[3] women were (only just – since the previous year) being made presbyters in the national church, a cause Loades supported from her lay location – as she also gave her support toward women in the episcopate – though interestingly and in some contrast to contemporaneous writing by Anglican women in the 1980s,[4] the ordination of women is not a focus of Loades' first book on feminism, *Searching for Lost Coins* (Loades 1987), which takes up wider perspectives.

Loades' work over time takes in impressively wide-ranging foci and genres: philosophy of religion, Christian ethics, biblical hermeneutics, the legacy of Anglican forebears, feminist theology, and sacramental spirituality being just some of her interests. Her work as an editor, earlier on the team responsible for *Modern Church* and especially later in charge of *Theology* (which led to an entry in *Who's Who*[5]), helped to make her well-known – though so too did her work in television, as a presenter on the then-new Channel 4 program *Seven Days*. When presented with a CBE ("Commander of the British Empire") medal, in the 2001 Honors list, she was the first woman to be recognized for "services to theology" (the only other person being C. F. D. [Charlie] Moule) – likely in recognition of her extensive work with the Arts and Humanities Research Council, which took her influence well beyond Durham. And when she became the first female president of the Society for the Study of Theology, in 2005, she was about to move out of Durham and launch into an active retirement in which she made her home just outside St. Andrews, Scotland, in whose university she became honorary professor and member of its Institute of Theology, Imagination and the Arts, carrying forward a strand of her work that came into focus in the final decade of her teaching career, on the arts. During her retirement, she became one of the first professional theologians to write on dance (see Loades 2018b), drawing on her long-term engagement with teaching classical ballet, which has been a preoccupation for much of her time in retirement even as she continues to write, speak, and preach.

Feminist Theology

Searching for Lost Coins (Loades 1987) was the first monograph on Christian feminism to emerge from a British university theologian, and resulted from her Scott Holland Lectures in Newcastle-upon-Tyne in 1986. The Scott Holland Trust had requested her thought on "theology and the significance of gender" – a particular take on the trust's defining concern with "the religion of the Incarnation in its bearing on the social and economic life of man" (sic, somewhat ironically). The book's title is a clue to its approach to the Christian tradition, seeking rehabilitation of insights and resources that might be missed in a merely contemporary perspective. She deals in particular with what she identifies as core symbols: (perhaps unfashionably for the time) articulating reserve about depiction of the divine as feminine ("god and god/ess"), uncluttering confusion about the figure of Mary, and scrutinizing the spirituality of some historical figures in a particularly moving chapter on the imitation of Christ, "Christ also suffered," with its stinging subtitle, "why certain forms of holiness are bad for you." Noted by numerous commentators for being "calm" and "gentle" (though inevitably by others "disturbing"[6]), the book concludes with the point that how the institutional church might welcome or welcome back women mistrustful of its "means of grace" is "unclear" to her (Loades 1987, p. 99). On the way to this, with respect to the idea that naming God as "mother" will effect change for the better for women, she echoes philosopher Anthony Flew:

> Someone tells us that God loves us as a father loves his children. We are reassured. But then we see a child dying of inoperable cancer of the throat. His earthly father is driven frantic in his efforts to help, but his Heavenly Father reveals no obvious signs of concern,

adding in her own voice, "substitute 'mother' all through, and the child will still die. . ., just as one singer of Psalm 22 dies on the cross" (Loades 1987, pp. 96–97). In her view, if language is to make a difference, churches will first need to "become the kinds of communities where there are genuine attempts to try to repair the damage done to women" (Loades 1987, p. 98). On the tropes of sacrifice that oftentimes link discipleship to the mystery of the cross, she focuses on Simone Weil as a troubling example of "the last kind of Christianity that women may need," discussing not so much the merits of "attention" for which Weil is so widely lauded, but rather the "holy anorexia" that manifest in her refusal to eat anything other than eucharistic elements, and so "close down [her] senses." No doubt Weil's was indeed an extreme embodiment of an affliction more widely appropriated in less shrill, but in the long term perhaps little less damaging, ways. At the heart of Loades' caution is that

> it is one thing to employ the metaphors of the "imitation of Christ" as the context of love and then be sustained by it in a situation of extremity, but quite another to make the bare possibility of being in that situation a focus of attention outside the context of love (Loades 1987, p. 57).

As Weil, in Loades' view, shows, without love the imitation of Christ can test persons to destruction, be "lived and died" (Loades 1987, p. 57).

Loades' extensive editorial commentary throughout *Feminist Theology: A Reader* (Loades 1990b, relating to Loades 1989b) built upon *Searching for Lost Coins'* initial discussions of contemporary feminist theologians, and included the primary sources of a wide range of feminist theology, introducing to British audiences[7] a heft of perspectives. While "balanced" (Brown 2008a, p. 273), it did not note the ecclesial allegiances if any, of the essayists included, though only three of twenty-two – Sara Maitland, Janet Morley, Nicola Slee – were Anglicans[8]). A second monograph on feminist theology, *Feminist Theology: Voices from the Past* (Loades 2001a), took more of its light from another dimension of *Searching for Lost Coins*: attention to historical figures. Alongside Weil in the earlier book, Elizabeth Cady Stanton, Helen Waddell, Virginia Woolf, and several others all find a place in Loades' discussion. For its part, *Voices from the Past* focuses on just three, each themselves Anglican: Mary Wollstonecraft (so returning Loades' focus to the eighteenth century), Josephine Butler (nineteenth century), and Dorothy L. Sayers. Each of the three is then related to a particular theme, as Loades seeks wisdom she deems at risk of being forgotten but that they may yet bring to contemporary issues: Wollstonecraft apropos abortion, Butler concerning the sexual abuse of children, and Sayers on a sacramental view of work and the world. The "issues" are all themes on which Loades had herself already written, and now directed into dialogue with these forebears. In the case of child sexual abuse, Loades was also the first British academic theologian to tackle the problem (Loades 1994b, 1996, 2001a). Loades' correlations each exemplify what *Voices from the Past* dubs "enlarged" feminism, concerned with women's self-governance and also with the vulnerable who may well be dependants of women and whose own flourishing rests on women's capacity to act with resolve beyond the realm of their own rights:

> As equality becomes increasingly a reality, there is a real danger that it will involve leaving some still on the margins of our attention – in some contexts, women themselves, in some others, those for whom they should have legitimate concern (Loades 2001a, p. 1).

Notably, while in writing like *Voices from the Past* Loades is unflinching from difficult issues relating to the abuse of children, in other places she gives strong hints on how children may bring "inchoate grace" (Loades 1997, p. 580) to others' lives, even be "living prayers" of the ones in whose loving care they are raised (Loades 1985a).

Loades' denouement to *Searching for Lost Coins*, on her unclarity as to how women may recognize means of grace in the Christian tradition, appears in hindsight to have been a provisional conclusion, as she comes to reassert the path she made her own in terms of:

> struggl[ing] hard with the devaluation of women for which the Christian tradition is in its own way responsible, but . . . assum[ing] that the tradition also contains resources for transformation and change, despite the weight of criticism levelled against it (Loades 2001a, p. 5).

Ever ready to say what she thinks stands in need of correction, Ann Loades herself could never be described as an uncritical or deferential participant in the life of the church, yet she nevertheless found her own way to stay engaged, and as well as exercising an extensive ministry of preaching that in no way quietened her questions, she was also the first ever female lay member of Chapter (the governing body) in Durham Cathedral's more than nine-hundred year history, and one of two first Lay Canons.[9] Intriguingly for what follows, Daniel Hardy, her one-time colleague and priest at the cathedral, noted that "the strength of her presence" could become unusually "subdued" in worship (Hardy 2008, p. 103).

Voices from the Past

One of Loades' first books was a co-edited collection of papers on Austin Farrer, *For God and Clarity* (Eaton and Loades 1983; see also Hebblethwaite 2008), and she has been a regular contributor to subsequent studies of Farrer such that he features in her thinking right up to her most recent writing (Loades 2018a). She has also written on a number of persons in the circle around him (Loades 2004b), The Inklings, drawing particular attention to women in or close to that group of Oxford intellectuals – Iris Murdoch and Helen Oppenheimer, for example – and also focusing her sights on its best known member, C. S. Lewis. Her contributions to understanding Lewis have two foci: first complexifying ways in which he is widely regarded as a Christian apologist by (albeit empathically) probing the difficulties he expressed in his book about the loss of his spouse Joy to cancer, *A Grief Observed*, which he initially published under a pseudonym. Then expressing little patience with his views about gender. It is here that the ordination of women does come to the fore in Loades' writing, locating Lewis' failure to recognize the capacity of women to serve as priests co-terminously with a 1936 Archbishop's Commission about the trouble it thought women would cause if made leaders of worship. Loades writes that the commission was "most foolish" (Loades 2010c, p. 83) – and when her turn came to join a commission on women in the episcopate, she did so only on the proviso that it be made known from the start that her mind was made up about the capacity of women to take a lead (Loades 2004c).

While *Voices from the Past* focused on Wollstonecraft, Butler, and Sayers, Sayers especially preoccupies a number of other writings. "Are Women Human?" and "The-Human-Not-Quite-Human" were Loades' entry point into Sayers' theological essays, and led her to appreciation of Dante, whose *The Divine Comedy* Sayers had translated and in whom Loades also found ideas to take into her own. Loades had already established a strong proclivity to "not conceive resources for theological reflection in too narrow terms" (Loades 1987, p. 15) so including many kinds of literature, and Sayers' attempts to convey Christian doctrine in a range of genres (not least novels) and including media beyond print (theater arts, and radio plays) resonates strongly with Loades' own penchants. Above all, though, via Sayers' explorations of Dante, the figure of Beatrice (Loades 1987, p. 35) becomes a focus for some of Loades' own ideas, as an example of how persons may mediate grace to one another, their presence central to an expansive view of sacramentality, notwithstanding all the ambiguities of human intent and action. Overriding reserve about the latter is Loades' view that "if the horrors of judicial execution can be the means of divine revelation so might the boring, the banal, the squalid, the morally problematic," with grace in any case never self-made as "a human self-making of divine presence is a contradiction in terms and a thoroughly futile endeavour" (Loades 2000, p. 31).

Evelyn Underhill became another key figure in Loades' thinking. Beginning from her observation that, as a woman, Underhill had neither an ecclesial nor academic base from which to do theology, Loades writes about Underhill's own development, including her achievements as a "first" in various ways that foreshadow the firsts Loades was herself to achieve in her own day. The shifts between Underhill's two most significant publications, *Mysticism* of 1911 and *Worship* of 1936, and Underhill's conversion to Christianity, commitment to the Church of England (which was not without considerable tensions), and increasing Christocentricism are of particular interest to Loades, as are Underhill's approaches to war and eventual pacifism, and Underhill's writing as a novelist (Loades 2019), as well as Underhill's particular appreciation of the role of the presider in Christian worship as an image of other members of the assembly in their movement toward God (Loades 2010a).

One other "voice from the past" invites mention in surveying Ann Loades' contributions: that is, that of Mary the mother of Jesus, an almost silent and deeply ambiguous figure in and for much of Christianity. *Searching for Lost Coins* discusses Mary particularly in terms of disentangling traditions about the mother of Jesus and Mary of Magdala, and elsewhere, Loades writes (as Janet Martin Soskice says in her introduction, "amusingly and perceptively") on "the Virgin Mary in the feminist quest" (Loades 1990a; Loades 2021). In fact over time Loades yielded a cluster of essays on Mary, in which she stresses Mary's focal role at Pentecost as depicted in the iconography of the Rabulla Gospels, and in which she applies a phrase appropriated from the Dominican thinker Cornelius Ernst to the mother of Jesus: "grace is not faceless" (e.g., Loades 1990a, p. 173). This term, itself akin to what Dante learned from Beatrice, is a link into the third major feature of Loades' work: an emphasis on the sacramental, not least with respect to human persons.

Sacramental Spirituality

In the early 1990s, Loades gained a new colleague at Durham, David Brown, who came to the Van Mildert chair as canon-professor previously occupied by Daniel Hardy. Together Loades and Brown embarked on a major collaboration to mark the nine-hundredth anniversary of the cathedral where Brown worked in his joint post, and where Loades was herself a long-term worshipper. Their "sacramental spirituality" project entailed a series of public events engaged with the arts (such as poetry readings, and both temporary installations and commissioning of painting and sculpture) as well as an extensive lecture series resulting in two books: *The Sense of the Sacramental* (Brown and Loades 1995) and *Christ: The Sacramental Word* (Brown and Loades 1996). Both Brown and Loades went on to develop their thinking on sacramentality individually, as well as to some extent collaboratively (Brown and Loades 2006), with Loades' writing pushing forward with her characteristic emphasis on the social, ever present in her work since at least the Scott Holland invitation. As she states bluntly, "much discussion of sacramentality avoids even beginning to grapple with the 'graces' of institutional and political life" (Loades 2004a, p. 172). So she insists that the biblical list of "fruit of the Spirit" – love, joy, peace, and so on – needs to be complemented or expanded as "we need new ways of thinking and living in the *polis* which elicit from us new 'fruits of the Spirit' if we are to negotiate what is likely to remain a very complex and mistake-ridden world" (Loades 2000, p. 33; Loades 2005, p. 261; see Loades 1991, 2001b, for examples of attention to economic justice).

Another dimension of her sense of the sacramental is expressed in her view that "one of the reasons that our sense of liturgy is so poor is that . . . we have lost the sense of what it is to be an artist, and have lost the artists themselves" (Loades 2000, pp. 45–46). Yet her striking stress on divine presence being "associated with the fleeting, the contingent, here today and gone tomorrow, with 'travelling light'" leads her to openness to including all kinds of arts in liturgy, and not least ones unjustly neglected in an all-too-common liturgical fetishism for the fixed:

> After all, most of the "material signs" of specific sacraments are fluid, consumable, transient, except for their immediate or longer term effects on the persons concerned, themselves the pilgrims (Loades 2000, pp. 33–34).

Hence, music, dance, visual and plastic arts, poetry, and literature all have a place in "allowing for the possibility of [divine presence], relishing it whenever it just so happens to be around, to surface perhaps, to be not merely unmistakably but perhaps even ambiguously just 'there'" (Loades 2000, p. 31).

Taking together her concern with the social and then with the arts, many forms of *poesis* (that is, "human making," and an emphasis no doubt influenced at least in part by Sayers on creativity) lead Loades to "Christ as sacrament" (Loades 2005, pp. 266–267): one in whom her religion of the Incarnation affirms God "not merely flesh-makes but flesh-takes" (Loades 2004a, p. 162), and whose "grace and glory" can be seen "on one another's faces" (Loades 1994a, p. 13). Ann Loades would echo Evelyn Underhill that "God extends an invitation to be loved to each and every human being" (Loades 1997, p. xii), adding that "God does not leave human beings to flounder in their pains and difficulties but seeks them out" (Loades 2004a, p. 161) – an interesting turning of the importance of "searching" – with God becoming "sayable in [the] seeking" as God "initiates such mediation of divine presence as may be possible to us and for us" (Loades 2004a, p. 162).

Dante's *Paradiso* at the end of *The Divine Comedy* itself ends with a prayer to the Virgin Mary in which a trinitarian image comes into focus. "The love that moves the sun and the other stars" depicted as three spheres of light, one of which is "limned with our image," as Dorothy L. Sayers translated "*pinta de la nostra effige.*" Loades evidently likes this "limned" image as Sayers had done before her, as she quotes it in various places and cites it in her sermons (Loades 1993, p. 170; Loades 1994a, p. 12). This depiction of a doctrine, glimpsed in a grace-bearing image – anatomy or face perhaps, even a smile?[10] – is a fitting picture of Loades' own strong convictions about blessing enabled by divine generosity to and through human persons.

Conclusion

What emerges from attention to Ann Loades' writings is an awareness of its interconnections. Sacraments are considered not only in the confines of Christian assembly, but as clues to grace at play in the care of children, the workplace, social change, and other things besides. Feminism is no exercise in self-referentiality, but an activity that must both keep shifting norms in public life and shelter the vulnerable. And forebears sometimes have startling aptness, because tradition

> is not to be construed as "the dead hand of the past" which will prevent us from thinking afresh, but a life-giving source of vitality . . . of its essence creative and innovative, mustering every grace of intelligence and skill in enabling us to learn from the past, generate critical dissonance with the present, open up new vistas and walkways, generate new insights, negotiate dead ends, endure experiences of profound alienation, and live with criteria which themselves may change (Loades 2004a, p. 164).

Apparently Stephen Sykes[11] once suggested to Ann Loades that her thinking could be likened to a rabbit warren (Brown 2008b, p. 9): above ground as it were not at first always seeming to be linked, but under the surface all of a piece. It is her non-compartmentalized sensibility toward "grappl[ing] with a relationship with God in one's present context" (Loades 2015, p. 150) that makes both her approach and her convictions so rich.

Notes

1 www.churchtimes.co.uk/articles/2016/12-february/features/interviews/interview-ann-loades-theologian-professor-emerita-in-divinity-durham (accessed July 17, 2020).

2 Coleridge and Kierkegaard are both present. For a full bibliography of Ann Loades' writings up to 2008, see Watson and Burns (2008, pp. 276–284).

3 Though another Anglican woman, Sarah Coakley, had been made so abroad and women from traditions other than Anglicanism had been so in other British universities – for example Lisa Isherwood and Ursula King, both Roman Catholics.

4 Monica Furlong's efforts are most notable, as those of Daphne Hampson who at that time was an Anglican before later identifying as post-Christian, in an example of the kind of shift Loades saw that many other women either had and might yet make (see Loades 1987, p. 1).

5 http://www.ukwhoswho.com/view/10.1093/ww/9780199540884.001.0001/ww-9780199540884-e-24809/version/4 (accessed July 17, 2020).

6 Reviews *Religious Studies, Contact, and Churchman*, respectively.

7 The book, as a number of her others, was co-published in North America, and in this case translated into Spanish.

8 Maitland later became a Roman Catholic.

9 N. T. Wright's sermon at her installation: www.durhamcathedral.co.uk/worship-music/regular-services/sermon-archive/worrying-prophecy-wonderful-grace (accessed July 17, 2020).

10 The word "*effige*" appears just twice in the *Comedy*, the other time in clear connection with Beatrice (*Paradiso*, Canto 31).

11 Sykes was another former Van Mildert Professor.

References

Brown, D. (2008a). Biographical Epilogue. In: *Exchanges of Grace: Essays in Honour of Ann Loades* (eds. N. Watson and S. Burns), 271–275. London: SCM Press.

Brown, D. (2008b). Introduction. In: *Exchanges of Grace: Essays in Honour of Ann Loades* (eds. N. Watson and S. Burns), 1–8. London: SCM Press.

Brown, D. and Loades, A. (eds.) (1995). *The Sense of the Sacramental: Movement and Measure in Art and Music, Time and Place.* London: SPCK.

Brown, D. and Loades, A. (eds.) (1996). *Christ – The Sacramental Word: Incarnation, Sacrament, and Poetry.* London: SPCK.

Brown, D. and Loades, A. (2006). Learning from the arts. In: *Who Is this Man? Christ in the Renewal of the Church* (eds. J. Baker and W. Davage), 67–102. London: Continuum.

Eaton, J. and Loades, A. (eds.) (1983). *For God and Clarity: Essays in Honour of Austin Farrer.* Eugene, OR: Pickwick Publications.

Hardy, D.W. (2008). Theology and spirituality: a tribute to Ann Loades. In: *Exchanges of Grace: Essays in Honour of Ann Loades* (eds. N. Watson and S. Burns), 103–119. London: SCM Press.

Hebblethwaite, B. (2008). Ann Loades and Austin Farrer. In: *Exchanges of Grace: Essays in Honour of Ann Loades* (eds. N. Watson and S. Burns), 130–141. London: SCM Press.

Leech, K. (1985). *True God: An Exploration in Christian Spirituality.* London: Sheldon Press.

Loades, A. (1985a). Death and disvalue: some reflections on "sick" children. *Hospital Chaplain* 93: 5–11.

Loades, A. (1985b). *Kant and Job's Comforters.* Newcastle-upon-Tyne: Avero.

Loades, A. (1987). *Searching for Lost Coins: Explorations in Christianity and Feminism.* London: SPCK.

Loades, A. (1989a). C. S. Lewis: grief observed, rationality abandoned, faith regained. *Journal of Literature and Theology* 3: 107–121.

Loades, A. (1989b). Feminist theology. In: *The Modern Theologians: An Introduction to Christian Theology in the Twentieth Century*, vol. 2 (ed. D.F. Ford), 235–253. Oxford: Blackwell.

Loades, A. (1990a). The Virgin Mary in the feminist quest. In: *After Eve: Women, Theology and the Christian Tradition* (ed. J.M. Soskice), 156–178. London: Collins.

Loades, A. (ed.) (1990b). *Feminist Theology: A Reader.* London: SPCK.

Loades, A. (1991). A feminist perspective on the morality of the new right. In: *The Renewal of Social Vision* (ed. M. Northcott), 49–61. Edinburgh: Centre for Theology and Public Issues.

Loades, A. (ed.) (1993). *Dorothy L. Sayers: Spiritual Writings.* London: SPCK.

Loades, A. (1994a). The face of Christ. In: *Silence in Heaven: A Book of Women's Preaching* (eds. H. Walton and S. Durber), 9–13. London: SCM Press.

Loades, A. (1994b). *Thinking About Child Sexual Abuse.* London: University of London.

Loades, A. (1995). Are women human? Dorothy L. Sayers as a feminist reader of Dante's Beatrice. *Feminist Theology* 8: 21–38.

Loades, A. (1996). Dympna revisited: thinking about the sexual abuse of children. In: *The Family in Theological Perspective* (ed. S.C. Barton), 253–272. Edinburgh: T & T Clark.

Loades, A. (1997). *Evelyn Underhill.* London: Fount.

Loades, A. (2000). Word and sacrament: recovering integrity. In: *Faith in the Public Forum* (eds. N. Brown and R. Gasgoine), 28–46. Adelaide: ATF Press.

Loades, A. (2001a). *Feminist Theology: Voices from the Past.* Oxford: Polity.

Loades, A. (2001b). From Kant to Fukuyama and beyond: some reflections. In: *Public Theology in the Twenty-First Century: Essays in Honour of Duncan B. Forrester* (ed. W. Storrar), 143–158. London: T & T Clark.

Loades, A. (2004a). Finding new sense in the sacramental. In: *The Gestures of God: Explorations in Sacramentality* (eds. G. Rowell and C. Hall), 161–172. London: Continuum.

Loades, A. (2004b). The vitality of tradition: Austin Farrer and friends. In: *Captured by the Crucified: The Practical Theology of Austin Farrer* (eds. D. Hein and E.H. Henderson), 15–46. London: Continuum.

Loades, A. (2004c). Women in the Episcopate. *Anvil* 21: 113–119.

Loades, A. (2005). Sacramentality and Christian spirituality. In: *The Blackwell Companion to Christian Spirituality* (ed. A. Holder), 254–268. Oxford: Blackwell.

Loades, A. (2010a). Evelyn Underhill (1875-1941): *Mysticism* and *Worship*. *International Society for the Study of the Christian Church* 10: 51–70.

Loades, A. (2010b). On Gender. In: *The Cambridge Companion to C. S. Lewis* (eds. R. MacSwain and M. Ward), 160–173. Cambridge: Cambridge University Press.

Loades, A. (2010c). Unequivocal affirmation of the saving significance of difference. In: *Presiding Like a Woman* (eds. N. Slee and S. Burns), 77–87. London: SPCK.

Loades, A. (2011). Dorothy L. Sayers: War and Redemption. In: *C. S. Lewis and Friends: Faith and the Power of Imagination* (eds. D. Hein and E. Henderson), 53–70. London: SPCK.

Loades, A. (2015). Anglican spirituality. In: *The Oxford Handbook of Anglican Studies* (eds. M.D. Chapman, S. Clarke and M. Percy), 149–164. Oxford: Oxford University Press.

Loades, A. (2018a). Lazarus without limits: scripture, tradition, and the cultural life of a text. *International Journal for the Study of the Christian Church* 18: 252–264.

Loades, A. (2018b). Some straws in the wind: reflections towards theological engagement with theatre dance. In: *Christian Theology and the Transformation of Natural Religion: From Incarnation to Sacramentality: Essays in Honour of David W. Brown* (ed. C.R. Brewer), 191–206. Peeters: Leuven.

Loades, A. (2019). Evelyn Underhill: Mysticism explored through the novel. In: *Anglican Women Novelists: From Charlotte Bronte to P.D. James* (eds. J. Maltby and A. Shell), 73–86. London: Bloomsbury.

Loades, A. (2020a). *Grace and Glory in One Another's Faces: Preaching and Worship* (ed. S. Burns). Norwich: Canterbury.

Loades, A. (2021). *Grace is Not Faceless: Reflections on Mary*. London: DLT.

Loades, A. and MacSwain, R. (eds.) (2006). *The Truth-Seeking Heart: Austin Farrer and His Writings*. Norwich: Canterbury Press.

Loades, A. and Rue, L. (eds.) (1991). *Contemporary Classics in Philosophy of Religion*. La Salle, Ill: Open Court.

Watson, N.K. and Burns, S. (eds.) (2008). *Exchanges of Grace: Essays in Honour of Ann Loades*. London: SCM Press.

Kenneth Leech (1939–2015)

Stephen Burns

Kenneth (often known as Ken) Leech (1939–2015) was born and died in Manchester in the north-west of England. Educated at grammar school in Hulme (an area near the city center), he then went to King's College, London, and Trinity College, Oxford, before training for ordination at St. Stephen's House, also in Oxford. Leech then worked mainly in parish ministry (in one place, St. Anne's, Soho, where Dorothy L. Sayers had earlier been a churchwarden), only ever holding one teaching post in theology, at St. Augustine's College, Canterbury, and then for just three years. Apart from his years in Oxford and Canterbury, almost his entire working life[1] (as undergraduate study before it) was spent in London's East End, the part in which he lived longest giving the title to his last book: *Doing Theology in Altab Ali Park* (Leech 2006a). Leech noted that his brief stint in Canterbury was the first time in his life that he had not lived on a main road, and also that it was impossible for him to write theology without constantly referring back to the context of Whitechapel Road on which Altab Ali Park is situated (Leech 2001, pp. 2, 4). Notably for what follows, Leech was conscious both that the East End of London is one of the most ethnically mixed areas of the world (Leech 2001, p. 136), and also "the heartland of British fascism" (Leech 2001, p. 156). In his later years, Leech retired back to Manchester, where he married again in what was the very last year of his life.

The Manchester home in which Leech was raised was nominally Methodist, his engineer father being a "convert" to socialism and via that commitment being at least somewhat open to what he regarded as the working-class sympathies of the Methodist Church – though he never attended worship. Ken Leech was to inherit his father's strong socialist leanings, but also to make an active Christian commitment, commenting that "Christian faith and socialism have been equally central" in his life, with his own Christian faith especially shaped by a justice-oriented version of the anglo-catholic tradition of Anglicanism he knew to have been embodied by the "red vicar"

Twentieth Century Anglican Theologians: From Evelyn Underhill to Esther Mombo, First Edition.
Edited by Stephen Burns, Bryan Cones, and James Tengatenga.

of his hometown (Leech 2006b, p. 307), and then which, from his undergraduate days, he was able to make his own as he found himself in an East End "full of left-wing Christians," as he put it. While Leech made his own alliance with the socialism of his father, he also, from an early age, worried about the racism he encountered in the home in which he grew up, which was, he noted, specifically directed at Poles resettled in his town. Against this background, one might appreciate how anti-racism was to become an abiding theme in Leech's writing, as would "forging connections"[2] between Christian faith and what he cited as his other commitments: "equality, justice, human dignity and common ownership" (Leech 2006b, p. 308) alongside what he called the work of "discerning the signs of the times."[3]

The title given to the stipended position from which he wrote in the last stage of his working life – "community theologian" – is also a significant indicator of Leech's stances, pointing not only to his long-time rootedness in the local communities of the East End but also to his strong ecclesial consciousness, and likely his own appropriation of the notion of the scholar-priest. It was meant to show how he was critical of the idea of "an individual theologian," insisting instead that "theology is a corporate project" (Leech 2001, p. 126). He also appropriated (citing) Johan Baptist Metz's conviction: "The important questions to be asked by theology . . . are: who should do theology, and where, and in whose interest, and for whom?" (Leech 2001, p. 121). And he said in his own voice, "if theology does not help to liberate human beings and the created order, it helps to oppress them" (Leech 1997, p. 50). It was, for him, not only that theology is committed, partisan, and biased, but that theology claiming any sort of detachment was only likely to be profoundly attached to majoritarian values and whatever the mores of the *status quo* (Leech 2006a, pp. 70–71).

It is notable also that though oftentimes claiming that his work was not "addressed to academics" (Leech 1985, p. vii) it was widely feted as "enormously learned,"[4] "amazing in its many-sidedness and depth,"[5] and such like. A prolific – if sometimes repetitive, or differently put, thematically persistent – wrtier and thinker, as parish priest and then community theologian Leech found an audience for his writing not only in Britain but also abroad. From 1978 he began visiting the United States, first of all Chicago (he relates this first visit in Leech 1988, pp. 151–164), followed by many other places, and his influence became arguably stronger in the United States than in England (Leech 2006a, pp. 191–194). Either way, his work reached a wide readership around the North Atlantic.

In the context of *Twentieth Century Anglican Theologians*, Kenneth Leech particularly represents a kind of theology produced outside – though connected to – the academy. As he put it in his own words, he valued "close links" (Leech 2006a, p. 163) with academic theology, though worked from other settings, his own reasons for this no doubt at least in part betrayed in his skeptical assessment both of the capacity of academic theology to lose moorings in ministry and to tend to speak largely to other professional theologians (Leech 2006a, p. 145). Of his own writing, he said, "Writing was central to my work in the East End, but couldn't have been done, or had any substance, without the work or life that nourished it" (Leech 2006a, p. 145). And in another place, "It seems better always to write from the situation one knows best, and it is often when one speaks most personally and concretely that one finds connections being forged with people from very different backgrounds" (Leech 1992a, p. ix).

Although not always employed as parish priest (because "community theologian," for example) he was always attentive to the parish context of Anglican ministry in its English context. Leech's writings frequently reference Alan Ecclestone, another exemplar of theological writing from a parish base. Another contemporary, W. H. Vanstone, might also be identified as another leading example of such. In Leech's writings, concern with ecclesial contexts manifests especially in his longstanding interest in liturgy – and not least his assertion that "the faith is about worship before it is about doctrine" (Leech 2006a, p. 55) – and his many perspectives on the work of the pastor (Leech 1986; Leech 1990 – and Leech 1998 as just three of his books that foreground pastoral work in their titles alone). But given his East End emphasis, Leech's writings do not imagine a generic parish setting, and he was especially preoccupied with deeply urban experience like his own as well as issues that surge up within such environments. The racism inhabiting urban (as well, of course, other) settings is a signal instance, and his work is marked by a range of foci not always the concern of academic theologians. So especially in his early work he engaged with what he termed the "youthquake" (Leech 1973) of the times, and as part of (though larger) than his exploration of youth culture, he wrote about the drug scene in which young people (among others) were participating.[6] He also tackled homelessness, migration, and multiculturalism, among many other concerns about social justice that emerged from the localized struggles in which he became involved (Leech 1990, p. 104).

Leech's many-sided writings take the shape of over twenty books at his own hand, many of which reflect directly on the East End, even as some are based on lecture series' in universities such as Durham, Edinburgh, and Toronto; one based on preaching (Leech 1994) – while sermons are also scattered across the whole; contributions to and editing of anthologies; pieces for national newspapers;[7] and pamphlets, some of which were published by the Sisters of the Love of God – the anglo-catholic religious community with whom he himself took retreats for years – and many others put out (notably, for free, without copyright restriction) by the "dissident anglo-catholic" (Leech 2006a, p. 33) Jubilee Group, which he chaired (Leech 1990, pp. 129–134). Across his transatlantic readership, he remains perhaps best known for a trilogy of works that came early in his writing career – that is, *Soul Friend* (Leech 1977), *True Prayer* (Leech 1980), and *True God* (Leech 1985) – each in their own way concerned with spirituality, and part of what might be said to be a renaissance of the study of Christian spiritual traditions in which Leech's friend and fellow Jubilee Group member Rowan Williams' *The Wound of Knowledge* (Williams 1979) is contemporaneous and also important. It was especially *Soul Friend*, about spiritual direction, which was best to provide Leech with entrée to a North American readership, with much of his work not only being co-published in North America (though sometimes books came out under different names from their British editions) and also later republished there, but occasionally only published there.

Leech's enduring popularity in Canada and the United States is important not least given his "prophetic" critique of what he saw as the preoccupation with individualistic self-development in forms of pastoral care and counseling in North America. In the United Kingdom, however, it tends to be Leech's contributions to "urban theology" that have been especially appreciated, with *Through Our Long Exile* (Leech 2001) – the basis of a PhD he never completed – claiming to be the first of a kind in the UK (Leech 2001, p. 3), and certainly important in the genre. Whereas some North American forms of pastoral theology have sometimes tended to the individualistic approach Leech critiques,[8] while British forms have perhaps typically more strongly accented social conditions (though often with urban experience defined, including in church reports, in terms of unfortunate expressions like "social deprivation," "special disadvantage," and so on), Leech's work encircles the whole, and it is his persistent integration of Christian spirituality and social contexts that marks his work and merits his inclusion in a shortlist of notable twentieth century Anglican theologians

Spirituality and Social Justice

In one place Leech relates an anecdote about visiting a group to speak about justice and being told that he must often be "confused with the other Kenneth Leech who writes books on prayer and spirituality" (Leech 2006a, p. 92). Sometimes his writing is blistering about the constructed nature of the supposed distinction: "I am frankly appalled at the way in which 'spirituality' is being promoted as a way of avoiding and evading the demands of justice and of struggle for a more equal world" (Leech 1992b, p. ix). Leech emphatically rejected lines between them, noting that he never thought about his apparent "holding together" or "bringing together" of the two until he went to the United States: "prior to this I simply thought of Christian faith and practice as a life which involved prayer, worship and action for justice for the world" (Leech 2006a, p. 91). Some of his work, though, written in the period of Margaret Thatcher's prime-ministership of Britain through the 1980s, squarely identifies her views with the limited individualistic perspectives he takes to be contrary to Christianity and akin to the division of the spiritual and the social he tracks in US settings (Leech 1985, pp. 381–382, 387). At other times he also cites "waves of activism" presumed to be accompanied by neglect of personal devotion as problematic in the 1960s (Leech 1992b, p. 25). Sometimes again his writing indicts very influential twentieth century theologians – or at least ways in which their work was appropriated – as culprits in unhelpful resistance to the "theological wholeness" (Leech 1992b, p. ix) he prizes. Most notable, perhaps, is his citing of Karl Barth's argument in 1940s Germany that "it was essential to carry on theological work *as if nothing had happened*" (Leech 1985, p. 386, italics in original). This is to say that Leech may have found a heightened awareness of an issue he wanted to tackle in the United States but he could also identify European examples, closer to home.

The least that might be said, then, is that Leech's diagnosis of the problems he perceives is multifaceted. It is remedied in his own thought by very frequent use of various related juxtapositions that appear consistently right across his work. So, one reads of prayer – or spirituality, or ministry, or theology – and politics, prayer and conflict, or darkness, or marginality, or struggle. *True God* is particularly striking for juxtaposing "God" with desert and abyss, among other things, ending characteristically with a chapter called "God of justice." Such pairings point to Leech's insistence on seeing together what are sometimes perceived as different domains, and this pairing dynamic is so prevalent in framing his thinking that it is apt that a similar juxtaposition, "prayer and prophecy," is the title given to a reader on him.

Notably, Leech's understanding of this "wholeness" rests on both his understanding of the Bible and his sense of tradition. His writing makes very much and wide use of the Bible. It is a theology "above all grounded in scripture" (Leech 2006b, p. 5) – though it is also notable that he doesn't much refer to commentaries. As to his own theological position, he described it in his own words as "subversive orthodoxy" (Leech 1992a). Orthodoxy, he reminds, "is about being consumed by glory," not so much right belief as right praise (Leech 1985, p. 11). Yet it is striking that his main recurring theological emphases are creedal, with much stress on incarnation, and – after it being pointed out to him that some readers missed a focus on the cross (Leech 2006a, p. 144) – also paschal. Above all, though, and by his own admission, his main motif was the symbol of the "kingdom" (commonwealth/beloved community of God): his "regulative principle," with this (biblically funded) notion of divine reign gathering in his socialist convictions while being for him the center of the gospel (Leech 2006a, pp. 208–214). He undoubtedly believed that "there is a received tradition" (Leech 2006a, p. 24) and his criticism of liberalism (reasserting the view that "liberal Christians often give atheists less and less in which to disbelieve" [Leech 2006a, p. 22, with the quote scribed to Alistair McIntyre]) was that it was not strong enough to "confront . . . monsters" (Leech 1992a, p. 22; Leech 2005, pp. 68, 85) that would need to be tackled for God's reign to manifest. Yet while critical of liberalism, his spirituality of glory disdained "false backwardness" (Leech 2006a, p. 23), "static and propositional" (Leech 2006a, p. 25) approaches in theology, instead suggesting that a "dynamic, liberating" praise would enable both rootedness and impetus for change (Leech 1992a, p. 9). Hence, he saw "theology [a]s a movement, not a position" (Leech 2006a, pp. 20, 24) and as responsive (Leech 2006a, p. 25), questioning, and rethinking (Leech 2006a, p. 24). His own rethinking – always orthodox, not least for its strong emphasis on praise and prayer – was not so much revisionist, as evident in turning out Christian doctrine in response to human life in specific social situations. As Alasdair McIntyre lauded Leech, he had "an unusual ability to identify what is going on in the world and to respond to it" (Leech 2006b, p. 5).

Racism

As noted, Leech had been aware since his youth of the racism in his own home and community (Leech 2006b, p. 307).[9] Later, in the East End, he had much opportunity to deepen and practice his own contrary convictions, in close association with various ethnic minority groups – notably the Bengali community that settled in the environs of what became known as Altab Ali Park, so named after the brutal murder of a local Bengali man.

While *Race* (Leech 2005) is the straightforward title of one of Kenneth Leech's last books, its themes were present in much of his writing from the start. Especially notable is *Struggle in Babylon* (Leech 1988), written after he finished a term as Race Relations Field Officer for the Church of England's Board of Social Responsibility, and during which he had raised his voice to ask questions of the 1985 report *Faith in the City*.[10] While appreciative of some aspects of the report he pointed out it was weak in its treatment of racism: so "while it devotes a number of pages to the role of black people in the Church of England, and contains various references to racial discrimination, it has nothing to say about racism as a structural reality in Church and nation" (Leech 1988, p. 143). The heart of his critique was that it is "missing something of the heart of gospel conflict" (Leech 1992a, p. 23), with racism the main "monster" it failed to confront as the gospel demands. He was not shy of making known his view that the report's failure to look critically at structures related to the church's leadership being largely drawn from the public school and Oxbridge educated, "a Church of the wealthy and the genteel" (Leech 1990, p. 19). In comments that might suggest some leads as to why he himself was never "preferred" to a bishopric, "people are appointed bishops partly because they are believed – usually rightly – to be 'safe' and support the current line in duplicity." He liked to situate himself away from what he called "the dominant dishonesty" (Leech 2006a, p. 40), holding that while leaders were drawn from elites, understanding of oppression would falter. He also later came to see that the history of colonialism in shaping the practices of the church had not been examined as it needs to be.

Leech's work asserts both that race is a myth, a "biological fiction" (Leech 2005, p. 20) and that racism is an absolute affront to the gospel of Jesus. He followed Ruth Benedict's categorization of racism as a religion (Leech 2005, p. 19) – in his own words, an "alternative gospel" (Leech 2005, p. 108) – and was clear that "while the concept of 'race' is imprecise and full of uncertainties, there is no uncertainty, except among the wilfully ignorant, that racism as a practised and lived reality is alive and well" (Leech 2005, p. 22). He could be critical of established studies of racism,[11] which may well claim (falsely, he would hold) to be "objective" (Leech 2006a, p. 42) just as he was of therapeutic "racism awareness training" and such like, which while doing good work needed, he thought, to ask "why black people and others on the receiving end of [. . .] prejudice should be expected to wait until these people have been persuaded to undergo such therapy, and until the process has had some effect" (Leech 2005, p. 44). Likewise, his work offers caution about terms such as "inclusion," "diversity," and "pluralism," as potentially ways of evading engagement with the reality of structural oppression. His own insistence was always instead on historical consciousness, so as to "locate racism within the wider framework of injustice and oppression outside which it is incomprehensible and apart from which it cannot be resisted and defeated" (Leech 2005, p. 97). Nevertheless, historical consciousness might better lead to "small scale, local and provisional action," responsive to current forms of racist organizing that need to be combatted in the cause of God's reign. Moreover, Leech's doctrinal emphasis on incarnation came into play in a very significant way in his thinking on race, as an unequivocal affirmation of the inherent equality of every human being. And as for the schema of thought that that affirmation guides, his "own view [wa]s that the Church will never make progress in this area until we see opposition to racism as being central to biblical faith, incorporated at the heart of its liturgy and life, repeated regularly in creedal commitment." Notably, in a late piece of writing, "putting on Christ: race and the Christian community," he worked through what he called "four central questions" – the nature of humanity, the potential for human love, the nature of grace, and the purpose of the church – in ways that gather up his longstanding efforts to confront racism in church and nation (Leech 2006a).

Catholic Anglicanism

Leech's emphasis on the local was wrapped up with one on the parish – the etymology of which he tracked to its meanings as "exile," and "living away from home," far from settled (Leech 2006a, p. 22) – but he characteristically combined this with wide-ranging exploration of Christian traditions and a strong self-identification with Anglicanism's catholic strand. He was by no means uncritical of this tradition, though, and could only commend aspects of it. He was particularly withering about ritualism that showed no corresponding verve for social justice, and which he deemed "genteel, precious and dainty," "camp/kitsch," "sectarian," "archaic and insular," and "obsessed with trivia," among other things, and he had intense dislike of a liturgical "correct-ness" that could dominate the liturgy, and even, he would say, occlude the faith itself. Indeed, it was the "sickly piety" and "right wing" stances of some anglo-catholics that the Jubilee Group pitted itself against (Leech 1990, p. 129). He defined his own, and the group's, position as "jubilee catholic," marked by being liturgically more given to communalizing worship[12] and more importantly outward facing and active in the pursuit of social justice in the parish and the wider world. To vivify a sense of what this might look like, his writing offers many vignettes of parish priests who enacted such a vision of catholic Anglicanism (note especially Leech 1986, pp. 85–126; Leech 2006b, pp. 259–287), through which he intended to offer concrete hope that the jubilee tradition might again flourish as a liturgical and ecclesial movement allied to combatting the monsters his work names.

Conclusion

A strong feature of Leech's work is his revision of his own writing, even to a point that Leslie Houlden in a review Leech commissioned called "excessive" (Leech 2006a, p. 81). Evidently, Leech took critique of his work seriously, for instance, telling of carrying around "for a long time" a letter that unsettled him (Leech 2006a, pp. 78–82), while he thought it through.

The strongest questions of Leech are probably those that begin from note of his consistent self-positioning on the underside – though this is likely to be something that he himself would have regarded as required by God's commonweal. Yet there is some force in recognition that his work is often oppositional, while giving voice to the weak, sometimes offering less clues to the powerful on practices to recalibrate what has gone wrong. Certainly, he writes a lot of the like of ministry as marginal (e.g., Leech 1990, pp. 1–33), and his vision of the church at its best is of a creative minority active for justice within larger society. Within the church, he could be sharply critical of leaders. As seen above, within anglo-catholicism, he was far from uniformly appreciative.

While he did much revising of his own writing, he did not always draw in new themes as wider contexts changed, so globalization, and diaspora dynamics, do not feature in his work, nor does black theology as it became more robust in its own voice. Later forms of urban and practical theology may have become better at recognizing such things than Leech ever did (Shannahan 2010, p. 101). What is beyond doubt is that he not only pioneered but remarkably popularized the genres.

Notes

1 Leech (2006, p. 112) tells that he spent forty-six of his years in London.
2 An apt chapter title in the Reader, *Prayer and Prophecy*, edited by Bunch and Richie.
3 The subtitle of Leech (1997).
4 See the review of 1977, cited inside the back cover of Leech (1985).
5 Leslie Houlden, cited in Leech (2006, p. 81).
6 Leech (1998) reveals that his interest came about because his churchwarden's children were heroin users. The 1998 edition is an updated and revised version of an earlier text published twice already, in 1970 and 1973.
7 Loades (1995) has inclusions from Leech's newspaper pieces, while others are gathered into Bunch and Richie (2006).
8 That Leech (1998, p. 86) quotes US practical theologian Don Browning's assertion that "a practical theology of care" should attempt to "critique and fulfill the care structures of the larger society" is just one instance that gives pause to escalating this sense into a blanket statement.
9 As a teenager, he heard Trevor Huddleston witness to an anti-racist Christian ministry, and this abided with him.
10 Sometimes deemed to be the most important statement of the Church of England in the twentieth century, e.g., Ford (1989, p. 255).
11 And the lack of them, noting that a seminary textbook for trainee ministers "dealt with" racism in a wholly inadequate eight lines.
12 An example he gives is preference for processions involving of all, not reserved for clergy, though the inclusive impulse is rooted in his understanding of Trinitarian theology.

References

Ford, D.F. (1989). Faith in the Cities: Corinth and the Modern City. In: *On Being the Church: Essays on the Christian Community* (eds. C.E. Gunton and D.W. Hardy), 225–256. Edinburgh: T & T Clark.

Leech, K. (1973). *Youthquake: Spirituality and the Growth of a Counter-Culture*. London: Sheldon Press.

Leech, K. (1977). *Soul Friend: Spiritual Direction in the Modern World* (2nd edn 1984). London: DLT.

Leech, K. (1980). *True Prayer: An Introduction to Christian Spirituality*. London: Sheldon Press.

Leech, K. (1985). *True God: An Exploration in Spiritual Theology*. London: Sheldon Press.

Leech, K. (1986). *Spirituality and Pastoral Care*. London: Sheldon Press.

Leech, K. (1988). *Struggle in Babylon: Racism in the Cities and Churches of Britain*. London: Sheldon Press.

Leech, K. (1990). *Care and Conflict: Leaves from a Pastoral Notebook*. London: DLT.

Leech, K. (1992a). *Subversive Orthodoxy: Traditional Faith and Radical Commitment*. Toronto: ABC.

Leech, K. (1992b). *The Eye of the Storm: Spiritual Resources for the Pursuit of Justice*. London: DLT.

Leech, K. (1994). *We Preach Christ Crucified: The Proclamation of the Cross in a Dark Age*. London: DLT.

Leech, K. (1997). *The Sky Is Red: Discerning the Signs of the Times*. London: DLT.

Leech, K. (1998). *Drugs and Pastoral Care*. London: DLT.

Leech, K. (2001). *Through Our Long Exile: Contextual Theology and the Urban Experience*. London: DLT.

Leech, K. (2005). *Race*. London: SPCK.

Leech, K. (2006a). *Doing Theology in Altab Ali Park*. London: DLT.

Leech, K. (2006b). *Prayer and Prophecy: The Essential Kenneth Leech* (eds. D. Bunch and A. Richie). London: DLT.

Loades, A. (ed.) (1995). *Spiritual Classics from the Late Twentieth Century*. London: CHP.

Shannahan, C. (2010). *Voices from the Borderland: Re-Imagining Cross-Cultural Urban Theology in the Twenty-First Century*. Sheffield: Equinox.

Williams, R. (1979). *The Wound of Knowledge: Christian Spirituality From the New Testament to St. John of the Cross*. London: DLT.

Carter Heyward (1945–)

Stephen Burns and Bryan Cones

A look at Carter Heyward's book-list of "resources" for her memoir *She Flies On* (Heyward 2017, pp. 227–232) suggests that not many of her resources are Anglican. Among those from "earlier periods" only Frederick Denison Maurice, with mention of him in the main text (Heyward 2017, p. 169) relating his expulsion from his teaching role at King's College, London, for his refusal to assent to certain Christian doctrines. Charles Williams (for whose significance, see Heyward 1976, pp. 23–24), John A.T. Robinson and Desmond Tutu are among a short list of modern Anglicans, then just a few contemporaries from US-based Episcopal Church contexts – all associated one way or another with New England (and even more narrowly either Boston or New York), and notably Episcopal Divinity School (EDS): Patrick Cheng, Kelly Brown Douglas, Kwok Pui-lan – EDS being the institution at which Heyward herself taught from 1975 to 2005. Rather than Anglican forebears (or even too many Anglican contemporaries), Heyward's resources include writings by Holocaust survivors (especially Elie Weisel, see Heyward 1982; Heyward 2010a, pp. 17–18) and above all texts of liberation theology, supremely those of US Presbyterian laywoman Beverly Wildung Harrison (Heyward 2010b, pp. 190–199) and German Lutheran laywoman Dorothee Soelle (Heyward 2003, pp. 221–238; Heyward 2010b, pp. 223–227), each Heyward's teachers at Union Theological Seminary in New York. Heyward herself became Anglicanism's foremost "radical" liberation theologian, associated with various causes that have placed her ahead of the curve, as it were, of developments in her own Episcopal Church and often near the storm center of wider controversies in the Anglican Communion in both twentieth and twenty-first centuries. These aspects of her work merit her inclusion in *Twentieth Century Anglican Theologians*.

Carter Heyward's writings are in the mode of essays, books (sometimes collections of essays; e.g., Heyward 1984, 1989b, 1995b), sermons (Heyward 1989a), and liturgical resources such as eucharistic prayers (e.g., Heyward 1984, pp. 49–51, 148–150, 254–255;

Twentieth Century Anglican Theologians: From Evelyn Underhill to Esther Mombo, First Edition.
Edited by Stephen Burns, Bryan Cones, and James Tengatenga.

Heyward 1999, pp. 204–215). Although there is development in her thinking, and expanding concerns (notably latterly trans issues), there is also remarkable consistency of perspective, with striking themes reiterated, albeit sometimes slightly recast, over time. Her writing is often quite personal, dealing forthrightly with, for example, her experience of therapy, and in which autobiography is central to her method. For Heyward, "sharing one's own religious history, one's own theological questions, one's own ethical commitments, has long seemed to me an honest way of *beginning* theological conversation" (Heyward 2010a, p. 11). In addition to describing her own theology as "liberal, feminist, LGBTQ, and liberationist" (Heyward 2017, p. xviii), she also suggests it is "rather traditionally shaped" – hence *She Flies On* (Heyward 2017) is in three-parts, turning its focus around the doctrine of the Trinity. She writes that she "love[s] God but not the God of patriarchal Christianity" (Heyward 2017, p. 131), "love[s] Jesus" with her "life wrapped around images and stories of a human Jesus" (Heyward 2017, p. 69), and is "filled with Spirit. . . filled, that is, with zest and gratitude, and energised for whatever might come next" (Heyward 2017, p. 216). Yet lurking alongside what she makes of Christian doctrines is always "an unholy trinity of injustice," "race, class, gender" (Heyward 2017, p. 29) afflicting her own society in the United States – and of course elsewhere. A telling comment in her memoir, though, illumines Heyward's attention to the United States, in that she notes that liberation theologies are concerned with "two great goods": first "the common good" and then "the relative freedom of individuals to speak, write, worship and build associations with whomever we please, much as the Constitution [of the USA] and its Bill of Rights promises" (Heyward 2017, p. 114; cf. p. 192) – with each of the two "measured and balanced by the other." This search for measure and balance directs her critique of race, class and gender in the United States and her thinking through long struggles in which she has immersed herself (in addition to work in her own name, Mudflower Collective 1985). Her perspectives are both and at once deeply affected by her North American setting and also strikingly countercultural, contrary to many presumed norms.

Born in 1945 to a homemaking mother "renowned for her optimism" (Heyward 2017, p. 22) and a father in whom "there was nothing harsh or authoritarian" – making him a "lousy patriarch" (Heyward 2017, p. 11) – Carter is the eldest of three children. Their father was employed by oil-giant Esso such that his work required several moves, so the household lived in various parts of North Carolina in the South of the US. Heyward writes with appreciation of her "unusually open-minded and socially progressive white Christian family" (Heyward 2017, p. 13) involved as it was in the Episcopal Church, keeping family prayer times at home, and in which "if God had been given any other name . . ., it would have been kindness" (Heyward 2017, p. 14). In her early years, however, Heyward also became aware of racism, herself "hurting" the family maid with a jump-rope song about a "nigger," and being "molested" by a black gardener at their home (Heyward 2017, pp. 17, 18; with related footnotes carefully explaining her deliberate decision to use the "n-word") and "knowing full well at age six that God the Father did not like the way we white people treated colored people" (Heyward 2017, p. 23). Significantly, her childhood "imaginary playmate" was black (Heyward 2017, p. 18), and equally important, a girl who wanted to be a priest (Heyward 1976, p. 7). Meanwhile, throughout Heyward's childhood, elsewhere in the South, Rosa Parks' refusal to give up her seat on a bus to a white traveler sparked protest in Montgomery, Alabama, while in Lynchburg, Virginia, Jerry Falwell was among Christian leaders calling on others to shun racial justice (Heyward 2017, pp. 29, 54). A teacher from her own high school later self-immolated outside the Pentagon in protest at the Vietnam War (Heyward 2017, 52–53). And against this socio-political background in which she was acutely aware of her own "unearned benefits" (Heyward 2017, p. 55), Heyward's own growing pains through adolescence were marked by a struggle with bulimia, gender confusion, and "ardent" religious engagement as means of trying to tackle addictive behaviors to do with body image and sexual identity, on the one hand "turn[ing] earnestly to a traditional Anglo-Catholic understanding of the Trinitarian God," on the other hand "'giv[ing her] life to Christ' at a Billy Graham rally" (Heyward 2017, pp. 28, 32) and – perhaps heralding what was to come in terms of her ordination as a priest – celebrating holy communion in the "back yard, consecrating Vienna sausages and coconut milk as the Body and Blood of Christ" (Heyward 2010a, p. 24; Heyward 2017, p. 32).

After undergraduate studies at a women's college, Heyward went to Union Theological Seminary in New York, where she "learned well that the struggles for justice are foundational for all theology worth doing" (Heyward 2017, p. 58). She joined anti-racist demonstrations, met an Australian priest, David, who asked her to marry him – whom she declined realizing that she was lesbian (and him gay), met Beverly Wildung Harrison who was to become one of her "life companions," and had a breakdown, confused (her word: Heyward 1982, p. xv) about both her sexuality and vocation. She identifies this breakdown as "a beginning of [her] adulthood" (Heyward 2017, p. 57), with her decision not to go to Australia with David bringing clarity to her own vocation to be a priest. It also initiated "exhaustion" that "propelled [her] into therapy," which would become important for some of her writing (e.g., Heyward 1993, 2017, p. 127) and shape her key ideas to do with boundaries and mutuality – on which, see below.

Several years later she was turned down for ordination as a deacon in the diocese of North Carolina because she had "an authority problem" (Heyward 2017, p. 38; though see Heyward 1975, p. 31) and this was to prove instrumental in her own part as one of the so-called "Philadelphia 11" who proceeded to ordination as priests at a service on June 29, 1974 (Heyward having been made deacon in New York in June 1973), even against the vote of a General Convention of the Episcopal Church (see Heyward 1976). This was, Heyward notes, a fortnight before Watergate, and an event in which she learned "the sacred power of collective action" (Heyward 2017, p. 84). Although her ordination was not regularized for another two years, it brought a sea-change to the Anglican tradition. Before that time, Florence Li-Tim Oi (1907–1992) had been the first woman to be ordained priest, in Hong Kong in the year before Carter Heyward was born, but also in "irregular" circumstances – to provide sacramental ministry in war-time extremities. After the war, Oi resigned her license to officiate and it was then not until 1971 that Hong Kong ordained other women and Oi was again recognized. These early 1970s ordinations sparked debate in the newly formed, global-scope, Anglican Consultative Council, and also in the Episcopal Church and its General Convention, which after debate voted against women's ordination as priests. The 1974 priesting of the Philadelphia 11 was conducted by three retired bishops and the ordination sermon (not by one of the bishops but a Harvard academic) included this justification: "as blacks refused to participate in their own oppression by going to the back of the bus in 1955 in Montgomery, women are refusing to cooperate in their own oppression by remaining on the periphery of full participation in the Church" (Hein and Shattuck 2004, p. 141). One of the other 11 was Ella Reneé Bozarth, a poet, whose striking poem "Before Jesus" is suggestive of the rearrangement of symbols that went on for some with these women's ordination:

Before Jesus was his mother.
Before supper in the upper room,
breakfast in the barn.

Before the Passover Feast,
a feeding trough.
And here, the altar of Earth,
fair linens of hay and seed.

Before his cry, her cry.
Before his sweat of blood,
her bleeding and tears.
Before his offering, hers.

Before the breaking of bread and death,
the breaking of her body in birth.

Before the offering of the cup,
the offering of her breast.
Before his blood, her blood.

And by her body and blood alone,
his body and blood and whole human being.

The wise ones knelt
to hear the woman's word
in wonder.

Holding up her sacred child,
her spark of God in the form of a babe,
she said: "Receive and let your hearts be healed
and your lives be filled with love, for
This is my body, This is my blood."[1]

Bozarth's focus is of course Mary, but the centrality of women to the Christian story of salvation and its ritual celebration in eucharist is evident, and the ordination as a signal of this was variously celebrated and vilified. As Heyward herself recounts, "we ordinands were blasted all over the world by bishops and others who called us 'hostile', 'arrogant', 'selfish', 'sick', 'spoiled', 'women on power trips', 'women who couldn't take no for an answer.'" Yet: "In the midst of the turmoil, one of the bishops who ordained us wrote that we need to bear in mind that you don't shake an institution to its foundations and expect those in authority to thank you." And: "A few months later this same man ended a letter to me, 'Stay in the saddle and enjoy the ride'. This gentle admonition has stayed with me" (Heyward 1995a, p. 108).

Two of the other Philadelphia 11, Alison Cheek and Susan Hiatt (Heyward 2010b, pp. 218–22; Heyward and Lehane 2014), were, with Carter Heyward, hired by EDS in Cambridge (part of the Boston metro area), Massachusetts, so that they had an institutional base. Alongside her teaching role there, Heyward undertook doctoral studies, back at Union, with Tom Driver, publishing *The Redemption of God: A Theology of Mutual Relation* in 1982 (Heyward 1982), a book that would introduce themes elaborated through her subsequent writings. In the meantime, she published various articles, including two co-terminously in July 1979, in one of which she "came out" as lesbian, the other as bisexual (Heyward 2010a, p. 24; Heyward 2017, pp. 91–94; also Heyward 1989b pp. 20–36). Then in 1980, she and Beverly Wildung Harrison began a "special relationship" as "partners," "lovers" (Heyward 2017, pp. 89–90, 126, 128, 166) in what they intentionally set up as a non-monogamous "not closed or coupled" arrangement, and in which they remained "life companions" (Harrison died in 2012) even as Heyward entered another life partnership, with Sue Slasser, from the 1990s. From 1996, the three lived together, with others – at times twenty-five or so others – in an intentional community in North Carolina, "Redbud Springs," from which in 2000 Heyward also set up the Free Rein Center for Therapeutic Riding and Education, in which "horses help humans heal," through "mutuality and the courage to step through fear, crossing boundaries and cultures – in this case, between horse and human – and learning to listen and speak in ways new to one another" (Heyward 2017, p. 218). In her later years, Heyward abandoned both alcohol and meat (Heyward 2017, pp. 124–129, 212–214), the latter at least no doubt part of her commitment "to god."

God/ding

For Carter Heyward, "God" is "an active verb," rather than "a noun, much less a proper name." (Heyward 2017, p. 10). This abiding emphasis of Heyward's work emerged early, in her doctoral thesis, and she relates it to various forebears: first to Paul Tillich's idea of God as "the ground of our being" and then more particularly Mary Daly's notion of God as verb – though Daly does not speak, as Heyward does, of "godding." Asserting that "there is no unchanging deity in or beyond the universe," Heyward holds that godding is what Jesus did, teaching and embodying passion for justice. But the dynamic of godding is by no means unique to him, as "incarnation includes all humans and other creatures, bearers of God and able 'to god'" (Heyward 2017, p. xix). "We god in love, a common awareness that no one of us is alone, and that in the relation between subject and subject, there is power"; and "we god toward justice, moved by and moving the God given voice by the prophets, the God moving transpersonally in history, by us, through us" (Heyward 1982, p. 153). Succinctly, "godding is a mutual process of co-creating right-relation" (Heyward 1996, p. 85), and "God is our power for generating mutuality" (Heyward 2017, p. 46).

Heyward most controversially explored mutuality in a book about experience of therapy, *When Boundaries Betray Us* (Heyward 1993). Recounting her "yearning to be-friend" her therapist, dubbed "Elizabeth Farro," beyond the therapeutic relationship, this book relates how Heyward wished "Elizabeth could let me know how our relationship had been changing her, what she had experienced during my therapy, how she really felt about me, what she had been given through our work together, what difference my passion and questions and struggles and celebrations had made to her" (Heyward 1993, p. 11). Moreover, it conveys her belief that these wishes were mutual. As it happened, the therapist, despite apparently speaking of "seriously considering" becoming friends, resisted, so held boundaries conventional in her profession. For Heyward, though, friendship beyond therapy had "to do with everything I hold as sacred" (Heyward 1993, p. 71), and as she conveys a key exchange during the therapy in a poem in the book:

> *you say*
> *you're not sure*
> *we can move*
> *beyond our*
> *clinical beginnings.*
>
> *i say*
> *this is*
> *a crock.*
>
> *. . . where's your*
> *faith in*
> *the power*
> *already*
> *transforming*
> *us*
> *both?*
> (Heyward 1993, pp. 70–71,
> italics in original)

Heyward regarded Farro's refusal as "abuse – not sexually, but emotionally," asserting that "harm, damage, violence – can result from a professional's refusal to be authentically present with those who seek help; and . . . such abuse can be triggered as surely by the drawing of boundaries too tightly as by failure to draw them at all" (Heyward 1993, p. 137). In the furore following the book's publication (with feminists among others distancing themselves from it: Hunt 1995; Lunn 1995), Heyward contended all the more adamantly that therapy relationships like her own may "reify patriarchal/kyriarchical power," promoting "structures of domination and control" (Heyward 1995a, p. 108), and she later took another gloomier view, reflecting on the book as one about mutuality *not* always being possible (Heyward 2010a, p. 21).

Christa and Gender Queering

Just as Heyward reconfigures traditional understanding of God, so she does of Jesus, insisting from her very earliest writing that "any church doctrine built, maintained and employed to facilitate exclusion and separation rather than inclusion and unity is a doctrine unworthy of the name of Jesus" (Heyward 1976, p. 143), or more abruptly: whose name she does not wish to be used "as an excuse for being a narrow-minded bigoted asshole" (Heyward 2017, p. 52, citing a gift she was sent by a friend). From Dorothee Soelle, she adopts and makes her own the term "christo-fascism" to contest "unbridled capitalism," "the worship of wealth over human well-being," and "significant numbers of white Christians – in the United States and globally – who tilt fascist in their hatred of black and brown people, Muslims, Jews, gays, abortion providers, and feminists, as well as in their belief that God has a preference for them and their faith" (Heyward 2017, pp. 99–100). Then from Edwina Sandys' sculpture of a naked, crucified woman, she adopts the term "Christa" to speak of her "contemporary forms" in enslaved, abused, exploited, unwanted, powerless women (and men): such that "Christa is an appropriate image for that which is sacred in our midst. Recognising her reality . . . is basic to our ability to live in spiritual continuity with Jesus" (Heyward 1995b, p. 126).[2] And in some ways akin to the bishop's admonition to her after ordination, "like Christa, and with her, we cannot expect simultaneously to help make God incarnate in the world and be affirmed by those holding patriarchal power in place" (Heyward 1995b, pp. 123–124).

In these and other ways, Jesus is a central figure in Heyward's thinking, albeit one about whom she thinks Christian tradition has "misled" in its suggestion that "incarnation" refers "specifically, or solely" to him (Heyward 2017, p. 80). Bluntly, "classical christology . . . is dead," in need of redefinition if "the Jesus story is to be redemptive for Christian women of different colors, cultures, and classes" (Heyward 1990, p. 193). Rather, for Heyward "christic meanings" emerge from right relation, "christic power" being her way of referring to "God's taking shape among us" (Heyward 2017, p. 80), coming forth as a result of godding. "God is incarnate in all creation insofar as we love one another, participate in healing and liberating our sisters and brothers, and extend compassion to neighbours and kindness to the whole inhabited earth" (Heyward 2017, p. 80). And: "If we see God as a power incarnate primarily (or exclusively) in one historical (or heavenly) figure, then we miss our own vocation to god" (Heyward 1999, p. 61).

Horse as Priest

Heyward's own ordination as priest was significant for the Anglican Communion, propelling women's ministry forward by pressing against conventions – and consensus. Despite her sense of sacred power in common action against the status quo, Heyward has maintained a view of priesthood that she relates clearly to her notions of mutuality. So "the ordained priest, like Jesus, is not set above brothers and sisters, but among them." And: "there is no one special son – or daughter" (Heyward 2017, p. 85). Her own views of priesthood are no doubt in part a response to the force of the challenge

Dorothee Soelle put to her on their first meeting: "why would any justice-loving woman want to be a priest?" (Heyward 2017, p. 85).

Heyward's ongoing reflection on priesthood is manifest not least in sermons preached at others' ordinations (Heyward 1989a, pp. 64–69; Heyward 1995b, pp. 49–58). We see in those sermons an inclusivizing of priesthood, with the ordained person and other people always said to be sharing the same vocation to "be dressed" in garments of creation, liberation, and peace; of LGBTQIA+ clergy among other things now "staring down" the church which has so long turned its back on queer people (Heyward 1995b, pp. 55–56).

A most important aspect of her ongoing reflection on priesthood is a further inclusive move: to consider non-human creatures also as priests. So she extends "creation-affirming threads" of Christian tradition to insist on "connection between how the church has treated *women, sex,* and *bodies* and how it views non-human members of creation" (Heyward 1995a, p. 104). She and Bev Harrison had long prayed together at table, "Some have food. Some have none. God bless the revolution" (Heyward 2017, p. 213), but meat-eaters might also need to hear: "Take. Eat. Is this not my body?" (Heyward 1995a, p. 107), then turning to animals not as food, not in domination, but according to notions of mutuality and right-relation consistent with her wider work, attentive to the ecosystem humans and non-human creatures share. "The root of our salvation, call it Christ/Christa or God or love or justice, whatever names we may give it, does not have a single face. It has countless, different human faces and arms and amputations and also the faces and bodies of lambs and falcons and scorpions" (Heyward 1995b, p. 110). In particular, at Free Rein, Heyward discovered "horse as priest," "at the altar of the therapeutic arena – bringing together the human rider and her, or his, restorative, healing power" – manifest in examples of young riders becoming able to speak their first words in contact with Free Rein animals (Heyward 2010b, p. 119). Elaborating this conviction, Heyward typically pushes beyond convention, "beyond Catholicism" she says in that human rider – autistic child, at-risk teen, addicted adult, another with special needs – can be priest as well as horse, given "God . . . sparks between and among all" (Heyward 2010b, p. 120); and "beyond Protestantism" as non-human creatures emphatically have as much to do with God's healing as humans do. So in her view of the mutuality possible between human and non-human creatures, "arrogant" human-centered views are relinquished, and animals are to be loved "as sisters and brothers."

Conclusion

In her later years, Heyward has said that for all she is "still a Jesus person," loving the story of "the man from Nazareth whom I experience as a brother and friend, and whose Sacred Spirit does indeed 'walk and talk' with me," she "seldom goes to church," too "weary," "worn down," "depressed" by its patriarchal ways (Heyward 2017, p. xviii). With the significance of her own priestly ordination, she latterly locates the key priestly ministry she receives from a "mystery simultaneously divine and equine" (Heyward 2010a, p. 27). At the "altar" of therapeutic riding, she now perceives herself as "acolyte" (Heyward 2010b, p. 120) to horse and rider, godding together. A prayer at the close of her refection on horses ends this exploration of her thinking, distilling as it does a number of her key ideas:

> Elephant God, forgive us.
> Holy mountain, shelter us.
> Sister spirit stream, carry us on.
> Tiny sparrow, sing to us your favourite hymn.
> Pelican brother Jesus, cover us with your wings.
> Bid us goodnight and raise us in the morning
> in your christic power to recreate the world.
>
> (Heyward 2010b, p. 117)

Notes

1 Used by permission of Alla Renée Bozarth, with this note: The poem, "Before Jesus—Mary, Protopriest of the New Covenant" is in these books by Alla Renée Bozarth: Accidental Wisdom, iUniverse 2003, and This is My Body— Praying for Earth, Prayers from the Heart, iUniverse 2004.

2 On Christa in later theology by Anglican Nicola Slee, see Slee (2011, 2012, 2018).

References

Hein, D. and Shattuck, G.H. Jr. (2004). *The Episcopalians*. New York: Church Publishing.

Heyward, C. (1976). *A Priest Forever: The Formation of Woman and a Priest*. New York, NY: Harper and Row.

Heyward, C. (1982). *The Redemption of God: A Theology of Mutual Relation*. Lanham, MD: University of America Press.

Heyward, C. (1984). *Our Passion for Justice: Images of Power, Sexuality, and Liberation*. New York, NY: Pilgrim Press.

Heyward, C. (1989a). *Speaking of Christ: A Lesbian Feminist Voice* (ed. E.C. Davies). New York, NY: Pilgrim Press.

Heyward, C. (1989b). *Touching Our Strength: The Erotic as Power and the Love of God*. San Francisco, CA: HarperCollins.

Heyward, C. (1990). Jesus of Nazareth/Christ of Faith: Foundations of a Reactive Christology. In: *Lift Every Voice: Constructing Christian Theologies from the Underside* (eds. S.B. Thistlethwaite and M.P. Engel), 191–200. San Francisco, CA: HarperCollins.

Heyward, C. (1993). *When Boundaries Betray Us: Beyond Illusions of What Is Ethical in Therapy and Life*. San Francisco, CA: HarperCollins.

Heyward, C. (1995a). A response to Pam Lunn and Mary Hunt. *Theology and Sexuality* 3: 104–108.

Heyward, C. (1995b). *Staying Power: Reflections on Gender, Justice, and Compassion*. Cleveland, OH: Pilgrim Press.

Heyward, C. (1996). Godding. In: *A-Z of Feminist Theology* (eds. L. Isherwood and D. McEwan), 85. Sheffield: Sheffield Academic Press.

Heyward, C. (1999). *Saving Jesus From Those Who are Right*. Minneapolis, MN: Fortress Press.

Heyward, C. (2003). Crossing over: Dorothee Soelle and the Transcendence of God. In: *The Theology of Dorothee Soelle* (ed. S.K. Pinnock), 221–238. Valley Forge, PA: Trinity Press International.

Heyward, C. (2010a). Breaking points: shaping a relational theology. In: *Through Us, with Us, in Us: Relational Theologies in the Twenty-First Century* (eds. L. Isherwood and E. Bellchambers), 9–32. London: SCM Press.

Heyward, C. (2010b). *Keep Your Courage: A Radical Christian Feminist Speaks.* London: SCM Press.

Heyward, C. (2017). *She Flies on: A White Southern Christian Debutante Wakes Up.* New York, NY: Seabury.

Heyward, C. and Lehane, J. (eds.) (2014). *The Spirit of the Lord Is Upon Me: The Writings of Sue Hiatt.* New York, NY: Seabury.

Hunt, M. (1995). Review article: *When Boundaries Betray Us. Theology and Sexuality* 3: 105–111.

Lunn, P. (1995). Boundaries and transference. *Theology and Sexuality* 3: 112–117.

Mudflower Collective (1985). *God's Fierce Whimsy: Christian Feminism and Theological Education.* Cleveland, OH: Pilgrim Press.

Pears, A. (2004). *Feminist Christian Encounters: The Models and Strategies of Feminist Informed Christian Theologies.* Aldershot: Ashgate.

Slee, N. (2011). *Seeking the Risen Christa.* London: SPCK.

Slee, N. (2012). Visualizing, conceptualizing, imagining and praying the Christa: in search of her risen forms. *Feminist Theology* 21: 71–90.

Slee, N. (2018). Reimaging Christ as a coming girl: an advent experiment. In: *Future Present: Embodying a Better World Now* (ed. J. Baker), 118–131. London: Proost.

David W. Brown (1948–)

Christopher R. Brewer

David William Brown was born on July 1, 1948 in Galashiels, a prominent town in the Borders of Scotland.[1] His mother, Catherine Brown née Smith (1917–2002), was trained as a nurse, and, with the outbreak of World War II, joined Queen Alexandria's Royal Army Nursing Corps. That is when she met Brown's father, also named David William Brown (1907–1973). After the war, Brown's mother worked as a midwife, and his father as an electrical engineer. With the nationalization of the electrical supply in July 1948, it had become viable to distribute electricity to the western isles, and so Brown's father moved his family from Gattonside just outside Melrose, which is just east of Galashiels, to Bowmore – the largest town on Islay and home to the famed Bowmore Distillery – where he worked for the North of Scotland Hydro-Electric Board. Brown's sister, Elaine, was born in 1951.

As the result of a job promotion for Brown's father, the family moved to Campbeltown in 1956. Brown attended the primary school of Dalintober (through 1960), and then Keil School in Dumbarton (through 1966), now defunct. He then moved further east, matriculating at the University of Edinburgh. After completing his degree in Classics at Edinburgh in 1970, Brown had every intention of going to Coates Hall, the theological college in Edinburgh, to train for the ministry. Brown's professor of Greek, Arthur Beattie (1914–1996), however, encouraged him to apply for the new degree in philosophy and theology at Oxford, and so Brown wrote to Basil Mitchell (1917–2011), who was putting the program together. Mitchell recommended that Brown apply to Oriel College. Beattie then discovered funds for him to do so, something called the Alexander Campbell Fraser scholarship, awarded to a graduate in philosophy at Edinburgh who wished to continue studies in philosophy at Oxford. Mitchell later wrote:

Twentieth Century Anglican Theologians: From Evelyn Underhill to Esther Mombo, First Edition.
Edited by Stephen Burns, Bryan Cones, and James Tengatenga.
© 2021 John Wiley & Sons Ltd. Published 2021 by John Wiley & Sons Ltd.

When the new school was first examined in 1972 there were seven candidates in all, including one David Brown from Oriel. The number being so small, the papers had to be marked by examiners in other schools of which philosophy formed a part. David Brown was awarded a First and, moreover, shared the Henry Wilde Prize, which went to the best performance in philosophy in the University. Freddy Ayer's argument could not have been answered more conclusively, and so I have always said that, when I die, David Brown's name will be found engraved upon my heart (Mitchell 2009, p. 273).

High praise from the Nolloth Professor of the Philosophy of the Christian Religion, and according to Mitchell the Chair of the Examiners, Sir Anthony Quinton (1925–2010), subsequently Lord Quinton, described Brown's performance as "like a Rolls Royce in first gear," presumably the idea being that there was plenty of power still in reserve.

It should come as no surprise, then, that Mitchell wrote in support of Brown's PhD application to Cambridge. Brown also applied to the prestigious BPhil in Philosophy at Oxford, and was accepted by both universities, but opted for Cambridge where he was initially assigned Donald MacKinnon (1913–1994) and Geoffrey Lampe (1912–1980) as supervisors. For a variety of reasons, Brown eventually transferred to the philosophy faculty where he wrote a thesis on "Naturalism in Ethics" under the supervision of Elizabeth Anscombe (1919–2001) and Bernard Williams (1929–2003). Professor J. Kemp (*b.* 1920) of Leicester University and Michael Tanner served as examiners, and Brown graduated in 1976. After Cambridge, Brown had every intention of going into parish ministry, but – as the result of Geoffrey Cuming's (1917–1988) persistence in suggesting that Kenneth Turpin (1915–2005), then Provost of Oriel, not only write to the Principal of Wescott to enquire after Brown, but also subsequently to insist upon an interview – Brown returned to Oriel as Fellow, Chaplain, and Tutor in Theology and Philosophy. As Robert MacSwain has noted:

In keeping with the heritage of Oriel, Brown deliberately identified his work with two of the college's most prominent past members: Joseph Butler (undergraduate, 1715–1718) and John Henry Newman (fellow, 1822–1845). However, Brown was also associated closely with two successive Nolloth Professors of the Philosophy of the Christian Religion who were also fellows of Oriel, Basil Mitchell (1917–2011) and Richard Swinburne. He was thus generally affiliated with the analytic movement in contemporary Anglo-American philosophy of religion, and his early work was in this mode primarily (MacSwain 2016, p. vii).

Along these lines, Brown's first major work, *The Divine Trinity*, begins with "A Task for the Philosophical Theologian," Brown arguing "that philosophy and theology cannot be kept artificially apart, as they are at present within the Anglo-Saxon tradition" (Brown 1985, p. x). He called for "the founding of a new discipline of philosophical theology (or the widening of the horizons of the philosophy of religion) to apply more widely the type of penetration of theology by philosophy" (Brown 1985, p. x). In a more recent volume, Brown says that his "concern over the years has been to value the contribution of both disciplines" (Brown 2016, p. 3). In fact, his concern is broader still, rooted in what he refers to as "an open tradition" (Brown 1999a, p. 7), i.e., open not only to philosophy, but also to other religions and cultures, and the arts in particular.

Brown left Oxford for Durham in 1990 where, as Van Mildert Professor Divinity in the University of Durham and Canon of Durham Cathedral, he lived in the canonry just steps from the cathedral, perched high above the River Wear. During this time, Brown served as Canon Librarian, and was also responsible for a number of artistic commissions, including Paula Rego's portrait of Margaret and David (as well as the refurbishment of the Nine Altars Chapel), the Stella Maris window (designed by Leonard Evetts), the Transfiguration window (designed by Tom Denny), and the Millennium window (designed by Joseph Nuttgens). Brown also oversaw the reordering of Cuthbert's shrine, including two large banners of Cuthbert and Oswald (designed by Thetis Blacker) (for illustration and discussion, see Brown, R. 2010).

Until 1999, Brown was – and to some still is – most well-known for *The Divine Trinity*, but with an essay on "The Trinity in Art," (Brown 1999b; Brown 2016, pp. 130–149), and then a major volume exploring the relationship of tradition and imagination (Brown 1999a), it could be said that Brown shifted from a Butlerian defense of divine intervention (later interaction), to – without forsaking Butler – a Newman-inspired consideration of the "moving text" and "an open tradition" that seeks to highlight God's active and continuing involvement through nature, culture, and the arts. As a result, there is a tendency to distinguish between the early Brown and the later Brown, but as I have argued previously there is no sharp distinction between these two phases of Brown's work. No doubt development took place, but divine interaction has always been Brown's focus. In any case, and returning now to the details of Brown's biography, shortly after the publication of two volumes with Oxford University Press (Brown 1999a, 2000), Brown was elected as a Fellow of the British Academy in 2002.

After seventeen years at Durham, Brown continued his northward pilgrimage, moving back to Scotland (2007); more specifically, to St. Mary's College, University of St Andrews as Wardlaw Professor of Theology, Aesthetics and Culture, and Professorial Fellow of the Institute for Theology, Imagination, and the Arts (ITIA). He was awarded a DLitt from Edinburgh University in 2012, and in that same year, was elected as a Fellow of the Royal Society of Edinburgh. Brown retired in September 2015.

Key Themes

Brown begins with an interactionist God, as well as an accompanying twin-commitment to divine generosity and human freedom.[2] He argues that stress on divine respect for human freedom is the only plausible way to maintain the notion of an interactionist God while acknowledging the fallibility of scripture (Brown 2013). Against conservatives, who seek "to retain the old model of inspiration," and also against radical critics, who "tend to move the locus of authority to divine acts in history," Brown argues for revision of the concept of revelation in light of religious experience (Brown 1985, p. xii). Revelation is, according to Brown's incarnational logic (Brown 1999a),[3] historically situated and culturally conditioned. It is, in other words, an interactionist, kenotic, sensitive/adaptive, progressive/developmental theory of revelation as divine dialogue, an address adapted to specific situations that because of human freedom and its limitations may also regress as well as advance.

Given that Brown emphasizes the conditioned character of all thought (including scripture and revelation), it should come as no surprise that he thinks the Bible fallible, but for Brown this means potential for development. He explains: "Close attention to original context can uncover open trajectories as it were, pressure points that almost demand further development" (Brown 1999a, p. 54). I will return to this idea in a moment, and more specifically, the related concepts of triggers and criteria, but the point to be made here is that while some would think fallibility a sign of weakness, perhaps even grounds for rejecting the faith, it is for Brown part and parcel of the divine dialogue that constitutes *living* faith. Brown explains:

> [Dialogue] suggests, on the one hand, accommodation to one's interlocutor – expressing oneself at a level at which he can understand and, on the other hand, some contribution from that interlocutor, some explication of the point which he believes the dialogue to have reached, which will then in turn elicit a further response and so on. Or, putting it another way, the notion of dialogue fully acknowledges that God's communication with man takes place in very specific contexts with certain things already assumed at each stage, an already existing canon of assumptions, as it were, – a canon that has shaped the community's conception of God, and thus inevitably shapes both the present experient's response to a particular experience and also what it is possible for God to put into that particular experience by way of content (Brown 1985, p. 70).

Fallibility is, from Brown's perspective, to be preferred, and this for logical as well as moral reasons (Brown 1985, pp. 71–74). To be more specific, the logical reason is that God works with existing thought patterns, and so reveals within a tradition of understanding that is developed over time. The moral reason, on the other hand, has to do with human freedom, as Brown explains: "For it might be that God deliberately refrains from ever imposing a particular viewpoint on a recipient, but always wishes that it should become, as it were, internalised or, putting it another way, experienced as the recipient's own insight" (Brown 1985, p. 72). In any case, fallibility means openness to change, and this development occurs when "triggers" (i.e., external stimuli, beyond scripture) lead to reinterpretation. Brown thus concludes: "What we therefore seem to have is a community of faith in continual process of change as fresh contexts trigger fresh handlings of inherited traditions." (Brown 1999a, p. 57). This process of change no doubt raises the question of criteria – i.e., which changes are legitimate and upon what basis? – and though Brown has identified nine types of criteria (Brown 2000, pp. 389–405), critics have continued to press the issue. This is not the place to adjudicate, and more work certainly needs to be done by Brown and others to address this issue, but surely, as Brown has noted, "we must not use that as an excuse for not facing the more complex reality which we find" (Brown 1999a, p. 127).

To summarize: Brown accepts the findings of biblical criticism, and more specifically the fallibility of the Bible, but thinks fallibility not only acceptable but also preferable in light of his developmental theory of revelation which, together with fallibility, maintains divine interactionism and human freedom.

At this point, several things should be noted. First, Brown rejects any sharp distinction between natural and revealed theology, emphasizing the role of reason as well as the wider context of religious experience in any adequate account of revealed theology. Second, he distinguishes revelation from the canon of scripture. Third, he expands the notion of canon to include not only the biblical canon, but also the canon of interpretation. Fourth, he relocates revelation to the act of interpretation. Tradition (i.e., interpretation) is thus, for Brown, potentially revelatory, and, I might add, imaginatively mediated. He thus speaks of tradition as "the motor that sustains revelation both within Scripture and beyond" (Brown 1999a, p. 1) and, additionally, suggests that "the truth of imaginative 'fit'" may well be preferable to the criterion of "literal fact" (Brown 1999a, p. 7; also Brown 1985, pp. 103–105; Brown 2000, pp. 402–403). It is for this reason that Brown speaks of "Art as revelation" (Brown 1999a, pp. 322–364) and elsewhere, "Artists as Theologians" (Brown 2017a, pp. 99–149), i.e., because ongoing imaginative mediation is, from Brown's perspective, more than reception or illustration, but, instead and more significantly, has the potential to innovate and reinvigorate. Going further, Brown argues that these later developments might even correct or "critique" the scriptural text (Brown 1999a, pp. 1, 5).[4] All of this is part of what Brown calls "the moving text" that spans scriptural and interpretive canons, i.e., "a shifting real text whose actual content at any particular moment could only be determined by careful analysis of its social setting" (Brown 1999a, p. 127).

Brown's attention to a given text's social setting may, at first glance, seem to privilege history – i.e., insofar as he wishes to draw attention to the text's intervening history – and this is in one sense true,[5] but he ultimately gives priority to questions of meaning and significance rather than history or canon. As he explains: "Neither history nor canon can be allowed to function as final arbiters, since more fundamental are questions of significance. What we need to consider is whether theologically or spiritually the new versions of a story or a new use to which it is put had something valuable to say in its new context, and so perhaps also to us today" (Brown 1999a, p. 208). Brown is, in other words, concerned with relevance, or as he puts it, "spiritual significance." As he explains in the introduction to his first collections of sermons,

> when I became a priest, I determined that – no matter how difficult it should prove – I would attempt to integrate fully these two areas of my life: study and pulpit. To my delight this seemed to enable me to communicate the good news of Jesus Christ *more* effectively, not less. But this should not have surprised me, for the biblical writers themselves had thought spiritual significance more important than a literal recording of events. . ... Through acknowledging this, the text ceased to be a burden upon me; instead it insisted that I too spoke of God's power of healing and renewal for my own day (Brown 1995, pp. ix–x).

And so we have come full circle, back to an interactionist God who is involved in an ongoing dialogue with humanity through "the moving text."

Brown speaks also of "an open tradition that is willing to learn from approaches beyond the narrow compass of the Christian community itself" (Brown 2000, p. 7) and this "open tradition" is more or less synonymous with his notion of "the moving text," albeit framed in terms of "tradition" rather than "text." The point here is that tradition is more indefinite than definite, supple rather than static or unchanging. And while innovation may well come from within the tradition itself, change might just as easily come from external stimuli, including other religions. Brown explains: "The Christian story has thus acquired new insights not merely through recovery of neglected aspects of its past but also through external stimuli necessitating fresh thought and with it rather different imaginative appropriations of the Christian message from what the primitive community would have envisaged" (Brown 2000, p. 8).

Brown's career is most often divided into two halves: the early Brown, who was concerned with matters of philosophical theology, and the later Brown, more interested in the arts and culture. The fact that two volumes of essays have recently been published – the first comprising essays on philosophical theology, and the second volume essays on the arts and culture – might seem to reinforce this division of Brown's work into two halves (Brown 2017a).[6] While there is some truth to this two-halves characterization, there is a more fundamental unity underlying Brown's corpus that might be described from one side as a sustained argument *against* deism and for a generous God or, from the other side, a sacramental vision of reality, that is mediated through inspired human creativity. Admittedly, to sustain this claim I will need to use "deism" in a more extended meaning than is commonplace (and indeed more widely than Brown himself) but the continuities are nonetheless remarkable.

While Brown's argument no doubt has its roots in Bishop Butler's response to seventeenth century deism (Brown 1985, p. vii),[7] the deism against which Brown now argues is, from his perspective, the result of theologians excluding from divine activity a wide range of human experience once thought significant. Previously concerned with the proponents of explicit forms of contemporary deism (e.g., Maurice Wiles, John Hick), Brown is now rooting out implicit forms of deism rife in contemporary theology (as seen in Karl Barth and his heirs). Whereas he once argued for divine "intervention," against an explicit deism's non-interventionist stance, he now argues for a continuing process of divine "interaction" (Brown 1986, p. 264) and this against an implicit deism's restrictive notion of revelation. In its current form, then, Brown's argument against deism has less to do with some abstract philosophical notion of non-intervention than it does with a very real pastoral concern for those negatively affected by the Church and its theologians' unwillingness to recognize God at work more broadly. "There is," according to Brown, "too much of a mismatch between what the Church takes to be significant and the actual experience of the wider population" (Brown 2004, p. 2). The result is that the unchurched either think God irrelevant (i.e., functional deism) or opt for their experience of God outwith the Church (i.e., spiritual but not religious). Brown thinks this a sad state of affairs, and one that is completely unnecessary given that the Church once took seriously a wide range of human experience, and could do so once more (Brown 2004, p. 6; also

Brown 2007). Drawing upon Augustine's analogy, Brown wants to acknowledge "God . . . already everywhere in the world like the water in a sponge" (Brown 2017a, p. 15).

In his earlier work, Brown was thus seeking to argue, *against* deism, that a general pattern of divine interventionism applies, and that, as he puts it, "the debate with deism must take account of the whole range of religious experience and its interpretations" (Brown 1985, pp. 52–53). This desire to "take account" – with reference to religious experience as *revelation* – is, I argue, the thread connecting the so-called early and later Brown. Ever the accountant of religious experience, Brown's hyper-empirical method is concerned with "the whole range of data" (Brown 1985, p. 53; also Brown 2004, pp. 1–3), i.e., as relevant to constructive theology, and more specifically, "a satisfactory counter-case to deism's view of the material" (Brown 1985, p. 53).

Getting down to the details, Brown's fundamental desire to "take account" has "four important consequences" (Brown 1985, p. 53). These consequences are significant in supporting my argument for continuity rather than evincing any real discontinuity of method, so much so that, frankly, I wonder how anyone could think Brown's more recent work a departure from his earlier commitments. The four consequences are as follows: first, "the question of evidence for intervention and the nature of the theistic model cannot be disentangled." Second, "the philosophical theologian will need to engage very closely with the material in question" (Brown 1985, p. 53). Third, "the traditional procedures of the philosopher will need to be reversed. . .. [W]e will have to assume in advance that the material under investigation is . . . most likely to fall under the rubric of 'revelation', without the application of any proposed tests for revelation being made in advance" (Brown 1985, p. 54). Fourth, "no precise signification can be attached to the term 'revelation' until the investigation is complete" (Brown 1985, p. 54). One need only compare these four consequences from *The Divine Trinity* in 1985 with the Introduction to Brown's 2004 monograph, *God and Enchantment of Place*, to see my point. Brown has consistently sought to draw attention to "the evidence," and not only as a means to the proximate end of rethinking the theistic model, but, more importantly, as a sustained and pastoral argument against deism. As Brown writes:

> People still find God in the great range of human experience that their ancestors once did. It is just that serious consideration is no longer given to such experience within the Church. Instead, an intellectual system is offered that now hangs free of the once universally shared assumptions on which it was based: the divine reality available everywhere to be encountered (Brown 2008, p. 271).

Put simply: the church and its theologians have failed to account for the evidence, and in so doing dismiss not only the experience, but also the claimant. The same could be said with reference to many theologians' response to Brown: i.e., that theology has been guilty not only of the sin of ignoring the wide range of material to which Brown seeks to draw attention, but also the sin of killing, or in any case attempting to kill, the messenger in the form of calls for criteria. These calls – most often for Christological criteria – are, however, less than clear for as Brown notes, "there is the whole question of what is meant by a christological criterion" (Brown 2017a, p. 75; also Brown 2000, p. 400–402). There is, one might say, an impatience in theology that masquerades as a desire for clarity vis-à-vis criteria. Against this tendency, Brown calls for "a careful listening exercise, the final result of which cannot be predetermined" (Brown 2004, p. 2). To illustrate Brown's approach in the negotiation of a current topic, I turn now to his discussion of homosexuality.

Negotiating a Current Topic: Homosexuality

Given that Brown thinks of revelation as a moving rather than a static text, it should come as no surprise that he would suggest that "we need to think of a continuous dynamic of tradition operating both within the Bible and beyond" (Brown 1999a, p. 365). What this means is that, from Brown's perspective, the reader of scripture shouldn't feel the need to force a static text to take on new meaning, as if that is what it meant all along, but rather to acknowledge the ongoing nature of God's revelation, and so accept that a renegotiation, and perhaps even critique or correction, is necessary. As Brown suggests, this approach "can release those of us who are Christians from constantly trying to find in Scripture justifications for positions that are more naturally read as later self-understandings" (Brown 1999a, p. 365). Brown outlines several advantages of this approach, the second (and most significant in this context) being that "the Bible ceases to have an impossible burden placed upon it, as somehow transcendent to all history" (Brown 1999a, p. 365). Now, this could easily sound as though Brown is operating without criteria, but, in fact, he has outlined nine types of criteria operative in his discussion of the development of tradition (Brown 2000, pp. 389–405) and the second – empirical criteria – is particularly relevant here. Brown begins with the equality of the sexes, arguing that

> the reason why the sexes were treated differently over the centuries, including during the scriptural period, was not simply because of prejudice but also because there were assumed to be relevant differences between the sexes that justified such treatment. That is something which most people now no longer believe to be the case . . . . (Brown 2000, p. 393).

Brown argues that this is the result of "empirical discovery, as experience has demonstrated women to be no less effective in positions of leadership, education, and so forth" (Brown 2000, p. 394). And this leads him to conclude: "The more fundamental New Testament principle of equality of regard could then be invoked to require equality of status, once deep-seated assumptions about underlying differences justifying differences of status has been undermined" (Brown 2000, p. 394). That being said, Brown adds:

> In making such discoveries, though, it is important that we do not pretend that such truths were after all hidden in the scriptural text. That is why I want to protest against any unqualified use of Galatians 3:28 that failed to acknowledge its more limited meaning in its original context. God has enabled a new meaning to be given to the text in quite a new situation. Again, to take

another example not previously discussed, our understanding of homosexuality and its causes is in the process of transformation. What the final result will be I leave to others to reflect. It remains important, though, that, in trying to understand potential implications, pronouncements of Bible and modern period alike are set against the backdrop of the way the issue was experienced at the time (Brown 2000, p. 394).

Here we see how Brown navigates current reality with reference to "the moving text." Empirical discoveries can trigger new meaning, but it is a *new* meaning rather than recovery of the original meaning (to the exclusion of all previously claimed meanings), that is being claimed, and this is a significant difference, but it is this difference that makes Brown's approach compelling (see also Brown 2017b).

Notes

1 This section is from Brewer 2018a, pp. 7–12.
2 The first half of this section is from Brewer (2018b, pp. x–xiii). The second half is from Brewer (2018b, pp. ix–xi).
3 Brown explains: "[T]he incarnation involved a more radical kenosis than Christianity has assumed throughout most of its history, with Jesus very much conditioned by the culture of which he was part. But if this was true at the point of God's deepest disclosure and involvement with humanity, then *a fortiori* one would expect matters to proceed similarly elsewhere in revelation, and this is in fact what we find as we study the origin of the various biblical ideas. Revelation was thus a matter of God taking seriously our historical situatedness, our dependence on our own particular environment and setting, rather than attempting to override it" (Brown 1999a, pp. 7–8).
4 Important to note is that this process of critique works in both directions, and also that progress is not inevitable (Brown 1999a, pp. 1, 51, 207).
5 I say "in one sense" as Brown does, in fact, wish to draw attention to "the intervening

history." He explains: "Present-day Christianity, it seems to me, will go badly wrong, if it attempts an unmediated dialogue with the biblical text rather than recognizing also the intervening history that has helped shape its present perception of the text's meaning" (Brown 1999a, p. 2. See also Brown 1999a, p. 117).
6 Brown himself has commented: "Those familiar with my academic history will be aware that my career divides effectively into two halves, the first primarily concerned with relations between theology and philosophy and the second with the arts and culture more generally" (Brown 2010). That said, he continues: "Not that I have abandoned interest in philosophy but I have come to see some of the issues raised by the arts as more fundamental" (Brown 2010).
7 Brown acknowledges Butler in the Preface to (Brown 1985), noting that "his earlier refutation of deism has helped to inspire my own" (Brown 1985, p. vii).

References

Brewer, C.R. (2017b). Editor's introduction. In: *Divine Generosity and Human Creativity* (David Brown; eds. C.R. Brewer and R. MacSwain), ix–xv. London: Routledge.

Brewer, C.R. (ed.) (2018a). Editor's introduction. In: *Christian Theology and the Transformation of Natural Religion: From Incarnation to Sacramentality – Essays in Honour of David Brown*, 7–12. Leuven: Peeters.

Brewer, C.R. (2018b). Editor's introduction. In: *The Moving Text: Interdisciplinary Perspectives on David Brown and the Bible* (eds. G.V. Allen, C.R. Brewer and D.F. Kinlaw III), ix–xx. London: SCM Press.

Brown, D. (1985). *The Divine Trinity*. London: Duckworth.

Brown, D. (1986). Wittgenstein against the "Wittgensteinians": a reply to Kenneth Surin on *The Divine Trinity*. *Modern Theology* 2: 257–276.

Brown, D. (1995). *The Word to Set You Free: Living Faith and Biblical Criticism*. London: SPCK.

Brown, D. (1999a). *Tradition and Imagination: Revelation and Change*. Oxford: Oxford University Press.

Brown, D. (1999b). The trinity in art. In: *The Trinity: An Interdisciplinary Symposium on the Trinity* (eds. S.T. Davis, D. Kendall and G. O'Collins), 329–356. New York: Oxford University Press.

Brown, D. (2000). *Discipleship and Imagination: Revelation and Change*. Oxford: Oxford University Press.

Brown, D. (2004). *God and Enchantment of Place: Reclaiming Human Experience*. Oxford: Oxford University Press.

Brown, D. (2007). Experience skewed. In: *Transcending Boundaries in Philosophy and Theology: Reason, Meaning and Experience* (eds. K. Vanhoozer and M. Warner), 158–175. Aldershot: Ashgate.

Brown, D. (2008). *God and Mystery in Words: Experience through Metaphor and Drama*. Oxford: Oxford University Press.

Brown, David. (2010). In the Beginning was the Image: Why the Arts Matter to Theology. Presented at the Society for the Study of Theology conference in Manchester, April 12–14.

Brown, D. (2013). God and symbolic action. In: *Scripture, Metaphysics, and Poetry: Austin Farrer's the Glass of Vision With Critical Commentary* (ed. R. MacSwain), 133–147. Farnham: Ashgate.

Brown, D. (2016). *God in a Single Vision: Integrating Philosophy and Theology* (eds. C.R. Brewer and R. MacSwain). London: Routledge.

Brown, D. (2017a). *Divine Generosity and Human Creativity: Theology through Symbol, Painting and Architecture* (eds. C.R. Brewer and R. MacSwain). London: Routledge.

Brown, D. (2017b). The equal marriage debate: a view from the margins. *Theology* 120 (6): 412–418.

Brown, R. (2010). *Post-War Art in Durham Cathedral: Telling the Christian Story*. Durham: Durham Cathedral.

MacSwain, R. (2016). Editor's introduction. In: *David Brown, God in a Single Vision: Integrating Philosophy and Theology* (eds. C.R. Brewer and R. MacSwain), vii–x. London: Routledge.

Mitchell, B. (2009). *Looking Back: On Faith, Philosophy and Friends in Oxford*. Langley Park, Durham: The Memoir Club.

David F. Ford (1948–)

Ashley Cocksworth

In a sermon preached in 2011 in the Chapel of Trinity College, Cambridge, David F. Ford said this of one of the most important Reformed theologians of the twentieth century: the aim of Karl Barth's theology is to "soak us so thoroughly in a God-centered understanding of reality that we too become inebriated with this sober intoxication" (Ford 2011a). You could hardly find a better description of Ford's own life and work. The first reading that Evensong was taken from the seventeenth chapter of the Gospel of John (the high priestly prayer of Jesus) and the second from the *Church Dogmatics* itself (the climactic passage in Barth's celebrated meditation on the theme of glory). The special status of the Gospel of John, the theology of Karl Barth, the ministry of preaching, the theme of God's glory, the University of Cambridge, the quest for "sober intoxication" worked out over a lifetime in constant dialogue with God through prayer and scripture, the sermon reflects many of the distinctively Fordian themes that will be discussed below.

Born in Dublin in 1948 into a "not particularly practicing" Irish Anglican family, Ford describes his relationship with Irish Anglicanism as one of fondness for *The Book of Common Prayer* but otherwise somewhat "tenuous" (Cunningham 2003; Ford 2010). Following his first degree in Classics at Trinity College, Dublin, and before taking up the career in business that lay before him, he accepted a two-year scholarship to St. John's College, Cambridge, to study anything; and he chose theology. "David Ford's illustrious academic career is, by his own publicly stated account, an indefinitely extended interruption of his path to business management" (Greggs et al. 2013, p. 14). His initial excursion into academic theology was followed by a STM (Master of Sacred Theology) degree at Yale Divinity School. There, under the close supervision of Hans W. Frei and the teaching of George Lindbeck, David Kelsey, and Henri Nouwen, Ford came into deep and lasting contact with the writings of Karl Barth. Arriving back at Cambridge as a doctoral student Ford returned with the

Twentieth Century Anglican Theologians: From Evelyn Underhill to Esther Mombo, First Edition.
Edited by Stephen Burns, Bryan Cones, and James Tengatenga.
© 2021 John Wiley & Sons Ltd. Published 2021 by John Wiley & Sons Ltd.

narrative theology that was being developed by and would become synonymous with the Yale school and set about applying it to Barth's hermeneutics, this time under the supervision of Stephen Sykes and Donald M. MacKinnon (and, during his spell in Tübingen, with Eberhard Jüngel).

Before the completion of his doctoral work, Ford took up a lectureship in theology at the University of Birmingham in 1976 and remained there until 1991 when he succeeded Sykes (the newly consecrated Bishop of Ely) as the Regius Professor of Divinity at Cambridge – the first lay incumbent of the chair. He spent over twenty-five years in Cambridge, retiring in 2015 having quite literally altered the Cambridge theological landscape: not least in the sense that under his tenure and oversight the Divinity Faculty moved to a new building. His entrepreneurship helped to raise over £30 million for various projects, including the founding of several significant interfaith initiatives that would take place within the new faculty building and wider university.

Although Ford continued to publish on Barth and supervise successive generations of doctoral theses on him, his own intellectual labors would reach considerably beyond than the world of Barth studies (Ford's own thesis on Barth would be published as Ford 1981). His publications, too numerous to list here, include work on modern theology, 2 Corinthians with his Birmingham colleague and long-term conversation partner Frances M. Young, the doctrines of anthropology and salvation, the theme of Christian wisdom (which would prove endlessly generative), the role of the university, contemporary Irish poetry, interfaith engagement, and the theological, spiritual, and practical dimensions of the Christian life in books aimed at non-academic audiences. Across many of his recent writings, a constant reference point is the Gospel of John. In 2015 Ford gave the prestigious Bampton lectures in Oxford on John and has been working for many years on a commentary on the gospel to be published by Baker Academic. Besides ongoing work on John, the interfaith practice of Scriptural Reasoning (SR), education, and new work on the theology of reconciliation in the Anglican context, in his "retirement" Ford is working on a theological understanding of disability in a book he is co-editing with Deborah Hardy Ford and Ian Randall on Lyn's House, the L'Arche-inspired Christian community in Cambridge, and a theological engagement with "The Five Quintets," the *magnum opus* of another of his long-term dialogue partners Micheal O'Siadhail (who have been first readers of each other's work for over fifty years) (O'Siadhail 2018).

Publications aside, much of Ford's theological legacy is bound up with the Cambridge Interfaith Programme,[1] which he established in 2002 in the new Faculty of Divinity building, and its flagship practice of SR (on this, more later), which emerged out of the Jewish Textual Reasoning Group that began to convene at the American Academy of Religion in the early 1990s.[2] For his contribution to interfaith engagement, Ford received the 2011 Coventry International Prize for Peace and Reconciliation and three years later was honored with an OBE (Order of the British Empire). The overriding concern for better quality dialogue across the Abrahamic faiths is a good example of the unmistakably "public" dimension of Ford's life and work. He sees being drawn into the sober intoxication of God through Jesus Christ as simultaneously being drawn more intensively into the world and into the church. In all he does, he seeks to work out how theology can help shape practice as wisely as possible. Perhaps reflecting his deep formation in postliberal theology while at Yale, there is also, then, a discernibly ecclesial shape to his theological outlook: he works his theology out in relation to the church.

In his Anglicanism – as indeed in his theology, which is intrinsically border crossing – Ford does not rest content with party categories and established boundaries. Faithfully non-sectarian, he is deeply committed to the whole church. While in Cambridge he, for many years, attended and regularly preached at St. Benet's, which until recently was led by Anglican Franciscans, and his time in the multifaith city of Birmingham was spent at an inner-city Anglican church in the evangelical tradition where he was a warden for five years and a member of Diocesan Synod. In Birmingham, he was especially energized by relationships outside Anglicanism, including with several Pentecostal and Black-led churches. The theme of the Holy Spirit and charismatic practice has remained central to Ford's theological imagination ever since (Ochs 2011, pp. 195–221).

Beyond his local church involvement, Ford has given himself to the service of the Church of England and the wider Anglican Communion. He has led several diocesan clergy study events, worked (with Bishop Lesslie Newbigin) on the *Faith in the City of Birmingham Report*, and served as a theological consultant to the 1998 Lambeth Conference. There, Ford was an observer of the main sessions, present at the lunchtime meetings of the steering group of the Conference, and part of the group that produced the opening and closing Plenary Sessions, at both of which he spoke. He remained variously involved in the four subsequent Primates' Meetings held in Porto, Kanuga, Canterbury, and Gramado – including leading the daily Bible studies and contributing to the drafting of the pastoral letters issued by the meetings (Ford 2006c). We'll interact with Ford's (mostly unpublished) engagements with Lambeth 1998 toward the end of the chapter. Beyond Lambeth, he has chaired the Council of Westcott House, Cambridge, has been a Council Member of Ridley Hall, Cambridge (both theological colleges), served for many years on the Doctrine Commission of the Church of England and on the Archbishop of Canterbury's Urban Theology Group, and, more recently, turned his attention to the Church of England's vision for primary and secondary education in the United Kingdom. The vision statement, "Deeply Christian, Serving the Common Good" (2016), has all the signs of Fordian theology: the flourishing of the common good in our complexly multifaith and multisecular society, the theme of wisdom, and the Gospel of John.[3]

Despite the important contributions he has made to the shaping of so much contemporary theology in the British context and his longstanding involvement in life of the Church of England and the Anglican Communion, like others featured in this volume, Ford is rarely read as an *Anglican* theologian.[4] Yet while his theological interests do not lie in producing a distinctively Anglican theology for Anglicans, Ford's theology bears many of the classic characteristics of a deep formation in Anglican theological sensibilities. In what follows, I discuss Ford's Anglican identity in respect of two themes drawn from his own vision for the future of Christian theology as described in *Christian Wisdom* (Ford 2007). During the final year of writing *Christian Wisdom*, Ford formulated twelve theses to articulate the shape of a contemporary theology rooted in the wisdom of God (Ford 2007, p. 4). Ford has returned to these theses in many other writings too, and we will focus on two of them to help expose the deep-seated Anglican undercurrents in his theology. The first concerns the need for theology to be immersed in praying and the second is about the utter centrality of reading scripture. The two themes – praying and reading scripture – are typically Anglican and fully Fordian.

"Prayer is the beginning, accompaniment and end of theology: Come, Holy Spirit! Hallelujah! and Maranatha!" (Ford 2007, p. 4)

It is a truth (nearly) universally acknowledged that Anglicanism doesn't really do theology in any systematically recognizable way. To cite Sykes' 1978 indictment of Anglican theology: "Anglicans are not supposed to know about, or to be interested in, systematic theology" (Sykes 1978, p. ix).[5] Equally suggestive is the omission of "doctrine" from the list of the characteristics Michael Ramsey, another sometime occupant of Ford's Regius chair, thinks makes Anglican theology *Anglican*. Ramsey does, however, cite the "sensitivity to the significance of spirituality, the life of prayer, for theology" as one of markers of Anglican self-understanding (Ramsey 1960, p. 164). "Accordingly," as the Report of the Lambeth Conference of 1978 concludes, "in order to find out what characterizes Anglican doctrine, the simplest way is to look at Anglican worship and deduce doctrine from it" (Anglican Commission 1978, p. 99). It is more in common prayer than common doctrine that Anglicans of different doctrinal stripes grow into deeper communion with each other.

To lay claim to the Anglican commitment to the significance of prayer for theology it has become customary to invoke the early church maxim: the *lex orandi, lex credendi* ("the law of prayer is the law of belief"). So central to Anglican theological identity is the law of prayer that Phyllis Tickle argues that "there is no Anglicanism without it" (Tickle 2015, p. 517). Usually attributed to Prosper of Aquitaine (circa 390–455), who first used the phrase (rather casually, it should be said, and in a different form) in the context of the semi-Pelagian controversy of the fifth century to settle a doctrinal debate over grace, the *lex orandi, lex credendi* makes the case that the performance of the church's practices – in its prayer life and liturgy – is inherently connected to its beliefs. Beyond a general appeal to the *lex orandi*, however, what remains somewhat under theorized when taken up in Anglican theology is the question of what, theologically speaking, the *lex orandi* actually does; and here we turn to Ford's writings to put some theological flesh on this backbone of Anglican theology and in the process expose something of Ford's own Anglican character.

The thesis from Ford with which this section began states that the future of Christian theology depends on the reintegration of prayer and theology, much like the integration embodied by Anglican theology. These are not empty words. Ford is a theologian who prays and is completely unembarrassed about doing theology as a form of prayer. "I remember the transformation in my prayer when an old Anglican monk explained the wisdom of following a particular pattern of prayer and Bible readings – a 'daily office' . . . [S]ince then it has been like a basic rhythm" (Ford 2004, p. 89). The practice of prayer provides Ford with a "basic rhythm" for his theology. It is a habit: he inhabits prayer. Thus, Ford says, prayer not simply begins and ends theological work as the doxological bookends of Christian wisdom but also accompanies the work of theology throughout.

Like Barth, who provided him with his theological apprenticeship, Ford didn't set out to write a spiritual theology.[6] It is more that his theology is integrated with spirituality. As he works the *lex orandi* into and through his writings, weaving spirituality into all he says and thinks about God, the nature of Christian theology starts to look different. Again, perhaps reflective of the post-liberalism of Yale, Ford is suspicious of "cognitive-propositional" approaches to theology that see "doctrines as informative propositions to be assessed cognitively" (Ford 1986, p. 277). He sees Christian doctrine as infinitely more encompassing than "information" about God. Doctrines are integrally related to spirituality, the affections, and the living out of the Christian life in the messy realities of human existence. And this makes theology to be ultimately concerned with, to cite the subtitle of his *Self and Salvation* (Ford 1999), nothing less than "being transformed." There is something deeply Anglican about Ford's location of theology, as it were, beyond (cognitive) belief (see Coakley 2013). The genius of Thomas Cranmer's vision for the renewal of society was that it would be driven by the things people did in prayer rather than the beliefs people held. "Worship rather than doctrinal precision shapes a holy life," Ellen Charry writes (Charry 2014, p. 196). Ford's elegant integration of "knowing and praising," and the reformulation of "belief" it brings about, releases theology "from the fixations and obsessions of reason" and gently opens the theologian "to being knit into a reality that is delightful as well as true" (Hardy and Ford 1984, p. 113). To do theology is not, then, for Ford about assenting to a set of propositional statements; hence unlike other churches, Anglicanism doesn't privilege a magisterium, confessional documents, or canonical writings of key theologians. Instead, Anglican theology is principally about breaking bread together, it is about that characteristically Johannine verb *menein* – "dwelling, abiding, remaining, lasting, inhabiting, 'living in'" God (Ford 2011b, p. 31).

From the highly developed notion of the "worshipping self" around which his theological anthropology pivots in *Self and Salvation* (Ford 1999), the frequent appeals to the close relation between prayer and the ever resourceful category of Christian wisdom, the forwarding of prayer as crucial for the flourishing of the future of Christian theology, to the centrality of prayer in the Christian life in both *The Shape of Living* (Ford 1997) and *The Drama of Living* (Ford 2014), the doxological nature of theology is a persistent theme in every one of Ford's major publications. No more so, however, than in *Jubilate: Theology in Praise* (Hardy and Ford 1984), co-authored with his Birmingham colleague, and by then father-in-law, Daniel W. Hardy.

Jubilate presents an exhilarating exploration of just what is possible when theology is conducted in prayer and shaped fundamentally by the liturgy. Although its authors do not put it in quite these terms, the book can be read as the product of Anglican reasoning. The reintegration of prayer and doctrine reorientates theology toward its proper end: the praise of God, making theology a joyous, celebratory, doxological undertaking. The *lex orandi* functions, then, as a constant reminder of theology's vocation, which is to give glory to God and to be led deeper into the delight of that life. In this sense, Ford's infectious enthusiasm for the sheer delight of theology makes him a theologian *par excellence*. *Jubilate* also, importantly for our purposes, sheds further light on the theological role of the law of prayer. There is one theological feature of the *lex orandi* in particular I would like to draw out in dialogue with Ford's theology in the remainder of this section: how the *lex orandi* "radicalizes" Christian doctrine.

In an age when prayer often is seen to get in the way of critical enquiry, Ford celebrates theological thinking as not only integral to prayer but dependent on it (Ford 2011b, p. 91). As suggested in the subtitle to the revised edition of *Jubilate*, "knowing" (*lex credendi*) and "worshipping" (*lex orandi*) God belong together (Ford and Hardy 2005). Put simply, "theological thinking both helps to shape it [prayer and worship] and is shaped by it" (Ford 2011b, p. 92). It is in this "wise" interaction between prayer and theology, stimulated by the *lex orandi*, that doctrinal thinking is "radicalized." How so?

In *Jubilate*, prayer and praise, the constituent elements of the *lex orandi*, are said to gain access to a certain kind of theological truth. In fact, "there is a knowledge of God that can only come in praising God," Ford writes (Hardy and Ford 1984, p. 10). The *Jubilate* book can be read as a doctrinal outworking of this central theological conviction: classical Christian doctrines are read and reread in the blindingly bright light of prayer. New depths to the doctrines of God, creation, pneumatology, eschatology, and (especially) Christology are discovered in prayer. In each case, the role of the *lex orandi* is to push theological discourse into new areas, allow for "fresh creativity," rework tradition, and improvise on what has come before (Hardy and Ford 1984, p. 7). For Ford, there is a "mind-stretching" logic to prayer and praise (Ford 2007, p. 238). In praying to God, language expands and "stretches." Traditional ways of thinking about God "grow in content" (Hardy and Ford 1984, p. 14). In doxology, "language overflows, old expressions are renewed and filled with fresh meaning, and new expressions are inspired" (Hardy and Ford 1984, p. 14). Conversely, without prayer, theology grows to a standstill, uncritically repeating the past – it makes an idol of its very self.

A good example of the *lex orandi* in action, and its belief-stretching logic, can be seen in Ford's discussion of the formation of the doctrine of God's incarnation in Jesus Christ. Since the publication of *Lux Mundi* (1881), attention to the doctrine of the incarnation has been firmly established as one of the hallmarks of Anglican theology. As is Anglican theology, so too Ford's theology is characterized by a constant return to incarnational theology. The striking feature of the development of Christian doctrine, according to Ford, is its "daring innovation" beyond the Jewish tradition in relation to God's incarnation in Jesus Christ (Ford 2007, p. 202). What is striking for us is the role Ford allocates to prayer in the development of these doctrinal innovations: practices of prayer stimulated, he says, "'what if . . ..' exploratory thinking" (Ford 2011b, p. 74). More specifically, "the explosion of thanks and praise in the early Church unavoidably raised the question of God and especially of the relation of Jesus to God" (Hardy and Ford 1984, p. 54). These practices of praying to Jesus, praying through Jesus, and praising Jesus as Lord "had radical consequences" for the doctrine of God (Hardy and Ford 1984, p. 8). They led theologians, beginning with Paul and the Gospel writers, to confront the difficult question: *what if* because we pray to Christ in these ways Jesus is divine? Here we are catching sight of the *lex orandi* deepening and extending Christian belief into new areas, forcing early Christian theology to confront difficult questions concerning the reality of multiple divinities, and leading to daring doctrinal affirmations of Jesus Christ's full divinity. As Ford says, the *lex orandi* brought about "a revolution in the concept of God" and in so doing radicalized our speech of God – making it stranger (Hardy and Ford 1984, p. 54).

For Ford, Christian doctrine, in turn, has a "radicalizing" effect on the practice of prayer. It makes the human activity of prayer more than simply a human activity. There is a "transformation" of worship to expand prayer into the participation in the "worship within God, the dynamic of love and glorification" (Ford 1999, p. 214). Indeed, one of the earliest definitions of prayer was "conversation." When people in the early church spoke of prayer as conversation with God they meant more than a dialogue between the pray-er and God. They meant that to pray is to be caught up into this "worship within God." To pray means to be united with God in Christ. It involves the con-versing of the divine and the human, of God and humanity together "perfecting perfection" (Hardy and Ford 1984, p. 8).[7] In practice, for the early church and probably for Ford too, conversing with God in prayer likely meant entering into dialogue with the text of scripture in which the Word of God is to be heard; and it is to Ford's engagement with scripture that we now turn.

The "study of scripture is at the heart of theology" (Ford 2007, p. 4)

Immediately following the thesis on prayer in Ford's vision for the future of Christian theology is one on scripture. The "study of scripture is at the heart of theology," and especially of Anglican theology. Anglicanism, as Ford notes, has a "rich tradition of inhabiting scripture" (Ford 2001, p. 6). Part of Cranmer's vision for the Church of England was to be united in common prayer and enlivened by the "sober intoxication" of the Bible. The Prayer Book "was the wise gathering up of scripture and a long tradition of worship into a form which could be performed in worship in 17th century England in native tongue" among all the people of God (Ford 2001, pp. 5–6). Cranmer's lectionary ran through the New Testament twice a year, the Old Testament (and Apocrypha) once a year, and the Psalter once a month – and this patterned reading of scripture is situated in the liturgical context of praise and prayer. There is a profound integration of praying and reading scripture in the Anglican imagination, as there is in Ford's theology. Ford is a God-intoxicated theologian fueled by habitual prayer and the energetic reading of the Bible, and most recently by the Gospel of John.[8]

Ford's fascination with the Fourth Gospel says something of his Anglican identity. It locates him in a long line of Anglican exegetes of the Gospel of John (on this, see Williams 2014, pp. 121–137). The Gospel of John, with its radical affirmation of the incarnation of God, has "probably been more formative of Anglicanism . . . than any other text. It does not just lead into the profundities of the tradition; it also (together with the Letters of John) both poses problems about divisiveness and is extraordinarily encouraging in facing the future" (Ford 2006a, p. 153). For Ford, the Bible, which is so often at the heart of disagreements in the life of the church, also offers the main way through them. His repeated plea to the primates of the Anglican Communion in his engagement with the 1998 Lambeth Conference is for Anglicanism to appropriate afresh holy scripture. One way of making good on Ford's plea to appropriate the Bible afresh for the sake of the future of the Anglican Communion is through the practice of SR. Cofounded by Ford, SR is a practice of Jews, Muslims, and Christians reading each other's sacred texts together. "It allows for both deep particularity . . . and is open to seeing the Spirit at work across boundaries, including religious boundaries; and it entails face-to-face encounter and is deeply orientated toward friendship and collegiality" (Gregg, Muers, and Zahl 2013, p. 11).

SR is very much bound up with Ford's Anglican instincts and, as he has explained elsewhere, has its origins in Anglicanism and has strong Anglican participation.[9] What I want to press in this section is not so much what SR reveals of Ford's Anglican identity and the ways it accords with the heart of Anglicanism but what SR might offer to the Anglican Communion – particularly in terms of the theme of unity as expressed in the final of prayer of Jesus in John 17 and its vision for radically reconciled relationships. Indeed, and to be more specific, there is a double dynamic involved in the biblical therapy SR offers Anglicanism (Ford 2013, p. 150).

First, in the mode of Fordian "what if . . ." thinking (for Ford's discussion of "moods of faith," see Ford 2007, pp. 46–50), *what if* the core logic of SR could be reappropriated *intra*-religiously as well as across religions. What if the other side of the promise of SR is to move the Anglican Communion beyond the hermeneutical impasse that seems to lie at the root of many of its disputes and into a place of deeper understanding and richer disagreement. SR allows for deep differences to be faced but not necessarily resolved. "The aim is *not consensus*," Ford writes, but the deepening in both understanding and disagreement (aiming to improve the quality of both). Anglicans might further learn from SR's willingness to repair one's own tradition by drawing on the resources within it, to read beyond the "plain sense" of scripture, and to keep multiple readings in play (Ford 2006b, p. 5). The preference for the particular would encourage Anglicans who think differently from each other to speak from their own particular place, distinctive viewpoint, and specificity of context, to be listened to and to be open to have their own wisdom questioned and transformed in engagement with others. The result is what Ben Quash calls "double deepening": a deeper inhabiting of one's own tradition by means of a deepening of one's experience of another (Quash 2013, p. 206). At its best it does not conceal conflict or tension but makes public the depths of disagreement through mutual hospitality, friendship, and conversation (those most distinctively Fordian themes), and the promise of fostering enduring forms of unity within the Anglican Communion in tangible anticipation of future peace.

Second, as well as practicing SR between Anglicans to strengthen communion, SR should be practiced by Anglicans with those of other faiths. For Ford, unity within the Anglican Communion might well be dependent on reconciliation *across* religions and the peaceable sociality within the Abrahamic faiths to which SR reaches. *What if* "our intrafaith relations will not come right apart from our interfaith relations? It is not a matter of first trying to sort out the Church of England, or the Anglican Communion, or ecumenical relations among Churches, and then addressing relations with other faiths" (Ford 2013, p. 159). Instead, for Ford, addressing relations with other faiths, and as a priority, might prove crucial in the hastening toward peace within the Anglican Communion. And finally, *what if* joint studies of our scriptures "is as near as we can come to [interfaith] worship while being true to deeply differing faiths" (Ford 2013, p. 164)? This double dynamic of peaceful diversity within Anglicanism and across religions leads Ford to conclude that the time is "ripe for the practice of Scriptural Reasoning to spread more widely through the Anglican Communion" to serve the common good (Ford 2013, p. 163).[10]

Conclusion

In his published reflections on Lambeth 1998, Ford finds in (the now infamous, though at the time much-lauded) John Vanier's commentary on John 17 what he believed to be "God's call to the Anglican Communion at this time" (Ford 2006a, p. 155). His call throughout his Lambeth engagement was for Anglicanism to be *more* Anglican precisely by returning to the Anglican basis of reading scripture in the living tradition of the church and informed (spiritual) reason. But to what end? For Ford, it is to be united in the glory of God given to us in Jesus Christ so that we may "reflect the infinite beauty of God, the unity in God" (Vanier 2004, pp. 297–299).

Notes

1 https://www.interfaith.cam.ac.uk (accessed July 20, 2020).

2 For more on SR, see http://www.scripturalreasoning.org.uk/ (accessed July 20, 2020).

3 https://www.churchofengland.org/media/2532839/2016-church-of-england-vision-for-education-web-final.pdf (accessed July 20, 2020).

4 Aspects of his theology, such as his eucharistic theology and his rich theology of friendship, have proved highly amenable to Anglican theologians conducting distinctively Anglican theology. See Gittoes (2008), Thomson (2015, pp. 121–132). More generally, the Anglican shape of his "systematic theology" has been identified and drawn out in King et al. (2012, p. 319).

5 It is important to note that Sykes' denouncement of the state of Anglican theology has not stood the test of time. Ford's theology certainly breaks this characterization. The field of systematic theology is now flourishing and interestingly Anglican theologians have taken a lead in its regeneration. At least three substantial systematic theological projects are currently underway by Anglican theologians: Sarah Coakley, Graham Ward, and Katherine Sonderegger. More interesting still, for reasons that will soon become clear, is the role prayer plays in each of their distinctive methodologies.

6 The closest he comes to writing a dedicated "spirituality" is Ford (1997), the first in his "of Living" series, which Ford once remarked was his "favourite book." The first edition of the *Shape of Living* was the Archbishop's Lent Book for 1998 commissioned by the then Archbishop of Canterbury George Carey. In his Foreword, Carey describes the book to be "an example of Anglican theology at its best," perhaps because of its eloquent integration of theology, spirituality, and the living of the Christian life. In 2014, Ford produced a sequel to Ford (1997), and is currently working on a third book provisionally called *The Wonder of Living* based on his aforementioned theological engagement with O'Siadhail's "The Five Quintets."

7 Ford's anthropology, which is grounded in the vision that to be human means to participate in the praise of God, taps into a central strand of the Anglican theological tradition. The strand has been brilliantly pulled together by Ford's sometime spiritual director, A. M. Allchin, in his classic, Allchin (1988).

8 I say "most recently" because the Gospel of John is the latest in a series of intensive readings of biblical texts that have accompanied Ford's theological writing. For example, Jubilate (Hardy and Ford 1984) is worked out in intensive dialogue with the Psalms, Philippians, and the Gospel of Mark; *Meaning and Truth in II Corinthians* (Ford and Young 1987) dialogs, of course, deeply with 2 Corinthians; *Self and Salvation* (Ford 1999) is bound up with close readings of the Synoptics and Ephesians; and then there is the close studies of Job, the Gospel of Luke, and Revelation in *Christian Wisdom* (Ford 2007).

9 Ford guest-edited and contributed to an issue of the *Journal of Anglican Studies* in 2013 on SR and Anglicanism. For Ford's article on how SR and Anglicanism go together, see Ford (2013).

10 The promise of SR is being pragmatically tested in some of Ford's retirement projects, which include the co-chairing of the Global Covenant of Religions, the Faith in Leadership project, and the Rose Castle Foundation. Related to these, Ford has been working on a theology of reconciliation to inform Justin Welby's new "Reconciling Leaders Network." The Network aims to train emerging leaders, mentors, and "women on the front line" in reconciliation, mediation, conflict stabilization, and peacebuilding both within the church and beyond it in the many settings where conflict happens. SR has been intrinsic to all these activities: Rose Castle is the new hub for SR beyond the university, it is a basic practice in the programs run by Faith in Leadership, and it has informed the Global Covenant.

References

Allchin, A.M. (1988). *Participation in God: A Forgotten Strand in Anglican Tradition*. New York, NY: Morehouse.

Charry, E.T. (2014). The beauty of holiness: practical divinity. In: *The Vocation of Anglican Theology: Sources and Essays* (ed. R. McMichael), 196–243. London: SCM Press.

Coakley, S. (2013). Beyond "belief": liturgy and the cognitive apprehension of God. In: *The Vocation of Theology Today: A Festschrift for David Ford* (eds. T. Greggs, R. Muers and S. Zahl), 130–145. Eugene, OR: Cascade.

Cunningham, D.S. (2003). The practical theology of David F. Ford. *The Christian Century* 120 (9): 30–37.

Ford, D.F. (1981). *Barth and God's Story: Biblical Narrative and the Theological Method of Karl Barth in the Church Dogmatics*. Frankfurt: Peter Lang.

Ford, D.F. (1986). Review of *the Nature of Doctrine*, by George Lindbeck. *Journal of Theological Studies* 37: 277–282.

Ford, David F. (1997). *The Shape of Living*. London: Fount. Second edition: *The Shape of Living: The Spiritual Directions of Daily Life*. London: SPCK.

Ford, D.F. (1999). *Self and Salvation: Being Transformed*. Cambridge: Cambridge University Press.

Ford, David F. (2001). Looking Ahead. Unpublished lecture delivered at the Primates of the Anglican Communion Meeting in Kanuga, North Carolina, March 8.

Ford, D.F. (2004). *Shape of Living: The Spiritual Directions for Everyday Life*. Norwich: Canterbury Press.

Ford, D.F. and Hardy, D.W. (2005). *Living in Praise: Worshipping and Knowing God*. London: Darton, Longman and Todd.

Ford, D.F. (2006a). A wisdom for Anglican life: Lambeth 1998 to Lambeth 2008 and beyond. *Journal of Anglican Studies* 4 (2): 137–156.

Ford, D.F. (2006b). An interfaith wisdom: scriptural reasoning between Jews, Christians and Muslims. In: *The Promise of Scriptural Reasoning* (eds. C. Pecknold and D.F. Ford), 1–22. Oxford: Wiley Blackwell.

Ford, D.F. (2006c). A wisdom for Anglican life: Lambeth 1998 to Lambeth 2008 and beyond. *Journal of Anglican Studies* 4 (2): 137–156.

Ford, D.F. (2007). *Christian Wisdom*. Cambridge: Cambridge University Press.

Ford, D.F. (2010). Faith seeking wisdom: how my mind has changed. *The Christian Century* 127 (24): 30–34.

Ford, David F. (2011a). Karl Barth's Sober Intoxication. Unpublished sermon preached at Trinity College, Cambridge, Sunday February 27.

Ford, D.F. (2011b). *The Future of Christian Theology*. Oxford: Wiley Blackwell.

Ford, D.F. (2013). Scriptural Reasoning: its Anglican origins, its development, practice and significance. *Journal of Anglican Studies* 11 (2): 147–165.

Ford, D.F. (2014). *The Drama of Living: Becoming Wise in the Spirit*. Norwich: Canterbury Press.

Ford, D.F. and Young, F. (1987). *Meaning and Truth in 2 Corinthians*. London: SPCK.

Gittoes, J. (2008). *Anamnesis and the Eucharist: Contemporary Anglican Approaches*. Aldershot: Ashgate.

Greggs, T., Muers, R., and Zahl, S. (2013). Introduction. In: *The Vocation of Theology Today: A Festschrift for David Ford* (eds. T. Greggs, R. Muers and S. Zahl), 1–24. Eugene, OR: Cascade.

Hardy, D.W. and Ford, D.F. (1984). *Jubilate: Theology in Praise*. London: DLT. (US title: (1985) *Praising and Knowing God*. Louisville, KY: Westminster John Knox Press.) (Second UK edition: Ford, D. F. and Hardy, D. W. (2005). *Living in Praise: Worshipping and Knowing God*. London: DLT.).

King, B.J., MacSwain, R., and Fout, J.A. (2012). Contemporary Anglican systematic theology: three examples in David Brown, Sarah Coakley, and David F. Ford. *Anglican Theological Review* 94 (2): 319–334.

O'Siadhail, M. (2018). *The Five Quintets*. Waco, TX: Baylor University Press.

Ochs, P. (2011). *Another Reformation: Postliberal Christianity and the Jews*. Grand Rapids, MI: Baker Academic.

Quash, B. (2013). Abrahamic scriptural reading from an Anglican perspective. *Journal of Anglican Studies* 11 (2): 199–216.

Ramsey, M. (1960). *From Gore to Temple: The Development of Anglican Theology between* Lux Mundi *and the Second World War, 1889–1939*. London: Longmans.

Sykes, S. (1978). *The Integrity of Anglicanism*. Oxford: Mowbray.

Anglican Communion (1978). *The Resolutions of the Lambeth Conference 1978*. London: Church Information Office.

Thomson, J.B. (2015). *Sharing Friendship: Exploring Anglican Character, Vocation, Witness and Mission*. London: Routledge.

Tickle, P. (2015). Prayer. In: *The Oxford Handbook of Anglican Studies* (eds. M.D. Chapman, S. Clarke and M. Percy), 517–526. Oxford: Oxford University Press.

Vanier, J. (2004). *Drawn into the Mystery of Jesus through the Gospel of John*. London: DLT.

Williams, R. (2014). *Anglican Identities*. London: DLT.

N. T. (Tom) Wright (1948–)

Sean Winter

It would be hard to think of a more prolific and influential Anglican theologian than Nicholas Thomas Wright (1948–), formerly Bishop of Durham and, after several years as Research Professor of New Testament and Early Christianity at the University of St. Andrews, now relocated to Wycliffe Hall, Oxford, as Senior Research Fellow. It is tempting to think that this influence is simply the result of his prodigious output: upwards of ninety scholarly and popular books with his name on the front cover, an equivalent number of major scholarly articles, not to mention more popular reviews and opinion pieces, a healthy collection of letters to *The Times* and *The Telegraph*, and a couple of oratorio libretti for good measure.[1] Alternatively, and recognizing that numbers are not everything, one could interpret Wright's influence primarily by reference to the controversy that his work has generated; mainly, though not exclusively, in the earnest and diverse halls of contemporary evangelicalism. Undoubtedly, Wright's literary and rhetorical skills are also a part of the equation. Rarely has a New Testament scholar addressed their peers with such confidence, while at the same time writing for a popular audience with such clarity and verve. The argument of this chapter, however, will be that Wright's influence, for good or for ill, is ultimately the product of his determination to place his own ideas at the center of ongoing conversations about questions that stand at the heart of Christian faith: who was Jesus?; what is salvation?; how do we understand history?[2] His views, whatever one thinks about their relative merits, are presented in such a way as to make it clear to the reader that they make a difference to the way that Christian faith is understood and practiced. My further proposal is that Wright answers these questions in what can be read as a distinctively Anglican mode, in each case articulating a coherent and committed *via media* that preserves and restates many of the historical and theological convictions of the Christian tradition, while at the same time pushing in the direction of revision and reform.[3]

Twentieth Century Anglican Theologians: From Evelyn Underhill to Esther Mombo, First Edition.
Edited by Stephen Burns, Bryan Cones, and James Tengatenga.
© 2021 John Wiley & Sons Ltd. Published 2021 by John Wiley & Sons Ltd.

Wright's treatment of the three themes of history, Christology, and salvation are most fully worked out in the pages of his *magnum opus*, the series "Christian Origins and the Question of God," currently in four volumes, with a further two volumes awaiting completion (Wright 1992, 1996, 2003, 2013a).[4] Given the centrality of this project to Wright's overall contribution, the discussion will focus on the relevant volumes and critical responses to them.

Wright's biography is the story of someone who has confidently occupied key roles within the church and the academy by dint of their intellectual ability and fervent passion for scripture and the Christian faith. This combination of confidence, intellect, and fervor provides a partial explanation for the scale of Wright's output and influence. It also helps us to understand why Wright is a controversial theologian: the focus of sharp critique and loyal support, and a lightning rod for ongoing debates about the nature of Christian faith, the significance of Jesus, and the understanding of salvation and its consequences.

Wright was raised in what might be referred to in England as "middle Anglicanism" (as Kuhrt 2011, p. 11). He was educated at the historic Sedbergh school and went up to Oxford in 1968 to read "Greats." This classical education path, once common for New Testament scholars (less so today) undoubtedly set into place the fundamental linguistic, textual, and historical skills that undergird Wright's New Testament scholarship. He excelled academically (graduating with a first-class degree in 1971), combining his studies with leading the evangelical Oxford Inter-Collegiate Christian Union. This was followed by studies at Wycliffe Hall toward Anglican ministry and ordination as a deacon in 1975, priest in 1976. From this point, Wright's career as an academic theologian took him from Oxford (Junior Research Fellow at Merton College, 1975–1978), to Cambridge (Chaplain at Downing College, 1978–1981), and back again (Chaplain and Tutor at Worcester College, 1986–1993). Wright's Oxbridge existence was interrupted only by a five-year appointment to McGill University in Canada (1981–1986), to take up a position in New Testament, and so follow in the footsteps of his own doctoral supervisor, George Bradford Caird (1917–1984). This period, from the early 1970s to the early 1990s, can be seen as deeply formative but largely preparatory in relation to Wright's subsequent career. He completed his doctorate, taught New Testament, and published relatively little.[5] Undoubtedly, however, this was also a time in which the main contours of his overall theological project began to take shape, and build momentum.

Arguably, the turning point came with a period of sabbatical leave in Jerusalem in 1989 where Wright was able to write the first drafts of what became *The New Testament and the People of God* (Wright 1992), *Jesus and the Victory of God* (Wright 1996), and some of *Paul and the Faithfulness of God* (Wright 2013a).[6] As yet unfinished, this ambitious project offers a comprehensive account of the development of early Christian theology and literature. The halting progress of the project is partly explained by Wright's decision in 1994 to take up the position of Dean of Lichfield Cathedral, the first in a trio of appointments within the Church of England that would, via a stint at Westminster Abbey (2000–2003), end up with his appointment as Bishop of Durham (2003–2010). Yet, despite the demands of ecclesial office, Wright continued to publish; particularly more popular works such as the "For Everyone" commentary series, published sermons and lecture series, and Wright's own translation of the New Testament.[7]

In 2010 Wright moved back into academia with his appointment to St. Andrews, enabling him to complete his major study of Paul, teach and supervise doctoral students, and revisit and rearticulate ideas first explored in earlier works, especially in relation to Jesus and history (see, for example Wright 2012, 2016, 2019).[8] Throughout this time, Wright has placed or found himself at the center of major scholarly debates. He is best known as a proponent of the "New Perspective on Paul" (discussed below), and as a key figure in the "Third Quest" for the Historical Jesus, in each case shaping the scholarly conversation while at the same time making the implications of the debates clear for a wider readership. Behind both of these contributions, however, lies Wright's commitment to the importance of history.

History and Hermeneutics

Wright has placed the task of "doing history" at the heart of his theological work, insisting that "the Christian theologian is committed to speaking true words about the past" (Wright 1992, p. 136). The nature of Christian claims about God as the "lord of history" who has "acted climatically, *and not merely paradigmatically*, in Jesus of Nazareth . . . will drive the Christian to history," Wright claims (Wright 1992, p. 136). This commitment to a form of historical enquiry that can be reconciled with the theological truth claims of Christian faith undergirds Wright's entire project, and is the main focus of his large-scale works on the New Testament, Jesus, the resurrection, and Paul.

The success of this quest – for a commitment to history that illuminates and even provokes, rather than detracts from, Christian faith – depends on Wright's ability to navigate the tricky waters of contemporary or, to adopt an oft-used Wright-ian phrase, post-Enlightenment historiography. Samuel Adams provides a recent account of this navigation, demonstrating that Wright's appeal to the notion of "critical realism . . . attempts to resolve the tension between realism and idealism in such a way that regains the central role of historical knowledge for theology and, at the same time, to justify theological inquiry as undertaken by the historian" (Adams 2015, pp. 40–41). In study after study, Wright articulates the need for history and argues for a historical method that moves beyond the enlightenment quest for objectivity, and the post-modern collapse of all such quests into the discourse of subjectivity and power. We need to recognize that historical knowledge is relational, in so far as it only emerges out of the "appropriate dialogue or conversation between the knower and the thing known," but remain committed to the "reality of the thing known, as something other than the knower" (Wright 1992, p. 35 [emphasis removed]; see also Wright 1992, Chapter 4). This can be achieved if we substitute the search for "facts" with the exploration of "worldviews" by means of the iterative (Wright's word is "spiral") processes of hypothesis and verification. To access the "worldview" of Jesus, or Paul and the other writers of the New Testament, is to make contact not only with historical reality, but with that history's meaning.

We return to Jesus and Paul below. So it is appropriate to illustrate these claims at this point with reference to Wright's major study of the resurrection (Wright 2003), a work that, notably, emerged from what was to be the final chapter of Wright's study of the historical Jesus. Moving beyond (or behind) those works of New Testament scholarship that explore the question of the resurrection by interrogating the nature of early Christian belief, Wright sets out to answer the question: "So what did happen on Easter morning?" (Wright 2003, p. 4). Wright's answer to this question is established over more than seven-hundred pages of analysis of the relevant data from pagan, Jewish and Christian sources from antiquity, and culminates in the argument of Chapter 18, "Easter and History" (Wright 2003, pp. 685–718). This exhaustive historical work leads Wright to conclude that we can indeed "know" with a chastened but nonetheless real level of confidence that Jesus' tomb was found to be empty and that the early Christians had "meetings" with Jesus after his crucifixion:

> I conclude that the historian, of whatever persuasion, has no option but to affirm both the empty tomb and the "meetings" with Jesus as "historical events" . . . I regard this conclusion as coming in the same sort of category, of historical probability so high as to be virtually certain (Wright 2003, pp. 709–710).

Furthermore, Wright claims that the only viable historical explanation of these "events," their necessary and sufficient "cause," is that Jesus was raised bodily from the dead. This claim is made not within the epistemological boundaries of Enlightenment historiography, but precisely as a challenge to those boundaries. And yet, Wright insists that such a claim can be understood to be historical.

Wright's insistence on the virtues of critical realism promotes the ongoing significance of history as the ground and, in important ways, the norm for Christian faith. This emphasis drives his interpretation of Jesus and Paul (to be explored below), and offers a fixed point from which, Wright believes, subsequent theological claims emerged, and against which they may be tested. It also provides a reminder that there is no conversation about history that is not also a conversation about hermeneutics. Critical realism tells us that here, as elsewhere, interpretation (and therefore the subjectivity of the "knower") goes all the way down. Or does it? Some (from either end of the theological spectrum) may seek to cling to a form of the historical positivism that Wright rejects. Yet, even within the terms of critical realism, many have the sense that, for Wright, it is the quest for realism that wins. Put another way, Wright's version of critical realism remains optimistic, too optimistic perhaps, about the confidence we can have in historical enquiry and its capacity to ground the truth claims of Christian faith (see Bockmuehl 2004, p. 501). For some, Wright's clear commitment to history is misplaced in so far as affords it a theological significance that history does not deserve in the light of our understanding of the reality of God and the nature of the Christ event; as straightforwardly the location of divine action, and the vehicle of divine revelation (see Adams 2015; Johnson 2013). For others, the problems are more directly related to the kinds of historical arguments that Wright deploys in his account of Jesus and the early Christian movement. To that account we now turn.

Jesus and Eschatology

In *Jesus and the Victory of God* (Wright 1996) Wright entertains the possibility that the task of discovering the historical reality of Jesus of Nazareth is "prodigal son" to the "elder son" of orthodoxy and Christian theology. The task is to enable history to give up the "dissolute methodologies that have made it appear so bankrupt" and for theology to overcome its own "inverted arrogance." Reconciliation is possible through (studying) Jesus (Wright 1996, p. 137).

The account of Jesus that effects this reconciliation is laid out in detail in the next six-hundred pages of Wright's influential contribution to the quest for the historical Jesus that makes two basic claims. The first is that Jesus was a Jewish eschatological prophet who understood his own ministry to be the inauguration of the reign of God, a witness to "his belief and claim that Israel's god was fulfilling his promises and purposes in and through what he himself was doing" (Wright 1992, p. 473, summarizing Part II). Jesus' aim in making such claims was to "bring about a radical shift within, not an abandonment of, the worldview of his hearers" by offering them a new account of Israel's hope for "the great redemption, the restoration, the return from exile, the 'forgiveness of sins'" (Wright 1996, p. 473; yet note that Wright's claim that Jews of Jesus' day regarded themselves as still somehow "in exile," anticipating a future restoration, has been the focus of significant critique; see Scott 2017). The second claim is that Jesus understood his own vocation to not only "evoke" that hope, but to "enact" and "embody" it by going to Jerusalem, challenging the Temple, and being crucified in the hope of vindication (Wright 1996, p. 651, summarizing Part III). In holding such beliefs, Jesus remains a loyal first-century Jewish prophet, critical of alternative understandings of Israel's history and hope (Wright 1996, p. 652 speaks of Jesus' "critique and renovation from within," "challenge to traditions and institutions whose true purpose . . . had been grievously corrupted and distorted: and of new proposals which, though without precedent, were never mere innovation.") They also provide a historical fixed point from which church's Christological confession could appropriately emerge, in that his entry into Jerusalem constituted not only a messianic claim but also a claim about the return of Israel's God to Zion, "embodying in himself the returning and redeeming action of the covenant God" (Wright 1996, p. 653).

Scholarly reception of Wright's description of Jesus has been mixed (on which, see Newman 1999). The claim that Jesus saw himself and was seen by others as an eschatological prophet calling for the renewal of Israel and proclaiming the imminence of God's reign is a well-established position, shared by many, perhaps even the majority of New Testament scholars.[9] The main alternative view, represented in different but related ways by various scholars associated with the Jesus Seminar, seems now to be fading from view, and with good reason (see the discussion in Wright 1996, pp. 29–82).[10] But major reservations remain. Luke Timothy Johnson accuses Wright of various historiographical fallacies, including overly hasty moves from what is plausible to what is probable, and stretching the limits of evidence (Johnson 2013, pp. 210–216).[11] We have noted above that Wright's central proposal about the importance of the return-from-exile theme for Jesus and his contemporaries has not secured widespread support. But perhaps the most damaging critique for Wright's project lies in the challenge to his view of Jesus' vocational self-understanding.

There are potential problems with the claim that Jesus was aware that his (implicit) claim to be Israel's Messiah encompassed a vocation to "enact in himself what, in Israel's scriptures, God had promised to accomplish all by himself" (Wright 1996, p. 653). Although this is an attempt to cross the gap between history and theology, the pre- and post-Easter Jesus, Jesus as proclaimer of the divine reign and as proclaimed in the gospel, it tends minimize the gap in the interests of preserving continuity between Jesus and Second Temple Judaism on the one hand and the emerging Christian movement on the other.

Furthermore, Wright's treatment of these themes depends on a major reinterpretation of the meaning of Jesus' eschatological teaching. Drawing on insights developed *in nuce* by his doctoral supervisor, George Caird, Wright argues that this material (which accounts for a substantial portion of the gospel tradition) has been largely misunderstood. Rather than referring to Jesus' imminent expectation of eschatological judgment and cosmic renewal, the symbolism of Mark 13 and related texts refer to Jesus' anticipation of events that connote the "climax" of Israel's history and the inauguration of a new phase in God's dealings with Israel and the world (see the helpful taxonomy in Wright 1996, p. 208).[12] Not only does this position suffer some exegetical problems, it has also been pointed out that it serves a possible apologetic role by absolving the historical Jesus from the possibility of holding eschatological expectations that turned out to be wrong (see Adams 2007; Allison 1999).

Wright's Jesus speaks to many people: to those acutely aware of the deficiencies of the "Cynic teacher" Jesus and his liberal Protestant ancestors; to those rightly suspicious of a de-Judaized Jesus, disconnected from a plausible historical context; to those searching for a Jesus strongly connected to Christian belief and practice today. It is likely that Wright's broad appeal as a theologian lies in his ability to describe Jesus in ways that are grounded in the scholarly debate, but that speak to the live questions of faith and mission. The issue here, as elsewhere, is the extent to which the theology drives and distorts the historical enquiry.

Paul and Salvation

Consideration of the nature of Jesus' eschatological vision provides an obvious link into Wright's treatment of the notion of salvation more generally, and this brings us, finally, to his treatment of the apostle Paul. Pauline theology is where Wright's work as a New Testament scholar began, and it is likely that his numerous contributions to the study of Paul will remain his most enduring legacy.[13] The central claim of Wright's work is that Paul is a theologian of Israel's covenant, who "reinterpreted" or "reworked" Jewish convictions about God, God's election of Israel, and Israel's hope for the future in the light of his own convictions about Jesus, Israel's vindicated Messiah, and the Spirit, God's transforming presence in the world (see Wright 2013a, pp. 46–47 and note headings from pp. 609–1265). Several aspects of this reading of Paul can be briefly identified.

First, and the thing for which Wright is most famous, it constitutes a direct challenge to readings of Paul shaped by the Lutheran tradition of justification by faith, placed at the center of Paul's concerns, and interpretations of that doctrine in narrowly forensic terms: justification as the acquittal of the sinner on the basis of the imputation of righteousness, secured through Christ's substitutionary death, and appropriated through faith as the response of trust in divine grace. This reading of Paul, and Paul's understanding of salvation, is of course a dominant lens through which the apostle is read within Wright's own evangelical tradition, not least in relation to the argument of his letter to the Romans. Building on the ground breaking work of E. P. Sanders, Wright, along with James D. G. Dunn in particular, provided a direct challenge to this reading on the basis of historical considerations and exegetical analysis, offering an alternative vision the basic shape of which remains largely consistent throughout Wright's career. For Wright, Paul's justification language is essentially Paul's way of talking about covenant membership, being "welcomed into the sin-forgiven family" of Abraham on the basis of faith alone (Wright 2013a, p. 1031).[14] It is not the gospel itself (which is primarily the proclamation that Israel's messiah is now Lord), but a consequence of the gospel related to the specific circumstances of the Jewish Paul's vocation to the "nations." Paul's question, therefore, is not so much "how does the sinner find a gracious God?" as "who now belongs to the people of God and on what basis?" In making such claims, and defending them exegetically and theologically at enormous length, Wright has become a target for substantial critique, as well as a leading figure for those experiencing a dissatisfaction with other-worldly, spiritualized, contractual, and individual accounts of salvation endemic within their evangelical heritage.

Secondly, Wright's account of salvation is set out in terms of "narrative." His is a theology of the story of God's dealings with the world from creation to eschaton with a strong emphasis on that story's fundamental coherence and linear unfolding through the pattern of promise and fulfillment. In an influential essay, Wright portrays the contemporary task of biblical interpretation (and patterns of faith and practice that ensue) as that of improvisation of the closing moments of the last act of a play. The "script" is provided (the "acts" are Creation; Fall; Israel; Jesus; Church) up to the point where the actors are invited to learn and inhabit the drama before creatively interpreting it for the final scenes. (Wright 1991b). Paul is the first Christian theologian in so far as he does just this. Paul is:

> able to reclaim and retrieve Israel's long history . . . as the story of promises kept at least, of genuine anticipations of the coming kingdom, of a covenant faithfulness which would result . . . in the sudden and surprising covenant renewal spoken of by Moses and the prophets (Wright 2013a, p. 1481).

This reading of Paul has placed Wright in direct conflict with those scholars who emphasize much more strongly the ways in which Paul's theology disrupts the story of Israel and so generates significant levels of discontinuity between Pauline Christianity and Judaism, not to mention alternative streams of the early Christian movement.[15]

Finally, this reading of Paul allows Wright to refocus on the ethical and political implications of Paul's gospel, especially through consideration of the counter-imperial significance of his claims about Jesus and salvation (Wright 2013a, pp. 1271–1320). Wright speaks about this aspect of Paul as a "different kind of revolution," avoiding the twin dangers of "escaping the life and rule of earth by being taken away into heaven in the future" or "anticipating that with a detached spirituality in the present." Paul's theological vision "remained emphatically this-worldly . . . the transformation, not the abandonment, of present reality" (Wright 2013a, p. 1307). Again, while a number of Wright's New Testament colleagues remain unconvinced about the explicit presence of such ideas in Paul, it is a reading that speaks to a broad range of Christian social, missional, and political commitments (for skepticism, see Barclay 2011).

These sweeping summary statements cannot possibly do justice to the nuances of Wright's reading of Paul. The exegetical work that lies behind them is substantial and the structural elegance of the overall account is obvious. Here, Paul's theology and the vision of salvation proclaimed within it is narratable, scriptural, communal, ethical, and political. For many the strength in Wright's reading of Paul is that it has these characteristics while remaining recognizably "evangelical." For others it renders Paul too safe, too coherent, a revisionist rather than a true revolutionary. It is beyond doubt, however, that Wright's "reworking" of Paul has been and will continue to be deeply influential, speaking across traditional demarcations of ecclesial and theological identity.

Conclusion

How might we explain Wright's attempts to navigate carefully between the fixed points of historical realism and post-modern chastening, the historical reality of Jesus of Nazareth and the truth of the church's claims about Jesus Christ, the future-oriented justification of the individual, and the this-worldly salvation of the people of God? It is possible, of course, that the positions that Wright adopts, and undoubtedly the reception of his work, are deeply affected by his determination to engage the academic world of biblical scholarship and the variegated world of contemporary evangelicalism (Kuhrt 2011, p. 10). The distinguished Professor of Early Christianity is in many ways still the President of the Oxford Inter-collegiate Christian Union, bringing evangelical fervor and persuasion to bear on the academy, and a keen critical eye to the easy assumptions and unexamined prejudices of the church.

But this search for a middle way is also distinctively Anglican, and this perhaps provides a further explanatory layer for Wright's appeal to a wide range of readers from across the spectrum of theological debate and ecclesial politics. Lest this point be misunderstood, I am not suggesting that Wright is content with the kind of anemic middle ground that takes no position, or that consistently seeks compromise. If, in Wright's work, we see evidence of what Alan Bartlett has named a "passionate balance," it is only reached through a rigorous commitment to the value of and relationship between things that are too often separated (see Bartlett 2007). In so far as Wright works for renewal from within his own religious tradition – generating controversy, to be sure, but all the while insisting that his position is a legitimate, faithful interpretation of the story thus far – he bears a striking resemblance to Wright's Jesus and Paul. To draw on a biblical example of which Wright himself is fond, he has in many ways become the father, standing between the academy and the church, the prodigal and the elder brother, welcoming and chastising where necessary, seeking reconciliation wherever possible; a theological project that is indeed intended "for everyone."

Notes

1 Counting such things is difficult. The figure of ninety or more books includes authored, co-authored, and edited works, as well as new and combined editions of previously published work. The most comprehensive list of publications can be found at http://ntwrightpage.com/2018/02/24/updated-publications-list-2018 (accessed July 20, 2020). This page does not include the most recent major studies: Wright 2019; Wright and Bird 2019. One feature of Wright's publication profile (other than its enormity) is its growing momentum over time. Between 1978 and 1990 he published or edited five books, between 1991 and 2000 twenty books, between 2000 and 2010 thirty-eight books, and between 2011 and 2018 twenty-nine books.

2 Of course, Wright has written about any number of issues that formally lie outside this threefold taxonomy of his work, most notably in the area of ethics. If pressed, I would argue that that his treatment of these other topics always betrays the generative influence of his work as a New Testament scholar for whom these three questions are *the* questions raised by the texts themselves. Wright himself prefers to reduce the crucial questions into two categories: "[h]ow did Christianity begin, and why did it take the shape that it did?," so my focus on Wright's account of history; and "[w]hat does Christianity believe and does it make sense?," hence my focus on core theological claims about Jesus and salvation. See Wright (1992), p. 10.

3 I am aware that the term *via media* is regarded by some as an "unacceptably crude" understanding of Anglicanism (so Sykes 1995, p. 82). I do not have in mind

so much the positioning of Anglicanism at the mid-point between Catholicism and radical Protestantism (my own tradition), so much as a stance in relation to tradition and history that accepts the need for continual reform, but is reluctant to consider the need for more fundamental theological and historical disruption.

4 In the latest volume on Paul an earlier decision to use the uncapitalized form "god" has given way to more traditional usage.

5 Notable from this period is the small commentary, Wright (1986), and significant revision of an earlier work on the history of New Testament scholarship, Neil and Wright (1988).

6 I base this on Wright's own description of the Jerusalem sabbatical in Wright (1992, p. xix) and Wright (1996, p. xix). Anecdotal evidence supports this. The present author arrived in Oxford in September 1990 to study with Wright who, at that time, was relatively unknown. The word around Oxford at that time was that Wright had been writing at a rate of five to ten-thousand words a day during his sabbatical. It was certainly clear to me that he was on the cusp of making an ambitious and major contribution to New Testament studies.

7 The commentary series was published between 2001 and 2008 and culminated in Wright (2011).

8 Wright has been honored by colleagues and former students in Dunne and Lewellen (2018).

9 Wright himself coined the phrase "Third Quest" to capture the recovery of Jesus' Jewishness and the centrality of his eschatological claims in recent Jesus' scholarship (see Wright 1996, pp. 83–124).

10 The approach to the historical Jesus represented by the Jesus Seminar collapses because of the misguided appeal to certain criteria for establishing authenticity of the tradition, and the associated severing of Jesus from the context of first century Judaism that inevitably results. Note also Wright's lengthy engagement with the position of his friend Marcus Borg in Wright and Borg (1999).

11 Note also the observation that Wright "relieves himself of the necessity of taking differences between [Synoptic] accounts seriously by appealing to the premise that stories circulated in oral tradition in slightly different forms" (Johnson 2013, p. 217).

12 Note also Wright's preference for position 3.

13 Wright's unpublished Oxford DPhil was entitled "The Messiah and the People of God: A Study in Pauline Theology with Particular Reference to the Argument of the Epistle to the Romans" (University of Oxford, 1980) and it sets out the main trajectories of interpretation for much of the ensuing, voluminous published work on Paul. See also Wright 1991a, 2002, 2005, 2009, 2013b, 2015, 2018).

14 Wright's understanding of justification is complex. The best way of getting a sense of how it differs from classic Protestant evangelicalism is to read his response to the critique of John Piper in Wright (2009).

15 Here I refer to what has become known as the "apocalyptic" school of Pauline interpretation, whose representatives are deeply critical of Wright's reading of Paul. This robust critique is mutual, see Wright (2013b).

References

Adams, E. (2007). *The Stars Will Fall from Heaven: Cosmic Catastrophe in the New Testament and its World*. London: Bloomsbury.

Adams, S.V. (2015). *The Reality of God and Historical Method: Apocalyptic Theology in Conversation with N. T. Wright*. Downers Grove, MI: IVP Academic.

Allison, D.C. Jr. (1999). Jesus and the victory of apocalyptic. In: *Jesus and the Restoration of Israel: A Critical Assessment of N. T. Wright's Jesus and the Victory of God* (ed. C.C. Newman), 126–141. Downers Grove, MI: IVP.

Barclay, J.M.G. (2011). Why the Roman Empire was insignificant to Paul. In: *Pauline Churches and Diaspora Jews*, WUNF 275, 363–387. Tübingen: Mohr Siebeck.

Bartlett, A. (2007). *A Passionate Balance: The Anglican Tradition*. London: DLT.

Bockmuehl, M. (2004). Compleat history of the resurrection: a dialogue with N. T. Wright. *JSNT* 26: 489–504.

Dunne, J.A. and Lewellen, E. (eds.) (2018). *One God, One People, One Future: Essays in Honour of N. T. Wright*. London: SPCK.

Johnson, L.T. (2013). A historiographical response to Wright's Jesus. In: *Contested Issues in Christian Origins and the New Testament: Collected Essays*, NovTSup 146, 51–70. Leiden: Brill.

Kuhrt, S. (2011). *Tom Wright for Everyone: Putting the Theology of N. T. Wright into Practice in the Local Church*. London: SPCK.

Neil, S. and Wright, T. (1988). *The Interpretation of the New Testament 1861–1986*. Oxford: Oxford University Press.

Newman, C.C. (ed.) (1999). *Jesus and the Restoration of Israel: A Critical Assessment of N.T. Wright's Jesus and the Victory of God*. Downer's Grove. MI: IVP.

Scott, J.M. (ed.) (2017). *Exile: A Conversation with N.T. Wright*. Downers Grove, MI: IVP.

Sykes, S. (1995). *Unashamed Anglicanism*. London: DLT.

Wright, N.T. (1986). *Colossians and Philemon*. Leicester: IVP.

Wright, N.T. (1991a). *The Climax of the Covenant: Christ and the Law in Pauline Theology*. Edinburgh: T & T Clark.

Wright, N.T. (1991b). How can the Bible be authoritative? Vox Evangelica 21: 7–21.

Wright, N.T. (1992). *The New Testament and the People of God*, Christian Origins and the Question of God 1. London: SPCK.

Wright, N.T. (1996). *Jesus and the Victory of God*, Christian Christian Origins and the Question of God 2. London: SPCK.

Wright, N.T. (2002). The letter to the Romans: introduction, commentary, and reflections. In: *New Interpreters' Bible*, vol. X (ed. L.E. Keck), 394–770. Nashville, TN: Abingdon.

Wright, N.T. (2003). *The Resurrection of the Son of God*, Christian Origins and the Question of God 3. London: SPCK.

Wright, N.T. (2005). *Paul: Fresh Perspectives.* London: SPCK.

Wright, N.T. (2009). *Justification: God's Plan and Paul's Vision.* Downers Grove, MI: IVP Academic.

Wright, N.T. (2011). *The New Testament for Everyone.* London: SPCK.

Wright, N.T. (2012). *How God Became King: The Forgotten Story of the Gospels.* New York, NY: HarperOne.

Wright, N.T. (2013a). *Paul and the Faithfulness of God*, Christian Origins and the Question of God 4. London: SPCK.

Wright, N.T. (2013b). *Pauline Perspectives: Essays on Paul, 1978–2013.* London: SPCK.

Wright, N.T. (2015). *Paul and His Recent Interpreters: Some Contemporary Debates.* London: SPCK.

Wright, N.T. (2016). *The Day the Revolution Began: Reconsidering the Meaning of Jesus' Crucifixion.* New York, NY: HarperOne.

Wright, N.T. (2018). *Paul: A Biography.* London: SPCK.

Wright, N. T. (2019). History and Eschatology: Jesus and the Promise of Natural Theology. London: SPCK.

Wright, N.T. and Borg, M. (1999). *The Meaning of Jesus: Two Visions.* London: SPCK.

Wright, N. T. and Bird, M. F. (2019). The New Testament in its World: An Introduction to the History, Literature and Theology of the First Christians. Grand Rapids: Zondervan.

Esther Mombo (1957–)

Emmy Corey

My favorite memory of Esther Mombo comes from a crisp, cold morning in the summer of 2018 during a service that she and others had planned to celebrate Lillian, a former student who was about to become the second woman ordained to the Reformed Church of East Africa (RCEA).[1] Lillian was among the many people who spent years lobbying for ordination in the RCEA. In just a few days, the struggle for ordination would end, bringing with it the many challenges of her new position. The service that morning, held at St. Paul's University in Limuru, Kenya, began with the soft, high-pitched voice of a current student, singing from the back of the room. The singer moved toward the front where Lillian stood, dancing along the way. Esther Mombo, donned in a black skirt and blazer with a starched white button-down shirt, joined in, moving with the student and beckoning other women to join along the way. As the lone, white, US woman in a room full of Kenyan women, I responded to this moment as any person in my position might – by staying on the sidelines, recording the dance with the camera on my phone. But by the time Mombo reached me, watching from the outside was no longer an option. She stretched out her hand, pulled me in, and I clumsily joined the line of women.

This moment stays with me because it represents so much of who Mombo is and the work of theological education and ministry to which she is committed. Admittedly, it also symbolizes the hesitancy I have in writing on her work for a collection on Anglican theologians. As an outsider to Esther's culture, my own preconceived notions of Anglican theology have often been shaped by images of the white, Westerners I read as a seminary student. Writing about Mombo's contributions is an invitation to merge worlds that I often keep separate. But one of the commitments of the Anglican Communion is just that: communion. And Mombo's life and work have been dedicated to creating the kind of Communion where all voices can be heard and taken

Twentieth Century Anglican Theologians: From Evelyn Underhill to Esther Mombo, First Edition.
Edited by Stephen Burns, Bryan Cones, and James Tengatenga.
© 2021 John Wiley & Sons Ltd. Published 2021 by John Wiley & Sons Ltd.

seriously. Neither supplemental nor secondary, her voice matters to Anglican theology for it serves as a constant reminder of both who we are and who we can become.

Esther Mombo's contributions to Anglican theology are best demonstrated by the spaces she creates for others. Building on the notion that the incarnate word of God is "a word for the whole world, for everyone," Mombo does not consider any Christian to be exempt from proclaiming that word (Mombo 2006). In fact, much of her work has centered around not only making sure that all *can* proclaim the word of God, which she believes offers liberation and reconciliation for those on the margins. Mombo challenges the various communities to which she belongs – pushing them to expand their borders and make room for those who are on the outside. I chronicle just a few of the ways Mombo has made space for others. Through her work at St. Paul's University, I address the ways that Mombo created an institutional place for women, in particular. Then, through her commitment to the Circle of Concerned African Women Theologians, I outline her emphasis on sources for theology that take the experiences of African women seriously. Next, I demonstrate the ways Mombo applies Circle methodologies by addressing poverty and HIV/AIDS as theological concerns. Finally, I discuss the ways that Mombo has made space in the wider Anglican Communion by calling for liturgical renewal and ownership of local communities that do not preclude a global sense of belonging.

Making Space at St. Paul's University

Esther Mombo was born in 1957 in the village of Birongo, located in Kisii County in Western Kenya. The oldest of eight children, Mombo was born into a Quaker family. She received her Bachelor's degree in Divinity from St. Paul's United Theological College (now known at St. Paul's University) before beginning her Master of Philosophy in Ecumenism at the University of Dublin, Trinity College in 1986. Upon completing her Master's degree, Mombo returned to Kenya and began teaching in an Anglican bible college. It was there that she became an Anglican herself. Mombo later returned to the United Kingdom to begin her doctorate in Church History at the University of Edinburgh. Upon completion of her doctorate in 1998, Mombo moved back to Kenya where she took a teaching position at St. Paul's United Theological College. Mombo quickly became instrumental to the small, but growing university and became academic dean in 1999.

In 2008, just after St. Paul's was awarded a university charter, Mombo was appointed as Deputy Vice Chancellor of Academic Affairs. In this role, the university saw tremendous institutional growth. The increase in female students at St. Paul's under Mombo's leadership was staggering. From just one female student in 1980 to three in 2001 to thirty-two in 2009, women now comprise a significant percentage of St. Paul's graduates (Mombo and Joziasse 2011). Many women credit Mombo with not only recruiting them to come to the university, but also for helping the university find ways to make sure they could attend without worrying about payment. Aware of the institutional support necessary to keep marginalized students in theological education, Mombo cultivated strategic partnerships with universities across the globe during her time as Deputy Vice Chancellor. She continues those relationships in her current post as Director of International Partnerships and Alumni Relationships, which she holds in addition to her role as Associate Professor.

Mombo is committed to students who have historically been disenfranchised from theological education. Drawing them in, she works to create a space for them. At St. Paul's, these students have predominantly been women. In her article, "Women in African Christianities," Mombo notes that women in Africa "are the Church," but their leadership is not always welcome (Mombo 2016, p.130). From the early days of Christian missions in the colonial period that emphasized an education focused on "domesticity," women were depicted to missionary supporters as captive to backward traditions. In need of rescue by the West, women were taught how to be good home-makers, mothers, and wives as a means of liberation. They were to preserve the moral integrity of the home, resisting the temptations of power and authority that accompanied formal leadership roles. The legacy of mission education continues today (Mombo 2016, p. 131). Because women's voices have historically been restricted, their inclusion into theological education reconstitutes our understanding of who and what constitutes church leadership.

Women and men across Sub-Saharan Africa have sparked efforts to "engender theological education," as women enroll in seminaries and colleges. For Mombo, this work should be twofold. First, theological education must not be held captive to clericalism. That is, it must be available to those who are not seeking ordination. Second, theological education must have a "gender sensitive" curriculum that includes the experiences of women, particularly those on the margins (Mombo 2016, p. 133). This work is not just a distant academic thesis for Mombo. Her entire career at St. Paul's University has been built on these two foundations for engendering theology. First, St. Paul's University created a place for women by delinking theological education from ordained ministry. This was an important shift in the social landscape of the university. Because some women came from churches that did not allow women's ordination, this new opening created a space for more lay women to begin their theological education regardless of whether their churches gave their permission.

The separation of theological education from ordination was vital for Mombo, who writes,

> The reason I felt it was important to give theology to the people of God, is because I no longer consider the ordained ministry as the pre-requisite to theological education. To me, ordination is just *one* of the ministries. If a woman is called to serve God . . . anything that a woman does to serve God is for me an important ministry in the Church (Mombo and Joziasse 2011, p. 113).

As a layperson herself, the significance of including women who do not intend to be ordained was a poignant one for Mombo, whose own contributions to the Anglican Church have outmatched many ordained clergy! The second task Mombo has undertaken to engender theological education is through her collaboration with the Circle of Concerned African Women Theologians. She and the Circle members have worked to produce theological curricula that center the experiences of women on the margins. Mombo's participation in the Circle has given her a space to tackle issues such as poverty and HIV/AIDS through a theological lens.

Rethinking Theological Sources: The Circle of Concerned African Women Theologians

Mombo is a dedicated member and leader of the Circle of Concerned African Women Theologians. Begun in 1989, this ecumenical group of women theologians across the continent has made its mark in both universities and global institutions. Members have served on the World Council of Churches, become key leaders in the YWCA (Young Women's Christian Association), and have taken university positions in their home countries. Born from the Ecumenical Association of Third World Theologians (EATWOT) and the World Council of Churches, the Circle began as African women theologians noticed how vastly under represented they were in these ecumenical spaces. Initiated by Ghanaian Mercy Amba Oduyoye, the Circle became a way of gathering women together in collective work that addressed the issues that were most pressing for their contexts. Distinguishing their work as "African women's theologies," the women of the Circle come from a variety of religious backgrounds (Mombo and Joziasse 2011, p. 4). They continue to write, research, and publish on issues such as HIV/AIDS, gender violence, poverty, environmental degradation, and other deeply rooted social issues that disproportionately impact the world's most vulnerable (Fiedler 2017).

As Circle members and theologians Isabel Phiri and Sarojini Nadar note, the women of the Circle do their work with careful attention to three elements. First, they interrogate the interlocking subjugations of gender, race, and class in their work. Doing theology from a lens, that is attentive to this "triple bind," Circle members consider the way their work impacts women on the margins. Second, they blend activism and theory in their work. Finally, they utilize for doing theology that are "appropriate to African modalities of theologizing that are distinctive from the West, but still maintain a critical approach." As they suggest, one of these sources is narrative storytelling that remains true to African roots while also pointing to those aspects of culture that demonize and oppress women (Phiri and Nadar 2006, pp. 3–4, 7–8). Circle members critique their culture as insiders, while acknowledging that their own communities are often marginalized in larger social, structural, and economic forces (see Dube 2006).

Mombo's work is deeply informed by sources and methods that the Circle uses for doing theology. Begun in 1996, her chapter of the Circle in Limuru is known for its emphasis on theological education and the ministerial training of women (Fiedler 2017). Emphasizing that theology is concretized through women's experience, Mombo encourages women at St. Paul's to draw on their experiences of marginalization as a source for doing theology. Using the Circle's emphasis on narrative storytelling, women that experience stigma have been able to declare that their voices matter at St. Paul's. From single women to widows to rape survivors, students mine their stories to explore the visible ways theology has impacted their lives, both positively and negatively. Often, theology is simultaneously the source of many women's stigmatization and the key to liberation. Women confront their own marginalization by telling their narratives alongside scripture. By interrogating texts that mimic their own experiences and challenging the ones that silence them, students have been able to declare that their voices matter at St. Paul's in a unique way. Just as Mombo and the Circle worked to make space for them, these women make space for others, challenging the parameters that diminish their voices while expanding the borders around what constitutes theological sources (Mombo and Joziasse 2011, pp. 11–13).

Poverty and Mission

Mombo's expansive understanding of borders challenges the wider Anglican Church in myriad ways. First, using missiology and theology, she calls for the Church's involvement in dismantling problems of poverty and HIV/AIDS. By tackling the concrete, but deeply rooted, problems of poverty and HIV/AIDS, Mombo notes that the Church has played a pivotal role in exacerbating these problems. At the same time, this is precisely why the Church can and should assume a transformative role in their undoing. In an essay for "Anglican Women on Church and Mission," Mombo (Mombo 2012) outlines poverty as a key concern for the Anglican Church. Despite the many interventions from non-governmental organizations (NGOs) and faith-based organizations (FBOs), poverty does not seem to be declining.

Perhaps this is because the issue is so deeply entrenched in Anglican colonial history.[2] Mombo suggests that Anglican mission stations facilitated the growth of material wealth in the colonial era that inadvertently created a wealth disparity that significantly impacted women. As Mombo writes, "During this period of mission establishment, there was a strong link between spirituality and materiality" (Mombo 2012, p. 136). As people passed through the "colonial and economic systems," they "managed to gain material things, which moved them from one class to another" (Mombo 2012, p. 139). Conversion to Christianity became connected with material wealth. Through evangelization, health, and education, the newly converted could become upwardly mobile, gaining skills in literacy and skilled labor (Mombo 2012, p. 137). Of course, not everyone advanced in this colonial setup. For one, as students of "domesticity," or midwifery women were often left behind in many of these efforts (Mombo 2009, p. 215). In effect, the mission stations inadvertently helped to facilitate a class stratification that remains today and disproportionately impacts women. The underclass ignited during the colonial period only became larger after independence as Kenyans moved from rural areas to newly formed cities. They lived in informal settlements (slums) across urban areas in hopes of finding work. Poverty and religion live alongside one another in these areas today. In some settlements, Mombo writes,

> there are more churches than toilets, and one wonders how the people cope with the call of nature . . . There is a connection [between religion and toilets] in that . . . if cleanliness is next to godliness, then a religion that ignores the living conditions of its members is deficient (Mombo 2009, p. 216).

Churches, Mombo argues, must be attentive to both the material and spiritual needs of humanity. Ultimately, Mombo suggests that the solutions to the problem of poverty should come from those on the continent rather than using traditional Western approaches to poverty alleviation. Genuine poverty alleviation, Mombo argues, comes in the form of programs that directly address the structural (and historical) conditions that have created poverty in the first place rather than placing the onus solely upon the individuals and communities that experience poverty (Mombo 2009, pp. 224–225).

A Christological Approach to HIV/AIDS

Just as poverty is a problem that concerns the Church, Mombo also notes that HIV/AIDS is a theological concern. Drawing on the life and ministry of Jesus, Mombo writes,

> As a sign to the world, the church – a missionary community, a mission – should face contemporary challenges in the same way that Christ approached the world of his day: first, as a human presence – a fellowship and offer of service responding to the people's real needs today (Mombo 2005, p. 60).

Just as Jesus spoke directly to the concrete realities of his time, so too must his followers find ways to respond to problems in their own time. For Mombo, this response should not come through distant charities or specialized HIV/AIDS ministries, instead it should come by becoming "the conscience of society – approving the good and correcting the evil, in a gentle way." This work necessarily involves reading scripture with an eye toward those infected and affected by HIV/AIDS. Mombo writes, "The church's first missiological challenge in the HIV/AIDS era is to rethink the gospel in light of contemporary cultures – especially cultures that promote death rather than life" (Mombo 2005, p. 60). For Mombo, the ministry of Jesus was connected to communal critique in an effort to create a more life-giving space for all.

Mombo's gentle approach of rethinking the gospel considering the realities of HIV/AIDS is perhaps best demonstrated through her discussion of widow inheritance. A tradition, that is still practiced in some African societies, widow inheritance was originally meant to promote life. It was a way of caring for a woman after her husband died. But as Mombo notes, the practice has contributed to an increase in HIV, as a woman can be inherited by a male relative of her deceased husband who already has another wife. Mombo's criticisms of this practice stems from a failure on the part of the Church to approach the issue "as Jesus would" (Mombo 2005, p. 61). Jesus, "showed a different way of dealing with gender issues, so that men and women would be regarded equally" (Mombo 2005, p. 61). The Church's silence over the issues that widows face from other relatives, as well as from the communities they live in, precludes the ability of abundant life for most widows. Widows often allow themselves to be inherited because there is no other viable financial option for them. As Mombo suggests, churches could meet the needs of these women by providing alternatives to inheritance. These alternatives should not come from a specialized "HIV ministry." Rather, by making HIV/AIDS a central concern of churches, they are subsequently drawing in from the periphery those who are infected and affected. Moreover, Mombo suggests that churches ought to establish support systems for those widows who do not agree to widow inheritance and are subsequently subject to ridicule and exploitation by landlords and employers. Offering gentle critique from within her community, Mombo pushes her own community to rethink practices like widow inheritance by attending to matters like social and financial support of women who have lost their husbands.

Anglicanism in Africa: Making Space for the Local in a Global Communion

Mombo's communal concerns expand beyond her local community through her participation in the Anglican Communion. As a contributor to ongoing debates and concerns around what it means to be Anglican, Mombo understands her local community to be imbedded in the ebbs and flows of a dynamic confederation of communities. For African Anglicans, this global relationship is multivalent, textured by a murky past and a complicated present, that is hardly simple or straightforward. From her calls for liturgical renewals that incorporate indigenous practices to her leadership in the Lambeth Commission in 2004, Mombo has emerged as a leader that takes local practices and global community seriously. This commitment is demonstrated in the recent conversations around sexuality in the Anglican Communion. Here, Mombo's leadership has been an important reminder that identity and belonging are complicated in our global world. As just one of nineteen members on the 2004 Lambeth Commission, Mombo was tasked to respond to the election of an openly gay bishop in the Episcopal Church just one year earlier.[3] Her response to the ensuing Windsor Report troubled any binary image of "backward Africans" and "progressive Westerners." As Mombo notes, Africa's role in the Anglican Communion is not monolithic. While there are some leaders whose voices are louder than others in Sub-Saharan Africa on the issue of homosexuality, Mombo suggests that many members of Anglican congregations on the continent are largely unconcerned with the "politics of sexuality" altogether (Mombo 2007, p. 77).

This does not mean that homosexuality is absent in Sub-Saharan Africa. But Mombo claims that the significant focus on the issue that has come from her region paradoxically interferes with the provincial autonomy that many Anglican churches in Africa favor. It eclipses other pressing social issues such as HIV/AIDS, poverty, and hunger to which local leaders should attend. Mombo suggests that homosexuality becomes a focus in African churches because of asymmetrical partnerships between African bishops and those who enjoy

> the comforts of the North, and the joys of being accountable to [those] bishops whom they see only when they want to, or when they bring them over . . . [but] are not subjected to the . . . struggles of the Christian church in those provinces (Mombo 2007, p. 75).

For Mombo, such partnerships are not mutually beneficial and remain largely unconcerned with the daily lives of African bishops. The people that suffer as a result are those members on the margins of the Anglican Church.

Conclusion

Esther Mombo has given her life and career to making room for others. Her voice is a soft, steady challenge to the Anglican Communion to find ways to bring the experiences of those on the sidelines into the center. This is not an easy or straightforward task. Making room for others necessarily involves readjustments; asking some to move aside so that those on the periphery can be included. Making space means being attentive to the complicated histories that bring us to where we are, as well as the asymmetries of power in our present moment. Whether she is creating space in our institutions for outside voices, advocating for more transformative practices to dismantle poverty and HIV, or calling for liturgical and ecclesial renewals that are attentive to local contexts, Esther calls all of us to transitions that can only make us stronger and more dynamic. For Esther is not challenging us to be the kind of Communion she wants us to be, she is challenging us to become the kind of Communion we claim to be. Whether we are in the center or on the sidelines, she calls us to the promise of unity, which never comes at the expense of diversity. Fragility and possibility are bound together in Mombo's conception of Anglican theology. Her voice is a reminder that we should never cease to remember both the peril and the promise of global Communion.

Notes

1 I have changed her name for this chapter.
2 The impact of mission history in colonial Kenya is hardly monolithic. But the connections between Christianity, class, and gender have been well documented. See Kanogo (2005) and Peterson (2016).
3 See "The Lambeth Commission on Communion" from Anglican Communion, https://www.anglicancommunion.org/media/100345/The-Lambeth-Commission-on-Communion.pdf (accessed July 20, 2020).

References

Dube, M. (2006). Adkinra! four hearts joined together. In: *African Women, Religion and Health: Essays in Honor of Mercy Amba Ewudziwa Oduyoye* (eds. I.A. Phiri and S. Nadar), 131–156. Maryknoll, NY: Orbis.

Fiedler, R.N. (2017). *A History of the Circle of Concerned African Women Theologians, 1989-2007.* Mzuzu, Malawi: Mzuni Press.

Kanogo, T.M. (2005). *African Womanhood in Colonial Kenya, 1900-50.* Oxford: Ohio University Press.

Mombo, E. (2005). Missiological challenges in the HIV/AIDS Era: Kenya. *Theology Today* 62: 58–66.

Mombo, E. (2006). Anglican liturgies in East Africa. In: *The Oxford Guide to the Book of Common Prayer: A Worldwide Survey* (eds. C. Hefling and C. Shattuck), 277–286. New York, NY: Oxford University Press.

Mombo, E. (2007). The Windsor report: a paradigm shift for Anglicanism. *Anglican Theological Review* 89: 69–78.

Mombo, E. (2009). Religion and materiality: the case of poverty alleviation. In: *Religion and Poverty: Pan-African Perspectives* (ed. P.J. Paris), 213–227. Durham, NC: Duke University Press.

Mombo, E. (2012). The Church and poverty alleviation in Africa. In: *Anglican Women on Church and Mission* (eds. P.-l. Kwok, J.A. Berling and J. Te Paa), 135–150. Harrisburg, PA: Morehouse.

Mombo, E. (2016). Women in African Christianities. In: *The Routledge Companion to Christianity in Africa* (ed. E.K. Bongmba), 173–186. New York, NY: Routledge.

Mombo, E. and Joziasse, H. (2011). *If You Have No Voice, Just Sing!: Narratives of

Women's Lives and Theological Education at St. Paul's University. Limuru, Kenya: Zapf Chancery.

Peterson, D.R. (2016). The politics of transcendence in colonial Uganda. *Past & Present* 230: 197–225.

Phiri, I.A. and Nadar, S. (2006). Introduction: treading softly but firmly: African women, religion, and health. In: *African Women, Religion and Health: Essays in Honor of Mercy Amba Ewudziwa Oduyoye* (eds. I.A. Phiri and S. Nadar), 1–18. Orbis: Maryknoll, New York.

Afterword: God's Gift in Every Voice

James Tengatenga

By the middle of the nineteenth century it was clear that the Anglo-Celtic dominance of thought and theology in the Church of England (and its Celtic manifestations) at home and abroad was under challenge. Interestingly, the challenge was coming from within but based on experience in the colonial context. The calling of the first Lambeth Conference (1867) was, in part, a way to gather around and decipher the signs of the times and live into the new reality of a world church, and articulate it. It thus raised the issue of an ecclesiology that recognized the new dynamic and to avoid becoming another Roman Catholic Church, at least in structure and governance, if not in theology as well or to go the confessional church way of most of the Reformed Churches. Hence, at the end of it, it was resolved that the imperial church it was not, but it was a communion of churches.

The issues at hand were not only ecclesiological. There were new methods of biblical interpretation and criticism that were afoot in addition to the theological questions of interface with new cultures and new religions. The Colenso affair is a perfect example of all that in one place (and in one person!). From then on, context becomes a key factor in doing theology. The assumption that there is "universal" theology done for all from one particular context was debunked. This did not only apply to the colonies but also in the heartlands of Anglicanism. The Church of England context provided many voices who spoke in context just as the rest of the world was experiencing.

The twentieth century was to make this even more pronounced as each independent church began to speak not only from within, and to, its context, but began to stake its place in the global theological discourse. Some of this was articulated during the discussions in the Anglican Congresses of 1908 (London), 1953 (Minneapolis), and 1963 (Toronto). The latter said it more pointedly through its theme of "Mutual Responsibility and Interdependence in the body of Christ" (see Bayne 1963;

Twentieth Century Anglican Theologians: From Evelyn Underhill to Esther Mombo, First Edition.
Edited by Stephen Burns, Bryan Cones, and James Tengatenga.

Zink 2011). The writings we have sampled in this collection are a vignette into that global discourse. Granted this is only the tip of an iceberg. There are many more voices that would be presented, as Stephen Burns and Bryan Cones say in the introduction to this volume. By voices we do not just mean the theologians profiled here but also the contributors. Due to exigencies of time and location we, unfortunately, were not able to keep up the ideal we had in mind on that latter score but nonetheless we tried to not only source from "the usual suspects."

This latter point is not a cop-out but was the very reason why this project came into being. The point is as much a confession of "things left undone" as much as it continues to expose the glaring absence of other voices of the Communion. As long as the contributions and writers continue to be from the West, Anglican theology will continue to be less Anglican. By saying that I am suggesting that a worldwide communion theology needs to reflect what it claims to be – worldwide – for "Anglican" is no longer in "English captivity." As such this compilation's title has yet to be lived into. The talk has yet to be walked, but it has surely begun.

It is easy to blame the colonial specter and ethos that still haunts the Communion but the quest is a challenge to all. Until the tri-continentals[1] take it upon themselves to speak for themselves, theological language and method will continue to be lopsided. Of course, such an observation begs the question of why the situation is so and why the reticence/silence on the part of tri-continentals? As Stephen Burns has observed:

> Even if we recognise – as we must – a shift in Christianity to the global south, as Jione Havea asserts, "It does not really matter that the Bible is in the hands of Africans, and of Asians and Islanders, if they are to interpret it according to the teachings of white men" – a point that can be elaborated from Bible to the tradition at large and to many ways of theologising (Burns Forthcoming).

This is not to deny that power dynamics are still at work here. It is simply to name them in an attempt to exorcize them from the theological enterprise. Our hope is that this is a beginning of going outside the theological envelope that Anglicans have lived in for so long and into the open sphere that Anglicans inhabit, by location, culture, color, language, and station in life.

That being said, my intention here is to attempt a synthesis of the contributions of this select group of theologians as a way of giving an overview of their contribution to Anglican theology in the twentieth century. What we presented here showcases not only method, language, sources, medium, and context in doing theology but also takes seriously the age-old observation that theology is a reflection on experience in the context of an encounter with God and God's relations with human beings, and indeed all creation. That articulation is of necessity multilingual, both literally and figuratively. The theologians are multiracial, multigender, and inhabit different (and for some multiple) contexts. If a picture tells a thousand stories, then a comparison of the Lambeth Conference picture of 1867 and that of 1998 is a photographic representation and reflection of the sources of, and interlocutors in, Anglican theology in the twentieth century and beyond.

What this illustrates is that it is very difficult to pin down what Anglican theology is. What one can say conclusively is that it is eclectic and comprehensive, in the sense that it covers the, apparently, disparate spectrum of Anglican voices (from conservative to progressive) that defy, if not resist, systematization. As Stephen Burns and Bryan Cones say (with special refence to current intra-Anglican discourse) in the introduction to this volume, "The current impasse is a signal instance of how 'Anglican theology' can be difficult to expound; a complete picture, were that to be possible, would be quite unlikely to reveal easy ways to agreement." They further observe that,

> While documents do exist in which convictions of the nascent new English church are specified – notably the Thirty-Nine Articles of Religion – their status in Anglican provinces around the world which inherited them has wavered, and certainly by today is quite diverse. This in part reflects ongoing dispute about what period or epoch of history is or might be key for Anglicanism, with more or less weight being placed on the Reformations-era, medieval continuities, and "the early church" with its ecumenical councils. It has often been noted that Anglicans have harbored an affection for "patristics," and also that Anglicans have rarely been recognized – or seen themselves – as "systematic" theologians like those spawned in other traditions, both Protestant and Catholic. "Untidiness," "baffling of neatness," and such like, echo in much theology by Anglicans. . .

As if in response to this John Macquarrie in the 1960s and '70s attempted a systematic theology in his *Principles of Christian Theology*. For many in other Christian traditions this seemed to be what they had been waiting for from the Anglicans. It came close, but never quite took root in the way they expected. There is a stubbornness in the way of doing theology in the Anglican tradition that defies such constructs. Even as Macquarrie did systematic theology, it did not quite come out as other traditions would have it. In more recent times Alister McGrath has come close to doing "systematic theology" along Macquarrie's lines but he too takes an approach that defies cookie-cutter and pigeonhole systematization as in some other traditions. Macquarrie's work is thus significant in that it demonstrates that even when Anglicans attempt to be like others it turns out different and distinctive.

As they say, "You cannot quite define Anglican theology but you know it when you see it." But what might that mean? The Anglican Communion has been exercised by this question for generations. More recently during Rowan Williams' tenure as Archbishop of Canterbury, the question was understood as that of Anglican self-understanding in the midst of the diversity that is. As one way of building a common understanding, Rowan Williams established the workgroup, Theological Education in the Anglican Communion (TEAC). This commission came up with what became known as "The Anglican Way: Signposts on a Common Journey," whose aim was to help with a common way of viewing/understanding "the Anglican way." The document says, in part:

> The journey is on-going because what it means to be Anglican will be influenced by context and history. Historically a number of different forms of being

Anglican have emerged, all of which can be found in the rich diversity of present-day Anglicanism . . . The Anglican Way is a particular expression of the Christian Way of being the One, Holy, Catholic and Apostolic Church of Jesus Christ. It is formed by and rooted in Scripture, shaped by its worship of the living God, ordered for communion, and directed in faithfulness to God's mission in the world. In diverse global situations Anglican life and ministry witnesses to the incarnate, crucified and risen Lord, and is empowered by the Holy Spirit. Together with all Christians, Anglicans hope, pray and work for the coming of the reign of God . . . As Anglicans, baptized into Christ, we share in the mission of God with all Christians and are deeply committed to building ecumenical relationships. Our reformed catholic tradition has proved to be a gift we are able to bring to ecumenical endeavour. We invest in dialogue with other churches based on trust and a desire that the whole company of God's people may grow into the fullness of unity to which God calls us that the world may believe the gospel (TEAC 2007).

I submit that this may be a helpful way of making sense of what may seem to some to be an unwieldy, cacophonous, and undecipherable Anglican theology. The theologians sampled in this collection reflect this way of doing theology within their times and contexts: be they liberal, progressive, evangelical, conservative, broad church, or whatever.

Belonging and Self-Designation

There are identifiers or characteristics that are common to Anglican theology. Generally speaking, the theologian is a member of an Anglican church and identifies as such. For some it is not so easy an identification because there is an uneasiness with denominationalism. A case in point (according to Mark Meynell) may be John Stott who

> for some . . . was too evangelical, for others too Anglican. This tension lay sometimes in parallel, sometimes in convergence, with his interlocutors from the liberal and conservative wings within Anglicanism. . . . [He] "pursue[d] truth and unity simultaneously, that is to pursue the kind of unity commended by Jesus Christ and his apostles namely unity in truth."[2]

Ramsey with his burden for ecumenism may also be identified as another such (from the liberal side) even though that would be a stretch because his vision of church is that division/denominationalism will eventually be swallowed up by the one united church Jesus prayed for. About him Lizette Larson Miller said,

> He felt that being Anglican was to turn naturally to ecumenism because Anglicanism was itself born of so many forces and directions and therefore had at its best the gift of comprehension necessary to name the essentials of

unity. . . . If the dominical call to "be one" is taken seriously then the reconciliation of all peoples must be a priority of the church catholic. But, each part of the body of Christ is lacking "unless it is united with the whole church" including in holy orders, where "all orders are deficient until the church is united." . . . "All that is Anglican or Roman or Greek or partial or local in any way must share by an agonizing death to its own pride."

This is also expressed among quite a few of the theologians we sampled here who have prized the "provisionality" of Anglican theology and for that matter, any other theology because there is a possibility of the traditional and the current being superseded by another better or improved understanding. There is thus an open ended-ness that leads David Brown to call for "a careful listening exercise, the final result of which cannot be predetermined in advance." Ann Loades in addressing the same suggests

> Forebears sometimes have startling aptness because tradition is not to be construed as "the dead hand of the past" which will prevent us from thinking afresh, but a life-giving source of vitality . . . of its essence creative and innovative, mustering every grace of intelligence and skill in enabling us to learn from the past generate critical dissonance with the present open up new vistas and walkways, generate new insights, negotiate dead ends, endure experiences of profound alienation, and live with criteria which themselves may change.

All that is influenced not only by developing thought but also by the global contexts that shape and improve upon the project and so avoid captivity to narrowness. As Titre Ande Georges says (with reference to John Pobee and regarding the African context),

> African theology must also be ecumenical to guard against Western factionalism. Pobee notes that theology has been for too long denominational partly because in the nineteenth century, when much mission in Africa was carried out, theologians and church leaders thought that their denomination was the true church. The younger churches in Africa have been cast as branches of European church organisations.

Sources, Medium, and Language of Anglican Theology

Theology is open to correction and improvement. As such Anglican theology does not ignore the past but makes use of it as it paves a way for future development. The language or words may not themselves change but their interpretation may change and, as others may say, the intercourse between God and creation has possibilities of morphing. Process theology, which is hinted at by some of the theologians we have sampled, may be one such way of theologizing. By and large there is also a tendency among Anglican theologians to demonstrate their dependency on earlier Anglican theologians and thus claim Anglican pedigree. This they do while at the same time also relying on those from other traditions (ancient creeds, Eastern and Western traditions, and indeed other faiths) and philosophy of all sorts. One example is the observation that John McDowell makes about Donald MacKinnon:

> One particular series of conversations that MacKinnon fruitfully had was with tragic dramas. Sophocles and Shakespeare, or at least Shakespeare as the author of Hamlet and King Lear, stand alongside the likes of Aristotle, Kant, von Balthasar, and Barth in MacKinnon's list of important educators and thinkers on the nature of human knowing and living without comforting illusion.

The sources of Anglican theology are thus eclectic in addition to the hallmark scripture, tradition, and reason.

Another characteristic theme in Anglican theology is that of the incarnation as a thread that runs through most (if not all) Anglican theologizing. In talking about the incarnation, William Temple said "the limitations are the means whereby the Eternal Son, remaining always in the bosom of the Father, lays bare to us the very heart of Godhead, in doing this, moreover the Son of God has made our condition a matter of His own experience." Adding her voice on the significance of the incarnation, Dorothy L. Sayers said that "Jesus' 'Manhood' was a real manhood, subject to the common realities of daily life; [and] that the men and women surrounding Him were living human beings, not just characters in a story: that in short He was born, not into 'the Bible,' but into the world. . ." It is for this reason, Stephen Burns says, that in her radio plays she "made shock-waves . . . because the characters in her renditions of gospel stories speak in then-contemporary British idioms and with regional accents, a jolt to listeners used to reading and hearing read the Authorized Version of the Bible."

There is not one "sacred" medium of presenting theology. As Christopher Brewer observes:

> [David] Brown argu[es] "that philosophy and theology cannot be kept artificially apart, as they are at present within the Anglo-Saxon tradition." He called for "the founding of a new discipline of philosophical theology (or the widening of the horizons of the philosophy of religion) to apply more widely the type of penetration of theology by philosophy." In a more recent volume, Brown says that his "concern over the years has been to value the contribution of both disciplines."

The maxim *lex orandi, lex credendi* has demonstrated that theology is expressed in worship and spirituality. Ashley Cocksworth, describing David Ford, says,

> Ford didn't set out to write a spiritual theology. It is more that his theology is integrated with spirituality . . . He sees Christian doctrine as infinitely more encompassing than "information" about God. Doctrines are integrally related to spirituality, the affections, and the living out of the Christian life in the messy realities of human existence . . . Ford's elegant integration of "knowing and praising," and the reformulation of "belief" it brings about, releases theology

"from the fixations and obsessions of reason" and gently opens the theologian "to being knit into a reality that is delightful as well as true". . . . The reintegration of prayer and doctrine reorientates theology toward its proper end: the praise of God, making theology a joyous, celebratory, doxological undertaking . . . Conversely, without prayer, theology grows to a standstill, uncritically repeating the past – it makes an idol of its very self.

Art, literature, music, dance and drama are also the kind of media through which theology is presented, expressed and taught. As Dorothy Sayers said, "the dogma is the drama."

What is more, Anglican theologians are drawn from many places – from the academy and from the parish, as lay and clerics (deacons, priests and bishops), and different genders. All can be theologians. However, this is not without its conundrums when it comes to the freedom of expression and responsibility to a tradition. As John McDowell observes in discussing Donald MacKinnon:

> What he most personally struggles with is how to be true to his academic "calling" that necessitates "follow[ing] the argument whithersoever it leads," while remaining a person of the church even when he has to be "particularly alert to the clerical bias which almost inevitably on occasion threatens objectivity of judgment". . . . To live as a Christian in the world today is necessarily to live an exposed life; it is to be stripped of the kind of security that tradition, whether ecclesiological or institutional, easily bestows.

John A. T. Robinson drew attention to himself not because what he said was novel but because of his station as a bishop in the church. In his own defense he says "My sole concern is to question whether the doctrine must necessarily be expressed in certain images and categories which might have the effect for many of our generation to make it unreal . . . I want God to be as real for our modern secular scientific world as it was for the 'ages of faith.'"

Contextualization

Anglican theologians are influenced by, speak from and to their context while they articulate to each other and other traditions what they believe and how they live into it. In other words, they speak from where they stand and to their times and in the language of their times. Two Chinese theologians in this collection, T. C. Chao and K. H. Ting, had to find a way of doing theology in China. Not only were they dealing with the question of sources of theology but also with relevance and language that would communicate. Chen Yongtao in his discussion of T. C. Chao observes:

> It is obvious that while Chao created his Chinese theology, he was greatly influenced by various Western philosophies and theologies that flourished in his time. However, Chao was not a follower of any Western school particularly, either philosophical or theological. The method that Chao adopted might be

called a "principle of taking," *nalai zhuyi*. *Nalai zhuyi* literally means "taking-from-ism" or "borrowing-ism," which was first put forward in 1934 by Lu Xun, a modern Chinese writer. For Lu Xun, this term means that in the process of China's development, Chinese people should take all the good parts of Western civilization for their own purpose. *Nalai zhuyi* is thus a selective taking, but not a blind following. Chao's approach to Western philosophical and theological sources is such a selective taking . . . There were two things that Chao strived for: one was the Christianization (基督化) of China, which was the aim of his efforts, the other was the Sinicization (中国化) of Christianity . . . Moreover, Chao's later soteriology indicates also his effort at theological contextualization, while it is somewhat influenced by the Anglican tradition.

T. C. Chao provides a vignette into the complexity of the "contextualization" enterprise in the political context that is China, with its suspicion of all things foreign. He thus creates a unique blending of the political and cultural in ways that are unique to China.

K. H. Ting's theology "emphasized social engagement and theological liberalism. It was also ecumenical and was a theology in dialogue with the times, and with people both inside and outside the church. Once religion was no longer seen as opium, and therefore inherently destructive, it could be understood as a legitimate part of culture." His "theology is grounded in China's post-denominationalism but its personal and ecclesiological roots are Anglican and episcopal, enhanced by ecumenical commitment and political participation. His was a particular variety of an Anglican modern theology, Comprehensive in scope and focused on its context," says Philip Wickeri.

In the United Kingdom, Donald MacKinnon, in a very different way, offers a critique of the established Church of England, which he considers captive to a Constantinian relationship of church and state. Desmond Tutu's political/liberation theology critiques his apartheid context. William Temple traveled the country speaking on behalf of the Life and Liberty movement, "including self-governance through a church assembly, the adoption of a new prayer book to better reflect the spirituality of the age, more equitable clergy salaries, and securing the vote for women in ecclesiastical matters." Kenneth Leech poignantly said, "The important questions to be asked by theology . . . are: who should do theology, and where, and in whose interest, and for whom?" For "if theology does not help to liberate human beings and the created order, it helps to oppress them." In the context of Africa, "Tutu vigorously defended the continued right of spiritual communities to become involved in political action in as clear a way as possible while remaining spiritual; for example, he constantly stressed that the church must remain autonomous and, in particular, must have just as much right now and in the future to act independently of political parties," says Michael Battle.

It is also true that contextualization does not mean the same thing in every context. This is especially so when one listens to the African context where Tutu is presented as the other: the political, while John Pobee is presented as another strand of contextualization: the cultural. Even though Tutu and Pobee would frown upon this classification (as they have both dealt with both aspects in their writings), it does depict what obtained in the development of "African theology" in the twentieth century.

John Mbiti, on the other hand, is one who championed the recovery of African Traditional Religions as not only *preparatio evangelica,* but as vehicles of divine revelation and interaction of the divine with Africans in ways that are not antithetical to Christian theology. Pobee says that

> the concern of African theology is to attempt to use African concepts and African ethos as vehicles for communication of the gospel in an African context . . . African persons should not be treated as museum pieces or anthropological curios but as person who grow in stature, mentality, culturally and in other ways . . . He explains that *Homo Africanus* is a multiheaded hydra, in much the same way as "*Homo sapiens*" is multiheaded hydra. Also, a *Homo Africanus* of 1976 is different from a *Homo Africanus* of 1876 because of the impact of Westernism expressed through laws, learning, art, and more. So, culture is understood to be what is happening here and now; it is the result of many different influences, the Western and the missionary influences as well as the result of the earlier traditions, and it is therefore living and contemporary.

Feminism

The African context is not only about cultural versus political theology (in Anglican fashion), it is also not immune to dividing over gender. In Esther Mombo we are presented with a theological activism that highlights the gender bias that dogs the African Anglican theological enterprise, both in the church and the academy. She not only addresses gender issues but the attendant social and economic woes created by historical and structural conditions. She says "there are more churches than toilets and one wonders how the people cope with the call of nature . . . There is a connection [between religion and toilets] in that . . . if cleanliness is next to godliness, then a religion that ignores the living conditions of its members is deficient."

It is not only in Africa that feminism has been an issue. Ann Loades adds her voice about the possible effect of language change, in the British context, by saying that churches will first need to "become the kinds of communities where there are genuine attempts to try to repair the damage done to women." The need remains for "struggl[ing] hard with the devaluation of women for which the Christian tradition is in its own way responsible," even if/when "assum[ing] that the tradition also contains resources for transformation and change, despite the weight of criticism levelled against it." Dorothy Sayers addressed the question of the place of women in 1938 and again in 1941, in her essays "Are Women Human?" and "The Human-Not-Quite-Human." She says, "There is no act, no sermon, no parable in the whole Gospel that borrows its pungency from female perversity; nobody could guess from the words and deeds of Jesus that there was anything 'funny' about women."

It is not only women who address the matter of the place of women. In 1916 William Temple wrote: "Personally I want . . . to see women ordained to the priesthood. But still more do I want to see both real advance toward the reunion of Christendom, and the general emancipation of women. To win admission now would put back the former and to moot it would put back the latter."

Revelation and Scripture

Theology does not drop from the skies nor is it simply an intellectual/philosophical exercise in articulating revelation. In any case, Matthew Caldwell says that "Temple argues that there are two dimensions to this revelation: divine self-disclosure and human perception. Revelation, at its most profound, is the coincidence of event (God's action) and appreciation (human perception). The theological task is discovering, trusting, and understanding God's self-disclosure." Temple himself wrote "faith is not the holding of correct doctrines but personal fellowship with the living God . . . I do not believe in any creed, but I use certain creeds to express, to conserve, and to deepen my belief in God. *What is offered to man's apprehension in any specific Revelation is not truth concerning God but the living God Himself.*"

Theology engages scripture and tradition with reason in the context of divine inter-action with humans and all creation. As such, it highlights the role and place of experi-ence. Christopher Brewer, discussing Brown, says, "First, Brown rejects any sharp distinction between natural and revealed theology, emphasizing the role of reason as well as the wider context of religious experience in any adequate account of revealed theology. Second, he distinguishes revelation from the canon of scripture. Third, he expands the notion of canon to include not only the biblical canon but also the canon of interpretation. Fourth, he relocates revelation to the act of interpretation."

Broadly speaking Anglican biblical theology accepts and uses historical and literary criticism and has embraced newer methods of reading and thus interpreting scripture. Austin Farrer is noted as one of the first to apply the methods of literary criticism to biblical texts. In this sample, David Brown represents the progressive side, while John Stott and Leon Morris the evangelical, and David Ford an innovative, ecumenical, and multifaith approach.

Discussing David Brown's reading of scripture, Christopher Brewer says that while Brown respects the traditional reading and interpretation of scripture he believes that scripture is fallible; by which he means that it is open to reinterpretation: "Brown accepts the findings of biblical criticism, and more specifically the fallibility of the Bible, but thinks fallibility not only acceptable but also preferable in light of his developmental theory of revelation that together with fallibility, maintains divine interactionism and human freedom." In Christopher Brewer's discussion, we learn that Brown holds the view that "fresh contexts trigger fresh handlings of inherited traditions." Tradition is "the motor that sustains revelation both within Scripture and beyond," and that "the truth of imaginative 'fit' is preferable to the criterion of 'literal fact'."

On a more conservative perspective we have John Stott about whom Mark Meynell says, "his new-found beliefs crystallized in what would come to be described by David Bebbington as the evangelical quadrilateral: *conversionism* (the need for all to be changed), *activism* (conversion results in service), *biblicism* (a high view of the Bible), and *crucicentrism* (stress on the centrality of Christ's sacrificial death on the cross)." He shares this stance with the Australian, Leon Morris. About the latter, Neil Bach observes that he concluded:

firstly, that the Bible does not come to us as a bare word and nothing more. God's Spirit still witnesses and applies the word to the devout reader's need. Final authority is not just paper and ink. God uses his word to effect his purpose.

Second the Bible's witness to itself must be taken with full seriousness. . . . Third, we need a way of looking at the Bible that holds it to be fully authoritative but is not distracted over minor points. The Bible writers do not speak of inerrancy. Our concern is not to prove inerrancy by lining up every statement in harmony; our concern is to show the Bible is eminently trustworthy.

From a more innovative perspective we have David Ford who developed "spiritual reading" of scripture, reading sacred texts ecumenically and together with other religions. Ashley Cocksworth reflecting on this method says of Ford,

"The aim is *not consensus*," Ford writes, but the deepening in both understanding and disagreement (aiming to improve the quality of both). Anglicans might further learn from [Scriptural Reasoning]'s willingness to repair one's own tradition by drawing on the resources within it, to read beyond the "plain sense" of scripture, and to keep multiple readings in play. The preference for the particular would encourage Anglicans who think differently from each other to speak from their own particular place, distinctive viewpoint, and specificity of context, to be listened to and to be open to have their own wisdom questioned and transformed in engagement with others. The result is what Ben Quash calls "double deepening": a deeper inhabiting of one's own tradition by means of a deepening of one's experience of another.

Conclusion

Ryan Kuratko's assessment of John Macquarrie's thought captures well what twentieth century Anglican theology is like:

Every voice, rightly heard, speaks of God, and the task of theology is finding hermeneutic methods that uncover God's gift in every voice. This principle invariably makes Anglican theology seem less distinctive – it unabashedly draws voices from outside itself, from history and from other disciplines. Nonetheless, this drawing is distinctively Anglican . . . In working to find a *via media*, . . . insisting that what theology needs is the ability to entertain multiple visions at the same time. This is true when working with Heidegger's philosophy, the council of Chalcedon, and biblical scholarship, but it is also true . . . upon encountering other religious communities and ideas.

As such Anglican theology is biblical, creedal, eclectic, incarnational, contextual, missional, and is open to change into a more inclusive ecumenical vision of God and all creation in response to the dominical imperative for unity. There is no part of human life and human concern it does not address. As *The Anglican Way: Signposts on a Common Journey* puts it (TEAC 2007), "[The Anglican way] is formed by and rooted in Scripture, shaped by its worship of the living God, ordered for communion, and directed in faithfulness to God's mission in the world." Anglican theology uses all media of communication available to society in popular and contextual language, albeit still captive to the English idiom. It is expressed not only in words and worship but by representative voices that the divine self-revelation elicits in humanity and all creation. It is not a special province of westerners and professionals (even though they abound) but engaged by all – female, male, academics, public figures, novelists, poets, parish priests, and bishops.

The Lambeth Conference of 1998 vividly demonstrated the passing of Anglican thinking from *modernity* to *post-modernity*. Despite the acrimonious fall out, it did usher in a new age of theological engagement that will continue to unfold. Many voices have yet to speak and those that have and are speaking are yet to be heard. I trust that the voices of both the theologians sampled herein and the contributors are an example of what that might look like. The silence of the absent, the unrecognized, tri-continentals and all those not yet in the discourse (theological *indaba*) is for us a loud *cri de coeur* for the fruition and coming into being of a more comprehensive Anglican theology. The purist of the old school will surely worry about whether the resultant Anglican theology will still be recognizably Anglican. The progressive pan-Anglican will respond by pointing out that it is, just as it has been over the ages since the first Ecumenical Councils, if not since the beginning of creation. The journey has begun and I pray that, following this kind of lead, there will be a proliferation of bringing these hidden Anglican gems into the public so that more in-depth theological *indaba* can flourish. I also hope that those who are now silent will speak without feeling judged for where they come from: location, linguistic, or worldview wise. Until *all* God's people speak, access the platforms and fora, and are heard, we have not finished doing theology. If we think we are there, we deceive ourselves and are caught in a "period captivity" from which stupor we need to be aroused. The eternal God will continue to reveal Godself to all and indeed, Anglican theology will be one among many ecumenical attempts at articulating humanity's experience of the divine. It is tempting and even hubris to say, "Watch this space!" but we will say it.

Notes

1 I prefer this descriptor to "Third World" or "Southern."
2 Where citations are taken from elsewhere in this volume, in this Afterword they have been stripped of references included in the other context in which they occur in this book.

References

Bayne, S. (1963). *Mutual Responsibility and Interdependence in the Body of Christ*. London: SCM Press.

Burns, S. (Forthcoming). Silence. In: *Bordered Bodies, Bothered Voices: Native and Migrant Theologies* (ed. J. Havea).

TEAC (Theological Education in the Anglican Communion). (2007). *The Anglican Way:*

Signposts on a Common Journey. (accessed July 20, 2020) https://www.anglicancommunion. org/media/39814/teac.pdf

Zink, J. (2011). Changing world, changing church: Stephen Bayne and "mutual responsibility and interdependence". *Anglican Theological Review* 93: 243–262.

Index

Page References to Notes will contain the letter 'n' followed by the Note number

Twentieth Century Anglican Theologians: From Evelyn Underhill to Esther Mombo, First Edition.
Edited by Stephen Burns, Bryan Cones, and James Tengatenga.
© 2021 John Wiley & Sons Ltd. Published 2021 by John Wiley & Sons Ltd.

Aotearoa New Zealand and Polynesia, Anglican
Church in, x
Appasamy, Aiyadurai Jesudason, 41
Sundar Singh: A Biography, 39–40
Archbishop of Canterbury, office of, xii, 13
Randall Davidson, 41
Arthur Michael Ramsey, xv, 65
William Temple, xv, 12, 15, 24, 103
Rowan Williams, 228
Archbishop of York, office of, William Temple, 12,
14, 24
Aristotle, 114
Articles of Religion, xi
atonement
individual theologians
T. C. Chao, 29
Leon Morris, 85–88
William Temple, 18–19
through cross, 85–87
Western interpretations, 29
Augustine, 5, 6, 191
Confessions, 4
Aulen, Gustav, 88
Austin, J. L., 57
Australia, Anglican Church in, xi
Avis, Paul, xii
Ayer, A. J., 58
Language, Truth, and Logic, 57

Bach, Neil, 235–236
Baldwin, Stanley, 14
Barth, Karl, xvi, 6, 56, 58, 131, 170, 195, 196, 199
Church Dogmatics, 195
influence on Chao, 22, 24, 30
neo-orthodoxy, 22, 24
Basham, A. L., *The Wonder that was India*, 35
Battle, Michael, 233
Beattie, Arthur, 185
Bebbington, David, 120
Beetge, David, 141
Bell, George, 103
Berlin, Isaiah, 74
Berrigan, Daniel, xvi, 132
Bible
Africa Bible Commentary, 149
and African theology, 148
authority of, 28, 29, 84
Authorized Version, 50
burning of, 38
Christology of, 150
literary criticism, 235
New English Bible, 104
as norm of faith, 28
Revised Version, 104
as Word of God, 29

see also Christianity; Christology; New
Testament scholarship; Old Testament
scholarship
biblicism, 120, 121
Bishop of Manchester, office of, William Temple, 12
Bloch, Ernst, *The Principle of Hope*, 78
Book of Common Prayer, xii, 195
Botha, P. W., 141, 142
Bozarth, Ella Renée, 178
Brewer, Christopher R., 231, 235
Breyfogle, T., 59–60
British Council of Churches, 3
Brown, David W., 60, 162, 185–194, 230, 235
biography, 185
career, split into two halves, 190, 191
Critical Catholicism, 61
on deism, 190, 191, 193n7
on fallibility, 188–189
on homosexuality, 192–193
natural theology of, xvi
New Testament scholarship, 192
theological themes, 187–192
on Trinity, xvi
as Van Mildert Professor of Divinity, Durham, 187
writings
"Art as Revelation," 189
"Artists as Theologians," 189
Divine Humanity, xvi
The Divine Trinity, xvi, 186, 187, 191
God and Enchantment of Place, 191
"The Trinity of Art," 187
Brown, Robert McAfee, xi
Browning, Don, 174n8
Buber, Martin, 103
Bujo, Bénézet, 151
Bultmann, Rudolph, 112
Burns, Stephen, 227, 228, 231
Butler, Josephine, 160

Caiaphas, 76
Caird, George, 211
Caldwell, Matthew, 235
Cambridge Interfaith Programme, 196
Carr, Paul, 124
Catholicism *see* Roman Catholic Church
"Catonsville Nine," 132
Chao, T. C., 22–33, 99, 232–233
on atonement, 29
attack by Anti-Rightist Movement (1957), 25
baptism, 23
Barth's influence on, 22, 24, 30
biography, 23–25
and Chinese Protestant Church, 25, 31
Christian nationalism concept, 26–27
and Confucianism, 23, 27

Made in the USA
Coppell, TX
19 January 2021